PRIVATE PAPERS OF
JAMES BOSWELL
FROM MALAIIIDE CASTLE

✵

ISHAM COLLECTION

✵

BOSWELL's JOURNAL

OF

A Tour to the Hebrides

WITH

SAMUEL JOHNSON, LL.D.

Now First Published from the Original Manuscript

❀ ❀

Prepared for the Press, with Preface and Notes

by Frederick A. Pottle *and* Charles H. Bennett

❀ ❀

The Literary Guild, Inc.
New York

The story of the manuscripts of James Boswell is one of the most dramatic among all the tales of book and manuscript collecting, and the manuscripts themselves are among the most valuable literary properties ever discovered. For more than a century it was believed by scholars that all Boswell's papers had been destroyed shortly after his death. A few years ago, however, it became known that there existed in Malahide Castle a large collection which had come down through the years by inheritance to Lord Talbot de Malahide, Boswell's great-great-grandson. In 1927 Lord Talbot, who had previously declined to entertain any suggestion of releasing the papers, agreed to sell the property, including the publishing rights. The entire collection was acquired by Lt.-Colonel Ralph H. Isham, who proceeded at once to arrange for printing it privately in a limited edition.

The editing of the manuscripts was entrusted to Mr. Geoffrey Scott, and after his death to Professor Frederick Pottle of Yale University, who is everywhere recognized as a leading authority on the period of Johnson and Boswell. The task of deciphering, arranging, and annotating the huge collection, comprising more than a million words, proved to be the work of years, and its progress has been followed with profound interest by scholars and the public. The eighteen volumes of the limited edition have appeared at irregular intervals, beginning in 1928; the nineteenth and final volume, containing the index, is now in preparation.

When Colonel Isham acquired the Malahide collection, it was assumed that it contained all of Boswell's manuscripts that had been preserved. In addition to a large number of very important letters by and to Boswell, it included most of his journal, which he had kept intermittently for 37 years. But in spite of the richness of the material thus made available to the world for the first time, it was a disappointment to discover that there were some serious gaps in the journal. A few years later, when the publication was already well under way, another extraordinary treasure-trove came to light at Malahide Castle, when through a happy accident an old croquet-box in an unused cupboard was found to contain another large batch of Boswell papers. First in importance among the documents—all of which are invaluable to students of the period—was the original manuscript of the *Journal of a Tour to the Hebrides.*

Colonel Isham was able to acquire this second lot of manuscripts also, and he arranged for the expansion of his privately printed edition to include much of the new material. But the work had already proceeded past the point at which the Hebridean Journal belonged chronologically; in any event its bulk and the added expense would have increased the set too far beyond the limits originally contemplated and promised to the subscribers.

It is now known also that Sir William Forbes, Boswell's executor, carried off a considerable portion of his friend's papers, and died without restoring them to the heir. These papers, of whose existence the public has only recently been informed, are now in the custody of a Judicial Factor appointed by the Court of Session of Scotland, and will remain inaccessible until their ownership has been determined.

The present publishers expect to issue, from time to time, additional volumes containing more of the Boswell papers, but they determined that the first book should be the hitherto unpublished *Journal of a Tour to the Hebrides.* It is their privilege thus to make available one of the great books of English literature in its original form, which, as it here appears, differs materially from the previously printed text.

After more than 150 years, the Journal as Boswell wrote it is published. Throughout the years of preparation the English and American publishers have worked closely together and have had the invaluable help of both Colonel Isham and Professor Pottle. The first edition is issued jointly by the English and American publishers in a large-paper limited edition; the first trade editions are issued separately by the publishers in their respective countries on the same day.

PREFACE

THE FIRST PRINTING of an important manuscript calls for a certain amount of bibliographical description. Johnson arrived in Edinburgh on 14 August 1773 and remained there until the morning of 18 August. Boswell kept rough notes on loose sheets of paper for the 14th, 15th, 16th, and 17th, and did not expand them into a fully-written narrative until he was preparing his book for the press in 1785. (These rough notes survive, and have been printed, or reproduced in facsimile, in the limited edition of the *Boswell Papers*. They are referred to hereafter as "Notes," the record from 18 August being styled "Journal.") On 18 August the pair set out from Edinburgh, Boswell carrying two blank notebooks, the leaves of which, in their present condition, measure about 7 by 4½ inches. In these books he kept the record of the tour, beginning in a style hardly different from the preceding rough notes, but gradually allowing himself more freedom, until the Journal, except for a few standard abbreviations, became as fully written as a printed book. In the middle of his entry for 28 September, recording the second visit to Coirechatachan, he came to the end of his second notebook, and Johnson gave him a third, the leaves of which were considerably smaller than those of the first two. This he exhausted in Coll, apparently in the middle of the entry for 12 October, but was able to buy some loose paper at the one shop on the island. On these loose sheets he continued the record to the middle of 22 October, at Lochbuie. From that point to the end of the tour he kept only rough notes—apparently very scanty—which he himself seems later to have destroyed. Some time in 1779 (more than five years later) he began to complete the Journal from these jottings, and came back to the task at intervals during 1780, 1781, and 1782, finally bringing the record down into the entry for 26 October. "The Journal which Dr. Johnson read" ended at this point, and there is no reason to suppose that Boswell had ever written more before he revised the text for the printer. The manuscript, consisting of the three bound notebooks and a sheaf of loose leaves of approximately the same size, was read not only by Johnson but by Sir William Forbes and Mrs. Thrale. Boswell had it with him on the last of his visits to London in Johnson's lifetime, and at Oxford, in June 1784, persuaded Johnson to write on a blank leaf the note concerning the Honourable Archibald Campbell which serves as one of the illustrations of this volume.[1]

Johnson died on 13 December 1784; on the day after he heard the news, Boswell received a letter from Charles Dilly asking him if he could have a biography of 400 pages ready by February, that is, within six weeks. Boswell replied that he would not be rushed, but should do the work "deliberately." He went about adding to his store of materials for the *Life*, but turned to the Hebridean Tour for immediate publication. During January and February he tried without success to apply himself to the task of revision. Two friends whose advice he sought—Cosmo Gordon, Baron in the Court of Exchequer, and Dr. Hugh Blair—confirmed him in thinking that the Journal might be printed with little change. He therefore resolved "to set himself down quietly in London and get the work executed easily."

He arrived in London on 30 March 1785, but instead of going quietly to work, allowed himself to be swept for a month into a wild eddy of dinners, executions, and girls. Then on 29 April he dined with Edmond Malone, and something happened to him. They talked until after midnight. Next day Boswell worked all the morning at the *Tour*, and arranged with Henry Baldwin for the printing. His attention was almost

---

[1] *Post*, facing p. 354.

immediately distracted by a Bill fathered by Henry Dundas, which proposed a reduction in the number of the Lords of Session. Three weeks were consumed in the writing of an extravagant pamphlet. The *Letter to the People of Scotland* was published on 26 May; that same day Boswell resumed work on the *Tour*. On the 28th he stayed "in all day in nightgown and wrote *Hebrides*." There is a hint that he was having difficulties. On the 29th he made a memorandum to call on Malone and engage him for breakfast on "Monday" (30 May). And then, on 3 June, we find him spending the morning with Malone "revising *Hebrides*." "From the moment Malone is seen at work on June 3," says Geoffrey Scott, "there is no record of Boswell devoting a single hour of *solitary* industry to the Hebridean Journal. He works with Malone, usually at Malone's; and, it appears, *he never works without Malone*." This is probably too strong, but the proof of Malone's collaboration appears throughout the manuscript, which Mr. Scott never saw. Before 3 June Boswell had prepared copy for at least pp. 3–37 of the present edition, since he refers in his Journal for 1 June to an unsuccessful search for the quotation from Butler's *Remains*.[2] The revision of such portions of the corresponding copy as have survived is entirely in his hand. But in the entry for 21 August (p. 54 of this edition), Malone's hand suddenly appears, and before long more of the revision is in his hand than in Boswell's. We knew that Malone suggested the greater part of the changes which Boswell made in the second edition. It is now abundantly clear that he suggested the greater part of the changes made in preparing the original Journal for publication.

Fresh copy was written for the portion up to 19 August. But beginning with the eighth page of the manuscript of the Tour proper (p. 38, line 22 of the present edition), Boswell, perhaps already working with Malone, decided that the original record would serve. The leaves were torn from their covers

---

[2] See *post*, p. 37, n. 8.

and interleaved with blanks of the same size. Contractions were expanded, and additions and substitutions made between the lines and in the margins of the original leaves. When the changes were too extensive to be managed in this fashion, the passage in the original was scored out, and the new matter written on the interleavings.

The revision was much more extensive than would be suspected by a reader of this edition who did not compare it minutely with Boswell's book. Hardly a paragraph was printed exactly as Boswell wrote it. Indiscreet and indelicate matter was excised. Boswell's topographical observations were generally deleted, since Johnson had published a topographical account, and Boswell, with some justice, was sceptical as to his powers of "expressing visible objects." Many passages of personal reflection were dropped, because the book was to be an essay in Johnsonian biography, not an autobiography. In the latter half of the book the revision was dictated partly by considerations of space. After the comfortable Eighteenth-Century fashion, Boswell had begun to print as soon as he had enough copy for a sheet or two. He misjudged the bulk of his material, and chose too generous a format. By the time he had reached the middle of the work, it became clear that he would have to condense more drastically if his volume were not to be unpleasantly thick, and he consequently began to throw out by handfuls material which would certainly have found a place if it had occurred in the earlier portion of the manuscript. The revision was by no means confined to excision. Matter was transposed, matter was added, whole paragraphs were recast, and every sentence scanned for informal syntax and "inelegant" phraseology. We have discussed elsewhere[3] Boswell's assurance to the public that he was presenting "*the very Journal which Dr. Johnson read*," and shall say here only that his statement is gravely misleading. At various places in the notes we have called attention to differences between the manuscript

---

[3] p. 54, n. 4.

and the published book. *The reader must not suppose that these exhaust the list; they are only a few striking instances*. Only a page-for-page collation will show how extensive and pervasive the changes were.

It has been our aim to print, from the point at which it becomes fully written, the Journal as Boswell wrote it. To recover the original text from the labyrinth of deleting strokes and interlinear additions would have been a task of some difficulty even if the manuscript had been in good condition. It is, unfortunately, in very bad condition. At some time it was allowed to become damp, and has rotted, so that a great many of the leaves—perhaps a third of them—show defects, some of them serious. Over seventy-five pages out of a total of about 675 are missing altogether. Fortunately, the published book supplies the substance (not always the exact phraseology) of many of the missing portions. Because the leaves are so narrow and Boswell's hand is so generous, the majority of the remainder can be filled in with perfect confidence. There remain a considerable number which have been supplied by pure editorial conjecture. Restorations extending beyond a few words have been indicated in the footnotes, but shorter ones have usually been made silently. It would undoubtedly have been a more scholarly proceeding to provide the first edition with an elaborate apparatus of brackets and textual notes, but a text of that character (*crede expertis*) could have been perused only by a hardened scholar. Readers have already shown some impatience to have Boswell's journals in a reading text. It has therefore seemed best to issue the present editions of the Hebridean Journal first, and to allow the more austere editing of the text to follow. We may remark, however, that we have prepared such a text in typescript, and that the copy for the present volume was transcribed from it.

Our editorial policy may be defined as follows:

(1) The text up to the point at which the Journal becomes fully written, and from the point at which the Journal lapses,

is that of Boswell's third edition, the last which he revised.
When, however, the published *Tour* is used for filling in defects in the manuscript, the first edition has been chosen, because its phraseology is likely to be nearer that of the original
record. When the manuscript gives a reading, it has invariably
been followed; that is, we have in no instance yielded to the
temptation to make up an eclectic text composed of "better
readings" from both manuscript and published *Tour*.

(2) In about twenty cases we have supplied silently an
article or some form of the verb "to be" where the manuscript
shows no defect. These omissions were not inadvertent on Boswell's part, but were due to a recrudescence of the condensed
style of the earlier portion of the record. A few genuine inad-
vertencies have also been set right without editorial comment.

(3) The original manuscript had no paragraph division.
We have broken the text into paragraphs, following, wherever
possible, the paragraph division of the published *Tour*.

(4) We have expanded abbreviations and contractions, and
normalized spelling, capitalization, and punctuation throughout. Otherwise the portion of the text taken from the published *Tour* would have followed one style (Boswell's printer's);
that from the manuscript a second (Boswell's); and our editorial restorations would have been in a third. This mixture would
be tolerable in a research edition, but hardly in one intended
for general reading. We have gone further than any previous
editor of the *Tour*, and have normalized personal names and
place-names; perhaps rashly, since the Eighteenth Century
permitted considerable latitude in these matters, and great
confusion still reigns as to the spelling of the place-names of
Gaelic origin.[4] The scholarly reader should not turn to this
text for evidence as to Boswell's habits of spelling, capitalizing,
or pointing.

---

[4] Our principal authorities are the *Dictionary of National Biography*, Mrs. Margaret
Stuart's *Scottish Family History*, J. G. Bartholomew's *Survey Gazetteer of the British Isles*,
and the Royal Scottish Geographical Society's *Atlas of Scotland* (ed. J. G. Bartholomew).

(5) The dozen or more diagrams and sketches which appear in the manuscript are of little value from any point of view—antiquarian, topographical, or artistic—and for that reason have generally been omitted in this edition.

(6) Boswell's footnotes in the published *Tour* have been handled with some freedom. We have included the majority of them, but have felt free to abridge or omit. It should be remembered that these notes were no part of the original record.

(7) Our annotation is intended rather for the general reader than for the scholar. We have drawn freely, sometimes without specific acknowledgment, on our predecessors—Croker, Hill, Chapman, and particularly Carruthers, whose edition has been too long neglected. Our edition and Dr. L. F. Powell's revision of Hill's fifth volume went to the printers at the same time, but we have been able to correct or amplify a few of our identifications by means of the proof-sheets which he has generously sent us. The great mass of entertaining anecdote that has gathered around the *Tour* may at times have betrayed us into discursiveness; we hope not too frequently.

That Boswell, on the whole, handled his revision wisely for readers of his own day, can hardly be doubted; that his original record, untrimmed and unpolished, is more entertaining to our age, seems equally certain. In the first place, we are now able to read the *Tour*, not as a book about Johnson, but as one of the best chapters in Boswell's autobiography. The sections of self-analysis in this Journal are among the keenest that we have from his pen, and they show him at the happiest and most innocent period of his life. To recover, in their complete frankness, all his and Johnson's comments on the men and women whom they met on the tour, is also a gain. *The Journal of a Tour to the Hebrides*, even after pruning, remained one of the most indiscreet books ever given to the world (did it not bring its author to the verge of a duel?), but beside the original record it seems decorous and even timid. And the personalities can now hurt nobody. The Journal "which Dr. Johnson read" is far fresher, far more intimate, far more detailed and picturesque. The "elegancy" which Malone imposed upon it was in the direction of that generalization dear to the Eighteenth-Century heart, which the modern temperament finds so uncongenial. Boswell's own instinct sometimes rebelled against it.[5] The reader who has perused the following pages will, we predict with some confidence, return with reluctance to the published *Tour*.

It remains only to make certain acknowledgments. The materials for the Index (which provides fuller identification of persons mentioned in the text than any hitherto published) were collected by Mr. John P. Kirby, Donald Grant Mitchell Fellow in English in the Yale Graduate School, and Marion S. Pottle. Professor George Watson of the University of Chicago has given us advice concerning Scotticisms. Professor John Macdonald of the University of Aberdeen has furnished many of the notes on Gaelic words and phrases, Gaelic being a language of which we know as little as Boswell did. Practically the entire typescript for the printer was prepared by Mr. Edwin J. Dryer, Jr., Yale '37, holder of a bursary in Davenport College.

F. A. P.
C. H. B.

New Haven, 25 August 1936.

---

[5] See *post*, p. 101, n. 4.

TABLE OF CONTENTS

TABLE OF ILLUSTRATIONS

The Journal of a Tour to the Hebrides

with

SAMUEL JOHNSON, LL.D.

He was of an admirable pregnancy of wit, and that pregnancy much improved by continual study from his childhood; by which he had gotten such a promptness in expressing his mind that his extemporal speeches were little inferior to his premeditated writings. Many, no doubt, had read as much, and perhaps more than he; but scarce ever any concocted his reading into judgment as he did.

BAKER'S *Chronicle.*

The Journal of a Tour to the Hebrides

with

SAMUEL JOHNSON, LL.D.[1]

DR. JOHNSON had for many years given me hopes that we should go together and visit the Hebrides. Martin's Account of those islands[2] had impressed us with a notion that we might there contemplate a system of life almost totally different from what we had been accustomed to see; and to find simplicity and wildness, and all the circumstances of remote time or place, so near to our native great island, was an object within the reach of reasonable curiosity. Dr. Johnson has said in his *Journey* that he scarcely remembered how the wish to visit the Hebrides was excited; but he told me, in summer 1763, that his father put Martin's Account into his hands when he was very young, and that he was much pleased with it. We reckoned there would be some inconveniencies and hardships, and perhaps a little danger; but these we were persuaded were magnified in the imagination of everybody. When I was at Ferney in 1764, I mentioned our design to Voltaire.[3] He

---

[1] Up to p. 56 the text is that of the third edition of Boswell's printed *Tour*, the significant variations in the original notes or Journal being recorded in footnotes. For a fuller statement of the editorial policy, see the textual note, pp. xii-xiii.

[2] In the National Library of Scotland is a copy of this book, bearing the following inscription in Boswell's hand: "This very book accompanied Mr. Samuel Johnson and me in our tour to the Hebrides in autumn 1773. Mr. Johnson told me that he had read Martin when he was very young. Martin was a native of the Isle of Skye, where a number of his relations still remain. His book is a very imperfect performance; and he is erroneous as to many particulars, even some concerning his own island. Yet as it is the only book upon the subject, it is very generally known. I have seen a second edition of it. I cannot but have a kindness for him, notwithstanding his defects.—JAMES BOSWELL. 16 April 1774."

[3] On 24 December 1764. The conversation was in French, Voltaire explaining that one could not talk English without putting the tongue between the teeth, and that he had lost his teeth. See *Boswell Papers*, iv. 130.

looked at me as if I had talked of going to the North Pole, and said, "You do not insist on my accompanying you?" "No, sir." "Then I am very willing you should go." I was not afraid that our curious expedition would be prevented by such apprehensions, but I doubted that it would not be possible to prevail on Dr. Johnson to relinquish for some time the felicity of a London life, which, to a man who can enjoy it with full intellectual relish, is apt to make existence in any narrower sphere seem insipid or irksome. I doubted that he would not be willing to come down from his elevated state of philosophical dignity; from a superiority of wisdom among the wise and of learning among the learned; and from flashing his wit upon minds bright enough to reflect it.

He had disappointed my expectations so long that I began to despair; but in spring 1773, he talked of coming to Scotland that year with so much firmness that I hoped he was at last in earnest. I knew that if he were once launched from the metropolis, he would go forward very well; and I got our common friends there to assist in setting him afloat. To Mrs. Thrale in particular, whose enchantment over him seldom failed, I was much obliged. It was: "I'll give thee a wind." "Thou art kind."[4] To *attract* him we had invitations from the chiefs Macdonald and MacLeod, and for additional aid I wrote to Lord Elibank, Dr. William Robertson, and Dr. Beattie.

To Dr. Robertson, so far as my letter concerned the present subject, I wrote as follows:

Our friend Mr. Samuel Johnson is in great health and spirits, and, I do think, has a serious resolution to visit Scotland this year. The more attraction, however, the better; and therefore, though I know he will be happy to meet you there, it will forward the scheme if, in your answer to this, you express yourself concerning it with that power of which you are so happily possessed, and which may be so directed as to operate strongly upon him.

His answer to that part of my letter was quite as I could

---

[4] *Macbeth*, I. iii, the first and second witches. Boswell is continuing the nautical figure implied in "launched" and "afloat."

have wished. It was written with the address and persuasion of the historian of America:[5]

When I saw you last, you gave us some hopes that you might prevail with Mr. Johnson to make out that excursion to Scotland with the expectation of which we have long flattered ourselves. If he could order matters so as to pass some time in Edinburgh about the close of the Summer Session, and then visit some of the Highland scenes, I am confident he would be pleased with the grand features of nature in many parts of this country; he will meet with many persons here who respect him, and some whom I am persuaded he will think not unworthy of his esteem. I wish he would make the experiment. He sometimes cracks his jokes upon us, but he will find that we can distinguish between the stabs of malevolence and *the rebukes of the righteous, which are like excellent oil,*[6] *and break not the head.* Offer my best compliments to him, and assure him that I shall be happy to have the satisfaction of seeing him under my roof.

To Dr. Beattie I wrote,

The chief intention of this letter is to inform you that I now seriously believe Mr. Samuel Johnson will visit Scotland this year, but I wish that every power of attraction may be employed to secure our having so valuable an acquisition; and therefore I hope you will without delay write to me what I know you think, that I may read it to the mighty sage, with proper emphasis, before I leave London, which I must do soon. He talks of you with the same warmth that he did last year. We are to see as much of Scotland as we can in the months of August and September. We shall not be long of being at Marischal College.[7] He is particularly desirous of seeing some of the Western Islands.

Dr. Beattie did better: *ipse venit.* He was, however, so polite as to waive his privilege of *nil mihi rescribas,*[8] and wrote from Edinburgh as follows:

Your very kind and agreeable favour of the 20th of April overtook me here yesterday after having gone to Aberdeen, which place I left about a week ago. I am to set out this day for London, and hope to have the honour of paying my respects to Mr. Johnson and you about a week or

---

[5] The *History of America* did not appear until 1777. Boswell, writing in 1785 (a year and a half after the close of the American War), selects from Robertson's works the one of greatest contemporary interest.

[6] "Our friend Edmund Burke, who by this time had received some pretty severe strokes from Dr. Johnson on account of the unhappy difference in their politics, upon my repeating this passage to him, exclaimed, 'Oil of vitriol!' "—BOSWELL.

[7] "This, I find, is a Scotticism. I should have said, 'It will not be long before we shall be at Marischal College.' "—BOSWELL. It should always be remembered that to Boswell literary English was something of a foreign tongue.

[8] A tag from Ovid (altered); the meaning of the original is approximately, "Don't reply to this; come yourself."

ten days hence. I shall then do what I can to enforce the topic you mention, but at present I cannot enter upon it, as I am in a very great hurry; for I intend to begin my journey within an hour or two.

He was as good as his word and threw some pleasing motives into the northern scale. But indeed, Mr. Johnson loved all that he heard from one whom he tells us in his *Lives of the Poets* Gray found "a poet, a philosopher, and a good man."

My lord Elibank did not answer my letter to his lordship for some time. The reason will appear when we come to the Isle of Skye. I shall then insert my letter, with letters from his lordship both to myself and Mr. Johnson.[9] I beg it may be understood that I insert my own letters, as I relate my own sayings, rather as keys to what is valuable belonging to others than for their own sake.

Luckily Mr. Justice (now Sir Robert) Chambers, who was about to sail for the East Indies, was going to take leave of his relations at Newcastle, and he conducted Dr. Johnson to that town. Mr. Scott of University College, Oxford (now Dr. Scott of the Commons), accompanied him from thence to Edinburgh. With such propitious convoys did he proceed to my native city. But lest metaphor should make it be supposed he actually went by sea, I choose to mention that he travelled in post-chaises, of which the rapid motion was one of his most favourite amusements.

Dr. Samuel Johnson's character—religious, moral, political, and literary—nay, his figure and manner, are, I believe, more generally known than those of almost any man, yet it may not be superfluous here to attempt a sketch of him. Let my readers then remember that he was a sincere and zealous Christian, of high-Church-of-England and monarchical principles, which he would not tamely suffer to be questioned; steady and inflexible in maintaining the obligations of piety and virtue, both

---

[9] Boswell, in the printed *Tour*, *did* insert the letters of Elibank and Johnson, which had been copied into the Journal, but forgot his promise to print his own, which had not been. It is supplied in this edition from a copy among the Malahide Papers. See *post*, p. 407.

from a regard to the order of society and from a veneration for the Great Source of all order; correct, nay stern, in his taste; hard to please and easily offended, impetuous and irritable in his temper, but of a most humane and benevolent heart; having a mind stored with a vast and various collection of learning and knowledge, which he communicated with peculiar perspicuity and force, in rich and choice expression. He united a most logical head with a most fertile imagination, which gave him an extraordinary advantage in arguing, for he could reason close or wide as he saw best for the moment. He could, when he chose it, be the greatest sophist that ever wielded a weapon in the schools of declamation, but he indulged this only in conversation, for he owned that he sometimes talked for victory; he was too conscientious to make error permanent and pernicious by deliberately writing it. He was conscious of his superiority. He loved praise when it was brought to him, but was too proud to seek for it. He was somewhat susceptible of flattery. His mind was so full of imagery that he might have been perpetually a poet. It has been often remarked that in his poetical pieces (which it is to be regretted are so few, because so excellent) his style is easier than in his prose. There is deception in this: it is not easier but better suited to the dignity of verse; as one may dance with grace whose motions in ordinary walking—in the common step—are awkward. He had a constitutional melancholy the clouds of which darkened the brightness of his fancy and gave a gloomy cast to his whole course of thinking; yet, though grave and awful in his deportment when he thought it necessary or proper, he frequently indulged himself in pleasantry and sportive sallies. He was prone to superstition but not to credulity. Though his imagination might incline him to a belief of the marvellous and the mysterious, his vigorous reason examined the evidence with jealousy. He had a loud voice and a slow deliberate utterance which no doubt gave some additional weight to the sterling metal of his conversation. Lord Pembroke said once to me at Wilton, with a happy pleasantry

and some truth, that "Dr. Johnson's sayings would not appear
so extraordinary were it not for his *bow-wow way*," but I admit
the truth of this only on some occasions. The *Messiah* played
upon the Canterbury organ is more sublime than when played
upon an inferior instrument, but very slight music will seem
grand when conveyed to the ear through that majestic medium.
*While therefore Doctor Johnson's sayings are read, let his manner be
taken along with them.* Let it, however, be observed that the
sayings themselves are generally great; that, though he might
be an ordinary composer at times, he was for the most part
a Handel.—His person was large, robust, I may say approaching to the gigantic, and grown unwieldly from corpulency.
His countenance was naturally of the cast of an ancient statue,
but somewhat disfigured by the scars of that *evil* which it was
formerly imagined the *royal touch* could cure. He was now in
his sixty-fourth year, and was become a little dull of hearing.
His sight had always been somewhat weak, yet so much does
mind govern and even supply the deficiency of organs that
his perceptions were uncommonly quick and accurate. His
head and sometimes also his body shook with a kind of motion like the effect of a palsy; he appeared to be frequently
disturbed by cramps or convulsive contractions, of the nature
of that distemper called St. Vitus's dance.[10] He wore a full
suit of plain brown clothes with twisted-hair buttons of the
same colour, a large bushy greyish wig, a plain shirt, black
worsted stockings, and silver buckles. Upon this tour, when
journeying, he wore boots and a very wide brown cloth greatcoat with pockets which might have almost held the two volumes of his folio dictionary, and he carried in his hand a large
English oak stick. Let me not be censured for mentioning such

---

[10] "Such they appeared to me; but since the first edition, Sir Joshua Reynolds has observed to me that Dr. Johnson's extraordinary gestures were only habits, in which he indulged himself at certain times. When in company where he was not free, or when engaged
earnestly in conversation, he never gave way to such habits, which proves that they were
not involuntary. I still however think that these gestures were involuntary; for surely
had not that been the case, he would have restrained them in the public streets."—Bos-
WELL.

minute particulars.[11] Everything relative to so great a man is
worth observing. I remember Dr. Adam Smith, in his rhetori-
cal lectures at Glasgow, told us he was glad to know that
Milton wore latchets in his shoes instead of buckles.[12] When I
mention the oak stick, it is but letting Hercules have his club;
and by and by my readers will find this stick will bud and produce a good joke.

This imperfect sketch of "the *combination* and the *form*" of
that Wonderful Man whom I venerated and loved while in
this world, and after whom I gaze with humble hope now that
it has pleased ALMIGHTY GOD to call him to a better world,
will serve to introduce to the fancy of my readers the capital
object of the following Journal, in the course of which I trust
they will attain to a considerable degree of acquaintance with
him.

His prejudice against Scotland was announced almost as
soon as he began to appear in the world of letters. In his *London, a Poem*, are the following nervous lines:

> For who would leave, unbribed, Hibernia's land?
> Or change the rocks of Scotland for the Strand?
> There none are swept by sudden fate away,
> But all, whom hunger spares, with age decay.[13]

The truth is, like the ancient Greeks and Romans, he allowed himself to look upon all nations but his own as barbarians: not only Hibernia and Scotland, but Spain, Italy, and

---

[11] Boswell *was* severely ridiculed for this reason by Peter Pindar and others ("Who will
not, too, thy pen's minutiae bless, That gives posterity the Rambler's dress?"). He unfortunately felt these gibes, and omitted several vivid descriptions of Johnson's person
from his journals in preparing them for the *Life*. Notice, too, how in editing the Hebrides
Journal for the printer he generally strikes out his pleasant lists of what he and Johnson
ate and drank. The influence of Malone is probably to be discerned here; Malone, more
than Boswell, subscribed to the Eighteenth Century view, best expressed by Sir Joshua
Reynolds, that "the beauty of art consists in being able to get above all singular forms,
local customs, particularities, and details of every kind."

[12] Boswell attended the University of Glasgow as a student of civil law in 1759–60. He
never tired of repeating a compliment which Smith once paid him upon his "facility of
manners."

[13] Johnson's prejudice against Scotland was real, but these lines are poor evidence for it.
If read carefully, they will be found to say the direct opposite of what Boswell seems to
be quoting them to prove. The real object of attack in *London* is not Ireland, Scotland,
Spain, Italy, or France. It is London.

France are attacked in the same poem. If he was particularly prejudiced against the Scots, it was because they were more in his way; because he thought their success in England rather exceeded the due proportion of their real merit; and because he could not but see in them that nationality which I believe no liberal-minded Scotsman will deny. He was indeed, if I may be allowed the phrase, at bottom much of a *John Bull*, much of a *true-born Englishman*. There was a stratum of common clay under the rock of marble.—He was voraciously fond of good eating, and he had a great deal of that quality called *humour*, which gives an oiliness and a gloss to every other quality.

I am, I flatter myself, completely a citizen of the world. In my travels through Holland, Germany, Switzerland, Italy, Corsica, France, I never felt myself from home; and I sincerely love "every kindred and tongue and people and nation." I subscribe to what my late truly learned and philosophical friend Mr. Crosbie[14] said: that the English are better animals than the Scots; they are nearer the sun, their blood is richer and more mellow; but when I humour any of them in an outrageous contempt of Scotland, I fairly own I treat them as children. And thus I have, at some moments, found myself obliged to treat even Dr. Johnson.

To Scotland, however, he ventured; and he returned from it in great good humour, with his prejudices much lessened, and with very grateful feelings of the hospitality with which he was treated, as is evident from that admirable work, his *Journey to the Western Islands of Scotland*, which, to my utter astonishment, has been misapprehended, even to rancour, by many of my countrymen.

To have the company of Chambers and Scott, he delayed his journey so long that the Court of Session, which rises on the

---

[14] Andrew Crosbie, advocate, whose character is said to have furnished Scott with some hints for Counsellor Pleydell in *Guy Mannering*. When Boswell wrote these words, Crosbie had been dead less than four months. In his last years he had been harassed by financial troubles, and died bankrupt.

eleventh of August, was broke up before he got to Edinburgh.

On Saturday the fourteenth of August, 1773, late in the evening, I received a note from him that he was arrived at Boyd's Inn, at the head of the Canongate. I went to him directly. He embraced me cordially, and I exulted in the thought that I now had him actually in Caledonia. Mr. Scott's amiable manners and attachment to our Socrates at once united me to him. He told me that before I came in the Doctor had unluckily had a bad specimen of Scottish cleanliness. He then drank no fermented liquor. He asked to have his lemonade made sweeter, upon which the waiter with his greasy fingers lifted a lump of sugar and put it into it. The Doctor in indignation threw it out of the window. Scott said he was afraid he would have knocked the waiter down. Mr. Johnson told me that such another trick was played him at the house of a lady in Paris.[15] He was to do me the honour to lodge under my roof. I regretted sincerely that I had not also a room for Mr. Scott.[16] Mr. Johnson and I walked arm-in-arm up the High Street to my house in James's Court; it was a dusky night; I could not prevent his being assailed by the evening effluvia of Edinburgh. I heard a late baronet[17] of some distinction in the political world in the beginning of the present reign observe that "walking the streets of Edinburgh at night was pretty perilous and a good deal odoriferous." The peril is much abated by the care which the magistrates have taken to enforce the city laws against throwing foul water from the windows; but, from the structure of the houses in the old town, which consist of many storeys in each of which a different family lives, and there being no covered sewers, the odour still continues. A zealous Scots-

---

[15] Probably Mme du Boccage, of whom Baretti said that Johnson "hated her before he saw her."

[16] In the original notes at this point appears the following: "He said, 'Shall I see yᵉ Lady?' B. 'Yes.' 'Then I'll put on clean shirt.' I said, ' 'Tis needless. Either don't see her tonight, or don't put on clean shirt.' JOHNS. 'Sir, I'll do both.'"

[17] Perhaps Sir Gilbert Elliot, Bart., of Minto, who was a privy councillor and held various offices of state. He died in 1777.

man would have wished Mr. Johnson to be without one of his
five senses upon this occasion. As we marched slowly along, he
grumbled in my ear, "I smell you in the dark!" But he acknowledged that the breadth of the street and the loftiness of
the buildings on each side made a noble appearance.

My wife had tea ready for him, which it is well known he
delighted to drink at all hours, particularly when sitting up
late, and of which his able defence against Mr. Jonas Hanway
should have obtained him a magnificent reward from the East
India Company. He showed much complacency upon finding
that the mistress of the house was so attentive to his singular
habit; and as no man could be more polite when he chose to
be so, his address to her was most courteous and engaging,
and his conversation soon charmed her into a forgetfulness of
his external appearance.

I did not begin to keep a regular full journal till some days
after we had set out from Edinburgh, but I have luckily preserved a good many fragments of his *Memorabilia* from his very
first evening in Scotland.

We had, a little before this, had a trial for murder,[18] in which
the judges had allowed the lapse of twenty years since its commission as a plea in bar, in conformity with the doctrine of prescription in the civil law, which Scotland and several other
countries in Europe have adopted. He at first disapproved of
this, but then he thought there was something in it if there had
been for twenty years a neglect to prosecute a crime which was
known. He would not allow that a murder, by not being *discovered* for twenty years, should escape punishment. We talked
of the ancient trial by duel. He did not think it so absurd as is
generally supposed. "For," said he, "it was only allowed when
the question was *in equilibrio*, as when one affirmed and another denied; and they had a notion that Providence would in-

---

[18] An account of this cause, the King *versus* Callum Macgregor, is given in Maclaurin's
Criminal Cases, Edinburgh, 1774, pp. 595–615. Macgregor was indicted in May 1773 for
a murder committed in 1747. As Boswell says, the plea of prescription was admitted, and
the Court of Justiciary dismissed the indictment on 9 August 1773.

terfere in favour of him who was in the right. But as it was found that in a duel he who was in the right had not a better chance than he who was in the wrong, therefore society instituted the present mode of trial and gave the advantage to him who is in the right."

We sat till near two in the morning, having chatted a good while after my wife left us.[19] She had insisted that, to show all respect to the sage, she would give up her own bedchamber to him and take a worse. This I cannot but gratefully mention, as one of a thousand obligations which I owe her, since the great obligation of her being pleased to accept of me as her husband.

SUNDAY 15 AUGUST.[1] Mr. Scott came to breakfast, at which I introduced to Dr. Johnson and him my friend Sir William Forbes, now of Pitsligo, a man of whom too much good cannot be said; who, with distinguished abilities and application in his profession of a banker, is at once a good companion and a good Christian—which I think is saying enough. Yet it is but justice to record that once when he was in a dangerous illness he was watched with the anxious apprehension of a general calamity; day and night his house was beset with affectionate inquiries, and upon his recovery *Te Deum* was the universal chorus from the hearts of his countrymen.

Mr. Johnson was pleased with my daughter Veronica,[2] then

---

[19] The notes show that they revived the joke about Langton's will. "B. 'Langt. is a worthy man.' JOHNS. 'Sir, the earth has not a better man. But ridicule is inherent in him. There is no separating them.'"

[1] In the notes, the entry for this day begins thus: "I had a little of a headach. He had a Barber to shave him. The first rasor was bad. He was very angry. 'Sir, this is digging.'" Boswell must have omitted this through oversight.

[2] "The saint's name of *Veronica* was introduced into our family through my great-grandmother Veronica, Countess of Kincardine, a Dutch lady of the noble house of Sommelsdyck, of which there is a full account in Bayle's Dictionary. The family had once a princely right in Surinam. The governor of that settlement was appointed by the States General, the town of Amsterdam, and Sommelsdyck. The States General have acquired Sommelsdyck's right; but the family has still great dignity and opulence, and by intermarriages is connected with many other noble families. When I was at The Hague I was received with all the affection of kindred. The present Sommelsdyck has an important charge in the Republic, and is as worthy a man as lives. He has honoured me with his correspondence for these twenty years. My great-grandfather, the husband of Countess Veronica, was Alexander, Earl of Kincardine, that eminent Royalist whose character is given by Burnet in his *History of his own Times*. From him the blood of *Bruce* flows in

a child of about four months old. She had the appearance of listening to him. His motions seemed to her to be intended for her amusement, and when he stopped, she fluttered and made a little infantine noise and a kind of signal for him to begin again. She would be held close to him, which was a proof from simple nature that his figure was not horrid. Her fondness for him endeared her still more to me, and I declared she should have five hundred pounds of additional fortune.[3]

We talked of the practice of the Law. Sir William Forbes said he thought an honest lawyer should never undertake a cause which he was satisfied was not a just one. "Sir," said Mr. Johnson, "a lawyer has no business with the justice or injustice of the cause which he undertakes, unless his client asks his opinion, and then he is bound to give it honestly. The justice or injustice of the cause is to be decided by the judge. Consider, sir; what is the purpose of courts of justice? It is that every man may have his cause fairly tried by men appointed to try causes. A lawyer is not to tell what he knows to be a lie: he is not to produce what he knows to be a false deed; but he is not to usurp the province of the jury and of the judge and determine what shall be the effect of evidence, what shall be the result of legal argument. As it rarely happens that a man is fit to plead his own cause, lawyers are a class of the community, who, by study and experience, have acquired the art and power of arranging evidence and of applying to the points at issue what the law has settled. A lawyer is to do for his client all that his client might fairly do for himself if he could. If, by a superiority of attention, of knowledge, of skill, and a better method of communication, he has the advantage of his adver-

---

my veins. Of such ancestry who would not be proud? And, as *Nihil est, nisi hoc sciat alter*, is peculiarly true of genealogy, who would not be glad to seize a fair opportunity to let it be known?"—BOSWELL.

[3] Veronica was at this time Boswell's only child; with four others to provide for, he found it impossible to fulfil this enthusiastic declaration. Under the deed of settlement which he executed shortly before he began preparing the *Tour* for the press, Veronica received the same "fortune" as her sisters, *viz.*, an annuity of one hundred pounds a year. She outlived her father by only four months, dying of consumption on 26 September 1795.

sary, it is an advantage to which he is entitled. There must always be some advantage on one side or other, and it is better that advantage should be had by talents than by chance. If lawyers were to undertake no causes till they were sure they were just, a man might be precluded altogether from a trial of his claim, though, were it judicially examined, it might be found a very just claim." This was sound practical doctrine, and rationally repressed a too-refined scrupulosity of conscience.

Emigration was at this time a common topic of discourse. Dr. Johnson regretted it as hurtful to human happiness. "For," said he, "it spreads mankind, which weakens the defence of a nation and lessens the comfort of living. Men, thinly scattered, make a shift, but a bad shift, without many things. A smith is ten miles off; they'll do without a nail or a staple. A tailor is far from them; they'll botch their own clothes. It is being concentrated which produces high convenience."

Sir William Forbes, Mr. Scott, and I accompanied Mr. Johnson to the chapel founded by Lord Chief Baron Smith for the service of the Church of England. The Reverend Mr. Carr, the senior clergyman, preached from these words: "Because the Lord reigneth, let the earth be glad." I was sorry to think Mr. Johnson did not attend to the sermon, Mr. Carr's low voice not being strong enough to reach his hearing. A selection of Mr. Carr's sermons has, since his death, been published by Sir William Forbes, and the world has acknowledged their uncommon merit. I am well assured Lord Mansfield has pronounced them to be excellent.

Here I obtained a promise from Lord Chief Baron Ord that he would dine at my house next day. I presented Mr. Johnson to his lordship, who politely said to him, "I have not the honour of knowing you, but I hope for it and to see you at my house. I am to wait on you tomorrow." This respectable English judge will be long remembered in Scotland, where he built an elegant house and lived in it magnificently. His own ample fortune, with the addition of his salary, enabled him to be splendidly hospitable. It may be fortunate for an individual amongst ourselves to be Lord Chief Baron, and a most worthy man[4] now has the office; but in my opinion it is better for Scotland in general that some of our public employments should be filled by gentlemen of distinction from the south side of the Tweed, as we have the benefit of promotion in England. Such an interchange would make a beneficial mixture of manners, and render our union more complete. Lord Chief Baron Ord was on good terms with us all, in a country filled with jarring interests and keen parties; and, though I well knew his opinion to be the same with my own, he kept himself aloof at a very critical period indeed, when the Douglas Cause shook the sacred security of birthright in Scotland to its foundation; a cause, which had it happened before the Union, when there was no appeal to a British House of Lords, would have left the great fortress of honours and of property in ruins.[5]

When we got home, Dr. Johnson desired to see my books. He took down Ogden's *Sermons on Prayer*, on which I set a very high value,[6] having been much edified by them, and he retired with them to his room. He did not stay long, but soon joined us in the drawing-room.[7] I presented to him Mr. Robert Arbuthnot,[8] a relation of the celebrated Dr. Arbuthnot, and a man of literature and taste. To him we were obliged for a previous recommendation which secured us a very agreeable reception at St. Andrews, and which Dr. Johnson in his *Journey* ascribes to "some invisible friend."

Of Dr. Beattie[9] Mr. Johnson said, "Sir, he has written like a

---

[4] Sir James William Montgomery, Bart.   [5] See *post*, p. 351, n. 3.

[6] Boswell carried this book with him on the tour; his frequent references to it induced Collings and Rowlandson in their caricatures to show it peeping from his pocket.

[7] Boswell suppressed a compliment which Johnson paid to him on this room: "JOHNS. said of himself, without any prompting at all, my drawing-room was the pleasantest room he had ever been in." On the previous night, when Boswell had said "I'm glad to see you under my roof," Johnson had replied, "And 'tis a very noble roof."

[8] Probably Robert Arbuthnot, Esq., of Haddo, secretary to the board of trustees for fisheries and manufactures in Scotland, and a close friend of James Beattie's. He died in 1804.

[9] The reference is to Beattie's *Essay on Truth*, an attack on Hume's philosophy which had just brought its author an honorary D.C.L. from Oxford.

man conscious of the truth and feeling his own strength. Treating your adversary with respect is giving him an advantage to which he is not entitled. The greatest part of men cannot judge of reasoning, and are impressed by character; so that if you allow your adversary a respectable character, they will think that though you differ from him, you may be in the wrong. Sir, treating your adversary with respect is striking soft in a battle. And as to Hume—a man who has so much conceit as to tell all mankind that they have been bubbled for ages and he is the wise man who sees better than they, a man who has so little scrupulosity as to venture to oppose those principles which have been thought necessary to human happiness—is he to be surprised if another man comes and laughs at him? If he is the great man he thinks himself, all this cannot hurt him; it is like throwing peas against a rock." He added "*something much too rough*," both as to Mr. Hume's head and heart, which I suppress.[10] Violence is, in my opinion, not suitable to the Christian cause. Besides, I always lived on good terms with Mr. Hume, though I have frankly told him I was not clear that it was right in me to keep company with him. "But," said I, "how much better are you than your books!" He was cheerful, obliging, and instructive; he was charitable to the poor; and many an agreeable hour have I passed with him. I have preserved some entertaining and interesting memoirs of him, particularly when he knew himself to be dying, which I may some time or other communicate to the world.[11] I shall not, however, extol him so very highly as Dr. Adam Smith does, who says in a letter to Mr. Strahan the printer (not a confidential letter to his friend, but a letter which is published with all for-

---

[10] This can now be recovered: "B. 'But why attack his heart?' J. 'Why, Sir, because his head has corrupted it. Or perhaps it has perverted his head. I know not indeed whether he has first been a blockhead and that has made him a rogue, or first been a rogue and that has made him a blockhead.'"

[11] Boswell's last and most important interview with Hume took place on 7 July 1776, just seven weeks before Hume's death. Boswell never published his account of the conversation, which was first given to the world with the publication of the Malahide Papers (*Boswell Papers*, xii. 227–32).

mality), "Upon the whole, I have always considered him, both in his lifetime and since his death, as approaching as nearly to the idea of a perfectly wise and virtuous man as perhaps the nature of human frailty will permit." Let Dr. Smith consider: was not Mr. Hume blessed with good health, good spirits, good friends, a competent and increasing fortune? And had he not also a perpetual feast of fame? But, as a learned friend[12] has observed to me, "What trials did he undergo to prove the perfection of his virtue? Did he ever experience any great instance of adversity?" When I read this sentence, delivered by my old Professor of Moral Philosophy, I could not help exclaiming with the Psalmist, "Surely I have now more understanding than my teachers!"

While we were talking, there came a note to me from Dr. William Robertson:

Sunday.

DEAR SIR,—I have been expecting every day to hear from you of Dr. Johnson's arrival. Pray what do you know about his motions? I long to take him by the hand. I write this from the college, where I have only this scrap of paper. Ever yours,

W. R.

It pleased me to find Dr. Robertson thus eager to meet Dr. Johnson. I was glad that I could answer that he was come; and I begged Dr. Robertson might be with us as soon as he could.

Sir William Forbes, Mr. Scott, Mr. Arbuthnot, and another gentleman[13] dined with us. "Come, Dr. Johnson," said I, "it is commonly thought that our veal in Scotland is not good. But here is some which I believe you will like." There was no catching him. JOHNSON. "Why, sir, what is commonly thought I should take to be true. *Your* veal may be good, but that will only be an exception to the general opinion, not a proof against it."

Dr. Robertson, according to the custom of Edinburgh at that time, dined in the interval between the forenoon and afternoon service, which was then later than now; so we had not the pleasure of his company till dinner was over, when he came

---

[12] Probably Malone.
[13] He is named in the notes: Charles Hay, advocate, later Lord Newton.

and drank wine with us. And then began some animated dialogue, of which here follows a pretty full note.

We talked of Mr. Burke. Dr. Johnson said he had great variety of knowledge, store of imagery, copiousness of language. ROBERTSON. "He has wit too." JOHNSON. "No, sir, he never succeeds there. 'Tis low; 'tis conceit. I used to say Burke never once made a good joke.[14] What I most envy Burke for is his being constantly the same. He is never what we call humdrum; never unwilling to begin to talk, nor in haste to leave off." BOSWELL. "Yet he can listen." JOHNSON. "No, I cannot say he is good at that. So desirous is he to talk that if one is speaking at this end of the table, he'll speak to somebody at the other end. Burke, sir, is such a man that if you met him for the first time in a street where you were stopped by a drove of oxen, and you and he stepped aside to take shelter but for five minutes,[15] he'd talk to you in such a manner that when you parted you would say, 'This is an extraordinary man.' Now, you may be long enough with *me* without finding anything extraordinary." He said he believed Burke was intended for the Law, but either had not money enough to follow it or had not diligence enough. He said he could not understand how a man could apply to one thing and not to another. Robertson said one man had more judgment, another more imagination. JOHNSON. "No, sir; it is only one man has more mind than another. He may direct it differently; he may by accident see the success of one kind of study and take a desire to excel in it. I am persuaded

---

[14] "This was one of the points upon which Dr. Johnson was strangely heterodox. For, surely, Mr. Burke, with his other remarkable qualities, is also distinguished for his wit, and for wit of all kinds too; not merely that power of language which Pope chooses to denominate wit,

('True wit is Nature to advantage dressed;
What oft was thought, but ne'er so well expressed')

but surprising allusions, brilliant sallies of vivacity, and pleasant conceits. His speeches in Parliament are strewed with them."—BOSWELL. The latter part of this interesting but extremely long note, part of which was written by Malone, is here omitted.

[15] Boswell saw fit to alter Johnson's figure, as actually recorded in his notes: ". . . if you met him for the first time in a street where there was a shower of cannon bullets, and you and he ran up a stair to take shelter . . ." The result was unfortunate. As Dr. Chapman has pointed out, one does not "take shelter" from a drove of oxen.

that had Sir Isaac Newton applied to poetry, he would have made a very fine epic poem. I could as easily apply to law as to tragic poetry." BOSWELL. "Yet, sir, you *did* apply to tragic poetry, not to law." JOHNSON. "Because, sir, I had not money to study law. Sir, the man who has vigour may walk to the east just as well as to the west, if he happens to turn his head that way." BOSWELL. "But, sir, 'tis like walking up and down a hill; one man will naturally do the one better than the other. A hare will run up a hill best, from her forelegs being short; a dog, down." JOHNSON. "Nay, sir; that is from mechanical powers. If you make mind mechanical, you may argue in that manner. One mind is a vice, and holds fast; there's a good memory. Another is a file, and he is a disputant, a controversialist. Another is a razor, and he is sarcastical." We talked of Whitefield. He said he was at the same college with him and knew him "before he began to be better than other people" (smiling); that he believed he sincerely meant well, but had a mixture of politics and ostentation, whereas Wesley thought of religion only.[16] Robertson said Whitefield had strong natural eloquence, which, if cultivated, would have done great things. JOHNSON. "Why, sir, I take it he was at the height of what his abilities could do, and was sensible of it. He had the ordinary advantages of education, but he chose to pursue that oratory which is for the mob." BOSWELL. "He had great effect on the passions." JOHNSON. "Why, sir, I don't think so. He could not represent a succession of pathetic images. He vociferated and made an impression. *There*, again, was a mind like a hammer." Dr. Johnson now said a certain eminent political

---

[16] "That cannot be said now, after the flagrant part which Mr. John Wesley took against our American brethren, when, in his own name, he threw amongst his enthusiastic flock, the very individual combustibles of Dr. Johnson's *Taxation no Tyranny;* and after the intolerant spirit which he manifested against our fellow-Christians of the Roman Catholic communion, for which that able champion, Father O'Leary, has given him so hearty a drubbing. But I should think myself very unworthy, if I did not at the same time acknowledge Mr. John Wesley's merit, as a veteran 'Soldier of Jesus Christ,' who has, I do believe, turned many from darkness into light, and from the power of Satan to the living GOD."—BOSWELL.

friend[17] of ours was wrong in his maxim of sticking to a certain set of *men* on all occasions. "I can see that a man may do right to stick to a *party*," said he; "that is to say, he is a *Whig*, or he is a *Tory*, and he thinks one of those parties upon the whole the best, and that to make it prevail, it must be generally supported, though in particulars it may be wrong. He takes its faggot of principles, in which there are fewer rotten sticks than in the other, though some rotten sticks, to be sure; and they cannot well be separated. But to bind one's self to one man, or one set of men (who may be right today and wrong tomorrow), without any general preference of system, I must disapprove."[18]

He told us of Cooke who translated Hesiod and lived twenty years on a translation of Plautus for which he was always taking subscriptions; and that he presented Foote to a club in the following singular manner: "This is the nephew of the gentleman who was lately hung in chains for murdering his brother."[19]

In the evening I introduced to Mr. Johnson[20] two good friends of mine, Mr. William Nairne, advocate, and Mr. Hamilton of Sundrum, my neighbour in the country, both of whom supped with us. I have preserved nothing of what passed, except that Dr. Johnson displayed another of his heterodox opinions: a contempt of tragic acting. He said, "The action of all players in tragedy is bad. It should be a man's study to repress those

---

[17] Burke, as the original notes show.

[18] "If due attention were paid to this observation, there would be more virtue, even in politics. What Dr. Johnson justly condemned, has, I am sorry to say, greatly increased in the present reign."—BOSWELL. The latter part of this long note is here omitted.

[19] Samuel Goodere, commander of the *Ruby*, who had for many years been almost insanely jealous of his brother Sir John Dineley Goodere, finally caused him to be carried on board his vessel and strangled. This occurred in 1741.

[20] "It may be observed that I sometimes call my great friend *Mr.* Johnson, sometimes *Dr.* Johnson; though he had at this time a doctor's degree from Trinity College, Dublin. The University of Oxford afterwards conferred it upon him by a diploma, in very honourable terms. It was some time before I could bring myself to call him Doctor; but, as he has been long known by that title, I shall give it to him in the rest of this Journal."—BOSWELL. Since the original MS, however, almost everywhere gives "Mr. Johnson," that form appears in the present text where the MS is used.

signs of emotion and passion, as they are called." He was of a directly contrary opinion to that of Fielding in his *Tom Jones*, who makes Partridge say of Garrick, "Why, I could act as well as he myself. I am sure if I had seen a ghost, I should have looked in the very same manner, and done just as he did." For when I asked him, "Would not you, sir, start as Mr. Garrick does if you saw a ghost?" he answered, "I hope not. If I did, I should frighten the ghost."

MONDAY 16 AUGUST. Dr. William Robertson came to breakfast. We talked of Ogden on Prayer. Dr. Johnson said, "The same arguments which are used against GOD's hearing prayer will serve against his rewarding good and punishing evil. He has resolved, he has declared, in the former case as in the latter." He had last night looked into Lord Hailes's *Remarks on the History of Scotland*. Dr. Robertson and I said it was a pity Lord Hailes did not write greater things. (His lordship had not then published his *Annals of Scotland*.) JOHN-SON. "I remember I was once on a visit at the house of a lady for whom I had a high respect. There was a good deal of company in the room. When they were gone, I said to this lady, 'What foolish talking have we had!' 'Yes,' said she, 'but while they talked, you said nothing.'[1] I was struck with the reproof. How much better is the man who does anything that is innocent than he who does nothing. Besides, I love anecdotes. I fancy mankind may come in time to write all aphoristically, except in narrative; grow weary of preparation and connexion and illustration and all those arts by which a big book is made. If a man is to wait till he weaves anecdotes into a system, we may be long in getting them, and get but few in comparison of what we might get."

Dr. Robertson said the notions of Eupham Macallan,[2] a

---

[1] The notes corresponding to this passage have been preserved, but they do not supply the name. Possibly Mrs. Hester Chapone, who "had the assurance to dispute" with Johnson.

[2] Euphan McCullan, a fanatic of Covenanting times, believed that she received a direct answer to all her prayers. Lord Hailes, whose *Remarks on the History of Scotland* had just

fanatic woman of whom Lord Hailes gives a sketch, were still prevalent among some of the Presbyterians; and therefore it was right in Lord Hailes, a man of known piety, to undeceive them.

We walked out, that Dr. Johnson might see some of the things which we have to show at Edinburgh. We went to the Parliament House,[3] where the Parliament of Scotland sat and where the Ordinary Lords of Session hold their courts; and to the New Session House adjoining to it, where our Court of Fifteen (the fourteen Ordinaries with the Lord President at their head) sit as a court of review. We went to the Advocates' Library, of which Dr. Johnson took a cursory view,[4] and then to what is called the *Laigh* (or under) Parliament House, where the records of Scotland (which has an universal security by register) are deposited till the great Register Office be finished. I was pleased to behold Dr. Samuel Johnson rolling about in this old magazine of antiquities. There was by this time a pretty numerous circle of us attending upon him. Somebody talked of happy moments for composition, and how a man can write at one time and not at another. "Nay," said Dr. Johnson, "a man may write at any time if he will set himself *doggedly*[5] to it."

I here began to indulge old Scottish sentiments[6] and to express a warm regret that by our Union with England, we

---

appeared, had pointed out that her supposed "answers" led to the murder of Archbishop Sharp.

[3] Boswell omitted here an obscure passage from the notes. It may be expanded as follows: "Dr. Johnson asked why President Duncan Forbes had a statue and no one else. He agreed, however, that if others were admitted, there was danger lest they become too common." Roubiliac's statue of Forbes still stands in the Parliament House. Other statues were admitted in the Nineteenth Century, among them one of Boswell's particular aversion, Henry Dundas, first Viscount Melville.

[4] According to the notes, Johnson "would look at little."

[5] "This word is commonly used to signify *sullenly, gloomily;* and in that sense alone it appears in Dr. Johnson's Dictionary. I suppose he meant by it, 'with an *obstinate resolution,* similar to that of a sullen man.'"—BOSWELL. Johnson, whose conversations as reported by Boswell certainly gave currency to this word, seems, from the evidence of the *Oxford English Dictionary*, to have been the first to use it in this sense.

[6] He and Johnson, as the notes show, were at this moment looking at the Treaty of Union.

were no more—our independent kingdom was lost. JOHNSON. "Sir, never talk of your independency, who could let your Queen remain twenty years in captivity and then be put to death without even a pretence of justice, without your ever attempting to rescue her; and such a Queen, too!—as every man of any gallantry of spirit would have sacrificed his life for." Worthy MR. JAMES KER, Keeper of the Records: "Half our nation was bribed by English money." JOHNSON. "Sir, that is no defence; that makes you worse." Good MR. BROWN, Keeper of the Advocates' Library: "We had better say nothing about it." BOSWELL. "You would have been glad, however, to have had us last war, sir, to fight your battles!" JOHNSON. "We should have had you for the same price, though there had been no Union, as we might have had Swiss, or other troops. No, no, I shall agree to a separation. You have only to *go home*." Just as he had said this, I, to divert the subject, showed him the signed assurances of the three successive Kings of the Hanover family to maintain the Presbyterian establishment in Scotland. "We'll give you that," said he, "into the bargain."

We next went to the great church of St. Giles, which has lost its original magnificence in the inside by being divided into four places of Presbyterian worship. "Come," said Dr. Johnson jocularly to Principal Robertson,[7] "let me see what was once a church!"[8] We entered that division which was formerly called the New Church and of late the High Church, so well known by the eloquence of Dr. Hugh Blair. It is now very elegantly fitted up, but it was then shamefully dirty. Dr. Johnson said nothing at the time, but when we came to the great door of the Royal Infirmary, where, upon a board, was

[7] "I have hitherto called him Dr. William Robertson, to distinguish him from Dr. James Robertson, who is soon to make his appearance. But *Principal*, from his being the head of our college, is his usual designation, and is shorter; so I shall use it hereafter."—BOSWELL.

[8] From the notes we learn that Boswell remarked, "It is made into four kirks," and Johnson replied, "A Church will make many kirks." (An alternative reading of Johnson's remark is given: "It takes many kirks to make a church.")

this inscription, "*Clean your feet!*", he turned about slyly and said, "There is no occasion for putting this at the doors of your churches!"

We then conducted him down the Post House stairs, Parliament Close, and made him look up from the Cowgate to the highest building in Edinburgh (from which he had just descended), being thirteen floors or storeys from the ground upon the back elevation, the front wall being built upon the edge of the hill and the back wall rising from the bottom of the hill several storeys before it comes to a level with the front wall. We proceeded to the College with the Principal at our head. Dr. Adam Ferguson, whose *Essay on the History of Civil Society* gives him a respectable place in the ranks of literature, was with us. As the College buildings are indeed very mean, the Principal said to Dr. Johnson that he must give them the same epithet that a Jesuit did when showing a poor college abroad: "*Hae miseriae nostrae.*" Dr. Johnson was, however, much pleased with the library, and with the conversation of Dr. James Robertson,[9] Professor of Oriental Languages, the Librarian. We talked of Kennicott's edition of the Hebrew Bible and hoped it would be quite faithful. JOHNSON. "Sir, I know not any crime so great that a man could contrive to commit as poisoning the sources of eternal truth."

I pointed out to him where there formerly stood an old wall enclosing part of the College, which I remember bulged out in a threatening manner, and of which there was a common tradition similar to that concerning Bacon's study at Oxford—that it would fall upon some very learned man. It had some time before this been taken down, that the street might be widened and a more convenient wall built. Dr. Johnson, glad of an opportunity to have a pleasant hit at Scottish learning, said, "They have been afraid it never would fall."

We showed him the Royal Infirmary, for which, and for every other exertion of generous public spirit in his power,

---

[9] In the notes he is called "Little Robertson."

that noble-minded citizen of Edinburgh, George Drummond, will be ever held in honourable remembrance. And we were too proud not to carry him to the Abbey of Holyroodhouse, that beautiful piece of architecture, but, alas! that deserted mansion of royalty, which Hamilton of Bangour in one of his elegant poems calls

A virtuous palace, where no monarch dwells.

I was much entertained while Principal Robertson fluently harangued to Dr. Johnson upon the spot concerning scenes of his celebrated *History of Scotland*. We surveyed that part of the palace appropriated to the Duke of Hamilton, as Keeper, in which our beautiful Queen Mary lived, and in which David Rizzio was murdered, and also the State Rooms. Dr. Johnson was a great reciter of all sorts of things serious or comical. I overheard him repeating here in a kind of muttering tone a line of the old ballad, "Johnny Armstrong's Last Good-Night":

And ran him through the fair body![10]

We returned to my house, where there met him at dinner the Duchess of Douglas, Sir Adolphus Oughton, Lord Chief Baron, Sir William Forbes, Principal Robertson, Mr. Cullen, advocate. Before dinner he told us of a curious conversation between the famous George Faulkner and him. George said that England had drained Ireland of fifty thousand pounds in specie annually for fifty years. "How so, sir?" said Dr. Johnson. "You must have a very great trade?" "No trade." "Very rich mines?" "No mines." "From whence, then, does all this money come?" "Come! why, out of the blood and bowels of the poor people of Ireland!"

He seemed to me to have an unaccountable prejudice against Swift, for I once took the liberty to ask him if Swift had personally offended him, and he told me he had not. He

---

[10] "The stanza from which he took this line is,
'But then rose up all Edinburgh,
They rose up by thousands three;
A cowardly Scot came John behind,
And ran him through the fair body!'"—BOSWELL.

said today, "Swift is clear, but he is shallow. In coarse humour he is inferior to Arbuthnot; in delicate humour he is inferior to Addison. So he is inferior to his contemporaries, without putting him against the whole world. I doubt if the *Tale of a Tub* was his; it has so much more thinking, more knowledge, more power, more colour, than any of the works which are indisputably his. If it was his, I shall only say he was *impar sibi*."

We gave him as good a dinner as we could. Our Scotch moorfowl or grouse were then abundant and quite in season; and so far as wisdom and wit can be aided by administering agreeable sensations to the palate, my wife took care that our great guest should not be deficient.

Sir Adolphus Oughton, then our Deputy Commander-in-Chief, who was not only an excellent officer but one of the most universal scholars I ever knew, had learned the Erse language, and expressed his belief in the authenticity of Ossian's poetry. Dr. Johnson took the opposite side of that perplexed question, and I was afraid the dispute would have run high between them. But Sir Adolphus, who had a very sweet temper, changed the discourse, grew playful, laughed at Lord Monboddo's notion of men having tails, and called him "a Judge *a posteriori*,"[11] which amused Dr. Johnson, and thus hostilities were prevented.

At supper we had Dr. Cullen, his son the advocate, Dr. Adam Ferguson, and Mr. Crosbie, advocate.[12] Witchcraft was introduced. Mr. Crosbie said he thought it the greatest blasphemy to suppose evil spirits counteracting the Deity, and raising storms, for instance, to destroy his creatures. JOHNSON.

---

[11] "... Lord Monboddo, the Scotch judge, who has lately written a strange book about the origin of language, in which he traces monkeys up to men, and says that in some countries the human species have tails like other beasts. He inquired for these long-tailed men of Banks, and was not well pleased that they had not been found in all his peregrination" (Johnson to Mrs. Thrale, 25 Aug. 1773).

[12] Also Charles Hay, whose name Boswell has again suppressed. It is difficult to explain why Boswell twice deleted the name. For a year or two after the Hebrides jaunt, Hay was one of Boswell's most intimate friends. After 1780 he is not once mentioned in the journals.

"Why, sir, if moral evil be consistent with the government of the Deity, why may not physical evil be also consistent with it? It is not more strange that there should be evil spirits than evil men; evil unembodied spirits than evil embodied spirits. And as to storms, we know there are such things, and it is no worse that evil spirits raise them than that they rise." CROSBIE. "But it is not credible that witches should have effected what they are said in stories to have done." JOHNSON. "Sir, I am not defending their credibility. I am only saying that your arguments are not good, and will not overturn the belief of witchcraft." (Dr. Ferguson said to me aside, "He is right.") "And then, sir, you have all mankind, rude and civilized, agreeing in the belief of the agency of preternatural powers. You must take evidence; you must consider that wise and great men have condemned witches to die." CROSBIE. "But an Act of Parliament put an end to witchcraft." JOHNSON. "No, sir; witchcraft had ceased, and therefore an Act of Parliament was passed to prevent persecution for what was not witchcraft. Why it ceased, we cannot tell, as we cannot tell the reason of many other things." Dr. Cullen, to keep up the gratification of mysterious disquisition, with the grave address for which he is remarkable in his companionable as in his professional hours, talked in a very entertaining manner of people walking and conversing in their sleep. I am very sorry I have no note of this. We talked of the orang-outang, and of Lord Monboddo's thinking that he might be taught to speak. Dr. Johnson treated this with ridicule. Mr. Crosbie said that Lord Monboddo believed the existence of everything possible; in short that all which is in *posse* might be found in *esse*. JOHNSON. "But, sir, it is as possible that the orang-outang does not speak as that he speaks. However, I shall not contest the point. I should have thought it not possible to find a Monboddo, yet *he* exists." I again mentioned the stage. JOHNSON. "The appearance of a player with whom I have drunk tea counteracts the imagination that he is the character he represents. Nay, you know, nobody imagines that he is the character he represents. They say, 'See *Garrick*! How he looks tonight! See how he'll clutch the dagger!' That is the buzz of the theatre."

TUESDAY 17 AUGUST. Sir William Forbes came to breakfast and brought with him Dr. Blacklock, whom he introduced to Dr. Johnson, who received him with a most humane complacency: "Dear Dr. Blacklock, I am glad to see you!" Blacklock seemed to be much surprised when Dr. Johnson said it was easier to him to write poetry than to compose his *Dictionary*. His mind was less on the stretch in doing the one than the other. Besides, composing a dictionary requires books and a desk; you can make a poem walking in the fields, or lying in bed. Dr. Blacklock spoke of scepticism in morals and religion with apparent uneasiness, as if he wished for more certainty.[1] Dr. Johnson, who had thought it all over, and whose vigorous understanding was fortified by much experience, thus encouraged the blind Bard to apply to higher speculations what we all willingly submit to in common life; in short, he gave him more familiarly the able and fair reasoning of Butler's *Analogy*: "Why, sir, the greatest concern we have in this world, the choice of our profession, must be determined without demonstrative reasoning. Human life is not yet so well known as that we can have it. And take the case of a man who is ill. I call two physicians: they differ in opinion. I am not to lie down and die between them; I must do something." The conversation then turned on atheism; on that horrible book, *Système de la Nature*;[2]

---

[1] After the publication of the *Tour*, Boswell received a letter from Dr. Blacklock relative to this conversation in which Blacklock maintained that he had been misunderstood: he had expressed astonishment, not because Johnson said that it was easier to write poetry than a dictionary, but because he had said that the writing of the dictionary afforded him more pleasure. Moreover, Blacklock insisted that his remarks on scepticism had no bearing upon his own beliefs, but were general observations. Boswell printed this letter as an appendix to the second edition, politely refusing to alter his account. "I am slow to believe," he says, "that any man's memory, at the distance of several years, can preserve facts or sayings with such fidelity as may be done by writing them down when they are recent; and I beg it may be remembered that it is not upon *memory*, but upon what was *written at the time*, that the authenticity of my Journal rests."

[2] An atheistic book by Baron d'Holbach, recently published, which Voltaire called "a

and on the supposition of an eternal necessity, without design, without a governing mind. JOHNSON. "If it were so, why has it ceased? Why don't we see men thus produced around us now? Why, at least, does it not keep pace in some measure with the progress of time? If it stops because there is now no need of it, then it is plain there is and ever has been an all-powerful intelligence. But stay!" said he with one of his satiric laughs. "Ha! ha! ha! I shall suppose Scotchmen made necessarily, and Englishmen by choice."

At dinner this day we had Sir Alexander Dick, whose amiable character and ingenious and cultivated mind are so generally known (he was then on the verge of seventy, and is now —1785—eighty-one, with his faculties entire, his heart warm, and his temper gay); Sir David Dalrymple (Lord Hailes); Mr. Maclaurin, advocate; Dr. Gregory, who now worthily fills his father's medical chair; and my uncle, Dr. Boswell. This was one of Dr. Johnson's best days. He was quite in his element. All was literature and taste, without any interruption. Lord Hailes, who is one of the best philologists in Great Britain, who has written papers in the *World*, and a variety of other works in prose and in verse, both Latin and English, pleased him highly. He told him he had discovered the *Life of Cheynell*, in the *Student*, to be his. JOHNSON. "No one else knows it." Dr. Johnson had before this dictated to me a law paper, upon a question purely in the law of Scotland, concerning *vicious intromission*, that is to say, intermeddling with the effects of a deceased person without a regular title, which formerly was understood to subject the intermeddler to payment of all the defunct's debts. The principle has of late been relaxed. Dr. Johnson's argument was for a renewal of its strictness. The paper was printed, with additions by me, and given into the Court of Session.[3] Lord Hailes knew Dr. Johnson's part not to be mine, and pointed

---

philippic against God." It furnished the arguments for Shelley's *Necessity of Atheism*, and is lavishly quoted in the notes to *Queen Mab*.

[3] This document, a petition written for James Wilson of Haghouse, is preserved in the National Library of Scotland.

out exactly where it began and where it ended. Dr. Johnson said, "It is much, now, that his lordship can distinguish so."

In Dr. Johnson's *Vanity of Human Wishes* there is the following passage:

> The teeming mother, anxious for her race,
> Begs for each birth the fortune of a face;
> Yet Vane could tell what ills from beauty spring,
> And Sedley cursed the charms which pleased a king.

Lord Hailes told him he was mistaken in the instances he had given of unfortunate fair ones, for neither Vane nor Sedley had a title to that description. His lordship has since been so obliging as to send me a note of this, for the communication of which I am sure my readers will thank me.

The lines in the tenth Satire of Juvenal, according to my alteration, should have run thus:

> "Yet Shore[4] could tell . . .
> And Vallière[5] cursed . . ."

The first was a penitent by compulsion, the second by sentiment; though the truth is Mademoiselle de la Vallière threw herself (but still from sentiment) in the King's way.

Our friend chose Vane, who was far from being well-looked, and Sedley, who was so ugly that Charles II said his brother had her by way of penance.

Mr. Maclaurin's learning and talents enabled him to do his part very well in Dr. Johnson's company. He produced two epitaphs upon his father, the celebrated mathematician. One was in English, of which Dr. Johnson did not change one word. In the other, which was in Latin, he made several alterations.[6]

Mr. Murray, advocate, who married a niece of Lord Mansfield's, and is now one of the Judges of Scotland by the title of Lord Henderland, sat with us a part of the evening, but did not venture to say anything that I remember, though he is certainly possessed of talents which would have enabled

---

[4] "Mistress of Edward IV."—BOSWELL.
[5] "Mistress of Louis XIV."—BOSWELL.
[6] Boswell proceeds to specify the alterations, and in a footnote prints the entire epitaph.

him to have shown himself to advantage if too great anxiety had not prevented him.

At supper we had Dr. Alexander Webster, who, though not learned, had such a knowledge of mankind, such a fund of information and entertainment, so clear a head and such accommodating manners, that Dr. Johnson found him a very agreeable companion.

When Dr. Johnson and I were left by ourselves, I read to him my notes of the opinions of our judges upon the question of literary property.[7] He did not like them, and said, "They make me think of your judges not with that respect which I should wish to do." To the argument of one of them[8] that there can be no property in blasphemy or nonsense, he answered, "Then your rotten sheep are mine! By that rule, when a man's house falls into decay, he must lose it." I mentioned an argument of mine: that literary performances are not taxed. As Churchill says,

> No statesman yet has thought it worth his pains
> To tax our labours, or excise our brains,

and therefore they are not property. "Yet," said he, "we hang a man for stealing a horse, and horses are not taxed." Mr. Pitt has since put an end to that argument.[9]

WEDNESDAY 18 AUGUST.[1] On this day we set out from Edinburgh. We should gladly have had Mr. Scott to go with us, but he was obliged to return to England. I have given a sketch of Dr. Johnson; my readers may wish to know a little of his fellow-traveller. Think, then, of a gentleman of ancient blood, the pride of which was his predominant passion. He

---

[7] Boswell had just been arguing the case, which was decided on 20 July 1773. In January 1774 he published his "notes" as *The Decision of the Court of Session upon the Question of Literary Property.*
[8] Lord Gardenstone, as the notes show. Lord Hailes's speech is also specified as having disappointed Johnson.
[9] A tax was levied on horses in 1784.
[1] With this date Boswell began writing his journal in a bound notebook, but, as he says (*ante*, p. 12), it did not become a "regular full journal" for some days thereafter. Consequently the text of the published *Tour* is here continued, up to the point marked on p. 56.

was then in his thirty-third year, and had been about four years happily married. His inclination was to be a soldier, but his father, a respectable judge, had pressed him into the profession of the Law. He had travelled a good deal and seen many varieties of human life. He had thought more than anybody supposed, and had a pretty good stock of general learning and knowledge. He had all Dr. Johnson's principles, with some degree of relaxation. He had rather too little than too much prudence, and his imagination being lively, he often said things of which the effect was very different from the intention. He resembled sometimes

> The best good man, with the worst natured muse.

He cannot deny himself the vanity of finishing with the encomium of Dr. Johnson, whose friendly partiality to the companion of his tour represents him as one "whose acuteness would help my inquiry, and whose gaiety of conversation and civility of manners are sufficient to counteract the inconveniences of travel in countries less hospitable than we have passed."

Dr. Johnson thought it unnecessary to put himself to the additional expense of bringing with him Francis Barber, his faithful black servant, so we were attended only by my man, Joseph Ritter,[2] a Bohemian, a fine stately fellow above six feet high, who had been over a great part of Europe, and spoke many languages. He was the best servant I ever saw. Let not my readers disdain his introduction. For Dr. Johnson gave him this character: "Sir, he is a civil man, and a wise man."

From an erroneous apprehension of violence, Dr. Johnson had provided a pair of pistols, some gunpowder, and a quantity of bullets; but upon being assured we should run no risk of meeting any robbers, he left his arms and ammunition in an open drawer, of which he gave my wife the charge. He also left

---

[2] "Joseph Ritter afterwards undertook the management of the large inn at Paisley, called the Abercorn Arms, but did not succeed in that concern."—Sir WALTER SCOTT.

in that drawer one volume of a pretty full and curious Diary of his Life, of which I have a few fragments, but the book has been destroyed. I wish female curiosity had been strong enough to have had it all transcribed, which might easily have been done; and I should think the theft, being *pro bono publico*, might have been forgiven. But I may be wrong. My wife told me she never once looked into it. She did not seem quite easy when we left her, but away we went!

Mr. Nairne, advocate, was to go with us as far as St. Andrews. It gives me pleasure that by mentioning his *name* I connect his title to the just and handsome compliment paid him by Dr. Johnson in his book: "A gentleman who could stay with us only long enough to make us know how much we lost by his leaving us." When we came to Leith, I talked with perhaps too boasting an air how pretty the Frith of Forth looked; as indeed, after the prospect from Constantinople, of which I have been told, and that from Naples, which I have seen, I believe the view of that Frith and its environs from the Castle Hill of Edinburgh is the finest in Europe. "Ay," said Dr. Johnson, "that is the state of the world. Water is the same everywhere: 'Una est injusti caerula forma maris.'"[3]

I told him the port here was the mouth of the river or water of Leith. "Not *Lethe*," said Mr. Nairne. "Why, sir," said Dr. Johnson, "when a Scotchman sets out from this port for England, he forgets his native country." NAIRNE. "I hope, sir, you will forget England here." JOHNSON. "Then 'twill be still more Lethe." He observed of the pier or quay, "You have no occasion for so large a one, your trade does not require it; but you are like a shopkeeper who takes a shop, not only for what he has to put into it, but that it may be believed he has a great deal to put into it." It is very true that there is now compara-

---

[3] "Non illic urbes, non tu mirabere silvas:
Una est injusti caerula forma maris.—*Ovid. Amor.* L. II. El. xi.
Nor groves nor towns the ruthless ocean shows;
Unvaried still its azure surface flows."—BOSWELL.

tively little trade upon the eastern coast of Scotland. The riches of Glasgow show how much there is in the west; and perhaps we shall find trade travel westward on a great scale as well as a small.

We talked of a man's drowning himself. JOHNSON. "I should never think it time to make away with myself." I put the case of Eustace Budgell, who was accused of forging a will and sunk himself in the Thames before the trial of its authenticity came on. "Suppose, sir," said I, "that a man is absolutely sure that if he lives a few days longer, he shall be detected in a fraud, the consequence of which will be utter disgrace and expulsion from society." JOHNSON. "Then, sir, let him go abroad to a distant country; let him go to some place where he is *not* known. Don't let him go to the devil where he *is* known!"

He then said, "I see a number of people barefooted here; I suppose you all went so before the Union. Boswell, your ancestors went so when they had as much land as your family has now. Yet 'Auchinleck' is the 'Field of Stones': there would be bad going barefooted there. The Lairds, however, did it." I bought some speldings, fish (generally whitings) salted and dried in a particular manner, being dipped in the sea and dried in the sun, and eaten by the Scots by way of a relish. He had never seen them, though they are sold in London. I insisted on *scottifying*[4] his palate, but he was very reluctant. With difficulty I prevailed with him to let a bit of one of them lie in his mouth. He did not like it.

In crossing the Frith, Dr. Johnson determined that we should land upon Inchkeith. On approaching it, we first observed a high rocky shore. We coasted about, and put into a little bay on the northwest. We clambered up a very steep ascent, on which was very good grass but rather a profusion

---

[4] "My friend General Campbell, Governor of Madras, tells me that they make *speldings* in the East Indies, particularly at Bombay, where they call them *Bambaloes*."—BOSWELL. See the *Oxford English Dictionary* under *Bummalo*.

of thistles. There were sixteen head of black cattle grazing upon the island. Lord Hailes observed to me that Brantôme calls it *L'Isle des Chevaux*, and that it was probably "a *safer* stable" than many others in his time. The fort, with an inscription on it, *Maria Re.* 1564, is strongly built. Dr. Johnson examined it with much attention. He stalked like a giant among the luxuriant thistles and nettles. There are three wells in the island, but we could not find one in the fort. There must probably have been one, though now filled up, as a garrison could not subsist without it. But I have dwelt too long on this little spot. Dr. Johnson afterwards bade me try to write a description of our discovering Inchkeith, in the usual style of travellers, describing fully every particular, stating the grounds on which we concluded that it must have once been inhabited, and introducing many sage reflections; and we should see how a thing might be covered in words so as to induce people to come and survey it. All that was told might be true, and yet in reality there might be nothing to see. He said, "I'd have this island. I'd build a house, make a good landing-place, have a garden and vines and all sorts of trees. A rich man of a hospitable turn here would have many visitors from Edinburgh." When we had got into our boat again, he called to me, "Come now, pay a classical compliment to the island on quitting it." I happened luckily, in allusion to the beautiful Queen Mary, whose name is upon the fort, to think of what Virgil makes Aeneas say on having left the country of his charming Dido:

Invitus, regina, tuo de littore cessi.[5]

"Very well hit off!" said he.[6]

We dined at Kinghorn[7] and then got into a post-chaise. Mr. Nairne and his servant and Joseph rode by us. We stopped

[5] "Unwillingly, O queen, I left your shore."
[6] Boswell omitted a passage here: "It looked as if he and I had laid plan to have a good ready saying. Had we been little wits, it would have been believed. We spoke of the Glengore [syphilis]. He said we had a law to geld lepers, and a good one, as they cd do nothing but mischief. He was pleased wt the sailing."
[7] At Monro's, on fish with onion sauce, roast mutton, and potatoes (Boswell's Journal).

at Cupar and drank tea. We talked of Parliament, and I said I supposed very few of the members knew much of what was going on, as indeed very few gentlemen know much of their own private affairs. JOHNSON. "Why, sir, if a man is not of a sluggish mind, he may be his own steward. If he will look into his affairs, he will soon learn. So it is as to public affairs. There must always be a certain number of men of business in Parliament." BOSWELL. "But consider, sir, what is the House of Commons? Is not a great part of it chosen by peers? Do you think, sir, they ought to have such an influence?" JOHNSON. "Yes, sir. Influence must ever be in proportion to property, and it is right it should." BOSWELL. "But is there not reason to fear that the common people may be oppressed?" JOHNSON. "No, sir. Our great fear is from want of power in government. Such a storm of vulgar force has broke in." BOSWELL. "It has only roared." JOHNSON. "Sir, it has roared till the judges in Westminster Hall have been afraid to pronounce sentence in opposition to the popular cry. You are frightened by what is no longer dangerous, like Presbyterians by Popery." He then repeated a passage, I think in Butler's *Remains*, which ends, "and would cry 'Fire! Fire!' in Noah's flood."[8]

We had a dreary drive in a dusky night to St. Andrews, where we arrived late.[9] We found a good supper[10] at Glass's Inn, and Dr. Johnson revived agreeably. He said the collection called *The Muses' Welcome to King James* (first of England and sixth of Scotland), on his return to his native kingdom, showed that there was then abundance of learning in Scotland, and that the conceits in that collection, with which people find fault, were mere mode. He added, we could not now entertain

---

[8] Boswell adds a long note, furnished by Isaac Reed, giving the reference to Butler, but suggesting that the piece in which the passage occurs was really written by Sir John Birkenhead. The most interesting thing about this note is that Boswell seems to have gone to press without it, and to have cancelled two leaves to get it in.

[9] The following was omitted: "I *saw*, rather in a dream or vision, my child, dead, then her face eaten by worms, then a skeleton of her head. Was shocked and dreary.... I was sunk.... Mr. *J*. complained I did not hear in chaise, and said it was half abstraction. I must try to help this."

[10] "*Rissered* haddocks and mut. chops."—JOURNAL.

a sovereign so; that Buchanan had spread the spirit of learning amongst us, but we had lost it during the civil wars. He did not allow the Latin poetry of Pitcairne so much merit as has been usually attributed to it, though he owned that one of his pieces, which he mentioned but which I am sorry is not specified in my notes, was "very well." It is not improbable that it was the poem which Prior has so elegantly translated.

After supper we made a *procession* to St. Leonard's College, the landlord walking before us with a candle and the waiter with a lantern. That college had some time before been dissolved, and Dr. Watson, a professor here (the historian of Philip II), had purchased the ground and what buildings remained.[11] When we entered his court, it seemed quite academical; and we found in his house very comfortable and genteel accommodation.[12]

THURSDAY 19 AUGUST. We rose much refreshed.[1] I had with me a map of Scotland, a Bible which was given to me by Lord Mountstuart when we were together in Italy,[2] and Ogden's *Sermons on Prayer*. Mr. Nairne introduced us to Dr. Watson, whom we found a well-informed man of very amiable manners. Dr. Johnson, after they were acquainted, said, "I take great delight in him." His daughter, a very pleasing young lady, made breakfast. Dr. Watson observed that Glasgow University had fewer home-students since trade increased, as learning was rather incompatible with it. JOHNSON. "Why, sir, as trade is now carried on by subordinate hands, men in trade have as much leisure as others, and now learning itself is a trade. A man goes to a bookseller and gets what he can. We have done with patronage. In the infancy of learning we find some great man praised for it. This diffused it among others.

---

[11] "Mr. W. bought whole College for £400."—JOURNAL.

[12] "My Journal, from this day inclusive, was read by Dr. Johnson."—BOSWELL.

[1] This entry originally began thus: "Slept till near ten; waked well. Prayed fervtly; read new test. Found Mr. Johns. up. He shewed me his notes of yesterday's jaunt. Wonderfully minute, and exact except as to not seeing trees and hedges."

[2] For six weeks during the summer of 1765 Boswell travelled in Italy in the party of Lord Mountstuart, eldest son of the Earl of Bute.

When it becomes general, an author leaves the great and applies to the multitude." BOSWELL. "It is a shame that authors are not now better patronized." JOHNSON. "No, sir. If learning cannot support a man, if he must sit with his hands across till somebody feeds him, it is as to him a bad thing, and it is better as it is. With patronage, what flattery! what falsehood! While a man is *in equilibrio*, he throws truth among the multitude and lets them take it as they please. In patronage, he must say what pleases his patron, and it is an equal chance whether that be truth or falsehood." WATSON. "But is not the case now that, instead of flattering one person, we flatter the age?" JOHNSON. "No, sir. The world always lets a man tell what he thinks his own way. I wonder, however, that so many people have written who might have let it alone. That people should endeavour to excel in conversation, I do not wonder, because in conversation praise is instantly reverberated."

We talked of change of manners. Dr. Johnson observed that our drinking less than our ancestors was owing to the change from ale to wine. "I remember," said he, "when all the *decent* people in Lichfield got drunk every night, and were not the worse thought of. Ale was cheap, so you pressed strongly. When a man must bring a bottle of wine, he is not in such haste. Smoking has gone out. To be sure, it is a shocking thing—blowing smoke out of our mouths into other people's mouths, eyes, and noses, and having the same thing done to us. Yet I cannot account why a thing which requires so little exertion and yet preserves the mind from total vacuity, should have gone out. Every man has something by which he calms himself: beating with his feet or so.[3] I remember when people in England changed a shirt only once a week; a pandour, when he gets a shirt, greases it to make it last. Formerly, good tradesmen had no fire but in the kitchen; never in the parlour except on Sunday. My father, who was a magistrate of Lichfield, lived thus. They never began to have a fire in the parlour but on leaving

---

[3] "Dr. Johnson used to practice this himself very much."—BOSWELL.

off business or some great revolution of their life." Dr. Watson
said the hall was as a kitchen in old squires' houses. JOHNSON.
"No, sir. The hall was for great occasions, and never was used
for domestic refection." We talked of the Union, and what
money it had brought into Scotland. Dr. Watson observed that
a little money formerly went as far as a great deal now. JOHN-
SON. "In speculation, it seems that a smaller quantity of money,
equal in value to a larger quantity, if equally divided, should
produce the same effect. But it is not so in reality. Many more
conveniences and elegancies are enjoyed where money is plentiful than where it is scarce. Perhaps a great familiarity with it,
which arises from plenty, makes us more easily part with it."

After what Dr. Johnson has said of St. Andrews, which he
had long wished to see as our oldest university and the seat
of our Primate in the days of episcopacy, I can say little.[4]
Since the publication of Dr. Johnson's book, I find that he
has been censured for not seeing here the ancient chapel of
St. Rule, a curious piece of sacred architecture. But this was
neither his fault nor mine. We were both of us abundantly
desirous of surveying such sort of antiquities, but neither of
us knew of this. I am afraid the censure must fall on those who
did not tell us of it. In every place where there is anything
worthy of observation, there should be a short printed direc-
tory for strangers, such as we find in all the towns of Italy
and in some of the towns in England. I was told that there is
a manuscript account of St. Andrews by Martin, secretary to
Archbishop Sharp, and that one Douglas has published a
small account of it. I inquired at a bookseller's, but could not
get it. Dr. Johnson's veneration for the hierarchy is well
known. There is no wonder, then, that he was affected with

---

[4] In the MS there is a brief note about the old woman whom they found living in a vault,
which was omitted because Johnson had described her in his *Journey*, in a passage which
George Dempster called "the only silly thing in the book." Boswell's account he might
have considered even sillier, for it appears that he questioned her about second sight:
"Told me she never saw anything or heard, tho' she walked out in night-time. Only had
dreams before her relations died."

a strong indignation while he beheld the ruins of religious magnificence. I happened to ask where John Knox was buried. Dr. Johnson burst out, "I hope in the highway.[5] I have been looking at his reformations."

It was a very fine day. Dr. Johnson seemed quite wrapped up in the contemplation of the scenes which were now presented to him. He kept his hat off while he was upon any part of the ground where the cathedral had stood. He said well that Knox had set on a mob without knowing where it would end; and that differing from a man in doctrine was no reason why you should pull his house about his ears. As we walked in the cloisters, there was a solemn echo while he talked loudly of a proper retirement from the world. Mr. Nairne said he had an inclination to retire. I called Dr. Johnson's attention to this, that I might hear his opinion if it was right. JOHNSON. "Yes, when he has done his duty to society. In general, as every man is obliged not only to love GOD, but his neighbour as himself, he must bear his part in active life; yet there are exceptions. Those who are exceedingly scrupulous (which I do not approve, for I am no friend to scruples), and find their scrupulosity invincible, so that they are quite in the dark and know not what they shall do; or those who cannot resist temptations and find they make themselves worse by being in the world, without making it better, may retire. I never read of a hermit, but in imagination I kiss his feet; never of a monastery, but I could fall on my knees and kiss the pavement. But I think putting young people there, who know nothing of life, nothing of retirement, is dangerous and wicked. It is a saying as old as Hesiod,

Ἔργα νέων, βουλαῖτε μέσων, εὐχαῖτε γερόντων.[6]

That is a very noble line: not that young men should not

---

[5] In a sense, he *was*. St. Giles's churchyard, in which he was buried, became shortly after, and still remains, a thoroughfare.

[6] "Let youth in deeds, in counsel man engage;
   Prayer is the proper duty of old age."—BOSWELL.

pray, or old men not give counsel, but that every season of life has its proper duties. I have thought of retiring, and have talked of it to a friend, but I find my vocation is rather to active life." I said *some* young monks might be allowed, to show that it is not age alone that can retire to pious solitude, but he thought this would only show that they could not resist temptation.

He wanted to mount the steeples, but it could not be done. There are no good inscriptions here. Bad Roman characters he naturally mistook for half-Gothic, half-Roman. One of the steeples, which he was told was in danger, he wished not to be taken down; "for," said he, "it may fall on some of the posterity of John Knox—and no great matter!" Dinner was mentioned. JOHNSON. "Ay, ay; amidst all these sorrowful scenes, I have no objection to dinner."

We went and looked at the castle where Cardinal Beaton was murdered, and then visited Principal Murison at his college, where is a good library-room; but the Principal was abundantly vain of it, for he seriously said to Dr. Johnson, "You have not such a one in England."

The Professors entertained us with a very good dinner. Present: Murison, Shaw, Cook, Hill, Hadow, Watson, Flint, Brown. I observed that I wondered to see him eat so well after viewing so many sorrowful scenes of ruined religious magnificence. "Why," said he, "I am not sorry after seeing these gentlemen, for they are not sorry." Murison said all sorrow was bad, as it was murmuring against the dispensations of Providence. JOHNSON. "Sir, sorrow is inherent in humanity. As you cannot judge two and two to be either five or three, but certainly four, so, when comparing a worse present state with a better which is past, you cannot but feel sorrow. It is not cured by reason, but by the incursion of present objects, which wear out the past. You need not murmur, though you are sorry." MURISON. "But St. Paul says, 'I have learnt, in whatever state I am, therewith to be content.'" JOHNSON. "Sir, that relates to riches and poverty; for we see St. Paul, when he had a thorn in the flesh, prayed earnestly to have it removed, and then he could not be content." Murison, thus refuted, tried to be smart, and drank to Dr. Johnson: "Long may you lecture!" Dr. Johnson afterwards, speaking of his not drinking wine, said, "The Doctor spoke of *lecturing*" (looking to him). "I give all these lectures on water."

He defended requiring subscription in those admitted to universities thus: "As all who come into the country must obey the King, so all who come into an university must be of the Church."

And here I must do Dr. Johnson the justice to contradict a very absurd and ill-natured story as to what passed at St. Andrews. It has been circulated that after grace was said in English in the usual manner, he with the greatest marks of contempt, as if he had held it to be no grace in an university, would not sit down till he had said grace aloud in Latin. This would have been an insult indeed to the gentlemen who were entertaining us. But the truth was precisely thus: In the course of conversation at dinner, Dr. Johnson, in very good humour, said, "I should have expected to have heard a Latin grace among so many learned men; we had always a Latin grace at Oxford. I believe I can repeat it." Which he did, as giving the learned men in one place a specimen of what was done by the learned men in another place.

We went and saw the church in which is Archbishop Sharp's monument. I was struck with the same kind of feelings with which the churches of Italy impressed me. I was much pleased to see Dr. Johnson actually in St. Andrews, of which we had talked so long. Professor Hadow was with us this afternoon, along with Dr. Watson. We looked at St. Salvator's College. The rooms for students seemed very commodious, and Dr. Johnson said the chapel was the neatest place of worship he had seen. The key of the library could not be found, for it seems Professor Hill, who was out of town, had taken it with him.

Dr. Johnson told a joke he had heard of a monastery abroad where the key of the library could never be found.[7]

It was somewhat dispiriting to see this ancient archiepiscopal city now sadly deserted. We saw in one of its streets a remarkable proof of liberal toleration: a nonjuring clergyman strutting about in his canonicals with a jolly countenance and a round belly, like a well-fed monk.

We observed two occupations united in the same person, who had hung out two signposts. Upon one was, "James Hood, White-Iron Smith" (i.e. tin-plate worker). Upon another, "The Art of Fencing taught, by James Hood." Upon this last were painted some trees and two men fencing, one of whom had hit the other in the eye, to show his great dexterity; so that the art was well taught. JOHNSON. "Were I studying here, I should go and take a lesson. I remember Hope in his book on this art, says, 'The Scotch are very good fencers.'"

We returned to the inn where we had been entertained at dinner, and drank tea in company with some of the professors, of whose civilities I beg leave to add my humble and very grateful acknowledgment to the honourable testimony of Dr. Johnson in his *Journey*.

We talked of composition, which was a favourite topic of Dr. Watson's, who first distinguished himself by lectures on rhetoric. JOHNSON. "I advised Chambers, and would advise every young man beginning to compose, to do it as fast as he can, to get a habit of having his mind to start promptly. It is so much more difficult to improve in speed than in accuracy." WATSON. "I own I am for much attention to accuracy in composing, lest one should get bad habits of doing it in a slovenly manner." JOHNSON. "Why, sir, you are confounding *doing* inaccurately with the *necessity* of doing inaccurately. A man knows when his composition is inaccurate, and when he thinks fit he'll correct it. But if a man is accustomed to compose slowly and with difficulty upon all

7 "We saw the mace and silver arrows."—JOURNAL.

occasions, there is danger that he may not compose at all, as we do not like to do that which is not done easily; and at any rate, more time is consumed in a small matter than ought to be." WATSON. "Dr. Hugh Blair has taken a week to compose a sermon." JOHNSON. "Then, sir, that is for want of the habit of composing quickly, which I am insisting one should acquire." WATSON. "Blair was not composing all the week, but only such hours as he found himself disposed for composition." JOHNSON. "Nay, sir, unless you tell me the time he took, you tell me nothing. If I say I took a week to walk a mile, and have had the gout five days and been ill otherwise another day, I have taken but one day. I myself have composed about forty sermons. I have begun a sermon after dinner and sent it off by the post that night. I wrote forty-eight of the printed octavo pages of the *Life of Savage* at a sitting, but then I sat up all night. I have also written six sheets in a day of translation from the French."[8] BOSWELL. "We have all observed how one man dresses himself slowly and another fast." JOHNSON. "Yes, sir, it is wonderful how much time some people will consume in dressing: taking up a thing and looking at it, and laying it down, and taking it up again. Every one should get the habit of doing it quickly. I would say to a young divine, 'Here is your text; let me see how soon you can make a sermon.' Then I'd say, 'Let me see how much better you can make it.' Thus I should see both his powers and his judgment."

We all went to Dr. Watson's to supper. Miss Sharp, great-grandchild of Archbishop Sharp, was there, as was Mr. Craig, the ingenious architect of the new town of Edinburgh and nephew of Thomson, to whom Dr. Johnson has since done so much justice in his *Lives of the Poets*.

We talked of memory and its various modes. JOHNSON. "Memory will play strange tricks. One sometimes loses a single word.

---

[8] A translation with notes, of Crousaz's commentary on Pope's *Essay on Man*, first published in 1739. Boswell's Journal, under the date of 3 June 1781, shows that Crousaz's book was the work in question.

I once lost *fugaces* in the ode '*Posthume, Posthume*.'" I mentioned to him that a worthy gentleman[9] of my acquaintance actually forgot his own name. JOHNSON. "Sir, that was a morbid oblivion."

FRIDAY 20 AUGUST. Dr. Shaw, the Professor of Divinity, breakfasted with us. I took out my *Ogden on Prayer* and read some of it to the company. Dr. Johnson praised him. "Abernethy," said he, "allows only of a physical effect of prayer upon the mind, which may be produced many ways as well as by prayer; for instance, by meditation. Ogden goes farther. In truth we have the consent of all nations for the efficacy of prayer, whether offered up by individuals or by assemblies; and *Revelation* has told us it will be effectual." I said Leechman seemed to incline to Abernethy's doctrine. Dr. Watson observed that Leechman meant to show that, even admitting no effect to be produced by prayer respecting the Deity, it was useful to our own minds. He had given only a part of his system. Dr. Johnson thought he should have given the whole.

Dr. Johnson enforced the strict observance of Sunday. "It should be different," he observed, "from another day. People may walk, but not throw stones at birds. There may be relaxation, but there should be no levity."

We went and saw Colonel Nairne's garden and grotto. Here was a fine old plane-tree. Unluckily the Colonel said there was but this and another large tree in the county. This assertion was an excellent cue for Dr. Johnson, who laughed enormously, calling to me to hear it. He had expatiated to me on the nakedness of that part of Scotland which he had seen. His *Journey* has been violently abused for what he has said upon this subject. But let it be considered that when Dr. Johnson talks of trees, he means trees of good size, such as he was accustomed to see in England, and of these there are certainly very few upon the *eastern coast* of Scotland. Besides, he said that he meant

---

[9] His name is given in the MS, but the reading is uncertain: probably Robert Irving of Bonshaw, writer to the signet.

to give only a map of the road; and let any traveller observe how many trees which deserve the name he can see from the road from Berwick to Aberdeen. Had Dr. Johnson said, "There are *no* trees" upon this line, he would have said what is colloquially true, because by "no trees" in common speech we mean "few." When he is particular in counting, he may be attacked. I know not how Colonel Nairne came to say there were but *two* large trees in the county of Fife. I did not perceive that he smiled. There are certainly not a great many, but I could have shown him more than two at Balmuto, from whence my ancestors came, and which now belongs to a branch of my family.

The grotto was ingeniously constructed.[1] In the front of it were petrified stocks of fir, plane, and some other tree. Dr. Johnson said, "Scotland has no right to boast of this grotto; it is owing to personal merit. I never denied personal merit to many of you." Professor Shaw said to me as we walked, "This is a wonderful man; he is master of every subject he handles." Dr. Watson allowed him a very strong understanding, but wondered at his total inattention to established manners, as he came from London.

I have not preserved in my Journal any of the conversation which passed between Dr. Johnson and Professor Shaw, but I recollect Dr. Johnson said to me afterwards, "I took much to Shaw."

We left St. Andrews about noon, and some miles from it observing at Leuchars a church with an old tower, we stopped to look at it. The manse, as the parsonage-house is called in Scotland, was close by. I waited on the minister, mentioned our names, and begged he would tell us what he knew about it. He was a very civil old man, but could only inform us that it was supposed to have stood eight hundred years. He told us there was a colony of Danes in his parish; that they had landed at a remote period of time, and still remained a dis-

---

[1] They saw in it a "wonderful large lobster claw." This was preserved in the first and second editions, but deleted in the third.

tinct people. Dr. Johnson shrewdly inquired whether they had brought women with them. We were not satisfied as to this colony.[2]

We saw this day Dundee and Aberbrothock, the last of which Dr. Johnson has celebrated in his *Journey*. Upon the road we talked of the Roman Catholic faith.[3] He mentioned (I think) Tillotson's argument against transubstantiation: "That we are as sure we see bread and wine only as that we read in the Bible the text on which that false doctrine is founded. We have only the evidence of our senses for both." "If," he added, "GOD had never spoken figuratively, we might hold that he speaks literally when he says, 'This is my body.'" BOSWELL. "But what do you say, sir, to the ancient and continued tradition of the Church upon this point?" JOHNSON. "Tradition, sir, has no place where the Scriptures are plain; and tradition cannot persuade a man into a belief of transubstantiation. Able men, indeed, have *said* they believed it."

---

[2] The Rev. Mr. Kettle, author of the article on Leuchars in Sir John Sinclair's *Statistical Account of Scotland*, mentions the tradition that the eastern part of the parish was peopled by the crews of a Danish fleet wrecked on the coast, but finds no evidence to support the story. Sir Walter Scott called it "a vain imagination."

[3] The discussion was not so abstract as this suggests. The MS reads, "He asked me about Rom. Cath. in 1759, w^c I resumed [i.e. recapitulated]." (The date is wrong; it should be 1760. Boswell is usually correct in giving the day and hour of an occurrence, but he sometimes slips as to the year—e.g., in this very journal, he refers to his having first met Johnson in 1762.) The reference is to a period of Boswell's life of which certain aspects will perhaps always remain cloaked in mystery. What we know from Boswell himself is that in the spring of 1760 he ran off from Glasgow University to London, the centre of all his hopes of fame and fortune, and there took lodgings in the house of one Egan, a wig-maker and a Roman Catholic. He saw mass celebrated for the first time in the Bavarian Chapel, embraced Roman Catholicism, and entertained thoughts (as he afterwards told Rousseau) of going off to France and entering a monastery. Lord Auchinleck followed him to London, but went back to Scotland without him. Boswell had meanwhile fallen in with his father's Ayrshire neighbour, the Earl of Eglinton, who took him into his own house, introduced him into the circles of "the great, the gay, and the ingenious," and, Boswell says, "freed me from the gloom of superstition, although it led me to the other extreme." That is, Eglinton cured him of Romanism by turning him into a rake. From another source (Ramsay of Ochtertyre) we hear that Boswell's flight to London was made in the company of an actress, who was a Roman Catholic, and who has been thought to have been instrumental in effecting his conversion. He may, indeed, have carried on an intrigue with an actress after he reached London, but it is practically certain that he did not elope with one, for an unpublished anecdote in *Boswelliana* shows that he made the trip on horse-back in two days and a half, riding night and day. Boswell's adherence to Romanism was very brief, but it coloured the remainder of his exist-

This is an awful subject. I did not then press Dr. Johnson upon it, nor shall I now enter upon a disquisition concerning the import of those words uttered by our Saviour[4] which had such an effect upon many of his disciples that they "went back, and walked no more with him." The Catechism and solemn office for Communion in the Church of England maintain a mysterious belief in more than a mere commemoration of the death of Christ by partaking of the elements of bread and wine.

Dr. Johnson put me in mind that at St. Andrews I had defended my profession very well when the question had again been started whether a lawyer might honestly engage with the first side that offers him a fee. "Sir," said I, "it was with your arguments against Sir William Forbes, but it was much that I could wield the arms of Goliah."

He said our judges had not gone deep in the question concerning literary property. I mentioned Lord Monboddo's opinion that if a man could get a work by heart, he might print it, as by such an act the mind is exercised. JOHNSON. "No, sir, a man's repeating it no more makes it his property than a man may sell a cow which he drives home." I said printing an abridgment of a work was allowed, which was only cutting the horns and tail off the cow. JOHNSON. "No, sir, 'tis making the cow have a calf."

About eleven at night we arrived at Montrose. We found but a sorry inn,[5] where I myself saw another waiter put a lump of sugar with his fingers into Dr. Johnson's lemonade,

---

ence. He enjoyed devout feelings at St. Peter's in Rome; he had strong scruples against subscribing to the "formula" because it required him to profess an abhorrence of the doctrine of purgatory and the invocation of saints and angels. Throughout his life, he remained an occasional attendant at mass in the various Roman Catholic chapels in London. In an unpublished codicil to his Will, he requests the prayers of all his pious friends for his departed soul, "considering how reasonable it is to suppose that it may be detained some time in a middle state."

[4] "*Then Jesus said unto them, verily, verily, I say unto you, except ye eat the flesh of the son of man, and drink his blood, ye have no life in you.* See St. John's Gospel, chap. vi. 53 and following verses."—BOSWELL.

[5] They dined on haddocks, pickled salmon, veal cutlets, and fowl (Boswell's Journal).

for which he called him "Rascal!" It put me in great glee
that our landlord was an Englishman. I rallied the Doctor
upon this, and he grew quiet. Both Sir John Hawkins's and
Dr. Burney's *History of Music* had then been advertised. I asked
if this was not unlucky: would not they hurt one another?
JOHNSON. "No, sir. They will do good to one another. Some
will buy the one, some the other, and compare them; and
so a talk is made about a thing, and the books are sold."

He was angry at me for proposing to carry lemons with us
to Skye, that he might be sure to have his lemonade. "Sir,"
said he, "I do not wish to be thought that feeble man who cannot do without anything. Sir, it is very bad manners to carry
provisions to any man's house, as if he could not entertain
you. To an inferior it is oppressive; to a superior it is insolent."

Having taken the liberty this evening to remark to Dr.
Johnson that he very often sat quite silent for a long time,
even when in company with only a single friend, which I myself had sometimes sadly experienced, he smiled and said, "It
is true, sir. Tom Tyers" (for so he familiarly called our ingenious friend, who since his death has paid a biographical tribute
to his memory) "Tom Tyers described me the best. He once
said to me, 'Sir, you are like a ghost: you never speak till you
are spoken to.'"[6]

SATURDAY 21 AUGUST. Neither the Rev. Mr. Nisbet, the
established minister, nor the Rev. Mr. Spooner, the Episcopal
minister, were in town. Before breakfast we went and saw the
town hall, where is a good dancing-room and other rooms for
tea-drinking. The appearance of the town from it is very well,
but many of the houses are built with their ends to the street,
which looks awkward. When we came down from it, I met Mr.
Gleg, a merchant here. He went with us to see the English
chapel. It is situated on a pretty dry spot, and there is a fine

---

[6] "This description of Dr. Johnson appears to have been borrowed from *Tom Jones*, Book
XI, chap. ii. 'The other, who, like a ghost, only wanted to be spoke to, readily answered,'
&c."—BOSWELL.

walk to it. It is really an elegant building, both within and without. The organ is adorned with green and gold. Dr. Johnson gave a shilling extraordinary to the clerk, saying, "He belongs to an honest church." I put him in mind that Episcopals were but *dissenters* here; they were only *tolerated.* "Sir," said he, "we are here as Christians in Turkey." He afterwards went into an apothecary's shop and ordered some medicine for himself, and wrote the prescription in technical characters. The boy took him for a physician.

I doubted much which road to take, whether to go by the coast or by Laurencekirk and Monboddo. I knew Lord Monboddo and Dr. Johnson did not love each other, yet I was unwilling not to visit his lordship, and was also curious to see them together.[1] I mentioned my doubts to Dr. Johnson, who said he would go two miles out of his way to see Lord Monboddo. I therefore sent Joseph forward with the following note:

Montrose, 21 August.

My dear lord,—Thus far I am come with Mr. Samuel Johnson. We must be at Aberdeen tonight. I know you do not admire him so much as I do, but I cannot be in this country without making you a bow at your old place, as I do not know if I may again have an opportunity of seeing Monboddo. Besides, Mr. Johnson says he would go two miles out of his way to see Lord Monboddo. I have sent forward my servant, that we may know if your lordship be at home. I am ever, my dear lord, most sincerely yours,

James Boswell.

As we travelled onwards from Montrose, we had the Grampian Hills in our view, and some good land around us, but void of trees and hedges. Dr. Johnson has said ludicrously in his *Journey* that the *hedges* were of *stone*; for instead of the verdant *thorn* to refresh the eye, we found the bare *wall* or *dike* intersecting the prospect. He observed that it was wonderful to see a country so divested, so denuded of trees.

---

[1] "There were several points of similarity between them: learning, clearness of head, precision of speech, and a love of research on many subjects which people in general do not investigate. Foote paid Lord Monboddo the compliment of saying that he was 'an Elzevir edition of Johnson.' It has been shrewdly observed that Foote must have meant a diminutive or *pocket* edition."—Boswell.

We stopped at Laurencekirk, where our great grammarian, Ruddiman, was once schoolmaster. We respectfully remembered that excellent man and eminent scholar, by whose labours a knowledge of the Latin language will be preserved in Scotland, if it shall be preserved at all. Lord Gardenstone, one of our judges, collected money to raise a monument to him at this place, which I hope will be well executed. I know my father gave five guineas towards it. Lord Gardenstone is the proprietor of Laurencekirk, and has encouraged the building of a manufacturing village, of which he is exceedingly fond, and has written a pamphlet upon it, as if he had founded Thebes, in which, however, there are many useful precepts strongly expressed. The village seemed to be irregularly built, some of the houses being of clay, some of brick, and some of brick and stone. Dr. Johnson observed they thatched well here.

I was a little acquainted with Mr. Forbes, the minister of the parish. I sent to inform him that a gentleman desired to see him. He returned for answer that he would not come to a stranger. I then gave my name and he came. I remonstrated to him for not coming to a stranger, and by presenting him to Dr. Johnson proved to him what a stranger might sometimes be. His Bible inculcates "be not forgetful to entertain strangers," and mentions the same motive. He defended himself by saying he had once come to a stranger who sent for him, and he found him "a *little-worth person!*"

Dr. Johnson insisted on stopping at the inn, as I told him that Lord Gardenstone had furnished it with a collection of books, that travellers might have entertainment for the mind as well as the body. He praised the design, but wished there had been more books, and those better chosen.

About a mile from Monboddo, where you turn off the road, Joseph was waiting to tell us my lord expected us to dinner. We drove over a wild moor. It rained and the scene was somewhat dreary. Dr. Johnson repeated with solemn emphasis Macbeth's speech on meeting the witches. As we travelled on, he told me, "Sir, you got into our Club by doing what a man can do.[2] Several of the members wished to keep you out. Burke told me he doubted if you were fit for it, but now you are in, none of them are sorry. Burke says that you have so much good humour naturally, it is scarce a virtue." BOSWELL. "They were afraid of you, sir, as it was you who proposed me." JOHNSON. "Sir, they knew that if they refused you, they'd probably never have got in another. I'd have kept them all out. Beauclerk was very earnest for you." BOSWELL. "Beauclerk has a keenness of mind which is very uncommon." JOHNSON. "Yes, sir; and everything comes from him so easily. It appears to me that I labour when I say a good thing." BOSWELL. "You are loud, sir, but it is not an effort of mind."

Monboddo is a wretched place, wild and naked, with a poor old house; though, if I recollect right, there are two turrets which mark an old baron's residence. Lord Monboddo received us at his gate most courteously; pointed to the Douglas arms upon his house, and told us that his great-grandmother was of that family. "In such houses," said he, "our ancestors lived, who were better men than we." "No, no, my lord," said Dr. Johnson. "We are as strong as they, and a great deal wiser." This was an assault upon one of Lord Monboddo's capital dogmas, and I was afraid there would have been a violent altercation in the very close, before we got into the house. But his lordship is distinguished not only for "ancient metaphysics," but for ancient *politesse*—"*la vieille cour*"—and he made no reply.

His lordship was dressed in a rustic suit and wore a little round hat. He told us we now saw him as *Farmer Burnett*, and we should have his family dinner, a farmer's dinner. He said, "I should not have forgiven Mr. Boswell had he not brought you here, Dr. Johnson." He produced a very long stalk of corn as a specimen of his crop, and said, "You see here the

---

[2] "This, I find, is considered as obscure. I suppose Dr. Johnson meant that I assiduously and earnestly recommended myself to some of the members, as in a canvass for an election into Parliament."—BOSWELL.

*laetas segetes.*³" He added that Virgil seemed to be as enthusiastic a farmer as he, and was certainly a practical one. JOHNSON. "It does not always follow, my lord, that a man who has written a good poem on an art has practised it. Philip Miller told me that in Philips's *Cyder, a Poem* all the precepts were just, and indeed better than in books written for the purpose of instructing, yet Philips had never made cider."

I started the subject of emigration. JOHNSON. "To a man of mere animal life, you can urge no argument against going to America but that it will be some time before he will get the earth to produce. But a man of any intellectual enjoyment will not easily go and immerse himself and his posterity for ages in barbarism."

He and my lord spoke highly of Homer. JOHNSON. "He had all the learning of his age. The shield of Achilles shows a nation in war, a nation in peace; harvest sport, nay, stealing."⁴ MONBODDO. "Ay, and what we" (looking to me) "would call a Parliament-House scene: a cause pleaded." JOHNSON. "That is part of the life of a nation in peace. And there are in Homer such characters of heroes and combinations of qualities of heroes, that the united powers of mankind ever since have not produced any but what are to be found there." MONBODDO. "Yet no character is described." JOHNSON. "No, they all develop themselves. Agamemnon is

---

³ The "joy-giving corn" mentioned in Virgil's *Georgics,* I.1.

⁴ "My note of this is much too short. *Brevis esse laboro, obscurus fio.* Yet as I have resolved that *the very Journal which Dr. Johnson read* shall be presented to the public, I will not expand the text in any considerable degree, though I may occasionally supply a word to complete the sense, as I fill up the blanks of abbreviation in the writing; neither of which can be said to change the genuine Journal. One of the best critics of our age conjectures that the imperfect passage above has probably been as follows: 'In his book we have an accurate display of a nation in war, and a nation in peace; the peasant is delineated as truly as the general; nay, even harvest sport, and the modes of ancient theft are described.'"—BOSWELL. The critic was undoubtedly Malone. This note of Boswell's is misleading, and it is hard to convince oneself that it was not intended to mislead. It assures the reader that in preparing his journal for the press, Boswell has allowed himself no editorial latitude beyond expanding abbreviations and "*occasionally* supplying a word to complete the sense." As a matter of fact he supplied a great many words, occasionally added paragraphs of comment which had no source in the journal, and did not scruple to rewrite whole sections which he considered too crabbed or too verbose. He also made

always a gentleman-like character; he has always βασιλικόν τι.[5]
That the ancients held so is plain from this: that Euripides
in his *Hecuba* makes him the person to interpose."[6] MONBODDO.
"The history of manners is the most valuable. I never set a
high value on any other history." JOHNSON. "Nor I; and therefore I esteem biography, as giving us what comes near to ourselves, what we can turn to use." BOSWELL. "But in the course
of general history, we find manners. In wars, we see the dispositions of people, their degrees of humanity, and other particulars." JOHNSON. "Yes; but then you must take all the facts
to get this, and it is but a little you get." MONBODDO. "And it is
that little which makes history valuable." Bravo! thought I;
they agree like two brothers. MONBODDO. "I am sorry, Dr. Johnson, you were not longer at Edinburgh to receive the homage
of our men of learning." JOHNSON. "My lord, I received great
respect and great kindness." BOSWELL. "He goes back to Edinburgh after our tour." We talked of the decrease of learning in
Scotland, and of the *Muses' Welcome*. JOHNSON. "Learning is
much decreased in England in my remembrance." MONBODDO.
"You, sir, have lived to see its decrease in England, I its extinction in Scotland." However, I brought him to confess that
the High School of Edinburgh[7] did well. JOHNSON. "Learning

---

extensive deletions, frequently for no better reason than that he wished to make his book
shorter. What he really means is that he has scrupulously refrained from expanding his
condensed record of Johnson's conversation when he cannot confidently retrieve the
fuller form from his remarkable memory, which ordinarily required only a hint to bring
back the *ipsissima verba* of speeches made years before. In this sense his "accuracy" is undoubted, but it would have been more honest not to speak so emphatically of "what was
written at the time" and "*the very Journal which Dr. Johnson read.*"

[5] "A certain quality of kingliness."

[6] "Dr. Johnson modestly said he had not read Homer so much as he wished he had done.
But this conversation shows how well he was acquainted with the Moeonian bard; and
he has shown it still more in his criticism upon Pope's Homer, in his Life of that poet. My
excellent friend Mr. Langton told me he was once present at a dispute between Dr.
Johnson and Mr. Burke, on the comparative merits of Homer and Virgil, which was
carried on with extraordinary abilities on both sides. Dr. Johnson maintained the superiority of Homer."—BOSWELL.

[7] Which, by the way, it is certain that Boswell never attended, though Dr. William
Steven's history of the school represents him as a student there in 1756. The "James
Boswell" who appears in the lists was the biographer's first cousin, Dr. John Boswell's
eldest son.

has decreased in England, because learning will not do so much for a man as formerly. There are other ways of getting preferment. Few bishops are now made for their learning. To be a bishop a man must be learned in a learned age, factious in a factious age, but always of eminence. Warburton is an exception, though his learning alone did not raise him. He was first an antagonist to Pope, and helped Theobald to publish his Shakespeare; but seeing Pope the rising man, when Crousaz attacked his *Essay on Man* for some faults which it has and some which it has not, Warburton defended it in the Review of that time. This brought him acquainted with Pope, and he gained his friendship. Pope introduced him to Allen, Allen married him to his niece; so by Allen's interest and his own he was made a bishop. But then his learning was the *sine qua non*. He knew how to make the most of it, but I do not find by any dishonest means." MONBODDO. "He is a great man." JOHNSON. "Yes, he has great knowledge, great power of mind. Hardly any man brings greater variety of learning to bear upon his point." MONBODDO. "He is one of the greatest lights of your church." JOHNSON. "Why, we are not so sure of his being very friendly to us. He blazes, if you will, but that is not always the steadiest light. Lowth is another bishop who has risen by his learning."

Dr. Johnson examined young Arthur, Lord Monboddo's son, in Latin. He answered very well, upon which he said with complacency, "Get you gone! When King James comes back,[8] you shall be in the *Muses' Welcome!*" My lord and Dr. Johnson disputed a little whether the savage or the London shopkeeper had the best existence, his lordship, as usual, preferring the savage. My lord was extremely hospitable, and I saw both Dr. Johnson and him liking each other better every hour.

Mr. Johnson went downstairs a little.[9] My lord spoke of

[8] "I find some doubt has been entertained concerning Dr. Johnson's meaning here. It is to be supposed that he meant, 'when a king shall again be entertained in Scotland.'" —BOSWELL.

[9] With this sentence (near the bottom of p. 32 of the MS) the Journal becomes fully written, and furnishes the text from this point forward to p. 357. The footnotes signed BOSWELL are, however, from the printed *Tour*, unless the contrary is stated.

his conversation as I could have wished. Mr. Johnson had said, "I have done greater feats with my knife than this," though he had taken a very hearty dinner.[10] My lord, who affects or believes he follows an abstemious system, seemed struck with Mr. Johnson's manner of living. I had a particular satisfaction in being under the roof of Monboddo, my lord being my father's old friend, and having been always very good to me. We were cordial together. He asked Mr. Johnson and me to stay all night. When I said we *must* be at Aberdeen, he said, "Well, I'm like the Romans, 'happy to come, happy to depart.'" He thanked Mr. Johnson for his visit. MR. JOHNSON. "I little thought, when I had the honour to meet your lordship in London, that I should see you at Monboddo." After dinner, as the ladies were going away, Mr. Johnson would stand up. He insisted that good breeding was of great consequence in society. "'Tis fictitious benevolence. It supplies the place of it among those who see each other in public, or little. Depend upon it, the want of it always produces something disagreeable to one or other. I have always applied to good breeding what Cato says of honour" (repeated the lines nobly).

When he took up his large oak stick, he said, "My lord, that's *Homeric*."

Gory, the black, was sent as our guide so far. I observed how curious it was to see an African in the north of Scotland, with little or no difference of manners. A man is like a bottle, which you may fill with red wine or with white. He laughed to see Gory and Joseph: "Those two fellows, one from Africa, the other from Bohemia—quite at home." He was much pleased with Lord Monboddo today. He said he would have pardoned him for a few paradoxes when he found he had so much that was good. But that from his appearance in London he was all paradox, which would not do. He observed he had talked no

---

[10] Which included "admirable soup," ham, peas, lamb, and moor-fowl. (The menu is given at a previous point in the MS.)

paradoxes today; and as to the savage and the London shopkeeper, he did not know but he might have taken the side of
the savage equally, had anybody else taken the side of the
shopkeeper. He had said to my lord, in opposition to the value
of the savage's courage, that it was owing to his limited power
of thinking; and repeated Pope's four lines in which "Mace-
donia's madman" comes in, and the conclusion is "farther than
his nose." I objected to the last phrase being low. MR. JOHN-
SON. "'Tis intended, 'tis satire. The expression is debased to de-
base the character."

My lord showed Mr. Johnson *Hermes*, as the work of a living
author for whom he had great respect. Mr. Johnson said nothing. He afterwards told me that Harris was a coxcomb. Indeed,
I always thought so. I used to provoke my friend Temple by
laughing at the quaint affected style of his *Dialogues on Poetry,
Music, Painting, and Happiness*.[11]

When Gory was going to leave us, Mr. Johnson called to
him, "Mr. Gory, give me leave to ask you a question. Are you
baptized?" Gory told him he was—and confirmed by the Bishop
of Durham.

We had tedious driving this afternoon, and were a good
deal drowsy. Last night I was afraid Mr. Johnson was beginning to faint in his resolution, for he said, "If we must *ride*
much, we shall not go; and there's an end on't." Today when
he talked of Skye with spirit, I said, "Why, sir, you was beginning to despond yesterday. You're a delicate Londoner—
you're a macaroni! You can't ride!" JOHNSON. "Sir, I shall
ride better than you. I was only afraid I should not find a
horse able to carry me." I hoped then there would be no
fear of fulfilling our wild Tour.

We got to Aberdeen half an hour past 11. The New Inn,

---

[11] Boswell has carefully inked out this sentence and the preceding in a fashion quite unlike his deletions for the printer. He probably did this when (in 1775) he lent the MS to
Mrs. Thrale. Johnson's condemnation of Harris was also struck out when the Journal
was revised for the printer, but Boswell later changed his mind and brought the remark
in under date of 3 November, adding his own strictures in a considerably softened form.

we were told, was full. This was comfortless. The waiter, however, asked if one of our names was Boswell, and brought me a letter left at the inn. It was from Mr. Thrale, enclosing one to Mr. Johnson. Finding who I was, we were told they would contrive to lodge us by putting us for a night into a room with two beds. The waiter said to me in strong Aberdeenshire, "I thought I knew you, by your likeness to your fäther." My father puts up at the New Inn when on his circuit. We had a broiled chicken, some tarts, and crabs' claws. Little was said tonight. I was to sleep in a little box-bed in Mr. Johnson's room. I had it wheeled out into the dining-room, and there I lay very well.

SUNDAY 22 AUGUST. I sent a message to Professor Thomas Gordon, who came and breakfasted with us. He had secured seats for us at chapel. We went to it at ten. Good congregation, admirable organ. I was truly in a devout frame. Gordon, who officiated, had the most unhappy defects of speech. His tongue was too big. He made such efforts to articulate, 'twas like convulsions. There was no understanding him. 'Twas just the same as speaking in an unknown tongue. It was wrong to put him in orders.[1]

We walked down to the shore. Mr. Johnson laughed to hear that Cromwell's soldiers taught the Aberdeen people to make shoes and stockings, and brought in cabbages. He asked if weaving the plaids was ever a domestic art in the Highlands, like spinning or knitting. He could not be informed here. But he conjectured probably that where people lived so remote from each other, it would be domestic art, as we see it was among the ancients, as Penelope. I was sensible today, to a very striking degree, of Mr. Johnson's excellent English conversation. I cannot account for it, how

---

[1] A comparison between this paragraph and that in the published book will show the type of revision to which the MS was subjected throughout: "I sent a message to Professor Thomas Gordon, who came and breakfasted with us. He had secured seats for us at the English chapel. We found a respectable congregation, and an admirable organ, well played by Mr. Tait."

it struck me more now than any other day. But it was as if new to me; and I listened to every sentence which he spoke as to a musical composition. Professor Gordon gave him an account of the plan of education in his college. Mr. Johnson said 'twas similar to Oxford. Waller the poet's great-grandson was here. Mr. Johnson wondered how a man sent his son so far off, as there were so many good schools in England. He said at a great school there was all the splendour and illumination of many minds; that the radiance of all was concentrated in each, or at least reflected upon each. But he owned that neither a dull boy, nor an idle boy, would do so well at a great school as at a private one. That at a great school there were always boys enough to do well easily, who were sufficient to keep up the credit of the school; and after trying whipping to no purpose, the dull or idle boys were left at the end of a class, having the appearance of going through the course, but learning nothing at all. Such boys might do good at a private school, where constant attention was paid to them, and they were watched. So that the question of public or private education is not properly a general one. But whether is the one or the other best for *my* son.

We were told this Mr. Waller was just a plain country gentleman; and his son would be such another. I observed a family could not expect a poet but in a hundred generations. "Nay," said Mr. Johnson, "not one family in a hundred can expect a poet in a hundred generations." Then repeated "Three poets," etc., and part of a Latin translation of it done at Oxford—perhaps his own. I must ask.[2]

He received a card from Sir Alexander Gordon, who had been his acquaintance twenty years ago in London, and who,

---

[2] "London, 2d May, 1778. Dr. Johnson acknowledged that he was himself the author of the translation above alluded to, and dictated it to me as follows:

 Quos laudet vates Graius Romanus et Anglus
  Tres tria temporibus secla dedere suis.
 Sublime ingenium Graius; Romanus habebat
  Carmen grande sonans; Anglus utrumque tulit.

"if forgiven for not answering a line from him," would come in the afternoon. He was rejoiced to hear of him. We sent for him to come and dine with us. I was much pleased to see the kindness with which Mr. Johnson received Sir Alexander, a gentleman of good family (Lismore), but by the extravagance of his relations, to whom he left the care of his estate, had lost it. The King's College here made him Professor of Medicine, which affords him a decent subsistence. He told us Aberdeen exported stockings to the value of £100,000 in peace, and one hundred and seventy in war. Mr. Johnson asked what made the difference. Here we had a proof of the different sagacity of the two professors. Sir Alexander answered, "Because there's more occasion for them in war." Professor Thomas answered, "Because the Germans, who are our great rivals in the manufacture of stockings, are otherwise employed in time of war." "Sir, you have given a very good solution," said Mr. Johnson.

At dinner Mr. Johnson eat several platefuls of Scotch broth with pease in them, and was very fond of the dish. I said, "You never eat it before, sir." "No, sir, but I don't care how soon I eat it again." We had also skate, roasted lamb, roasted chickens, and tarts. My cousin and old flame at Inverness, Miss Dallas, was married to Mr. Riddoch, one of the ministers of the English Chapel here. He was ill and confined to his room. But we had a kind invitation to tea, and all went there. I was in a kind of uneasiness from thinking that I should see a great change upon her at the distance of twelve years.[3] But I declare

---

Nil majus Natura capit: clarare priores
  Quae potuere duos tertius unus habet."—Boswell.
The original lines, composed by Dryden, were first published under an engraved portrait of Milton prefixed to Tonson's folio edition of *Paradise Lost*, 1688:
  Three poets, in three distant ages born,
  Greece, Italy, and England, did adorn.
  The first, in loftiness of thought surpassed;
  The next, in majesty; in both, the last.
  The force of nature could no further go;
  To make a third, she joined the former two.
[3] Boswell met this "third cousin" while accompanying his father on the Northern Circuit

I thought she looked better in every respect, except that some of her fore-teeth were spoiled. She was the same lively, sensible, cheerful woman as ever. My mind was sensibly affected at seeing her. I believe there was sincere joy on both sides. Her youngest sister was gone to Maryland with her husband, also a clergyman. I saw her other two sisters. Kate I should not have known.——I recollected. Mr. Johnson did not talk much. He had only some jokes against Scotland: said, "You go first to Aberdeen; then to *Enbru*; then to Newcastle, to be polished by the colliers; then to York; then to London." And he laid hold of a little girl, Stuart Dallas, niece to Mrs. Riddoch, and said he'd take her with him, telling her in a hollow voice that he lived in a cave and had a bed in the rock, and she should have a little bed cut opposite to it.

Yet he spoke well on the point as to prescription of murder. He said a jury in England would make allowance for deficiencies of evidence on account of lapse of time. But that a general rule that a crime should not be punished or tried in order to punishment after twenty years was bad. That it was cant to talk of the King's Advocate delaying prosecution from malice. How unlikely was it the King's Advocate should have malice against people who commit murder, or should even know them at all. He said if the son of the murdered man should kill the murderer who got off merely by prescription, he would help him to make his escape; though were he upon his jury, he would not acquit him. That he would not advise him to do it. On the contrary, would bid him submit to the determination of society, because a man is bound to submit to the inconveniencies of it, as he enjoys the good. But that the young man, though politically wrong, would not be morally wrong. He would have to say, "Here I am amongst

---

in 1761. His journal of this jaunt, the first of his journals now preserved, is as yet unpublished. Under date of 16 May he wrote, "Breakfasted with Miss Dallas. . . . A charming creature indeed: excessively pretty, a most engaging manner. Great good sense, surprising propriety of language and facility of Expression. We were very merry. . . . Upon my soul, a delightfull Girl. Never has been at Edin^r, nor any where in a large Place. Was in raptures to myself w^t her."

barbarians who not only refuse to do justice, but encourage the
greatest of all crimes. I am therefore in a state of nature. For
where there is no law, it is a state of nature. I therefore upon
the eternal and immutable law of justice which requires that
he who sheds blood should have his blood shed, will stab the
murderer of my father."

We came to our inn quietly. Mr. Johnson borrowed at Mr.
Riddoch's a volume of Massillon, his discourses on the Psalms.
But I found he read little in it. Ogden too he sometimes took
up and glanced at, but threw it down again. I then entered
upon religious conversation. Never did I see him in a better
frame: calm, gentle, wise, holy. I said the same objection would
serve against the Trinity as against transubstantiation. "Yes,"
said he, "if you take Three and One in the same sense. If you
do so, to be sure, you cannot believe it. But they are Three in
one sense and One in another. We cannot tell how, and that is
the Mystery."

I spoke of the satisfaction of Christ. He said his notion was
that it did not atone for the sins of the world. But by satisfying
divine justice, by showing that no less than the Son of God
suffered for sin, it showed to men and innumerable created
beings the heinousness of sin, and therefore rendered it unnecessary for divine vengeance to be exercised against sinners, as it
otherwise must have been. In this way it might operate even in
favour of those who had never heard of it. As to those who did
hear of it, the effect it should produce would be repentance and
piety, by impressing upon the mind a just notion of sin. That
original sin was the propensity to evil, which no doubt was
occasioned by the Fall. He presented this great subject in a
new light to me, and rendered much more rational and clear
the ideas of what our Saviour has done for us, as it removed
the notion of imputed righteousness in the usual sense, and the
difficulty of our righteousness co-operating;[4] whereas by his

---

[4] In the first and all subsequent editions of the *Tour*, several words have been omitted in
this passage, so that it reads, nonsensically, "as it removed the notion of imputed righteousness in co-operating. . . ." In all the editions, too, the words immediately following

view Christ has done all already that he had to do, or is ever to do, for mankind, by making his great satisfaction, the consequences of which will affect each individual according to the particular conduct of each. I would illustrate this by saying that Christ's satisfaction is like there being a sun placed to show light to men, so that it depends upon themselves whether they will walk the right way or not, which they could not have done without that sun, "the sun of righteousness." There is, however, more in it than merely giving light—"a light to lighten the Gentiles." I must think of it at leisure and with attention. Mr. Johnson said, "Richard Baxter commends a treatise by Grotius, *De Satisfactione Christi*. I have never read it. But I intend to do it, and you may read it." I said upon the principle now laid down we might explain, "They that believe shall be saved," etc. They that believe will have such an impression made upon their minds as will make them act so as that they shall be accepted by GOD.

We talked of Langton's taking ill for a length of time a hasty expression. JOHNSON. "What is to come of society if a friendship of twenty years is to be broken off for such a cause? As Bacon says,

> 'Who then to frail mortality shall trust,
> But limns in water, or but writes in dust.'"

I said he should write expressly in support of Christianity, for that although a reverence for it shines through his works in several places, that is not enough. "You know," said I, "what Grotius has done, what Addison has done, you should do also." He said, "I hope I shall."

MONDAY 23 AUGUST. Principal Campbell, Sir Alexander Gordon, Professor Gordon, and Professor Ross came to us in the morning, as did Dr. Gerard, who had come in six miles from the country on purpose. We went and saw Marischal Col-

---

read, "whereas by this view" instead of "by his view," the reading of the MS. This is not certainly a misprint. Boswell may have changed "his" to "this" in the proofs to avoid ambiguity.

lege,[1] and at one we waited on the magistrates in the Town Hall, as they had invited us in order to present Mr. Johnson with the freedom of the city, which Provost Jopp did with a very good grace. Mr. Johnson was pleased with this mark of attention, and received it very politely. There was a pretty numerous company there. It was curious to hear all of them drinking "Dr. Johnson, Dr. Johnson" in the Town Hall of Aberdeen, and then to see him with his diploma in his hat, which he wore as he walked along the street, according to the usual custom. It gave me great satisfaction to observe the regard and indeed fondness, too, which everybody here had for my father.

While Sir A. Gordon conducted Mr. Johnson to Old Aberdeen, Professor Gordon and I called on Mr. Riddoch, whom I found to be a grave worthylike clergyman. He said that whatever might be said of Mr. Johnson while he was alive, after he was dead he would be looked upon by the world with regard and astonishment on account of his Dictionary.

Mrs. Riddoch, Professor Gordon, and I went and called for Mrs. Dallas, whom I had not seen since I was a mere child. Then he and I walked over to the Old College, which Mr. Johnson had seen by this time. I stepped a little into the chapel and looked at the tomb of the Founder, Archbishop Elphinstone, of whom I shall have occasion to write in my *History of James IV*.[2]

We dined at Sir A. Gordon's. The Provost, Professor Ross, Professor Dunbar, Professor Thomas Gordon were there. After dinner came in Dr. Gerard, Professor Leslie, Professor MacLeod. We had had little or no conversation in the morning.

---

[1] "Dr. Beattie was so kindly entertained in England, that he had not yet returned home."— BOSWELL.

[2] A projected work of Boswell's of which we hear no more. There are scattered references, in his journals, letters, and published writings, to more than fifty such projects, many of them being mentioned several times. They include poems, novels, pamphlets, and histories—but are chiefly biographies. Among the men of whom he planned to write a *Life* were Sir Joshua Reynolds, Thomas Ruddiman, Lord Kames, his friend John McAdam of Craigengillan, Steele, Gen. Oglethorpe, Lord Pitfour, Lord Covington, and Lord Eglinton. Sir Alexander Macdonald, not being a fit subject for serious biography, was to be dealt with in a novel.

Now we were but barren. The professors seemed afraid to speak.

Dr. Gerard told us that Strahan the printer was very intimate with Warburton. Mr. Johnson said, "He has printed some
of his works, and perhaps bought property of some of 'em. The
intimacy is as one of the professors here may have with one of
the carpenters who is repairing the College." "But," said Gerard, "I saw a letter from him to Strahan, in which he says that
the one half of the Church of Scotland are fanatics and the
other half infidels." Mr. Johnson said Warburton had accustomed himself to write letters just as he speaks, without thinking
any more of what he throws out. He said when he read Warburton first and observed his force and contempt, he thought
he had driven the world before him, but he found that was not
the case, for Warburton by his extensive abuse made it ineffectual.

He told me when we were by ourselves that he thought it
very wrong in Strahan to show Warburton's letter, as it was
raising him a body of enemies. He thought it foolish in Warburton to write so to Strahan, and he said the worst way of
being intimate is by scribbling. He said Warburton's essay on
Grace was a poor performance, and so was Wesley's answer.
(He was not in spirits somehow.) Warburton had laid himself
very open. In particular, he was weak enough to say that
in some disorders of the imagination people had spoken with
tongues—had spoken languages which they never knew before
—a thing as absurd as to say that in some disorders of the imagination people had been known to fly.[3]

Gerard said he had detected Thomas Warton in the most bare-
faced plagiarism in his Spenser. He copies a whole page from
Abbé du Bos, and to disguise it, quotes Du Bos for a sentence
in the middle of it.[4] I talked of difference of genius to try if I

---

[3] Percival Stockdale reports that Johnson once, in reply to Goldsmith's assertion that
Warburton was a weak writer, said: "Warburton may be absurd, but he will never be
weak; he flounders well" (*Memoirs*, ii. 64).
[4] This is a considerable overstatement of the seriousness of Warton's offence; indeed it
can hardly be called plagiarism at all. The passage referred to, concerning the plot of

could engage Gerard in a disquisition with Mr. Johnson. But it would not do. I mentioned Locke's writing verses. Mr. Johnson said he knew of none but a kind of exercise prefixed to T. Sydenham, about the dropsy—water, burning, both at once —and how Dr. Sydenham removed fire by drawing off water, contrary to the usual practice, which is to extinguish fire by bringing water upon it. "I know not," said he, "if there's a word of all this, but 'tis such kind of talk."[5]

We spoke of *Fingal*. He said, "If the poems were really translated, they were certainly first written down. Let Mr. Macpherson deposit the MS in one of the colleges at Aberdeen where there are people who can judge, and if the professors certify the authenticity, then there will be an end of the controversy. If he does not take this obvious and easy method, he gives the best reason to doubt, considering too how much is against it *a priori*."

We sauntered after dinner in Sir Alexander's garden and saw his little grotto, which is hung with pieces of poetry written in a fair hand. It was agreeable to see the contentment and

---

Orlando Furioso, occurs in the first edition (1754) of the *Observations on the Faerie Queene* on pp. 11–12. One sentence reads: "The ingenious Abbé du Bos observes happily enough, that 'Homer is a geometrician in comparison of Ariosto.'" The part immediately preceding this also reveals clearly Warton's reading of Du Bos's *Réflexions* (in Thomas Nugent's translation, 1748, as is shown by a later acknowledged quotation from Du Bos which is in Nugent's exact words); but there is only a portion of one sentence which can be said to have been "copied" from Du Bos:

"This poet is seldom read twice in order; that is, by passing from the first canto to the second, and from the second to the rest successively; but by pursuing (without any regard to the order of the books, or the stanzas) the different stories, which though all somewhere finished, yet are, at present, so mutually interwoven, that the incidents of one are perpetually clashing with those of another" (Warton).

"Ariosto is seldom read twice in order, that is, passing from the first canto to the second, and from the second to the rest successively, but by following, without any regard to the order of the books, the different stories, which he has rather incorporated than united" (Nugent, i. 243–4).

If Warton himself considered this a theft, it seems strange that he chose to "disguise" it by immediately giving the victim's name, with a chapter reference to the spot from which the material had been pilfered.

[5] "All this, as Dr. Johnson suspected at the time, was the immediate invention of his own lively imagination; for there is not one word of it in Mr. Locke's complimentary performance."—BOSWELL. He then proceeds to quote the verses—twenty-seven Latin couplets.

kindness of the worthy, harmless man. Professor MacLeod was brother to Talisker and brother-in-law to the Laird of Coll. He gave me a letter to young Coll. I was weary of this day, and began to think wishfully of the post-chaise. I was uneasy to think myself too delicate, and thought Mr. Johnson was quite satisfied. But he owned to me that he was fatigued. I said 'twas all kindness. "Yes, sir. But sensation is sensation." "Yes," said I, "you feel pain equally from the surgeon's probe as from the sword of the foe."

We tried two booksellers' shops and could not find Arthur Johnston's Poems. We went and sat near an hour at Mr. Riddoch's. He could not tell distinctly how much education at the college here costs, which disgusted Mr. Johnson. I had engaged to Mr. Johnson that we should go home to the inn, and not stay supper. They pressed us, but he was resolute. I saw Mr. Riddoch did not please him. He said to me, "Sir, he has no vigour in his talk." But it should have been considered that Mr. Johnson was not in good humour, so that it was not so easy to talk to his satisfaction. We sat quietly at our inn. He then became merry, and observed how little we had either heard or said at Aberdeen. That the Aberdonians had not started a single *mawkin*[6] for us to pursue.

TUESDAY 24 AUGUST. We set out about eight; morning fine. Breakfasted at Ellon. The landlady said to me, "Is not this the great Doctor that is going about through the country?" I said, "Yes." "Ay," said she, "we heard of him. I made an errand into the room on purpose to see him. There's something great in his appearance. It is a pleasure to have such a man in one's house; a man who does so much good. If I had thought, I would have shown him a child of mine who has had a lump on his throat for some time." "But," said I, "he's not a Doctor of Physic." "Is he an oculist?" said the landlord. "No," said I, "he's just a very learned man." Said the landlord: "They say he's the greatest man in England except

---

[6] Scottish for *hare*, as Boswell explains in the published *Tour*.

Lord Mansfield." Mr. Johnson was highly entertained with this, and I do think he was pleased too. He said he liked the exception, for that in Scotland it must be Lord Mansfield or Sir John Pringle.[1]

He told me a good story of Dr. Goldsmith. "Telemachus" Graham was sitting one night with him and Mr. Johnson, and was half drunk. He rattled away, and told Mr. Johnson, "You're a clever fellow, but you can't write an essay like Addison or verses like *The Rape of the Lock*." At last he said,[2] "Doctor, I will be happy to see you at Eton." "I shall be glad to wait on you," answered Goldsmith. "No," said Graham, "'tis not you I meant, Dr. Minor. 'Tis Dr. Major there." Goldsmith was prodigiously hurt with this. He spoke of it himself. Said he: "Graham is a fellow to make one commit suicide."

We had received a polite invitation to Slains Castle.[3] We arrived there just at three o'clock, as the bell for dinner was ringing. Though, from its being just on the Northwest[4] Ocean, no trees will grow here, Lord Erroll has done all that can be done. He has cultivated his fields so as to bear rich crops of every kind, and he has made an excellent kitchen-garden, with a hothouse. I had never seen any of the family. But there had been a card of invitation written by Mr. Charles Boyd, the Earl's brother. We were conducted into the house, and at the dining-room door were met by Mr. Charles Boyd, whom both of us at first took to be Lord Erroll, but he soon corrected our mistake. My lord was gone to dine in the neighbourhood at an

---

[1] Lord Mansfield, Lord Chief Justice of the King's Bench, and Sir John Pringle, physician to the King, and President of the Royal Society, were both Scotsmen.

[2] "I am sure I have related this story exactly as Dr. Johnson told it to me; but a friend who has often heard him tell it, informs me that he usually introduced a circumstance which ought not to be omitted. 'At last, sir, Graham, having now got to about the pitch of looking at one man, and talking to another, said *Doctor*, &c. What effect (Dr. Johnson used to add) this had on Goldsmith, who was as irascible as a hornet, may be easily conceived.'"—BOSWELL.

[3] "When I was at the English church in Aberdeen I happened to be espied by Lady Di. Middleton, whom I had sometime seen in London; she told what she had seen to Mr. Boyd, Lord Erroll's brother, who wrote us an invitation to Lord Erroll's house, called Slains Castle" (Johnson to Mrs. Thrale, 28 Aug. 1773).

[4] Corrected to "Northeast" in the published *Tour*, but not in the MS. Boswell must have made the correction in the proofs.

entertainment given by Mr. Irvine of Drum. Lady Erroll received us politely, and was very attentive to us in the time of dinner. There was nobody at table but she and Mr. Boyd and some of the children, their governor and governess. Mr. Boyd put Mr. Johnson in mind of having dined with him at Cumming the Quaker's, along with a Mr. Hall and Miss Williams. This was a bond of connexion between Mr. Boyd and Mr. Johnson. For me, my father's acquaintance was enough. After dinner my lady made her young family stand up in a row. There were eight, just steps of stairs, six girls and two boys, besides a young lady of four weeks old who did not appear. It was the prettiest sight I ever saw.[5]

Mr. Johnson proposed our setting out. Mr. Boyd said he hoped we would stay all night. His brother would be at home in the evening, and would be very sorry if he missed us. Mr. Boyd was called out of the room. I was very desirous to stay in so comfortable a house, and wished to see Lord Erroll. Mr. Johnson was right in resolving to go if we were not asked again, as it is best to err on the safe side and be sure that one is quite welcome at a house. To my great joy when Mr. Boyd returned he told Mr. Johnson that it was Lady Erroll who had called him out; that she would never let Mr. Johnson into the house again if he stirred that night, and that she had ordered the coach to carry us to see a great curiosity on the coast, after which we should see the house. We cheerfully agreed.

Mr. Boyd was out in the year 1745-6. He escaped and lay concealed for a year in the island of Arran, the ancient territory of the Boyds. He then went to France, and was about twenty years on the Continent. He married a French lady, and now he lives very comfortably at Aberdeen, and is much at Slains Castle. He entertained us with much civility. He had a pompousness or formal plenitude in his conversation.

---

[5] The MS is defective here, and the last three words are entirely conjectural, since Boswell revised the whole sentence in the published book.

Mr. Johnson said there was too much elaboration in his talk. I liked to see him a steady branch of the family, setting forth all its advantages with much zeal. My lady had hardly said anything. But he told me she was one of the most pious and most sensible women in the island; had a good head and as good a heart. He said she did not force her children in their education. Mr. Johnson said he would rather have the rod to be the general terror to all, to make them learn, than to tell children they should be more esteemed than their brothers or sisters. "The rod produces an effect which terminates in itself. A child is afraid of being whipped and gets his task, and there's an end on't; whereas by exciting emulation and comparisons of superiority, you lay the foundation of lasting mischief: you make brothers and sisters hate each other."

During Mr. Boyd's stay in Arran, he had found a chest of medical books left by a surgeon there, and had read them till he acquired some skill, in consequence of which he is often consulted. There were several women here waiting for him as patients. I thought this *practice* of Mr. Boyd's but a foolish amusement of vanity, and no doubt of benevolence too. We walked round the house till stopped by a gullet into which the sea comes. The house is built quite upon the shore. The windows look upon the main ocean, and the King of Denmark is Lord Erroll's nearest neighbour on the northeast.

We got into the coach and drove to Dunbuy, a rock near the shore, just an island covered with seafowl. Then to a circular basin of large extent, surrounded with tremendous rocks. On the quarter to the sea there is a high arch in the rock which the force of the tempest has driven out. This place is called Buchan's Buller, or the Bullers of Buchan, and the country people call it the Pot. Mr. Boyd said it was so called from the French *bouilloire*. It may be more simply traced from *boiler* in our own language.[6] We walked round this monstrous cauldron.

---

[6] The Oxford English Dictionary connects "buller" with Scandinavian words, but agrees with Boswell that the influence of "boil" is apparent.

In some places the rock is very narrow, and on each side you
have a sea deep enough for a man-of-war to ride in, so that it
is somewhat horrid to move along. However, there is earth
and grass upon the rock, and a kind of road marked out by
the print of feet, so that one makes it out pretty easily. It was
rather alarming to see Mr. Johnson poking his way. He insisted to take a boat and sail into the Pot. We did so. He was
stout and wonderfully alert. It was curious to me to observe
the Buchan men all showing their teeth and speaking with that
strange sharp accent which distinguishes them. Mr. Johnson
was not sensible of the difference of pronunciation in the north
of Scotland, which I wondered at.

As the entry into the Buller is so narrow that oars cannot
be used as you go in, the method taken is to row very hard
when you come near it, and give the boat such a rapidity
of motion that she glides in. Mr. Johnson observed what an
effect this scene would have had were we entering into an
unknown place. There are caves of considerable depth, I
think one on each side. The boatmen had never entered
either far enough to know the size. Mr. Boyd told us that it
is customary for the company at Peterhead Well to make parties and come and dine in one of the caves here.

He told us that as Slains is at a considerable distance from
Aberdeen, Lord Erroll, who has so large a family, resolved
to have a surgeon of his own. So he educated one of his
tenants' sons, and he is now settled in a very neat house and
farm just by, which we saw from the road. By the salary which
my lord allows him and the practice which he has had, he is
in very easy circumstances. He had kept an exact account
of all that had been laid out on his education, and he came
to my lord one day, told him that he had arrived at a much
higher station than ever he expected, that he was now able
to repay what my lord had advanced, and begged my lord
would accept of it. The Earl was pleased with the generous
gratitude and genteel offer of the man, but refused it. Mr. Boyd

told us Cumming the Quaker first began by writing against Dr. Leechman on Prayer, to prove it unnecessary, as GOD knows best what should be, and will order it without *us*.

When we returned we found coffee and tea in the drawing-room. My lady was not with us. There is a bow window in the drawing-room to the sea. Mr. Johnson repeated the ode, *Jam satis terris*,[7] while Boyd was with his patients. He spoke well to Mr. Boyd in favour of entails to preserve lines of men whom mankind are accustomed to reverence. He'd have as much land entailed as that they should never fall into contempt, and as much free as to give them all the advantages of property in case of any emergency. He said if the nobility were suffered to sink into indigence, they of course become corrupted; they are ready to do whatever the King chooses; therefore it is fit they should be kept from becoming poor, unless 'tis fixed that when they fall below such a standard of wealth, they shall lose their peerages. He said the House of Peers had made noble stands when the House of Commons durst not. The two last years of a session they dare not contradict the populace.

This room is ornamented with a number of fine prints. Mr. Johnson said Sir Joshua Reynolds was the most invulnerable man he knew, the man with whom if you should quarrel, you would find the most difficulty how to abuse. There is a whole-length of Lord Erroll by him in this room, and portraits of my lady and Lady ———, her cousin,[8] by Miss Read. At least my lady's is by her. Mr. Johnson said it wanted grace. I said the same of Lady ———'s. She has a Welsh harp before her. Her attitude is such as would as well have suited a spinning-wheel.

Mr. Johnson said the prospect here was the noblest he had ever seen—better than Mount Edgcumbe, reckoned the first

[7] Horace, *Odes*, I.ii.
[8] Conjectural; the MS is defective, preserving only "co" and uncertain fragments of other letters.

in England, because at Mount Edgcumbe the sea is bounded by land on the other side, and if you have a fleet, you have also the ideas of there being a dockyard, etc., which are not agreeable. Slains is an excellent old house. My lord has built of brick, round or along the square in the inside, a gallery both on the first and second storey, the house being no higher, so that he has always a dry walk, and the rooms, which formerly entered through each other, have now all separate entries from the gallery, which is hung with Hogarth's works and other prints. We went and sat awhile in the library. There is a valuable and numerous collection. It was chiefly made by Mr. Falconer, husband to the late Countess. This Earl has added a good many modern books.

About nine the Earl came home, and Captain Gordon of Park was with him. His lordship put Mr. Johnson in mind of their dining together in London, along with Mr. Beauclerk. I was excessively pleased with Lord Erroll. His stately person and agreeable countenance, with the most unaffected affability, gave me high satisfaction. There is perhaps a weakness, that is to say, more fancy or warmth of feeling than is quite reasonable in me, but there is much pleasure arising from it. I could with the most perfect honesty expatiate on Lord Erroll's good qualities as if I was bribed to do it. His agreeable look and softness of address relieved that awe which his majestic person and the idea of his being Lord High Constable of Scotland would have inspired. He talked very easily and sensibly with Mr. Johnson. I observed that Mr. Johnson, while he showed that respect to his lordship which he always does from principle to high rank, yet, when they came to argument, maintained that manliness which becomes the force and vigour of his understanding. To show external deference to our superiors is proper. To seem to yield to them in opinion is meanness.[9]

---

[9] "Lord Chesterfield, in his letters to his son, complains of one who argued in an indiscriminate manner with men of all ranks. Probably the noble lord had felt with some uneasiness what it was to encounter stronger abilities than his own. If a peer will engage at

The Earl said grace both before and after supper with much decency. He told us a story of a man who was executed at Perth some years ago for murdering a woman, who was with child to him, and a former child he had by her. His hand was cut off. He was then pulled up. But the rope broke, and he was forced to lie an hour on the ground till another rope was brought from Perth, the execution being in a wood at some distance—the place where the murders were committed. "There," said my lord, "I see the hand of Providence." I was really happy here. I saw in my lord the best dispositions and best principles; and I saw him *in my mind's eye* to be the representative of the ancient Boyds of Kilmarnock. I was afraid he might push the bottle about, as he, I believe, used formerly to do. But he drank port and water out of a large glass himself, and let us do as we pleased. He went with us to our rooms at night, said he took the visit very kind, told me my father and he were very old acquaintance; that I now knew the way to Slains, and he hoped to see me there again.

I had a most elegant room. But there was a fire in it which blazed, and the sea, to which my windows looked, roared, and the pillows were made of some sea-fowl's feathers which had to me a disagreeable smell. So that by all these causes, I was kept awake a good time. I began to think that Lord Kilmarnock might appear to me, and I was somewhat dreary. But the thought did not last long, and I fell asleep.[10]

---

foils with his inferior in station, he must expect that his inferior in station will avail himself of every advantage; otherwise it is not a fair trial of strength and skill. The same will hold in a contest of reason, or of wit.—A certain king entered the lists of genius with Voltaire. The consequence was, that, though the king had great and brilliant talents, Voltaire had such a superiority that his majesty could not bear it; and the poet was dismissed, or escaped, from that court."—BOSWELL. This note has been abridged. The passage alluded to in Lord Chesterfield's *Letters* is that concerning the "respectable Hottentot," a description which Boswell always thought intended for Johnson, though Johnson himself denied it.

[10] Lord Kilmarnock, Lord Erroll's father, was beheaded on Tower Hill for his part in the uprising of 1745. This passage (which appears almost *verbatim* in the published *Tour*) suggested one of Collings's and Rowlandson's caricatures. Boswell's editorial oscillation between decorum and extreme frankness seems purely capricious. He frequently deletes unflattering passages concerning persons for whom he can hardly have felt any tender-

WEDNESDAY 25 AUGUST. We got up between seven and eight, and found Mr. Boyd in the dining-room, with his great-coat by way of nightgown,[1] with tea and coffee before him, to give us breakfast. We were in admirable humour. Lady Erroll had given each of us a copy of an ode by Beattie on the birth of her son, Lord Hay.[2] Mr. Boyd asked Mr. Johnson what he thought of it, or how he liked it. Mr. Johnson, who was not very fond of it, got off very well by taking it out and reading the two second stanzas of it with much melody. This, without saying a word, pleased Mr. Boyd. He observed, however, to Mr. Johnson that the expression as to the family of Erroll, "*A thousand years* have seen it shine," was an anticlimax, and that it would have been better "ages." Mr. Johnson, however, said "a thousand" was better. "*Dolus latet in universalibus*.[3] Ages might be only two ages." Mr. Johnson talked of the advantage of keeping up the connexions of relationship, which produce much kindness. "Every man who comes into the world has need of friends. If he has to get them for himself, half his life is spent ere his merit is known. Relations are a man's friends who support him. When a man is in real distress, he flies into the arms of his relations. An old lawyer, who had much experience in making wills, told me that after people had deliberated long and thought of many for their executors, they settled at last by fixing on their relations. This shows the universality of the principle."

I regretted the decay of respect for men of family, and that a Nabob would carry an election from them. Said Mr. Johnson: "The Nabob will carry it by means of his wealth in a

---

ness (persons, indeed, who would probably never see his book), and then, as here, preserves worse passages concerning men for whom he expressed an extravagant regard.

[1] "Nightgown" in the Eighteenth Century meant "dressing-gown," not "sleeping-garment."

[2] "To hurl the dart, to ride the car,
To stem the deluges of war . . .
'Twas this that rais'd th'illustrious line
To match the first in fame!
A thousand years have seen it shine
With unabated flame. . . ."
(From *Ode on Lord Hay's Birthday*.)

[3] "General terms are treacherous."

country where money is highly valued, because nothing can be had without it; but if it comes to personal preference, the man of family will always carry it. There is a *scoundrelism* about a low man." Mr. Boyd said that was a good *ism*.

I said I believed mankind were happier in the ancient feudal state of subordination than when in the modern state of independency. Mr. Johnson said, "To be sure, the *Chief* was. But we must think of the number of individuals. That *they* were less happy seems plain; for that state from which all escape as soon as they can, and to which none return after they have left it, must be less happy; and this is the case with the state of dependence on a chief or great man."

I mentioned the happiness of the French in their subordination by the reciprocal benevolence and attachment between the great and those in lower ranks. Mr. Boyd gave us an excellent instance of gentility of spirit. An old Chevalier de Malthe, of ancient *noblesse* but in low circumstances, was in a coffee-house at Paris where was Julienne, the great manufacturer at the Gobelins of the fine tapestry, so much distinguished both for the figures and the *colours*. The Chevalier's carriage was very old. Says Julienne with a plebeian insolence, "I think, sir, you had better have your carriage new painted." The Chevalier looked at him with indignant contempt, and answered, "Well, sir, you may take it home and *dye* it." All the coffee-house rejoiced at Julienne's confusion.

We set out about nine. Mr. Johnson was curious to see a Druid's Temple. I had a recollection of one at Strichen which I had seen fifteen years ago.[4] So we went four miles out of our road after passing Old Deer, and went thither. Mr. Fraser was at home and showed it. But I had augmented it in my mind, for all that remains is the two stones set up on end with a long one laid between them, as was usual, and one stone due ———[5] from them. That stone was the capital one of the circle which

---

[4] In the course of his tour of the Northern Circuit with his father, in autumn 1758.
[5] Blank in the MS; in the printed *Tour* Boswell changes to "at a little distance from them."

surrounded what now remains. Fraser was very hospitable.[6] It was Strichen Fair, and he had several of his neighbours from it at dinner. One of them, Dr. Fraser, who had been in the army, remembered to have seen Mr. Johnson at a lecture on experimental philosophy at Lichfield. Mr. Johnson remembered being at the lecture, and he thought it curious that he should still find somebody who knew him.

Mr. Fraser sent a servant along to conduct us by a short passage into the high road. I observed that I had a most disagreeable idea of the life of a country gentleman; that I left Mr. Fraser just now as one leaves a prisoner in a jail. Mr. Johnson said that I was right in thinking them unhappy, for that they had not enough to keep their minds in motion.

I started a thought which amused us a great part of the way. "If," said I, "our Club should go and set up in St. Andrews as a college to teach all that each of us can in the several departments of learning and taste, we'd rebuild the city. We'd draw a wonderful concourse of students." Mr. Johnson entered fully into the spirit of this idea. We immediately fell to distributing the offices. I was to teach Civil and Scotch Law; Burke, Politics and Eloquence; Garrick, the Art of Public Speaking; Langton was to be our Grecian, Colman our Humanist; Nugent to teach Physic; Lord Charlemont, Modern History; Beauclerk, Natural Philosophy; Vesey, Irish Antiquities or Celtic Learning;[7] Jones, Oriental Learning; Goldsmith, Poetry and Ancient History; Chamier, Commercial Politics; Reynolds, Painting and the arts which have beauty for their ob-

---

[6] "He is the worthy son of a worthy father, the late Lord Strichen, one of our judges, to whose kind notice I was much obliged. Lord Strichen was a man not only honest, but highly generous; for after his succession to the family estate, he paid a large sum of debts contracted by his predecessor, which he was not under any obligation to pay."—BOSWELL. The remainder of Boswell's note is omitted.

[7] "Since the first edition, it has been suggested by one of the Club [probably Malone], who knew Mr. Vesey better than Dr. Johnson and I, that we did not assign him a proper place; for he was quite unskilled in Irish antiquities and Celtic learning, but might with propriety have been made professor of architecture, which he understood well, and has left a very good specimen of his knowledge and taste in that art. by an elegant house built on a plan of his own formation, at Lucan, a few miles from Dublin."—BOSWELL.

ject; Chambers, the Law of England. Mr. Johnson at first said,
"I'll trust Theology to nobody but myself." But upon due consideration that Percy is a clergyman, it was agreed that Percy
should teach Practical Divinity and British Antiquities, Mr.
Johnson himself, Logic, Metaphysics, and Scholastic Divinity.
In this manner did we amuse ourselves, each suggesting, and
each varying or adding. It was really a high entertainment.
Mr. Johnson said we only wanted a mathematician, since Dyer
died, who was a very good one. But as to everything else, we
would have a very capital university.[8] He said that we'd persuade Langton to lodge in the garret, as best for him, and if
he should take a fancy of making his Will, we'd get him to
leave his estate to the College.

We got at night to Banff. I sent Joseph on to Duff House,
but Earl Fife was not at home. We got but an indifferent inn.[9]
Mr. Johnson wrote a long letter to Mrs. Thrale. I wondered to
see him write so much so easily. He verified his doctrine that a
man "may always write when he will set doggedly to it."

THURSDAY 26 AUGUST. We got a fresh chaise here, a
very good one, and very good horses. William Bower, the
owner, drove it himself, and drove briskly. Our driver from
Aberdeen was rather slow. We breakfasted at Cullen. They
set down dried haddocks, broiled, along with our tea, etc. I
eat one. But Mr. Johnson disliked their presence, so they were
removed. Cullen has a snug, warm, comfortable appearance,

---

[8] "Our Club, originally at the Turk's Head, Gerrard Street, then at Prince's, Sackville
Street, now at Baxter's, Dover Street, which at Mr. Garrick's funeral acquired a *name*
for the first time, and was called THE LITERARY CLUB, was instituted in 1764, and now
consists of thirty-five members."—BOSWELL. Boswell proceeds to name twenty-six distinguished members of the Club, elected after the institution.

[9] "Here unluckily the windows had no pulleys; and Dr. Johnson, who was constantly
eager for fresh air, had much struggling to get one of them kept open. Thus he had a
notion impressed upon him, that this wretched defect was general in Scotland; in consequence of which he has erroneously enlarged upon it in his *Journey*. I regretted that he
did not allow me to read over his book before it was printed. I should have changed
very little; but I should have suggested an alteration in a few places where he has laid
himself open to be attacked. I hope I should have prevailed with him to omit or soften
his assertion that 'a Scotsman must be a sturdy moralist, who does not prefer Scotland
to truth,'—for I really think it is not founded; and it is harshly said."—BOSWELL.

though but a very small town and the houses mostly of a poor appearance. I observed upon one small thatched house a broad piece of freestone with an inscription bearing that this house and croft was *mortified*[1] to the poor of the parish by one Lawter, and that the house was repaired by the present minister of the parish, who, it seems, is the founder's representative.

I went and called for Mr. Robertson, who has the charge of my Lord Findlater's affairs, and was formerly Lord Monboddo's clerk, was three times in France with him, and translated Condamine's Account of the Savage Girl, to which my lord wrote a Preface containing several remarks of his own. Robertson said he did not believe so much as my lord did. That it was plain to him the girl confounded what she imagined with what she remembered. That besides she perceived Condamine and Mr. Burnett forming theories, and she adapted her story to them.

Mr. Johnson said it was a pity to see Lord Monboddo publish such notions as he has done, a man of sense and of so much elegant learning. That there would be little in a fool doing it. We would only laugh. But that when a wise man does it, we are sorry. "Other people," said he, "have strange notions, but they conceal them. If they have tails, they hide them." I shall here put down one or two more remarks on Lord Monboddo which were not made exactly at this time, but come in well from connexion. He said Monboddo was as jealous of his tail as a squirrel. He did not approve of a judge's being "*Farmer* Burnett"[2] and going about with a little round hat. He laughed heartily at his lordship's saying he was an *enthusiastical* farmer; "for," said he, "what can he do with his *enthusiasm?*" Here, however, I think Mr. Johnson mistaken. A man may be en-

---

[1] In a note inserted later in the MS, Boswell explains that this means "left in mortmain."

[2] "It is the custom in Scotland for the judges of the Court of Session to have the title of *lords*, from their estates; thus Mr. Burnett is Lord *Monboddo*, as Mr. Home was Lord *Kames*. There is something a little awkward in this; for they are denominated in deeds by their *names*, with the addition of 'one of the Senators of the College of Justice;' and subscribe their Christian and surname, as *James Burnett, Henry Home*, even in judicial acts."—BOSWELL.

thusiastical, that is to say, very keen in all the occupations or diversions of life. An ordinary gentleman farmer will be satisfied with looking at his fields once or twice a day. An enthusiastical farmer will be constantly employed on them, will have his mind earnestly engaged, will talk perpetually of them. But Mr. Johnson has much of the *nil admirari* in smaller concerns. *The Vanity of Human Wishes* early sobered his mind. Besides, so great a mind as his cannot be moved by inferior objects. An elephant does not run and skip like lesser animals.

Mr. Robertson sent a servant with us to show us through the wood, by which our way was shortened, and we saw so much of the place,[3] which is indeed admirably laid out. Mr. Johnson did not choose to walk about it. He always said that he was not come to Scotland to see fine places, of which there were enough in England, but wild objects—mountains, waterfalls, peculiar manners: in short, things which he had not seen before. I have a notion that he at no time has had much taste for rural beauties. I have very little.

Mr. Johnson said there was nothing more contemptible than a country gentleman living beyond his income and every year growing poorer and poorer. He spoke strongly of the influence which a man has by being rich. "A man," said he, "who keeps his money has in reality more use from it than he can have by spending it." I said this looked very like a paradox. But he explained it. "If," said he, "it were sure that a man is to keep his money locked up for ever, to be sure he would have no influence. But as so many want money, and he has the power of giving it, and they know not but by gaining his favour they may obtain it, the rich man will always have the greatest influence. He again who lavishes his money is laughed at as foolish, and in a great degree with justice, considering how much is spent from vanity. Even those who share of a man's hospitality have but a kindness for him in the

---

[3] Malone changed this to "we saw some part of his domain"—a typical example of the more elegant phraseology which resulted from his collaboration in the revision.

meantime. If he has not the command of money, people know
he cannot help them if he would. Whereas the rich man always can if he will, and for the chance of that will have
much weight." BOSWELL. "But philosophers and satirists have
all treated a miser as contemptible." JOHNSON. "He is so philo-
sophically, but not in the practice of life." BOSWELL. "Let me see
now. I do not know the instances of misers in England so as
to examine into their influence." JOHNSON. "We have had few
misers in England." BOSWELL. "There was Lowther, now."
JOHNSON. "Why, sir, Lowther, by keeping his money, had the
command of the county, which the family has now lost by
spending it.[4] I take it he lent a great deal; and that is the
way to have influence and yet preserve one's wealth. A man
may lend his money upon very good security and yet have
his debtor much under his power." BOSWELL. "No doubt, sir.
He can always distress him for the money, as no man borrows
who is able to pay on demand."

We dined at Elgin, and saw the noble ruins of the cathedral.
Though it rained much, Mr. Johnson examined them with a
most patient attention. He could not here feel an abhorrence
at the Scottish Reformers, for he had been told by Lord Hailes
that it was destroyed before the Reformation by the Lord of
Badenoch,[5] who had a quarrel with the Bishop. The Bishop's
house and those of the other clergy, which are still pretty en-

---

[4] "I do not know what was at this time the state of the parliamentary interest of the ancient family of Lowther, a family before the Conquest; but all the nation knows it to be
very extensive at present. A due mixture of severity and kindness, economy and munifi-
cence, characterizes its present Representative."—BOSWELL. This was a bid for the favour of Lord Lonsdale, upon whom Boswell fawned pathetically for some years, hoping
to be brought into Parliament, but receiving nothing but brutality and the recordership
of Carlisle. His breach with Lonsdale in 1790 nearly involved him in a duel. Lonsdale
may have been "munificent"; it is more to the point that he borrowed and never paid
back. Wordsworth's father, his law-agent, had died two years before the publication of
the *Tour*, leaving five young children. His estate consisted principally of claims on Lonsdale, who simply defied the executors. The Wordsworth children did not receive a penny of
their patrimony until after Lonsdale's death in 1802.
[5] "The cathedral of Elgin was burnt by the Lord of Badenoch, because the Bishop of
Moray had pronounced an award not to his liking. The indemnification that the see obtained, was, that the Lord of Badenoch stood for three days barefooted at the great gate
of the cathedral. The story is in the Chartulary of Elgin."—LORD HAILES.

tire, do not seem to have been proportioned to the magnificence of the cathedral, which has been of great extent, and had very fine carved work. In the ——— I was pleased to see the monument of a nun remaining. The ground within the walls of the cathedral is employed as a burying-place. The family of Gordon have their vault here. But it has nothing grand. I looked through a hole in the door of it. They just bury in the earth within it.

We passed Gordon Castle[6] this forenoon, which has a grand appearance: castle, planting, etc. Fochabers is a poorlike village, many of the houses ruinous. But it is remarkable they have in general orchards well stored with apple-trees. Elgin has piazzas in many places on each side of the street. It must have been a much better place formerly. Probably it had piazzas all along, as I have seen at Bologna. I approve much of this mode. It is so convenient in wet weather. Mr. Johnson disapproved of it because he said it made the under storey of a house very dark, which greatly overbalanced the conveniency, when it is considered how small a part of the year it rains; how few must then be upon the street, as many who are might as well be at home; and the small hurt supposing people to be as much wet as they commonly are in walking a street.

Baillie Leslie, at whose house we put up, gave us good fish, but beef collops and mutton chops which absolutely could not be eat. Mr. Johnson said this was the first time he had got a dinner in Scotland that he could not eat.[7]

---

[6] "I am not sure whether the Duke was at home. But, not having the honour of being much known to his grace, I could not have presumed to enter his castle, though to introduce even so celebrated a stranger. We were at any rate in a hurry to get forward to the wildness which we came to see. Perhaps, if this noble family had still preserved that sequestered magnificence which they maintained when Catholics, corresponding with the Grand Duke of Tuscany, we might have been induced to have procured proper letters of introduction, and devoted some time to the contemplation of venerable superstitious state."—BOSWELL.

[7] How much more interesting is this than the published text of this paragraph—"We fared but ill at our inn here; and Dr. Johnson said, this was the first time he had seen a dinner in Scotland that he could not eat." Baillie Leslie's inn, the Red Lion, was pronounced "good" by a writer in the *Gentleman's Magazine* for 1771 (p. 544), and he added that Leslie was "the only landlord in Scotland who wears ruffles." Dr. Hill, pursuing

We drove over the very heath where Macbeth met the witches, according to tradition. Mr. Johnson repeated solemnly again "How far is't called to Forres?" etc., parodying it to me: "All hail Dalblair!"[8]

We got to Forres at night. Found an admirable house kept by Lawson,[9] wine-cooper from London. By the road I had, from that strange curiosity which I always have about anything dismal, stepped out of the chaise and run up close to the gallows where Kenneth Leal hangs in chains for robbing the mail. As he had not hung but about two months, the body was quite entire. It was still a *man* hanging. The sight impressed me with a degree of gloom. Mr. Johnson did not know of this, or, he told me afterwards, he would not have talked as he did, for he diverted himself with trying to frighten me, as if the witches would come and dance at the foot of my bed. I said he would be the most frightened of the two. But that I would rather see three witches than one of anything else. I was really a little uneasy. However, the door of my room opened into his. This gave me a security, and I soon fell asleep.[10]

FRIDAY 27 AUGUST. It was dark when we came to Forres last night. So we did not see what is called King Duncan's Monument. I shall now mark some gleanings of Mr. Johnson's conversation. I spoke of *Leonidas*, and said there were some good passages in it. He said, "Why, you must *seek* for them." He said Paul Whitehead's *Manners* was a poor performance. He said I should write down all the particulars of my first coming to London, etc. He said he had a kindness

Johnson's footsteps more than a hundred years later, heard a story purporting to account for the poor dinner which was served to the travellers. It seems that the waiter, glancing hastily at Johnson, mistook him for one Paufer, a commercial traveller who frequented the inn and who spent as little as possible for food so that he might spend the more for drink. Johnson and Boswell were served accordingly.
[8] Expanded and explained in the published *Tour:* "I had purchased some land called Dalblair; and, as in Scotland it is customary to distinguish landed men by the name of their estates, I had thus two titles, 'Dalblair' and 'Young Auchinleck.'"
[9] This name has been heavily cancelled, and is doubtful.
[10] All of this paragraph except the first two sentences was omitted from the published *Tour*.

for Derrick;[1] and he had often said that if his letters had been written by one of a more established name, they would have been thought very pretty letters.

This morning we got upon the origin of evil. Moral evil, he said, was occasioned by free-will, which implies choice between good and evil. "And," said he, "with all the evil that is, there is no man but would rather be a free agent than a mere machine without the evil; and what is best for each individual must be best for the whole. If," said he, "a man says he would rather be the machine, I cannot argue with him. He is a different being from me." I said a man, as a machine, might have agreeable sensations; he might have music. "No," said he, "he could not have music, at least no power of producing music, for he who can produce music may let it alone. He who can play upon a fiddle may break it." The reasoning satisfied me. To be sure, there cannot be a free agent unless there is the power of being evil as well as good. We must take the inherent possibilities of things into consideration in our reasonings or conjectures concerning the works of GOD.

We came to Nairn to breakfast. It is a very poor place to be a county town and a royal burgh. Above the room where we were a girl was spinning wool on a great wheel, and singing an Erse song. "I'll warrant you," said Mr. Johnson, "one of the songs of Ossian." He then repeated these lines:

> Verse sweetens toil, however rude the sound.
> All at her work the village maiden sings;
> Nor, while she turns the giddy wheel around,
> Revolves the sad vicissitude of things.

I thought I had seen these lines before.[2] But Mr. Johnson fancied I had not, as they are in a detached poem by one Gifford, a parson, of which he does not remember the name.

I expected Kenneth Macaulay,[3] the minister of Cawdor,

---

[1] This follows naturally the preceding sentence, for it was Derrick who, in 1760, first introduced Boswell to the "many-coloured life" of London.

[2] He had perhaps seen them in Johnson's Dictionary, where they are quoted under "wheel."

[3] Grand-uncle of Lord Macaulay.

who published the *History of St. Kilda*, of which Mr. Johnson
is fond, would have met us here, as I had written to him from
Aberdeen. But I received a letter from him telling that he
could not come from home, as he was to have the sacrament
next Sunday, and earnestly begging to see us at his manse.
"We'll go," said Mr. Johnson, which we accordingly did. When
we came to it, Mrs. Macaulay received us, and told us he was
in the church distributing tokens.[4] We got there between twelve
and one, and it was near three before he came to us.

Mr. Johnson thanked him for his book, and said it was a
very pretty piece of topography. Macaulay did not seem much
to mind the compliment. From his conversation Mr. Johnson
was persuaded that he had not written the book which goes
under his name. I myself always suspected so. Mr. Johnson
said there was a combination in it of which Macaulay was not
capable, and he said to me privately, "Crassus homo est."[5]
However, he gave us a good hospitable dinner, and as we were
to get a route from him for our tour among the western isles,
we agreed to stay all night.

After dinner we walked to the old Castle of Cawdor, the
Thane of Cawdor's residence. The old tower must be of great
antiquity. There is a drawbridge, what has been a moat, and
a court. There is a hawthorn tree in one of the rooms, still
undecayed, that is to say, the stock still remains. The tower
has been built round it by a strange conceit. The thickness of
the walls, the small slanting windows, and a great iron door
at the entrance on the second storey, coming up the stairs,
all indicate the rude times in which this building has been
erected. There is a great deal of additional building 250 years

---

[4] "In Scotland, there is a great deal of preparation before administering the sacrament.
The minister of the parish examines the people as to their fitness, and to those of whom
he approves gives little pieces of tin, stamped with the name of the parish, as *tokens*,
which they must produce before receiving it. This is a species of priestly power, and
sometimes may be abused. I remember a law-suit brought by a person against his parish
minister, for refusing him admission to that sacred ordinance."—BOSWELL.

[5] "He is a coarse man." Johnson was to say worse later; see *post*, p. 215.

old: some large rooms, and an excellent kitchen partly cut out of rock, with a pump-well in it.

I was afraid Mr. Johnson would quarrel with poor Macaulay, who talked at random of the lower English clergy not being the most respectable. Mr. Johnson gave him a frowning look, and said, "This is a day of novelties: I have seen old trees in Scotland, etc., and I've heard the English clergy treated with disrespect." He did not perceive that honest Kenneth was not to be minded.

I dreaded that a whole evening at Cawdor manse would be heavy. However, Mr. Grant, minister at Daviot and Dunlichity,[6] was there, and helped us with conversation. Mr. Johnson said there was no harm in offices being hereditary, but it was wrong to force them so, and oblige a man to be a tailor or a smith or anything else because his father had been it. Mr. Grant told us a story of an apparition, which he had from the Rev. Mr. Grant at Nigg, *who saw it.* I shall write to Mr. Grant and have it from the fountain-head, if he will favour me with it.

Macaulay began a rhapsody against creeds and confessions. Mr. Johnson showed clearly that what he called *imposition* was only a voluntary declaration of agreement in certain articles of faith, which a Church had a right to require, just as any other society can insist on certain rules being observed by its members. Nobody is compelled to be of the Church, as nobody is compelled to enter into a society. This was a very clear and very just view of the subject. But poor Macaulay could not be driven out of his track. Mr. Johnson said well that he was a *bigot to laxness.*

As we had a great deal of conversation about the second sight, I mentioned to the company my uneasiness because I had seen, or had dreamed that I saw, my little daughter dead,

---

[6] The name of the parish is left blank in the MS; it is here supplied from Hew Scott's *Fasti Ecclesiae Scoticanae.* The Rev. Alexander Grant was transferred to Cawdor in 1780, and died in 1828.

the night that we were going from Cupar to St. Andrews; and I said I should not be easy till I got a letter. I thought it best to mention it to several people, because it made a strong impression upon my mind, and in case it should unhappily prove true, I might have witnesses to attest what I said. Yet I can hardly have any pretence to the second sight, being no Highlander. However, as others have had strange supernatural communications, I knew not but it might be my case. I endeavoured to prepare my mind by pious reflections for whatever might happen. Yet I remembered Mr. Johnson's doctrine among the St. Andrews professors, that grief for a loss must necessarily affect the mind of man.[7]

Mr. Macaulay and I laid the map of Scotland before us, and he mentioned a route for us from Inverness by Fort Augustus to Glenelg, Skye, Mull, Icolmkill, Lorne, Inveraray, which I wrote down. As my father was to set out for the North Circuit about the 18 of September, it was necessary for us either to make our tour with great expedition, so as to get to Auchinleck before he set out, or to protract it so as not to be at Auchinleck till his return, which would be about the 10 of October. By Macaulay's calculation, we were not to land in Lorne till the 20 of September. I thought that the interruptions by bad days, or by agreeable schemes of curiosity, might make it ten days later; and I thought too that we might perhaps go to Benbecula and visit Clanranald, which would take a week of itself.

Mr. Johnson went up awhile with Mr. Grant to the library, which consisted of a tolerable collection, but Mr. Johnson thought it rather a lady's library, with some Latin books in it by chance, than the library of a clergyman. It had only two of the Latin fathers, and one of the Greek ones in Latin. I doubted if Mr. Johnson would be present at a Presbyterian prayer. I told Macaulay so, and said that he might sit in the library. Macaulay said he'd let it alone rather than give Mr. Johnson offence. I spoke of it to Mr. Johnson, who said he had no objection.

---

[7] This paragraph was omitted from the printed *Tour*.

Accordingly Mr. Grant prayed. Mr. Johnson said it was a very good prayer, but objected to his not having introduced the Lord's Prayer. He told us that Baretti said once to him, "We have in our service a prayer called the *Pater Noster* which is a very fine composition. I wonder who is the author of it." Such a strange piece of ignorance may a man of literature and general inquiry happen to have.

Macaulay had a remarkably good manse. Mr. Grant and I slept in the same room. Mr. Johnson had a room to himself. The house was very decently furnished. Mrs. Macaulay is a MacLeod of a very good family. She seemed to have a little too much value for herself on that account.

SATURDAY 28 AUGUST. Mr. Johnson had brought a copy of Sallust with him in his pocket from Edinburgh. He gave it last night to Mr. Macaulay's son, a smart young lad about eleven. He had a governor in the house to teach him. Mr. Johnson had given an account of the education at Oxford in all its gradations. The advantages of being a servitor, to a youth of little fortune, struck Mrs. Macaulay much. I observed it aloud. Mr. Johnson very handsomely and kindly said that if they would send their boy to him when he was ready for the University, he would get him made a servitor, and perhaps would do more for him. He could not promise to do more, but would undertake for the servitorship.[1] This may be a most fortunate circumstance for the lad. The father did not take it so warmly as I should have thought he would, owing to the same cause which occasioned his invincible adherence to his notions against creeds and confessions. But Mrs. Macaulay was wisely and truly grateful.

I should have mentioned that Mr. White, a Welshman who has been many years factor on the estate of Cawdor, drank tea with us last night upon getting a note from Macaulay, and

---

[1] "Dr. Johnson did not neglect what he had undertaken. By his interest with the Rev. Dr. Adams, master of Pembroke College, Oxford, where he was educated for some time, he obtained a servitorship for young Macaulay. But it seems he had other views; and I believe went abroad."—BOSWELL.

asked us to his house. He gave us a letter to Mr. Fern, master of stores at Fort George. He showed it to me. It recommended "two celebrated gentlemen: no less than Dr. Johnson, *Author of his Dictionary*, and Mr. Boswell, known at Edinburgh by the name of Paoli."[2] He said he hoped I had no objection to what he had written. If I had, he would alter it. I thought it was a pity to check his effusions, and acquiesced, taking care, however, to seal the letter, that it might not appear that I had read it.

After breakfast and a conversation about saying grace to breakfast as well as dinner and supper, in which Mr. Johnson observed that it is enough if we have stated seasons of prayer, no matter when, and that a man may as well pray when he mounts his horse, or a woman when she milks her cow, as at meals, and that custom is to be followed,[3] we drove down to Fort George.

When we came into the square, I sent a soldier with the letter to Fern. He came to us immediately, and along with him came Major *Brewse* of the Engineers (pronounced *Bruce*). He said he believed it was originally the same Norman name with Bruce. That he had dined at a house in London where were three Bruces, one of the Irish line, one of the Scottish, and himself of the English line. He said he was shown it in the Herald Office spelled fourteen different ways. I told him the different spellings of my name. Mr. Johnson observed that there had been great disputes about the spelling of Shakespeare's name. At last it was thought it would be settled by looking at the original copy of his Will. But upon examining it, he was found to have written it no less than three different ways. This conver-

---

[2] Boswell's *Account of Corsica* (which contained "Memoirs of Pascal Paoli") had been published five years before. It had been very successful, and had made Boswell's name known throughout Great Britain and on the Continent.
[3] "He could not bear to have it thought that, in any instance whatever, the Scots are more pious than the English. I think grace as proper at breakfast as at any other meal. It is the pleasantest meal we have. Dr. Johnson has allowed the peculiar merit of breakfast in Scotland."—BOSWELL. "If an epicure could remove by a wish, in quest of sensual gratifications, wherever he had supped, he would breakfast in Scotland."—Johnson's *Journey*.

sation passed after we had been some time together. But it comes in well here.

Mr. Fern was a brisk civil man. He had been in the Fort for twenty years, but had been at different intervals in London and other places. Major Brewse was a man who seemed to be very intelligent in his profession, and spoke with uncommon deliberation and distinctness. They first carried us to wait on Sir Eyre Coote, whose Regiment (the 37) was lying here, and who commanded them. He asked us to eat a bit of mutton with him. Mr. Johnson said, "That, sir, is contrary to our plan." "Then," said Sir Eyre, "I hope you'll alter your plan." Mr. Johnson agreed, to my great joy.

Mr. Fern and Major Brewse showed us the fort very fully. The Major explained everything in fortification to us, as did Mr. Fern in stores. Mr. Johnson talked of the proportions of charcoal and saltpetre in making gunpowder, of granulating it, and of giving it a gloss. He made a very good figure upon these topics. He said afterwards that he had talked *ostentatiously*. We reposed ourselves a little in Fern's house. He had everything in neat order as in England. He had a tolerable collection of books. I looked at Pennant.[4] He says little of this fort but that the barracks, etc., form several streets. This is aggrandizing. Fern observed if he had said they form a square with a row of buildings before it, he would have given a juster description. Mr. Johnson observed, "How seldom descriptions correspond with realities; and the reason is that people do not write them till some time after, and then their imagination has added circumstances."

We talked of Sir Adolphus Oughton. The Major said he knew a great deal for a military man. "Sir," said Mr. Johnson, "you will find few men of any profession who know more. Sir

---

[4] Thomas Pennant's *Tour in Scotland*, the record of a tour of the mainland made in 1769, was published in 1771. In the summer preceding the expedition of Johnson and Boswell he had visited the western counties of Scotland and the Hebrides, but his book describing this tour did not appear until 1774. It was no doubt the publication of Pennant's first *Tour* and the news of his second which stimulated Johnson to realize his long-projected jaunt.

Adolphus is a very extraordinary man, a man of boundless curiosity and unwearied diligence."

I know not how the Major contrived to introduce the contest between Warburton and Lowth. Mr. Johnson said, "Warburton kept his temper all along, while Lowth was in a passion. Lowth published some of Warburton's letters. Warburton drew *him* on to write some very abusive letters, and then asked his leave to publish them, which he knew Lowth could not refuse after what *he* had done. So that he contrived it so that he should publish apparently with Lowth's consent what could not but show Lowth in a disadvantageous light." Mr. Johnson said the King did him the honour to ask him what he thought of that controversy. Mr. Johnson said he thought Warburton had most general learning, Lowth most scholastic learning. He did not know which of them called names best. The King said he judged of 'em very rightly. The King appeared to have read the controversy.

At three the drum beat for dinner. I could for a little fancy myself a military man, and it pleased me. We went to Sir Eyre's, in the Governor's house, and found him a most gentlemanlike man. His lady was, though not a beauty, one of the most agreeable women I ever saw, with an uncommonly mild and sweet tone in her conversation. She had a young lady, a companion, with her. There was a pretty large company: Fern, the Major of Engineers, and several officers. Sir Eyre had come from the East Indies by land, through the deserts of Arabia. He told us the Arabs could live five days without victuals, and subsist for three weeks with nothing else but the blood of their camels, who could lose so much of it as would suffice for that time, without being exhausted. He highly praised the virtue of the Arabs: their fidelity if they undertook to conduct you: that they'd lose their lives rather than let you be robbed. Mr. Johnson, who is always for maintaining the superiority of civilized men over uncivilized, said there was no superior virtue in this.

Colonel Pennington took up the argument with a good deal of spirit and ingenuity. Mr. Johnson said, "A sergeant and twelve men who are my guard will die rather than that I shall be robbed." "Ay," said the Colonel, "but the soldiers are compelled to do it." "Well," said Mr. Johnson, "the Arabs are compelled by the fear of infamy." COLONEL. "The soldiers have the same fear of infamy, and the fear of punishment besides; so have less virtue, because they act less voluntarily." Lady Coote observed very well that we ought to know if there is not among the Arabs some punishment for not being faithful on such occasions.[5]

We talked of the Stage. I observed that we had not now such a company of actors as in the last age: Wilks, Booth, etc. Mr. Johnson said, "You think so because there is one who excels all the rest so much. You compare them with Garrick and see the deficiency. Garrick's great distinction is his universality. He can represent all modes of life but that of an easy, fine-bred gentleman." The Colonel said he should give over playing young parts. MR. JOHNSON. "He does not take them now, but he does not leave off those which he has been used to play, because he does them better than any one else can do. If you had generations of actors, if they swarmed like bees, the young ones might drive off the old ones." He said he thought Mrs. Cibber got more reputation than she deserved, as she had a great sameness, though she had something very fine; though Mrs. Clive was the best player he ever saw. Mrs. Pritchard was a very good one, but had something affected. He imagined she had

---

[5] "Tafas was a Hazimi, of the Beni Salem branch of Harb, and so not on good terms with the Masruh. This inclined him towards me; and when he had once accepted the charge of escorting me to Feisal, we could trust him. The fidelity of road-companions was most dear to Arab tribesmen. The guide had to answer to a sentimental public with his life for that of his fellow. One Harbi, who promised to take Huber to Medina and broke his word and killed him on the road near Rabegh, when he found out that he was a Christian, was ostracized by public opinion, and, in spite of the religious prejudices in his favour, had ever since lived miserably alone in the hills, cut off from friendly intercourse, and refused permission to marry any daughter of the tribe."—T. E. Lawrence, *Seven Pillars of Wisdom*, copyright 1935 by Doubleday, Doran and Co., Inc., pp. 77–8.

some player of the former age in her eye, which occasioned it.

Pennington said Garrick sometimes failed in emphasis, as in *Hamlet*,

I will speak *daggers* to her, but I'll use *none*,

in place of

I'll *speak* daggers to her, but I'll *use* none.

Sir Eyre had something between the Duke of Queensberry and my late worthy friend Captain Cuninghame in his manner.

We had a dinner of two complete courses, variety of wines, and the regimental band of music playing in the square before the windows after it. I enjoyed this day much. We were quite easy and cheerful. Mr. Johnson said, "I shall always remember this fort with gratitude." I could not help being struck with the idea of finding upon that barren sandy point such buildings, such a dinner, such company. It was like enchantment. Mr. Johnson, on the other hand, said to me more rationally that it did not strike *him*, because he knew here was a large sum of money expended in building a fort. Here was a regiment. If there had been less than what he found, it would have surprised him. *He* looked coolly through all the gradations. *My* imagination jumped from the barren sand to the good dinner and fine company. Like the hero in *Love in a Hollow Tree*,

Without ands or ifs,
I leapt from off the sand upon the cliffs.[6]

I had a strong impression of the power and excellence of human art.

We left the fort between six and seven. Sir Eyre, the Colonel, etc., went downstairs and saw us into our chaise. There could not be greater attention paid to any visitors. Sir Eyre spoke of the hardships which Dr. Johnson had before him. Said I, "Considering what he has said of us, we must make him feel something rough in Scotland." Said Sir Eyre to him, "You must change your name." "Ay," said I, "Dr. Macgregor."

---

[6] In the third edition of the published *Tour* Boswell deleted the reference to *Love in a Hollow Tree*, and credited the lines merely to "an absurd poet," doubtless because he had looked into Lord Grimston's comedy of that name and could not find them there. The source is still to seek.

We got safely to Inverness, and put up at Mackenzie's at
the Horns. Mr. Keith, the Collector of Excise here, my old acquaintance at Ayr, who had seen us at the Fort, called in the
evening and engaged us to dine with him next day, and promised to breakfast with us and take us to the English Chapel; so
that we were at once commodiously arranged.

Mr. Johnson wrote tonight both to Mrs. Thrale and Mrs.
Williams, and I wrote to my wife. I value myself on having
as constant a regard—nay, love—for her as any man ever had
for a woman, and yet never troubling anybody else with it. I
was somewhat uneasy that I found no letter here from her,
though I could hardly expect it, as I had desired her to write
to Skye. I could not help my mind from imaging it as dreary
that I was to be yet for several weeks separated from her. Clouds
passed over my imagination, and in these clouds I saw objects
somewhat dismal. She might die or I might die; and I felt a
momentary impatience to be home, but a sentence or two of
the Rambler's conversation gave me firmness, and I saw that
I was upon an expedition which I had wished for for years,
and the recollection of which would be a treasure to me for
life. The inn was dirty and ill-furnished. The entertainment
pretty good.

SUNDAY 29 AUGUST. Mr. Keith breakfasted with us. Mr.
Johnson run out rather strongly upon the benefits derived to
Scotland from the Union, and the bad state of our people before it. I am entertained with his copious exaggeration upon
that subject. But I am uneasy when people are by who do not
know him as well as I do and may be apt to think him narrow-
minded.[1] I diverted the subject.

The chapel was but a poor one. The altar was a bare fir table,
with a coarse stool for kneeling on, covered with a piece of
coarse sail-cloth doubled by way of cushion. The lofts were at
each end, and one before the pulpit. At the left hand of it, when

---

[1] "It is remarkable that Dr. Johnson read this gentle remonstrance, and took no notice
of it to me."—BOSWELL.

you looked up to the loft, you saw just the uncovered joists. At
the right hand, where the altar was, they were covered with
white crown paper pasted upon them, which formed a ceiling.
The congregation was small. Tait, the clergyman, read prayers very well, though with much of the Scotch accent. He
preached on "Love your enemies." It was curious that when
talking of the connexions amongst men, he said that some
connected themselves with men of distinguished talents, and
since they could not equal them, tried to deck themselves with
their merit by being their companions. The sentence was to
this purpose. It had an odd coincidence with what might be
said of Mr. Johnson and me.

After church we walked down to the quay, where I met,
at Oliver's[2] fort, Mr. Alves the painter, whom I had not seen
since I was at Rome in 1765.[3] We then went to Macbeth's Castle. I had a most romantic satisfaction in seeing Mr. Johnson
actually in it. It answers to Shakespeare's description, "This
castle hath a pleasant," etc., which I repeated. When we came
out of it, a raven perched on one of the chimney-tops and
croaked. Then I repeated, "The raven himself is hoarse," etc.
I exulted in comparing my former hypochondriac state when
at Inverness with my present soundness and vigour of mind,
and I was thankful.

We dined at Keith's. A Miss Duff was there. Mrs. Keith
was officiously attentive to Mr. Johnson, asking him many questions about his drinking only water. He rebuked her by saying
to me, "You may remember that not[4] the least notice was
taken of this by Lady Erroll"—showing Mrs. Keith that she
was not so well-bred.

Mr. Johnson has the art for which I have heard my father
praise the old Earl of Aberdeen: *viz.*, that of instructing himself by making every man he meets tell him something of what

---

[2] i.e., Cromwell's.
[3] He at that time painted a miniature of Boswell, which has vanished.
[4] Omitted inadvertently.

he knows best. He led Keith to talk to him of the excise in
Scotland. Mr. Johnson told us that Mr. Thrale paid £20,000
a year; that he had four casks, each of which holds 1600 barrels—above a thousand hogsheads.

A young lady whose name I did not hear, and Mr. Grant,
the minister whom we had seen at Macaulay's, drank tea with
us. There was little conversation that can be written down. I
shall therefore here again glean what I have omitted on former days. Gerard told us that when he was in Wales he was
shown a valley inhabited by Danes who still retain their own
language, and are quite a distinct people. Mr. Johnson said it
could not be true, or all the kingdom must have heard of it.
He said to me as we travelled, "These people, sir, may have
somewhat of a *peregrinity* in their dialect, which is augmented
to a different language." I asked him if *peregrinity* was a word.
He laughed and said, "No." I told him this was just the second
time that I had heard him make a word. When Foote broke
his leg, I observed that this would fit him better for taking off
George Faulkner as Peter Paragraph. Mr. Johnson said,
"George will rejoice at the *depeditation* of Foote," and when I
asked him, laughed and owned he had made the word; and
that he had not made above three or four in the Dictionary.

Mr. Johnson told me that all the aid he had in compiling
the Dictionary was having about twenty etymologies sent him
by an unknown hand at the time, which he afterwards learned
was Dr. Pearce, Bishop of Rochester. Some of them he adopted.
He never lived a great deal with Lord Chesterfield, nor was
there any particular incident that produced a quarrel between
them, as has been erroneously propagated. My lord had made
him great professions. Yet for —— years, while Mr. Johnson
was engaged in his immense undertaking, the Dictionary, my
lord never took the least notice of him. When the work came
out, my lord fell a-scribbling in the *World* about it. Mr. Johnson, with a just indignation and contempt, wrote to him a letter which was civil but showed him that he did not mind what

he said or wrote, and that he had done with him. Mr. Johnson kept no copy of the letter. He could repeat it, and was once persuaded to write it down from memory, but he believes he has lost the copy. I have heard Langton repeat some of it; in particular a sentence to this purpose: that Lord Chesterfield, after leaving him to struggle with the waves unassisted, stretched out his hand to welcome him on shore.[5]

After tea Mr. Keith went with us to our inn. He and I left Mr. Johnson there a little and went and called for old Mr. Fraser, the minister; for Redcastle's family, where I found only Miss Murdoch, whom I had never seen before; and for Mrs. Anderson, formerly Miss Mackinnon, in whose mother's house I had formerly lodged along with my father at the Circuit. I am, as Mr. Johnson observed, one who has all the old principles, good and bad. That of attention to relations in the remotest degree, or to worthy people in every state whom I have once known, I inherit from my father. It gave me much satisfaction to hear everybody here speak of him with uncommon regard. Mr. Keith and Mr. Grant supped with us at the inn.[6] We had roasted kid.

MONDAY 30 AUGUST. This day we were to begin our *equitation*, as I said, for *I* would needs make a word too.[1] We might have taken a chaise to Fort Augustus. But we could not find

[5] "Is not a patron, my lord, one who looks with unconcern on a man struggling for life in the water, and, when he has reached ground, encumbers him with help?" This entire paragraph was omitted from the published *Tour*. Boswell merely referred to it in a footnote, saying that he was reserving the material for the *Life of Johnson*.

[6] "Mr. Grant used to relate that on this occasion Johnson was in high spirits. In the course of conversation he mentioned that Mr. Banks (afterwards Sir Joseph) had, in his travels in New South Wales, discovered an extraordinary animal called the kangaroo. The appearance, conformation, and habits of this quadruped were of the most singular kind; and in order to render his description more vivid and graphic, Johnson rose from his chair and volunteered an imitation of the animal. The company stared; and Mr. Grant said nothing could be more ludicrous than the appearance of a tall, heavy, grave-looking man, like Dr. Johnson, standing up to mimic the shape and motions of a kangaroo. He stood erect, put out his hands like feelers, and, gathering up the tails of his huge brown coat so as to resemble the pouch of the animal, made two or three vigorous bounds across the room!"—CARRUTHERS. One hopes that the Rev. Mr. Grant was not merely exercising his fancy when he told this story, but it seems strange that Boswell did not mention the incident.

[1] Dr. Chapman points out that the word had been in use since the Sixteenth Century.

horses after Inverness, so we resolved to begin here to ride. We should have set out at seven. But one of the horses needed shoeing; the smith had got drunk the night before at a wedding and could not rise early; so we did not get off till nine. We had three horses for Mr. Johnson, myself, and Joseph, and one which carried our portmanteaus; and two Highlanders who walked with us, John Hay[2] and Lauchlan Vass. Mr. Johnson rode very well.

A little above Inverness, I fancy about three miles, we saw just by the road a very complete Druid's temple; at least we took it to be so. There was a double circle of stones, one of very large ones and one of smaller ones. Mr. Johnson justly observed that to go and see one is only to see that it is nothing, for there is neither art nor power in it, and seeing one is as much as one would wish.

It was a delightful day. Loch Ness, and the road upon the side of it, between birch trees, with the hills above, pleased us much. The scene was as remote and agreeably wild as could be desired. It was full enough to occupy our minds for the time.

To see Mr. Johnson in any new situation is an object of attention to me. As I saw him now for the first time ride along just like Lord Alemoor,[3] I thought of *London, a Poem*, of the *Rambler*, of *The False Alarm*; and I cannot express the ideas which went across my imagination.

A good way up the Loch, I perceived a little hut with an oldish woman at the door of it. I knew it would be a scene for Mr. Johnson. So I spoke of it. "Let's go in," said he. So we dismounted, and we and our guides went in. It was a wretched little hovel, of earth only, I think; and for a window had just a hole which was stopped with a piece of turf which could be taken out to let in light. In the middle of the room

---

[2] The MS and the first edition read "Gray." The correction was made in the second edition.

[3] From what Boswell says later of Johnson's riding (*post*, p. 230, n. 2) it would appear that the comparison was not meant to be flattering. Lord Alemoor was one of the most respected members of the Scottish bench.

(or space which we entered) was a fire of peat, the smoke going out at a hole in the roof. She had a pot upon it with goat's flesh boiling. She had at one end, under the same roof but divided with a kind of partition made of wands, a pen or fold in which we saw a good many kids.

Mr. Johnson asked me where she slept. I asked one of the guides, who asked her in Erse. She spoke with a kind of high tone. He told us she was afraid we wanted to go to bed to her. This coquetry, or whatever it may be called, of so wretched a like being was truly ludicrous. Mr. Johnson and I afterwards made merry upon it. I said it was he who alarmed the poor woman's virtue. "No, sir," said he. "She'll say, 'There came a wicked young fellow, a wild young dog, who I believe would have ravished me had there not been with him a grave old gentleman who repressed him. But when he gets out of the sight of his tutor, I'll warrant you he'll spare no woman he meets, young or old.'" "No," said I. "She'll say, 'There was a terrible ruffian who would have forced me, had it not been for a gentle, mild-looking youth, who, I take it, was an angel.'"

Mr. Johnson would not hurt her delicacy by insisting to "see her bedchamber," like Archer in *The Beaux' Stratagem*. But I was of a more ardent curiosity, so I lighted a piece of paper and went into the place where the bed was. There was a little partition of wicker, rather more neatly done than the one for the fold, and close by the wall was a kind of bedstead of wood with heath upon it for a bed; and at the foot of it I saw some sort of blankets or covering rolled up in a heap. The woman's name was Fraser. So was her husband's. He was a man of eighty. Mr. Fraser of Balnain allows him to live in this hut and to keep sixty goats for taking care of his wood. He was then in the wood. They had five children, the oldest only thirteen. Two were gone to Inverness to buy meal. The rest were looking after the goats. She had four stacks of barley, twenty-four sheaves in each. They had a few fowls. They will live all the spring without meal upon milk and curd, etc., alone. What they get for

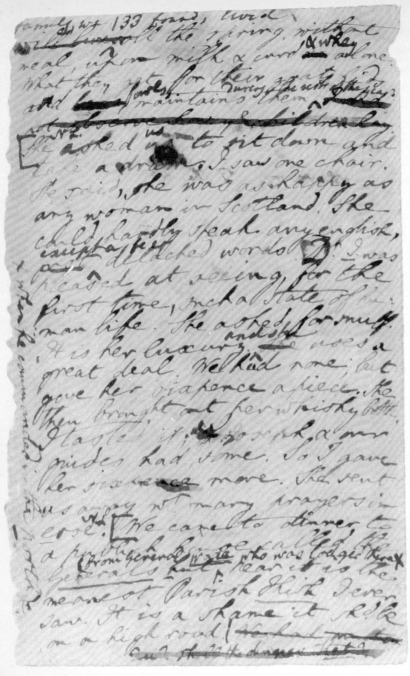

QUERY TO MALONE IN THE MANUSCRIPT

after dinner, we had a good deal of mountainous country. I had known Mr. Trapaud, at Fort Augustus twelve years ago, where my Father was Judge, a Circuit at Inverness. Joseph went forward one of our guides with a card to him, that he might know Dr. J & I were coming up leaving it to him to invite us or not. It was dark when we got there. The Inn was wretched. Government ought to build one, or give the president an additional salary, as he must in the present state of things necessarily be put to a great expence in entertaining travellers. Joseph announced to us, when we alighted, that the Governour waited for us at the gate of the fort. We walked to it. He met us with much civility conducted us to his house. It was comfortable to find ourselves in a well built little square and a really well-furnished house, in good company and with a good supper before us.

their goats, kids, and hens maintains them. I did not observe how the children lay.

She asked us to sit down and take a dram. I saw one chair. She said she was as happy as any woman in Scotland. She could hardly speak any English, just detached words. Mr. Johnson was pleased at seeing for the first time such a state of human life. She asked for snuff. It is her luxury. She uses a great deal. We had none, but gave her sixpence apiece. She then brought out her whisky bottle. I tasted it, and Joseph and our guides had some. So I gave her sixpence more. She sent us away with many prayers in Erse.

We came to dinner to a public house called the General's Hut. Near it is the meanest parish kirk I ever saw. It is a shame it should be on a high road. We had mutton-chops, a broiled chicken, and bacon and eggs, and a bottle of Malaga.[4] After dinner we had a good deal of mountainous country. I had known Governor Trapaud at Fort Augustus twelve years ago, at a Circuit at Inverness. I sent forward one of our guides and Joseph with a card to him, that he might know Mr. Johnson and I were coming up, leaving it to him to invite us or not. It was dark when we got up. The inn was wretched. Government ought to build one, or give the Governor an additional salary, as he must necessarily be put to a great expense in entertaining travellers. Joseph announced to us when we lighted that the Governor waited for us at the gate. We walked towards it. He met us, and with much civility conducted us to his house. It was comfortable to find ourselves in a well-built little square, a neat well-furnished house with prints, etc., a good supper (fricassee of moor-fowl, etc.); in short, with all the conveniencies of civilized life in the midst of rude mountains. Mrs. Trapaud and the Governor's daughter and her husband, Captain Newmarsh,

---

[4] There is a wistful marginal query by Boswell: "Shall the dinner *Stet?*" It was deleted. The query indicates that Boswell had edited this portion before submitting it to Malone; indeed this is the most obvious general explanation of the occurrence of corrections in both hands on many of the leaves. It is impossible to tell whether or not in this instance Boswell was present during Malone's revision.

were all most obliging and polite. The Governor, though near
seventy, had excellent animal spirits, the conversation of a soldier and somewhat of a Frenchman, talking with importance
of everything, however small. We passed a very agreeable evening till twelve, and then went to bed.

TUESDAY 31 AUGUST. The Governor has a very neat
garden. We looked at it and all the rest of the Fort, which is
but small and may be commanded from a variety of hills
around. We also looked at the galley or sloop belonging to
the Fort, which sails upon the Loch and brings what is wanted
for the garrison. Captains Ourry and D'Aripé and Lieutenant
Letch breakfasted with us. The two former had been in the
American War, and entertained Mr. Johnson much with accounts of the Indians. He said he could make a very pretty
book out of them were he to stay there. Governor Trapaud
was much struck with Mr. Johnson. "I like to hear him talk,"
said he. "It is so majestic. I should be glad to hear him speak
in your Court." He wanted us to stay dinner. But I considered
that we had a rude road before us, which we could easier encounter in the morning, and that it was hard to say when we
might get up were we to sit down to good entertainment and
good company. I therefore begged the Governor would just let
us slip away. Here too I had the satisfaction of another proof
how much my father is regarded. The Governor expressed the
highest respect for him, and bid me tell him that if he would
come that way on a Circuit to Inverness, he would do him all
the honours in his power.

Between twelve and one we set out and travelled eleven
wild miles till we came to a house in Glenmoriston kept by
one Macqueen.[1] Our landlord was a sensible fellow. He had

---

[1] The printed *Tour* changes this to "a Macqueen," with the following note: "*A* Macqueen is a Highland mode of expression. An Englishman would say *one* Macqueen. But
where there are *clans* or *tribes* of men, distinguished by *patronymic* surnames, the individuals of each are considered as if they were of different species, at least as much as nations
are distinguished; so that a Macqueen, a Macdonald, a Maclean, is said, as we say a
Frenchman, an Italian, a Spaniard."—BOSWELL.

learnt his grammar,[2] and Mr. Johnson justly observed that a man is the better for that as long as he lives. There were some books here: a treatise against drunkenness, translated from the French, a volume of the *Spectator*, a volume of Prideaux' *Connexion, Cyrus's Travels*. Macqueen said he had more volumes, and his pride seemed to be much piqued that we were surprised at his having books.

Near to this, we had passed a party of soldiers under a sergeant at work upon the road. We gave them two shillings to drink. They came to this house and made merry in the barn. We went out, Mr. Johnson saying, "Come, let's go and give 'em another shilling apiece." We did so, and he was saluted "MY LORD" by all of 'em. He is really generous, loves influence, and has the way of gaining it. He said he was quite feudal. Here I agree with him. I said I regretted I was not head of a clan. I would make my tenants follow me. I could not be a *patriarchal* chief. But I'd be a *feudal* chief.

The poor soldiers got too much liquor. Some of 'em fought and left blood upon the spot, and cursed whisky next morning. The house here was built of thick turfs and thatched with thinner turfs and heath. It had three rooms in length, and a little room projected. Where we sat, the side-walls were *wainscotted*, as Mr. Johnson said, with wands very well plaited. Our landlord had made all with his own hand. We had a broiled chicken, mutton collops or chops, mutton sausage, and eggs, of which Mr. Johnson eat five and nothing else. I eat four, some chicken and some sausage, and drank some rum and water and sugar. Joseph had lemons for Mr. Johnson, so he had lemonade. Mr. Johnson said he was a fine fellow: a civil man and a wise man.

Macqueen, our landlord, sat by us awhile and talked with us.

---

[2] i.e., he had studied Latin. Carruthers, who gives a long and interesting note on him, says he also wrote Gaelic verse. He "was a gentleman of the old Highland stamp, who considered himself a public benefactor by condescending to keep a change-house. He was married to a laird's daughter."

He said all Glenmoriston's people would bleed for him if they were well used. But that seventy men had gone out of the Glen to America. That he himself intended to go next year, for that his farm, which twenty-five years ago was only £5 a year, was now raised to £20. That he could pay £10 and live, but no more. Mr. Johnson said he wished Macqueen Laird of Glenmoriston, and Glenmoriston to go to America. Macqueen very generously said he should be sorry for it, for Glenmoriston could not shift for himself in America as he could do.[3]

I talked of the officers whom we had left today: how much service they had seen and how little they got for it, even of fame. Mr. Johnson said, "Sir, a soldier gets as little as any man can get." I observed that Goldsmith had more fame than all the officers last war who were not generals. JOHNSON. "Why, sir, you will get ten thousand to do what they did before you get one who does what Goldsmith has done. You must consider a thing is valued according to its rarity. A pebble that paves the street is in itself more useful than the diamond upon a lady's finger." I wish Goldie had heard this.

He said yesterday when I wondered how John Hay, one of our guides, who had been pressed aboard a man-of-war, did not choose to continue longer than nine months, after which time he got off: "Why, sir, no man will be a sailor who has contrivance to get himself into a jail, for being in a ship is being in a jail with the chance of being drowned."

We had tea in the afternoon, and our landlord's daughter, a modest civil girl very neatly dressed, made it to us. She told us she had been a year at Inverness and learnt reading and writing, sewing, knotting, working lace, and pastry. Mr. Johnson made her a present of a book of arithmetic[4] which he had bought at Inverness.

---

[3] Carruthers says that Macqueen was unjust to the Laird (Peter Grant), who had really made extraordinary efforts to hold his tenants. Macqueen himself "could not have had a very bad bargain." He did not emigrate, but stayed on fifteen years more at Anoch, then moved to another farm near by, "and survived till past ninety."

[4] The published *Tour* prints simply "book," with the following note: "This book has

The room had some deals laid as a kind of ceiling. There were two beds in the room. A woman's gown was hung on a rope to make a curtain of separation between them. Joseph had the sheets which we brought with us laid on them. We had much hesitation whether to undress or lie down with our clothes on. I said at last, "I'll plunge in! I shall have less room for vermin to settle about me when I strip!" Mr. Johnson said he was like one hesitating whether to go into the cold bath. At last he resolved too. I observed he might serve a campaign. Said he, "I could do all that can be done by patience. Whether I should have strength enough, I know not." He was in excellent humour. To see the Rambler as I saw him tonight was really a curiosity. I yesterday told him I was thinking to write an Epistle to him *on his return from Scotland,* in the style of Mrs. Gulliver to Captain Lemuel Gulliver—

Sullen you turn from both and call for *oats.*

He laughed and asked in whose name I'd write it. I said Mrs. Thrale's. He was angry and said, "Sir, if you have any sense of decency or delicacy, you won't do that." "Then," said I, "let it be Cole, the landlord of the Mitre Tavern." "Ay, that may do," said he.

Tonight each offered up his private devotions. After we had chatted a little from our beds, Mr. Johnson said, "GOD bless us both for Jesus Christ's sake. Good night." I pronounced "Amen." Mr. Johnson fell asleep immediately. I could not have

given rise to much inquiry, which has ended in ludicrous surprise. Several ladies, wishing to learn the kind of reading which the great and good Dr. Johnson esteemed most fit for a young woman, desired to know what book he had selected for this Highland nymph. 'They never adverted,' said he, 'that I had no *choice* in the matter. I have said that I presented her with a book which I *happened* to have about me.'—And what was this book?— My readers, prepare your features for merriment. It was Cocker's *Arithmetic!*—Wherever this was mentioned, there was a loud laugh, at which Dr. Johnson, when present, used sometimes to be a little angry. One day, when we were dining at General Oglethorpe's, where we had many a valuable day, I ventured to interrogate him, 'But, sir, is it not somewhat singular that you should *happen* to have Cocker's *Arithmetic* about you on your journey? What made you buy such a book at Inverness?'—He gave me a very sufficient answer. 'Why, sir, if you are to have but one book with you upon a journey, let it be a book of science. When you have read through a book of entertainment, you know it, and it can do no more for you; but a book of science is inexhaustible.' "—BOSWELL.

that good fortune for a long time. I fancied myself bit by innumerable vermin under the clothes, and that a spider was travelling from the *wainscot* towards my mouth.[5] At last I fell into insensibility.

WEDNESDAY 1 SEPTEMBER. I awaked very early. I began to imagine that the landlord, being about to emigrate, might murder us to get our money and lay it upon the soldiers in the barn. Such groundless fears will arise in the mind before it has resumed its vigour after sleep! Mr. Johnson had had the same kind of ideas; for he told me afterwards that he considered so many soldiers, having seen us, would be witnesses should any harm be done; and the thought of that, I suppose, he considered would make us secure. When I got up, I found him sound asleep in his miserable sty, I may say, with a coloured handkerchief tied round his head. With difficulty could I get him up. It put me in mind of Henry IV's fine soliloquy on sleep; for to be sure there was here an "uneasy pallet" with a witness.

A redcoat of the 15, whether officer or only sergeant I could not be sure, came to the house in his way to the mountains to shoot deer, which it seems Glenmoriston does not hinder anybody to do. Few indeed can do them harm. We had him to breakfast with us. We got away about eight. Macqueen walked some miles to give us a convoy. He had joined Prince Charles at Fort Augustus, and continued in the Highland army till after the battle of Culloden. As he narrated the particulars of that unlucky but brave and generous attempt, I several times burst into tears. There is a certain association of ideas in my mind upon that subject, by which I am strongly affected. The very Highland names, or the sound of a bagpipe, will stir my blood and fill me with a mixture of melancholy, and respect for courage; and pity for the unfortunate,[1] and superstitious re-

---

[5] This furnished the subject for another of Collings's and Rowlandson's caricatures.
[1] All the editions read "*an* unfortunate"—clearly a printer's error. Dr. Chapman was the first editor, apparently, to read the text closely enough to see that the passage, as printed, was nonsense. His ingenious emendation ("unfortunate *land*" for "unfortunate *and*") is now, unfortunately, shown to be mistaken.

gard for antiquity; and inclination for war without thought; and, in short, with a crowd of sensations.

We passed through Glen Shiel, with prodigious mountains on each side. We saw where the battle was in the year 1715.[2] Mr. Johnson owned he was now in a scene of as wild nature as he could see. But he corrected me sometimes in my observations. "There," said I, "is a mountain like a cone." "No, sir," said he. "It would be called so in a book; and when a man comes to look at it, he sees 'tis not so. It is indeed pointed at the top. But one side of it is much longer than the other." Another mountain I called immense. "No," said he, "but 'tis a considerable protuberance."

We came to a rich green valley,[3] comparatively speaking, and stopped at Auchnashiel, a kind of rural village, a number of cottages being built together, as we saw all along in the Highlands. We passed many many miles today without seeing a house, but only little summer-huts or *shielings*. Ewan Campbell, servant to Mr. Murchison, factor to the Laird of MacLeod in Glenelg, run along with us today. He was a fine obliging little fellow. At this Auchnashiel, we sat down on a green turf seat at the end of a house, and they brought us out two wooden dishes of milk. One of them was frothed like a sillabub. I saw a woman preparing it with such a stick as is used for chocolate, and in the same manner. That dish fell to my share; but I put by the froth and took the cream with some wheat-bread which Joseph had brought for us from Fort Augustus. Mr. Johnson imagined my dish was better than his, and desired to taste it. He did so, and was convinced that I had no advantage over him. We had there in a circle all about us, men, women and

---

[2] Corrected to 1719 in the published *Tour*.

[3] "Dr. Johnson, in his *Journey*, thus beautifully describes his situation here: 'I sat down on a bank, such as a writer of romance might have delighted to feign. I had, indeed, no trees to whisper over my head; but a clear rivulet streamed at my feet. The day was calm, the air soft, and all was rudeness, silence, and solitude. Before me, and on either side, were high hills, which, by hindering the eye from ranging, forced the mind to find entertainment for itself. Whether I spent the hour well, I know not; for here I first conceived the thought of this narration.'"—BOSWELL. Boswell continues with an encomium from the *Critical Review*.

children, all Macraes, Lord Seaforth's people. Not one of them could speak English. I said to Mr. Johnson 'twas the same as being with a tribe of Indians. "Yes," said he, "but not so terrifying." I gave all who chose it snuff and tobacco. Governor Trapaud had made us buy a quantity at Fort Augustus and put them up in small parcels. I also gave each person a bit of wheat-bread, which they had never tasted. I then gave a penny apiece to each child. I told Mr. Johnson of this, upon which he called for change for a shilling, and declared that he would distribute among the children. Upon this there was a great stir: not only did some children come running down from neighbouring huts, but I observed one black-headed man, who had been among us all along, coming carrying a very young child. Mr. Johnson then ordered the children to be drawn up in a row, and he distributed his copper and made them and their parents all happy. The poor Macraes, whatever may be their present state, were much thought of in the year 1715, when there was a line in a song,

"And aw' the brave McCraas is coming."[4]

There was great diversity in the faces of the circle around us. Some were as black and wild in their appearance as any American savages whatever. One woman was as comely as the figure of Sappho, as we see it painted. We asked the old woman, the mistress of the house where we had the milk (which, by

---

[4] "The McCraas, or Macraes, were since that time brought into the king's army, by the late Lord Seaforth. When they lay in Edinburgh Castle in 1778, and were ordered to embark for Jersey, they with a number of other men in the regiment, for different reasons, but especially an apprehension that they were to be sold to the East India Company, though enlisted not to be sent out of Great Britain without their own consent, made a determined mutiny, and encamped upon the lofty mountain, Arthur's Seat, where they remained three days and three nights; bidding defiance to all the force in Scotland. At last they came down, and embarked peaceably, having obtained formal articles of capitulation, signed by Sir Adolphus Oughton, commander-in-chief, General Skene, deputy commander, the Duke of Buccleuch, and the Earl of Dunmore, which quieted them. Since the secession of the Commons of Rome to the *Mons Sacer*, a more spirited exertion has not been made. I gave great attention to it from first to last, and have drawn up a particular account of it. Those brave fellows have since served their country effectually at Jersey, and also in the East Indies, to which, after being better informed, they voluntarily agreed to go."—BOSWELL. Boswell published an account of the mutiny in the *Public Advertiser*, 29 Sept. 1778.

the by, Mr. Johnson told me, for I did not observe it myself, was built not of turf but of stone), what we should pay. She said, what we pleased. One of our guides asked her in Erse if a shilling was enough. She said, "Yes." But some of the men bid her ask more. This vexed me, because it showed a desire to impose upon strangers, as they knew that even a shilling was high payment. The woman, however, honestly persisted in her first price. So I gave her half-a-crown. Thus we had one good scene of uncommon life to us. The people were very much pleased, gave us many blessings, and said they had not had such a day since the old Laird of MacLeod's time.

Mr. Johnson was much refreshed by this repast. He was pleased when I told him he would make a good chief. He said if he were one, he would dress his servants better than himself, and knock a fellow down if he looked saucy to a Macdonald in rags. But he would not treat men as brutes. He would let them know why all of his clan were to have attention paid to them. He would tell his upper servants why, and make them tell the others.

We rode on well till we came to the high mountain called the Rattachan, by which time both Mr. Johnson and the horses were a good deal fatigued. It is a terrible steep to climb, notwithstanding the road is made slanting along. However, we made it out. On the top of it we met Captain MacLeod of Balmeanach (a Dutch officer[5] come from Skye) riding with his sword slung about him. He asked, "Is this Mr. Boswell?" which was a proof that we were expected. Going down the hill on the other side was no easy task. As Mr. Johnson was a great weight, the two guides agreed that he should ride the horses alternately. Hay's were the two best, and Mr. Johnson would not ride but upon one or other of them, a black or a brown. But as Hay complained much after ascending the Rattachan, Mr. Johnson was prevailed with to mount one of Vass's greys.

---

[5] i.e., an officer of the Scots Brigade in Holland. He retired in 1787 with the rank of major.

As he rode upon it downhill, it did not go well, and he grumbled. I walked on a little before, but was excessively entertained with the method taken to keep him in good humour. Hay led the horse's head, talking to Mr. Johnson as much as he could; and just when Mr. Johnson was uttering his displeasure, the fellow says, "See such pretty goats." Then *whu!* he whistled, and made them jump. Little did he conceive what Mr. Johnson was. Here was now a common ignorant horse-hirer imagining that he could divert, as one does a child, *Mr. Samuel Johnson!* The ludicrousness, absurdity, and extraordinary contrast between what the fellow fancied and the reality, was as highly comic as anything that I ever witnessed. I laughed immoderately, and must laugh as often as I recollect it.

It grew dusky; and we had a very tedious ride for what was called five miles, but I am sure would measure ten. We spoke none. I was riding forward to the inn at Glenelg, that I might make some kind of preparation, or take some proper measures, before Mr. Johnson got up, who was now advancing in silence, with Hay leading his horse. Mr. Johnson called me back with a tremendous shout, and was really in a passion with me for leaving him. I told him my intentions. But he was not satisfied, and said, "Do you know, I should as soon have thought of picking a pocket as doing so." "I'm diverted with you," said I. Said he, "I could never be diverted with incivility." He said doing such a thing made one lose confidence in him who did it, as one could not tell what he would do next. I justified myself but lamely to him. But my intentions were not improper. I wished to be forward to see if Sir A. Macdonald had sent his boat; and if not, how we were to sail, and how we were to lodge, all which I thought I could best settle myself, without his having any trouble. To apply his great mind to minute particulars is wrong. It is like taking an immense balance, such as you see on a quay for weighing cargoes of ships, to weigh a guinea. I knew I had neat little scales which would do better. That his attention to everything in his way, and his uncommon desire to be always in the right, would make him weigh if he knew of the particulars; and therefore it was right for me to weigh them and let him have them only in effect. I kept by him, since he thought I should.

As we passed the barracks at Bernera, I would fain have put up there; at least I looked at them wishfully, as soldiers have always everything in the best order. But there was only a sergeant and a few men there. We came on to the inn at Glenelg. There was nothing to give the horses, so they were sent to grass with a man to watch them. We found that Sir Alexander had sent his boat to a point which we had passed, at Kintail, or more properly at the King's house—that it had waited several days till their provisions run short, and had returned only this day. So we had nothing to say against that Knight. A lass showed us upstairs into a room raw and dirty; bare walls, a variety of bad smells, a coarse black fir greasy table, forms of the same kind, and from a wretched bed started a fellow from his sleep like Edgar in *King Lear*: "Poor Tom's a-cold."[6]

The landlord was one Munro from Fort Augustus. He pays £8 to MacLeod for the shell of the house, and has not a bit of land in lease. They had no bread, no eggs, no wine, no spirits but whisky, no sugar but brown grown black. They prepared some mutton-chops, but we would not have them. They killed two hens. I made Joseph broil me a bit of one till it was black, and I tasted it. Mr. Johnson would take nothing but a bit of bread, which we had luckily remaining, and some lemonade which he made with a lemon which Joseph had for him,[7] and he got some good sugar; for Mr. Murchison, factor to MacLeod in Glenelg, sent us some, with a bottle of excellent rum, letting us know he was very sorry that his servant had not come and informed him before we passed his house; that we might have been there all night, and that if he were not obliged to set out early

---

[6] "It is amusing to observe the different images which this being presented to Dr. Johnson and me. The Doctor, in his *Journey*, compares him to a Cyclops."—BOSWELL.

[7] In the published *Tour* all this is condensed to a single sentence: "This inn was furnished with not a single article that we could either eat or drink."

next day for Inverness, he would come down and wait upon us.

I took some rum and water and sugar, and grew better; for after my last bad night I hoped much to be well this, and being disappointed, I was uneasy and almost fretful. Mr. Johnson was calm. I said he was so from vanity. "No," said he, "'tis from philosophy." It was a considerable satisfaction to me to see that the Rambler could practise what he nobly teaches.

I resumed my riding forward, and wanted to defend it. Mr. Johnson was still violent upon that subject, and said, "Sir, had you gone on, I was thinking that I should have returned with you to Edinburgh and then parted, and never spoke to you more."

I sent for fresh hay, with which we made beds to ourselves, each in a room equally miserable. As Wolfe said in his letter from Quebec, we had "choice of difficulties."[8] Mr. Johnson made things better by comparison. At Macqueen's last night he observed that few were so well lodged in a ship. Tonight he said we were better than if we had been upon the hill. He lay down buttoned up in his greatcoat. I had my sheets spread on the hay, and having stripped, I had my clothes and greatcoat and Joseph's greatcoat laid upon me, by way of blankets. Joseph lay in the room by me, upon a bed laid on the floor.

THURSDAY 2 SEPTEMBER. I had slept ill. Mr. Johnson's anger had affected me much. I considered that, without any bad intention, I might suddenly forfeit his friendship. I was impatient to see him this morning. I told him how uneasy he had made me by what he had said. He owned it was said in passion; that he would not have done it; that if he had done it, he would have been ten times worse than me. That it would indeed, as I

---

[8] "By the list of disabled officers (many of whom are of rank), you may perceive, Sir, that the army is much weakened. By the nature of the river, the most formidable part of this armament is deprived of the power of acting, yet we have almost the whole force of Canada to oppose. In this situation, there is such a choice of difficulties, that I own myself at a loss how to determine. The affairs of Great Britain, I know, require the most vigorous measures; but then the courage of a handful of brave men should be exerted only where there is some hope of a favourable event." From a letter from Gen. James Wolfe, 2 September 1759, describing his operations against Quebec (*Annual Register*, 1759, p. 246).

said, be "limning in water," should such sudden breaks happen (or something to that effect); and said he, "Let's think no more on't." BOSWELL. "Well then, sir, I shall be easy. Remember, I am to have fair warning in case of any quarrel. You are never to spring a mine upon me. It was absurd in me to believe you." JOHNSON. "You deserved about as much as to believe it from night to morning." Mr. MacLeod of Drynoch, to whom we had a letter from Kenneth Macaulay, breakfasted with us.

A quarter before nine we got into a boat for Skye. It rained much when we set off, but cleared up as we advanced. One of the boatmen who spoke English said that a mile at land was two miles at sea. I then said to him that from Glenelg to Armadale in Skye, which was our sail this morning and is called twelve, was only six miles. But this he could not understand. "Well," said Mr. Johnson, "never talk to me of the native good sense of the Highlanders. Here is a fellow who calls one mile two, and yet cannot comprehend that twelve such miles make but six." It was curious to think that now at last Mr. Johnson and I had left the mainland of Scotland and were sailing to the Hebrides, one of which was close in our view; and I had besides a number of youthful ideas, that is to say, ideas which I have had from my youth about the Isle of Skye. We were shown the land of Moidart where Prince Charles first landed. That stirred my mind.

We reached the shore of Armadale before one. Sir Alexander came down and received us. He was in tartan clothes. My lady stood at the top of the bank and made a kind of jumping for joy. They were then in a house built by a tenant at this place, which is in the district of Sleat. There was a house here for the family, which was burnt in Sir Donald's time. But there is really a good garden and a number of trees of age and size, mostly ash, and that too of a particular kind, the wood of which is very compact. There is a kind of recess here of land, as well as a kind of bay of the sea, more indeed the former. It is a pretty warm exposure. There is a little brook runs down from the hill through a tolerable bank of wood. I am a very imperfect topographer. The house is a very good tenant's house, having two storeys and garrets, but seemed very poor for a chief. Mr. Johnson and I were to have had but one room. But I made the plan be altered; so one of the beds was taken out of his room and put into the next, in which I and the overseer of the farm were to lie; but happily Joseph was put in the overseer's place.

We had at dinner a little Aberdeenshire man, one Jeans, a naturalist, with his son, a dwarf with crooked legs.[1] Jeans said he had been at Mr. Johnson's in London with Ferguson the astronomer. Mr. Johnson thought it strange how he found somebody in such distant places who knew him; that he should have thought he might hide himself in Skye. We had also Rorie Macdonald in Sandaig, an old brisk Highlander of 68, a near relation of Sir Alexander's, and his wife, a sister of Raasay's; Donald MacLeod, late of Canna, a very genteel man,[2] and Donald Macdonald, son to Rorie, who was Lieutenant of Grenadiers in Montgomerie's Regiment (I took a liking to him from his first appearance), as also ―― Macqueen, son to Rorie's wife by the first marriage, who was going to America, and a Captain MacLeod from Sutherland.

We had an ill-dressed dinner, Sir Alexander not having a cook of any kind from Edinburgh.[3] I alone drank port wine.

---

[1] The following note on John Jeans and his son is from a MS in the University Library, Aberdeen: "Being of an ingenious and active turn, he became an enthusiast for mineralogy, and travelled over the greater part of the mainland and the Highlands, collecting till he became eminent as a dealer, repairing annually to London, and being the first finder of numerous Scottish substances. He lived to old age, dying about 1804, aged about eighty.... A son succeeded him in the business of collecting and polishing, a coarse and contemptible character, who was drowned on a dark night by falling into the basin near the New Pier, 1809...." (*Notes and Queries*, ser. 10, vol. ii. 155–6.)

[2] Boswell deleted this compliment to Canna, apparently not long after writing it.

[3] Boswell's account of his and Johnson's reception at Armadale, and his personal observations on Sir Alexander and Lady Macdonald, were much abridged and softened in the first edition of the *Tour*. But enough remained to give Macdonald (he had been created a baron in 1776) just cause of offence, and on 26 November 1785 he sent to Boswell a long and angry letter filled with pedantic abuse. On 28 November Boswell wrote to his close friend William Bosville, Lady Macdonald's brother, asking him to wait upon Lord Macdonald and to inform him that he had suppressed several observations in the original manuscript for fear that they might give offence, which he was so anxious to avoid that he had even cancelled a leaf, "and had it reprinted free from a sentence or

No claret appeared. We had indeed mountain and Frontignac and Scotch porter. But except what I did myself, there was no hospitable convivial intercourse, no ringing of glasses. Nay, I observed that when Captain Macdonald and Mr. Macqueen came in after we were sat down to dinner, Sir Alexander let them stand round the room and stuck his fork into a liver pudding, instead of getting room made for them. I took care to act as he ought to have done. There was no wheat-loaf, but only a kind of bannock or cake, raw in the heart, as it was so thick. Sir Alexander himself drank punch without souring and with little spirits in it, which he distributed to those men who were accustomed even in their own houses to much better. He gave it with a pewter dividing-spoon which had served the broth. At tea there were few cups and no tea-tongs nor a supernumerary tea-spoon, so we used our fingers.

I was quite hurt with the meanness and unsuitable appearance of everything. I meditated setting out the very next day. At night we had only Rorie and spouse and the naturalist and his son. When Mr. Johnson and I retired for rest, he said it grieved him to see the chief of a great clan in such a state; that he was just as one in a lodging-house in London. However, he resolved that we should weather it out till Monday.

FRIDAY 3 SEPTEMBER. The day was very wet. Sir Alexander's piper plays below stairs both at breakfast and dinner, which is the only circumstance of a chief to be found about

---

two which were at first inserted." Having made this cancel, Boswell says (it is hard to believe him) that he supposed "that nothing remained that could possibly hurt his lordship." However, finding on revision that three exceptionable passages had escaped him, he had, some weeks before and entirely of his own accord, expunged them from the second edition, then in the press. In a postscript he added that sixteen sheets (256 pages) of the second edition were already printed off, and might be seen at the printer's. The sheet in question had been printed for some time. In consequence of this explanation and apology, Boswell asked that he be assured by Lord Macdonald that no use, public or private, would be made of the derogatory remarks in his letter. As Macdonald made no satisfactory answer, Boswell felt it necessary to appoint John Courtenay his second, and to entrust to him a formal challenge, which he was to present to Lord Macdonald if no means of compromise could be found. Macdonald however finally agreed to cancel or soften the harsher passages in his letter (which he thereupon, with a neat stroke of irony, referred to as a "second edition"), and to make no further use of them.

him. He had two chests of books, of which Mr. Johnson and I
ravenously seized some of the contents. It grew fair a little before dinner, and I took a little walk with Captain Macdonald,
from whom I found that Sir Alexander was quite unpopular,
and that all his deficiencies were well remarked. I made the
Captain drink port wine today. Mrs. Macdonald said that I
fitted Sir Alexander in several suits better than anybody—a
curious expression. I asked her how the old Laird of MacLeod
came to be so much in debt. She said, "You may as well read
the *Spectator* as begin to tell all that"; and she said it was a pity
that this young Laird should lose his *patronomic* estate when he
was in no fault; meaning that he was labouring under a load
of debt not contracted by himself.

When Sir Alexander was out of the room, I spoke of Sir
James. The Highlanders fairly cried. Neither my lady nor Mr.
Johnson were then present. I cried too, and we drank a bumper
to his memory. It was really melancholy to see the manly, gallant, and generous attachment of clanship going to ruin.

Sir Alexander composed today some Latin verses with which
he presented Mr. Johnson.[1] After dinner the Knight and I met
in Mr. Johnson's room, where I was looking for pen and ink.
I fell upon him with perhaps too great violence upon his behaviour to his people; on the meanness of his appearance here;
upon my lady's neither having a maid, nor being dressed better than one. In short, I gave him a volley. He was thrown into
a violent passion; said he could not bear it; called in my lady
and complained to her, at the same time defending himself
with considerable plausibility. Had he been a man of more
mind, he and I must have had a quarrel for life. But I knew he
would soon come to himself. We had moor-fowl for supper tonight, which comforted me.

We were advised by Rorie, by Donald MacLeod, and everybody to visit Raasay in our way to Dunvegan, MacLeod's
house, to which we looked wishfully forward as expecting more

---

[1] Boswell printed these verses in an appendix to the second edition of the *Tour*.

elegance and propriety. The Rev. Mr. Donald Macqueen I heard was the most intelligent man in the island. Sir Alexander should have had him here with us. I had a letter to him from Sir James Foulis. I sent an express to set off early next morning with a letter to him enclosing Sir James's and begging he'd meet us at Raasay on Monday or Tuesday, as also enclosing a card to MacLeod, to inform him that we were to be at Dunvegan.

Mr. Johnson was vexed that he could get no distinct information about anything from any of the people here. He wished that a good comedian saw Rorie and his wife, to take from them a Highland scene.

SATURDAY 4 SEPTEMBER. Sir Alexander was in my room before I got up, with a bowl of buttermilk, of which I drank. Our quarrel was already evanished. I set Mr. Johnson upon him this morning, who said that in seven years he would make this an independent island; that he'd roast oxen whole and hang out a flag as a signal to the Macdonalds to come and get beef and whisky. Poor Sir Alexander was always starting difficulties. "Nay," said Mr. Johnson, "if you're born to object, I have done with you." He would have a magazine of arms. Sir Alexander said they would rust. Said Mr. Johnson, "Let there be men to keep them clean. Your ancestors did not use to let their arms rust."[1]

It was in vain to try to inspirit him. Mr. Johnson said, "Sir, we shall make nothing of him. He has no more ideas of a chief than an attorney who has twenty houses in a street and considers how much he can make of them. All is wrong. He has nothing to say to the people when they come about him." My beauty of a cousin, too, did not escape. Indeed, I was quite disgusted with her nothingness and insipidity. Mr. Johnson said, "This woman would sink a ninety-gun ship. She is so dull—so heavy."

---

[1] "Dr. Johnson seems to have forgotten that a Highlander going armed at this period incurred the penalty of serving as a common soldier for the first, and of transportation beyond sea for a second offence. And as for 'calling out his clan,' twelve Highlanders and a bagpipe made a rebellion."—SIR WALTER SCOTT.

The naturalist and son have been gone two days. Nobody dined today but Rorie and his wife. Rorie was to be dispossessed of his farm in Glenelg at Whitsunday, and was trying to get one from Sir Alexander. He and his wife only dined today. In the afternoon came Rorie's two sons, James the factor and Captain Donald; Norman Macdonald, Sir James's old servant, who was in terms for a farm; and Donald MacLeod. They drank tea. The evening was heavy enough.

SUNDAY 5 SEPTEMBER. Sir Alexander and Rorie and I walked to the parish church of Sleat. It is a poor one; not a loft in it. There are no church-bells in the island. I was told there were once some. What has become of them I could not learn. The minister was from home, so there was no sermon. We went into the church and saw Sir James's monument. It is a very pretty one. The inscription is rather too verbose.[1] Mr. Johnson said it should have been in Latin, as everything intended to be universal and permanent should be.

It was a beautiful day. My spirits were cheered by the mere effect of climate. I had felt a return of spleen during my stay in this mean mansion, and had it not been that I had Mr. Johnson to contemplate, I should have been very sickly in mind. His firmness kept me steady. I looked at him as a man whose head is turning at sea looks at a rock or any fixed object. I wondered at his tranquillity. He however said, "Sir, when a man retires into an island, he is to turn his thoughts entirely on another world. He has done with this."[2] And although Mr. Johnson was calm, yet his genius did not shine as in companies where I have listened to him with admiration. It was enough if he was not weak.

After dinner Sir Alexander and I walked to Tormore, the

---

[1] "This extraordinary young man, whom I had the pleasure of knowing intimately, having been deeply regretted by his country, the most minute particulars concerning him must be interesting to many."—BOSWELL. There follow two letters from Sir James to his mother, Lady Margaret Macdonald, which are omitted in this edition.

[2] In the printed *Tour* the conversation is continued through an additional half-page—about one hundred and forty words which were certainly not in the "*very Journal which Dr. Johnson read.*"

house of James Macdonald, his factor. Here we had Rorie's
daughter, Miss Katie, a pretty girl enough, Captain Donald,
and the rest who were with us yesterday, and drank a couple
of bowls of punch. It was dark by the time we got back. I drank
freely of punch by way of being social, and after supper I
drank freely of port by way of keeping off a *taedium vitae*. Altogether, I had too much.

Mr. Johnson told us that Isaac Hawkins Browne drank hard
for thirty years, and that he wrote his poem, *De Animi Immorta-
litate*, in the last of these years. Sir Alexander and I had another
dispute tonight upon his method of proceeding, and he was
again in a passion.

MONDAY 6 SEPTEMBER. I awaked a good deal uneasy
from having drank too much. The morning too was very wet.
So I was in bad plight. About noon it cleared, and I grew better. Sir Alexander supplied us with horses, and we set out, accompanied by Mr. Donald MacLeod as our guide. The day
was exceedingly agreeable. We rode for some time along Sleat,
near the shore. The houses in general were made just of turf,
covered with grass, and the country seemed well peopled. We
came into Strath, and passed along a wild moorish tract of land
till we came to the shore at Broadford. There we found good
verdure and whin-rocks, or collections of stones like the ruins
of the foundations of old buildings. We saw, too, three cairns
of considerable size.

We came on a mile to Coirechatachan, a farm-house of Sir
Alexander possessed by Mr. Mackinnon,[1] a jolly big man who

---

1 "That my readers may have my narrative in the style of the country through which I
am travelling, it is proper to inform them, that the chief of a clan is denominated by his
surname alone, as MacLeod, Mackinnon, Mackintosh. To prefix *Mr.* to it would be a degradation from *the* MacLeod, &c. My old friend, the Laird of Macfarlane, the great antiquary, took it highly amiss, when General Wade called him Mr. Macfarlane. Dr. Johnson
said he could not bring himself to use this mode of address; it seemed to him to be too
familiar, as it is the way in which, in all other places, intimates or inferiors are addressed.
When the chiefs have *titles*, they are denominated by them, as *Sir James Grant, Sir Allan
Maclean*. The other Highland gentlemen, of landed property, are denominated by their
estates, as *Raasay, Boisdale;* and the wives of all of them have the title of *ladies*. The *tacksmen*, or principal tenants, are named by their farms, as *Kingsburgh, Coirechatachan;* and

received us with a kindly welcome. The house was of two storeys. We were carried into a low parlour, with a carpet on the
floor, which we had not seen at Armadale. We had tea in good
order, a *trea*,[2] silver tea-pot, silver sugar-dish and tongs, silver
tea-spoons enough. Our landlord's father had found a treasure
of old silver coins, and of these he had made his plate. Mr.
Johnson was quite well here. Mrs. Mackinnon was a decent
well-behaved old gentlewoman in a black silk gown. At night
we had of company Coirechatachan and his wife; Mrs. Mackinnon, daughter to his wife and widow of his son; Mr. Macpherson, minister of Sleat, and his wife, daughter of Coirechatachan; a niece of Coirechatachan's, Miss Mackinnon; Miss
Macpherson, sister to the minister; and Dr. Macdonald, a physician; as also young Mr. Mackinnon, son to Coirechatachan.
We had for supper a large dish of minced beef collops, a large
dish of fricassee of fowl, I believe a dish called fried chicken[3] or
something like it, a dish of ham or tongue, some excellent haddocks, some herrings, a large bowl of rich milk, frothed, as good
a bread-pudding as I ever tasted, full of raisins and lemon or
orange peel, and sillabubs made with port wine and in sillabub
glasses. There was a good table-cloth with napkins; china, silver spoons, porter if we chose it, and a large bowl of very good
punch. It was really an agreeable meeting.[4]

Old Coirechatachan had hospitality in his whole behaviour,
as had his wife, who was what we call a ladylike woman. Mr.
Pennant was two nights here. He and young Mackinnon went
to the top of Ben Caillich, a very high mountain just by, on the
top of which there is a cairn.

How superior was our reception here to that at Sir Alex-

---

their wives are called the *mistress* of Kingsburgh, the *mistress* of Coirechatachan.—Having given this explanation, I am at liberty to use that mode of speech which generally
prevails in the Highlands and the Hebrides."—BOSWELL. Mackinnon's first name, for
which Boswell left a blank which he neglected to fill, was Lachlan.

[2] i.e., tray. Boswell presumably meant to indicate a Hebridean pronunciation which differed from his own.

[3] Probably "friar's chicken," or chicken broth with eggs dropped in it.

[4] For this lyric paragraph the printed *Tour* substituted a sentence or two of generalized
language. The next paragraph but one was omitted altogether.

ander's! Mr. Johnson got a good bedroom to himself. When I went upstairs, Mrs. Mackinnon received me in an opposite bed-room with three beds in it, and with an air of hearty cordial-ity said, "Come away and see if you can sleep among a heap of folks"; then kissed me on each side of the face, and bid me good-night. I had a good clean bed with red and white check curtains to myself. In a bed with blue worsted stuff curtains lay Donald MacLeod and Dr. Macdonald; in a red one of the same kind, the minister and young Mackinnon.

TUESDAY 7 SEPTEMBER. Mr. Johnson was much pleased; said we had a genteeler supper than ever we saw at Sir Alex-ander's. There were several good books here: Hector Boethius in Latin, Cave's *Lives of the Fathers*, Baker's *Chronicle*, Jeremy Collier's *Church History*, Mr. Johnson's small Dictionary, sev-eral more books; a picture in oil colours, a mezzotinto of Mrs. Brooks (by some strange chance in Skye),[1] and a head of Prince Charles in Paris plaster. Also a print of Ranald[2] Mac-donald of Clanranald, with a Latin inscription about the Cul-loden cruelties.

It was a very wet, stormy day. So we were obliged to remain here, as it was impossible to cross the sea to Raasay. Mr. John-son called me to his bed-side this morning, and to my astonish-ment he *took off* Lady Macdonald leaning forward with a hand on each cheek and her mouth open—quite insipidity on a mon-ument grinning at sense and spirit. To see a beauty repre-sented by Mr. Johnson was excessively high. I told him it was a masterpiece and that he must have studied it much. "Ay," said he.

I put off a part of the forenoon in bringing up this Journal. The rest was a little dreary from the dulness of the weather and the uncertain state in which we were in, as we could not

---

[1] In editing the MS, Boswell described Mrs. Brooks as "the actress"; he also designated her "my fair friend." He later repented of the personal reference, and struck it out in the proofs. Mrs. Brooks was the wife of John Brooks the engraver. Mrs. Mackinnon later told Boswell (*post*, p. 228) that Coirechatachan bought the mezzotint at the sale of one of the emigrants.

[2] Boswell left a blank for this name, but neglected to fill it.

tell but it might clear up every hour. Nothing is more uneasy to the mind than a state of suspense, especially when it depends on the weather, as to which there can be so little calculation. As Mr. Johnson said of our weariness on the Monday at Aberdeen, "Sensation is sensation." Coirechatachan, which was last night a hospitable house, was in my mind changed today into a prison.[3] A Mr. Macdonald of Breakish came at dinner. We had a good plentiful one: roast mutton, a chicken-pie, and I forget how many good dishes. After it we had several Erse songs, and a bowl of stout punch. I was plagued somewhat with the toothache. I had a slight return of that spleen or hypochondria or whatever it should be called, which formerly made me so miserable, and which operates not only as to the present, but throws a gloom upon everything, whether past or future. The blackness of the imagination blackens every object that it takes in. How much reason have I to thank GOD that I have now hardly any remains of so direful a malady! The cheerfulness and constant good sense of my valuable spouse have had the happiest influence upon my mind.

After dinner I read some of Macpherson's *Dissertations on the Ancient Caledonians*, etc. I was disgusted at the unsatisfactory conjectures as to antiquity before the days of record. I was happy when tea came. Such, I take it, is the state of those who live in the country. Meals are wished for from the cravings of vacuity of mind as well as from the desire of eating. I was hurt to find even such a temporary feebleness, and that I was so far from being that robust wise man who is sufficient for his own happiness. I felt a kind of lethargy of indolence. I did not exert myself to get Mr. Johnson to talk, that I might not have the labour of writing down his conversation. Macpherson, the minister of Sleat, was a very poor companion. He teased us with pitiful scraps which he had picked up, such as, "Gay was a good poet. He made a great deal by the *Beggar's Opera*," etc. But what was worse, he told Mr. Johnson that there was an Erse

---

[3] The remainder of this paragraph was omitted from the published *Tour*.

Bible; that he had compared the new Erse Testament by Mr. Stuart with the former one; that there were many Erse manuscripts—all of which circumstances we afterwards found not to be true. Mr. Johnson inquired here if there were any remains of the second sight. Macpherson said he was *resolved* not to believe it, because it was founded on no principle. "Then," said Mr. Johnson, "there are many things which we are sure are true that you will not believe. What principle is there why the loadstone attracts iron? Why an egg produces a chicken by heat? Why a tree grows upwards, when the natural tendency of all things is downwards? Sir, it depends upon the degree of evidence that you have." Young Mr. Mackinnon told us of one Mackenzie who is still alive whom he had often seen faint, and when he recovered he told he had seen things. He told Mr. Mackinnon that on such a place he would meet a funeral, and that such and such people would be the bearers, naming four; and three weeks after he saw just what Mackenzie had told him. The naming the very spot in a country where a funeral comes a long way, and the very people as bearers when there are so many out of whom a choice may be made, seems curious. We would have sent for Mackenzie had we not been informed that he could speak no English. Besides, the young man seemed confused in his narration.

Mrs. Mackinnon, who was a daughter of old Kingsburgh, told us that her father was one day riding in Skye, and some women who were at work in a field on the side of the road told him they heard two *taisks*,[4] that is, two voices of persons about to die; "and what," said they, "is extraordinary, one of them is an *English taisk*, which we never heard before." When he returned, he at that very place met two funerals, and one of them was of a woman who had come from the mainland and could speak only English. This, she told us, made a great impression upon her father.

Between tea and supper, Coirechatachan and I and some

---

[4] Gaelic *taibhs*, *taibhse*: "ghost, vision, ghostly voice."

more of the gentlemen assembled round a good peat fire, and drank two or three bottles of porter. We had another excellent supper, and many lively Erse songs after it.

How all the people here were lodged, I know not. By putting a number of men in one room and another of women in another, thus separating men from their wives, a good deal was done.[5] Tonight Breakish was laid with Canna. What became of Dr. Macdonald, whose place was thus filled up, is more than I could guess. I observed the Highlanders were laid beside each other, and in sheets very dirty, without the least scruple. Joseph had a good bed with clean sheets made for him in the parlour. There were here two very good servants at table, a young lad bare-legged and a girl bare-headed but very decently dressed. She attended a company with uncommon alertness. I observed tonight a remarkable instance of the simplicity of manners or want of delicacy among the people in Skye. After I was in bed, the minister came up to go to his. The maid stood by and took his clothes and laid them carefully on a chair piece by piece, not excepting his breeches, before throwing off which he made water, while she was just at his back.

WEDNESDAY 8 SEPTEMBER. When I awaked, the rain was much heavier than yesterday, but the wind had abated. By breakfast, the day was better, and in a little it was calm and clear. The joy which I felt was very fine. The propriety of the expression, "the sunshine of the breast," was evident, for the brilliant rays penetrated into my very soul. We were all in better humour than before. Mrs. Mackinnon with unaffected hospitality and politeness expressed her happiness in having such company in her house, and really was capable of admiring Mr. Johnson; which indeed I must say all of them did according to their capacities. When I knew she was old Kingsburgh's daughter, I did not wonder at the good appearance which she made.

She had been much in Abercairney's family. She was at Kingsburgh the night that Prince Charles was there. She told me that

---

[5] In the published *Tour* the entry for Sept. 7 ended at this point.

next morning the Prince was sound asleep in a room upstairs. She went into her father's room, which was below, and waked him and suggested to him her apprehensions of a party's coming up. Her father said, "Let the poor man repose himself after his fatigues; and as for me, I care not though they take off this old grey head" (pulling off his night cap and showing it) "ten or eleven years sooner." He then pulled the clothes over his head and again fell fast asleep:

> Sweet are the slumbers of the virtuous man.

This worthy old gentleman lived to see the family of Macdonald, of which he had taken the most faithful charge in Sir James's minority, become what it now is in the person of this wretch Sir Alexander, who neglected Kingsburgh and has quarrelled with his son.

·I observed to Mr. Johnson that if Sir Alexander was a fierce barbarian, there might be something grand in observing his ravages; but that so much mischief should be produced by such an insect, really vexed one. At Coirechatachan the universal voice was against him. It was one of the farms upon the estate of Mackinnon, from whom it was purchased by the family of Macdonald by a strange sale which is well known. There are five years of the lease to run. By and by Sir Alexander will be harassing the people there too. But Mrs. Mackinnon talked as if their family would go to America rather than be oppressed by him. She said, "How agreeable would it be if these gentlemen should come in upon us when we're in America."[1] It was said Sir Alexander is very frightened at sea. Said Mr. Johnson, "*He's* frightened at sea; and his tenants are frightened when he comes to land." Coirechatachan pays but about £50 of rent. But by droving and selling meal, in the former part of his life, he has made as much money as that the interest of it will pay his rent.

---

[1] The Mackinnons never emigrated. When Carruthers published his edition of the *Tour*, in 1852, Coirechatachan was in the possession of a great-grandson of Johnson's entertainer. In 1889, however, Dr. Hill found the house a ruin, the yard in use as a sheepfold.

We resolved to set out directly after breakfast. We had about two miles to ride to the seaside, and there we expected to get one of the boats belonging to the fleet of bounty herring-ships[2] then on the coast, or at least a good country fishing-boat. But while we were preparing to set out, there arrived a man with the following card from the Reverend Mr. Donald Macqueen, to whom I had written to meet us at Raasay:

Mr. Macqueen's compliments to Mr. Boswell, and begs leave to acquaint him, that fearing the want of a proper boat, as much as the rain of yesterday, might have caused a stop, he is now at Sgianadan with Macgillicallum's[3] carriage, to convey him and Dr. Johnson to Raasay, where they will meet with most hearty welcome and where MacLeod, being on a visit, now attends their motions.

Wednesday forenoon.

This card was most agreeable. It was a prologue to that hospitable and truly polite reception which we were to have at Raasay. It added much to my good spirits. I was elated perhaps too youthfully. "This is right," said I. "We're now like ourselves." In a little arrived Mr. Donald Macqueen himself; a decent minister, an elderly man with his own black hair, courteous and rather slow of speech, but candid, sensible, and well-informed, nay, learned. Along with him came, as our pilot, a gentleman whom I had a great desire to see—Malcolm MacLeod, one of the Raasay family, celebrated in the year 1745 for his conducting the Prince with fidelity from Raasay to the Laird of Mackinnon's. He was now sixty-two years of age, quite the Highland gentleman; of a stout well-made person, well-proportioned; a manly countenance browned with the weather, but a ruddiness in his cheeks, a good way up which his rough beard extended; a quick lively eye, not fierce in his look, but firm and good-humoured. He had a pair of brogues, tartan hose which came up only near to his knees and left them bare, a purple kilt, a black waistcoat, a short cloth green coat with

---

[2] To encourage fisheries, an Act had been passed in 1750 placing a bounty of thirty shillings the ton on white herrings.

[3] "The Highland expression for Laird of Raasay."—BOSWELL. (Gaelic *Mac-Ghille-Chaluim*, "the son of the servant of Columba.")

gold cord, a large blue bonnet with a gold-thread button. I never saw a figure that was more perfectly a representative of a Highland gentleman. I wished much to have a picture of him just as he was. I found him frank and *polite*, in the true sense of the word.

The good family at Coirechatachan said they hoped to see us in our return. We rode down to the shore. But Malcolm walked with graceful vigour. We were accompanied on foot by young Mr. Mackinnon and Breakish.

We got into Raasay's *carriage*, which was a good stout open boat made in Norway. The wind had now risen pretty much. But we had four stout rowers, particularly a MacLeod, a fellow half naked, with a bare black head, robust and spirited, something half wild Indian, half English tar. Mr. Johnson sat high on the stern like a magnificent Triton.[4] Malcolm raised an Erse song, *Hatyin foam foam eri*,[5] to which he gave Jacobite words of his own. The tune was "*O'er the moor among the heather*," Highlandized. The boatmen and Mr. Macqueen chorused, and all went well. At length Malcolm himself took an oar and rowed like a hero. We sailed along the coast of Scalpay, an island belonging to Sir Alexander Macdonald, being part of the purchase from Mackinnon. It is four miles long and —— broad. Mr. Johnson was for him and me buying it and having a good school and an Episcopal church (Malcolm said he would come to it) and a printing-press where we should print all the Erse that could be found.

Here again I was strongly struck with the long-projected scheme of Mr. Johnson's and my visiting the Hebrides being realized. I called to him, "We are contending with seas," which I think were the words of one of his letters to me. "Not much," said he; and though the wind made the sea lash considerably upon us, he was not discomposed. After we were out of the shade

---

[4] A cancelled note in the MS after this sentence reads, "There is a blank in my Journal which I have thus filled up"—referring to the words "stern" and "Triton." The note was probably addressed to Malone.

[5] See *post*, p. 260.

of Scalpay, and in the sound between it and Raasay, which was for about a league, the wind made the sea really rough. I did not like it. Mr. Johnson said, "This now is the Atlantic. If I should tell at a tea-table in London that I have crossed the Atlantic in an open boat, how they'd shudder and what a fool they'd think me to expose myself to such danger." He repeated the ode, *Otium divos rogat*.[6]

In the confusion or hurry of this rough sail, Mr. Johnson's spurs, which Joseph had in his hand or on his knee, were carried overboard into the sea, and lost. This was the first misfortune that has befallen us. Mr. Johnson was a little angry at first, observing that there was something wild in a pair of spurs being carried into the sea out of a boat; but then he said that, as Jeans had said upon losing his pocket-book, "It was rather an inconvenience than a loss." He said he now recollected that the night before he dreamt that he put his staff into a river and chanced to let it go, and it was carried down the stream and he lost it. "So now you see," said he, "that I have lost my spurs; and this story is better than many of those which we have as to second sight and dreams." Mr. Macqueen said he did not believe the second sight; that he never met any well-attested instances; and if he did, he would impute them to chance, because all who pretend to that quality often fail in their predictions, though they take a wide range, and sometimes interpret literally, sometimes figuratively so as to suit the events. He told us that since he came to be minister of the parish where he now is, the belief of witchcraft or charms was very common, in so much that he had many prosecutions before his *session*[7] against women, for having by these means carried off the milk from people's cows. He disregarded them; and there is not now the least vestige of that superstition. He preached against it; and in order to give a strong proof to the people that there was nothing in it, he said from the pulpit that every woman in

---

[6] Horace, *Odes*, II.xvi.1. "Caught in the open Aegean, he implores the gods for rest."
[7] The parochial ecclesiastical court, as Boswell explains in the published text.

the parish was welcome to take the milk from his cows provided she did not touch them.[8]

Mr. Johnson asked him as to *Fingal*. He said he could repeat some passages in the original. That he heard his grandfather had a copy of the poem; but that he did not believe that Ossian composed that poem as it is now published. This came pretty much to what Mr. Johnson has always held, though he goes farther and maintains that it is no better than such an epic poem as he could make from the song of Robin Hood; that is to say, that, except a few passages, there is nothing truly ancient but the names and some vague traditions. Mr. Macqueen alleged that Homer was made up of detached fragments. Mr. Johnson denied it; said that it had been one work originally, and that you could not put a book of the *Iliad* out of its place; and he believed the same might be said of the *Odyssey*.[9]

Mr. Malcolm told us that he went with the Prince from Raasay in a boat, landed near Portree, and from thence they walked all night over the mountains till they came into Strath, and the Laird of Mackinnon received him. He said the Prince went as his servant, carrying a little bundle and a bottle with a little brandy in it. When the brandy was drank out, he was for throwing away the bottle. "No," said Malcolm, "since it has served your highness, I hope to drink a cask out of it yet," and kept it. He has it still, as also a silver stock-buckle which he got from the Prince. He said the Prince walked better than he did, and said he was not afraid of any party of soldiers if he was once at the distance of a musket-shot from them; but that he feared the Highlanders who were against him, as they could pursue so much better. He did not seem to be at all cast down.

I shall here put down all the particulars concerning the un-

---

[8] "Such spells are still believed in. A lady of property in Mull, a friend of mine, had a few years since much difficulty in rescuing from the superstitious fury of the people, an old woman, who used a *charm* to injure her neighbour's cattle. It is now in my possession, and consists of feathers, parings of nails, hair, and such like trash, wrapt in a lump of clay."—SIR WALTER SCOTT.

[9] Both these titles were filled in later, evidently because Boswell was not at first sure which was which.

fortunate Prince which I picked up at Raasay. He was two nights in a hut in that island. The present Raasay, Dr. Mac-Leod his brother, and Malcolm were with him. There came a man near to the hut whom they did not know. They were apprehensive he might be a spy; and the Raasay gentlemen were for shooting him directly. "No," said the Prince, "God forbid. Let us not take away a man's life who may be innocent." John Mackenzie, a common Highlander who was attending them, said in Erse, "Well, well, no matter. He must be shot. You are the King. But we are the Parliament." The Prince asked what the man said; and being told it in English, he, notwithstanding the peril which he was in, laughed loud and heartily. Luckily the unknown person did not perceive that there were people in the hut; at least did not approach it, but walked on past it, unknowing of his risk. Had he come to them, they were resolved to dispatch him, for as Malcolm said to me, "We could not keep him with us, and we durst not let him go. In such a situation I would have shot my brother if I had not been sure of him."

John Mackenzie is alive. I saw him.[10] About eighteen years ago he hurt one of his legs when dancing, and was obliged to have it cut off. So he was going about with a wooden leg. The story of his being a *member of Parliament* is always kept up. I took him out a little way from the house, gave him a shilling to drink Raasay's health, and talked to him of the story. With less foundation, some writers have traced the idea of Parliament and of the British Constitution in rude and early times. I was curious to know if John Mackenzie had really heard or understood anything of that subject, which, had he been a greater man, would have been strenuously maintained. "Why, John," said I, "did you think the King should be controlled by a Parliament?" He answered," I thought, sir, there were many voices against one."

The Prince asked Dr. MacLeod what kind of man Malcolm

---

[10] "This old Scottish *member of Parliament*, I am informed, is still living (1785)."—BOSWELL.

was, and Malcolm what kind of man the Doctor was, that he might know whom to trust. He told Malcolm, "Sir, I put myself into your hands. Only bring me to the Laird of Mackinnon." Malcolm proposed taking him by sea. He more wisely chose to go by land, after being in Skye. So Raasay, the Doctor, and Malcolm attended him in a boat which ferried him over. He told only Malcolm where he was to go, justly considering that it was safest to have the secret entrusted to as few as possible. He gave the Doctor a spoon and knife and fork in a shagreen case, and bid him keep them till they met again, and bid him be at Portree in a few days with some brandy and other things. Malcolm delivered him to Mackinnon, who went over with him to Morar, and delivered him to the present Morar, then a lad of seventeen. Malcolm told me that in the hut the Prince would start from broken slumbers and speak to himself in different languages: French, Italian, and English (though indeed it must be considered that my worthy friend Malcolm did not probably know the difference between French and Italian), and one of his expressions in English was, "O God! poor Scotland!" Malcolm said they had always a man keeping watch while they were in the hut, and that while they were crossing from Raasay to Skye it was somewhat rough, and the Prince asked if there was any danger; and upon being told there was none, he immediately sung an Erse song. He had learnt a good deal of Erse.

It was a most pleasing approach to Raasay. We saw before us a beautiful bay, well defended with a rocky coast; a good gentleman's house, a fine verdure about it, a considerable number of trees, and beyond it hills and mountains in gradation of wildness. Our boatmen sung with great spirit. Mr. Johnson observed that naval music was very ancient. As we came to shore, the music of rowers was succeeded[11] by that of reapers, who were busy at work, and who seemed to shout as much as to

---

[11] Here follows a page in the MS which is blank except for this note: "This page I missed inadvertently; not with any nonsensical purpose, as Tristram Shandy did."

sing, while they worked with a bounding vigour.[12] Just as we
landed, I observed a cross, or rather the ruins of one, upon
a rock, which had to me a pleasing vestige of religion. I perceived a large company coming out from the house. We met
them as we walked up. There were Raasay; his brother Dr.
MacLeod; his nephew the Laird of Mackinnon; the Laird of
MacLeod; Colonel MacLeod of Talisker, a genteel man and a
faithful branch of the family, an officer in the Dutch service;
Mr. MacLeod of Muiravonside, best known by the name of
Sandie MacLeod, who was aide-de-camp to the Prince in 1745,
and remained eighteen years in exile on that account; Mr. Macqueen, a young divine, son to the Reverend Mr. Donald Macqueen; Mr. James MacLeod, a boy about—years of age, the
future Laird of Raasay; and Mr. Macqueen, a genteel young
man, his tutor.[13] We were welcomed upon the green, and conducted into the house, where we were introduced to Lady Raasay, to Miss Flora Raasay (as she is called in this part of the
world for distinction), the eldest daughter or Princess, and to
nine other young ladies, viz., Janet, Katherine, Margaret, Isa-
bella, Jane, Julia, Anne, Mary, and Christian.[14] Raasay has
also three sons, James, Malcolm, and John, all boys. He himself is a sensible, polite, and most hospitable gentleman. I was
told that his island of Raasay, and that of Rona (from which
the eldest son of the family has his title), and a considerable extent of land which he has in Skye, do not altogether yield him
above £250 or at most £300 of rent; and yet he lives in the
greatest plenty; and so far is he from distressing his people, that,
in the present rage for emigration, not a man has left his estate.

   We found here coffee and tea in genteel order upon the table, as it was past six when we arrived: diet loaf, marmalade
of oranges, currant jelly; some elegantly bound books on a

---

[12] "They accompany in the Highlands every action, which can be done in equal time,
with an appropriate strain, which has, they say, not much meaning; but its effects are
regularity and cheerfulness" (Johnson's *Journey to the Western Islands*, Chapman ed., 56).
[13] The MS is defective here; "genteel" is conjectural.
[14] Boswell neglected to fill the blank which he left for these names; they have been supplied from Burke's *Landed Gentry*.

large table, in short, all the marks of improved life. We had a
dram of excellent brandy, according to the Highland custom,
filled round. They call it a *scalck*.[15] On a sideboard was served
up directly, for us who had come off the sea, mutton-chops
and tarts, with porter, claret, mountain, and punch.[16] Then
we took coffee and tea. In a little, a fiddler appeared, and a
little ball began. Raasay himself danced with as much vigour
and spirit as any man. Sandie MacLeod, who has at times an
excessive flow of spirits, was, in his days of absconding, known
by the name of McCruslick, which it seems was the designation of a kind of wild man in the Highlands, and so he was
called here. He made much jovial noise, but was too violent
for my nerves, though they are now pretty well stiffened. Mr.
Johnson[17] was so delighted with this scene that he said, "I
know not how we shall get away." It entertained me to observe him sitting by while we danced, sometimes in deep meditation, sometimes smiling complacently, sometimes looking upon
Hooke's *Roman History*, and sometimes talking a little, amidst
the noise of the ball, to Mr. Donald Macqueen, who anxiously
gathered knowledge from him. He was pleased with Macqueen, and said to me, "This is a critical man, sir. There must
be great vigour of mind to make him cultivate learning so
much in the Isle of Skye, where he might do without it. It is
wonderful how many of the new publications he has. There
must be a snatch of every opportunity." Mr. Macqueen told
me that his brother (who is the fourth generation of the family
following each other as ministers of the parish of Snizort) and
he joined together and bought from time to time such books as
had reputation. Soon after we came in, a black cock and grey
hen, which had been shot, were shown, with their feathers on,

---

[15] Gaelic *sgailc*.
[16] The printed *Tour* reads, "a substantial dinner, and a variety of wines." In the remainder of the Journal the reader may assume a similar suppression of detailed bills of fare.
[17] A leaf (pp. 201–2) of the MS is missing here; the text from this point down to that indicated by the next footnote has been supplied from the first edition. If the missing leaf
was written on both sides, it contained considerably more than the corresponding passage in the printed *Tour*.

to Dr. Johnson, who had never seen that species of bird before. We had a company of thirty at supper, and all was good humour and gaiety.[18] Many songs were sung, one in particular to encourage the emigrants, which had a chorus ending always with *Tullishole*.[19] The glass circulated briskly, but nobody was asked to drink more than he cared to, and there was no intemperance.

I had a very good room to myself. The house has eleven fine rooms. It was built by this Raasay. His father was out in 1745, but had previously conveyed the estate to him, so there was no forfeiture; but as the Prince was known to have had an asylum in Raasay, those employed under the Government burnt every house upon the island. The family house was then just new. The tower of three storeys, which Martin mentions, stood till within a little of those latter commotions, when it was taken down and the stones of it employed in building the present house, which was consumed with the fire, all but the walls, so that 'tis partly the work of the late Raasay, partly of this. Some of the rooms have a number of beds, and so they are able to have so extensive a hospitality. We were in a new state of existence tonight.

THURSDAY 9 SEPTEMBER. After a most comfortable sleep, I had goat's whey brought to my bedside. Then rose and partook of an excellent breakfast: as good chocolate as I ever tasted, tea, bread and butter, marmalade and jelly. There was no loaf-bread, but very good *scones*, or cakes of flour baked with butter. There was a plate of butter and curd mixed which they call ———;[1] cakes of what is called *graddaned* meal, that is, meal burnt with straw in place of being threshed and kiln-dried. This seems to be bad management, as so much fodder is con-

---

[18] So far from the printed text. The next four words have been supplied by the editors, to make a transition to the MS.
[19] Professor Macdonald suggests *tuillidh seòl*, "more sail," "more way, guidance," etc. "Can it be that the phrase meant 'further leading, guidance' as an exhortation to the singer or leader of the company, or, more simply, 'more': i.e., 'let us have more singing'?"
[1] The Gaelic word which Boswell could not recall was probably *gruitheam*.

sumed by it. Mr. Macqueen, however, defends it by saying that
it is doing the thing much quicker, as one operation serves for
what is otherwise done by two. His chief reason, however, was
that the servants in Skye are, according to him, a worthless,
faithless pack, and steal what they can; so that much is saved
by the corn passing but once through their hands, as at each
time they pilfer some. It appears to me that the graddaning is
a strong example of the laziness of the Highlanders, who will
rather let fire do for them, at the expense of fodder, than labour
themselves. There were also barley-bannocks of this year's meal,
and—what I cannot help disliking to have at breakfast—cheese.
It is the custom over all the Highlands to have it; and it often
smells very strong, and poisons to a certain degree the elegance
of an Indian[2] breakfast. The day was showery. However, Raasay and I took a walk and had a very solid, easy, feudal chat. I
conceived a more than ordinary regard for this worthy gentleman. He has had this island above four hundred years. It is
the remains of the estate of MacLeod of Lewis whom he represents; and there is a question with some whether MacLeod of
Harris or his family is the elder branch. However, he does not
contest the chieftainship with the Laird of MacLeod.[3] When we
returned, Mr. Johnson came out with us to see the old chapel.
But before quitting the island in my Journal (as I am now far
behind with it, for I am now writing on the 15 September), I
shall put down all my observations upon it at once. Mr. Johnson was in fine spirits. He said, "This is truly the patriarchal
life. This is what we came to find." Minute things mark civilized life. We had here variety of preserves, and two parrots in
cages were set out before the door to bask in the sun.

We had a plentiful and genteel dinner, after which McCruslick and I went out with guns to try if we could find any black
cock; but we had no sport, and there came a heavy rain, by

---

[2] i.e., luxurious, "Asiatic."
[3] Boswell deleted this reference to the rival claims of Raasay and the Laird of MacLeod.
Johnson had published a similar statement, and Raasay had objected. See the correspondence printed *post*, p. 398.

which we were a good deal wet. Malcolm had the best way of sheltering himself—under a dike with ferns upon it—that could be. We saw what is called a Danish fort.[4] Our evening was passed as last night was. The Laird of Mackinnon was a young man of small size, delicate constitution, feebleness of voice and nearness of sight, but I was told had great knowledge, and hurt himself by too much study, particularly of infidel metaphysicians. I had a small specimen of his improvement in that way when I spoke of the second sight. He immediately retailed some of the flimsy arguments of Voltaire and Hume against miracles in general. It was strangely offensive to hear infidelity from a Highland chief. It was like finding him toupé'd and essenced like a French fop. I was sorry for the young gentleman, who I heard was a worthy lad. I told Mr. Johnson he had studied himself into infidelity. "Then," said he, "he must study himself out of it again. That is the way. Drinking largely would sober him again."

Mr. Johnson showed me today two odes which he had written in Skye. One of them was to Mrs. Thrale. It was very pretty. I asked it from him. He said, "I'd as soon give you my ears." But he said I might get it from her if she pleased. He said he would not swear against giving me the other.[5] So I hope it shall enrich my Journal. I said I was entitled to have a diamond here and there in it. I would give him one[6] if I could.

I was in some doubt today whether to set out next day, in order that I might let Sir Alexander's horses get home to him the sooner, in which case I thought to return to Raasay in our way from Dunvegan to Sleat, whence we could have Sir Alexander's boat to Mull, and on return I might see the island fully. But I considered that we might perhaps get a boat from

---

[4] A *broch*, now known to have been constructed some centuries before the Scandinavian invasions. See Boswell's fuller description, *post*, p. 142.

[5] He let Boswell copy it on 20 September at Dunvegan. Both odes appear in the published text.

[6] This word was inadvertently omitted by Boswell, and has been supplied by the editors.

MacLeod's country, and it was better to make sure of seeing Raasay; so I resolved to have a great expedition tomorrow, and my friend Malcolm promised to call me before six.

FRIDAY 10 SEPTEMBER. Malcolm was at my bed-side between five and six.[1] I sprung up, and he and I and Donald Canna and Mr. Macqueen, the minister's son, and Joseph set out. We took a dram and a bit of bread directly. But Lady Raasay and some of her daughters were up, and a boy of the name of Stewart was sent with us as our carrier of provisions. We walked briskly along; but the country was very stony at first, and a great many risings and fallings lay in our way. We had a shot at a flock of plovers sitting. But mine was harmless. We came first to a pretty large lake, sunk down comparatively with the ground about it. Then to another; and then we mounted up to the top of Duncaan, where we sat down, eat cold mutton and bread and cheese and drank brandy and punch. Then we had a Highland song from Malcolm; then we danced a reel to which he and Donald Macqueen sang.[2] We then walked on over a much better country, very good pasture; saw many moor-fowl, but could never get near them; descended a hill on the ———[3] side of the island and went into a farm-house, a Maclean's. It was somewhat circular in its shape. At one end sheep and goats were lodged; at the other, the family. The man and his wife had a little bedstead. The place where the servants lay was marked out upon the ground with whinstones and strewed with fern. The fire was towards the upper end of the house. The smoke went out at a hole in the roof, at some distance and not directly above it, as rain would hurt it. I found here sacks made of rushes very well plaited, so as to be strong and very

---

[1] In the published *Tour*, Boswell condenses the account of his jaunt around Raasay into two sentences. The material was good, but it was not Johnsonian.
[2] The "reel" furnished Collings and Rowlandson with subject matter for a caricature. Boswell is waving his journal in his right fist; a portable ink-horn and pen dangle from his buttonhole.
[3] The hill must have been Beinn a Chapuill, on the east side of the island.

compact. They really looked well and made[4] very tolerable baskets. The art of *creeling* or working in wattles seems to be well practised among these islanders.

Let me here put down a local saying of mine against Sir Sawney. I said by driving away the gentlemen, the best people upon his estate, he would have no beams, no great timber—just a *creel clan*. He knew not well how to do about Mr. Johnson and me. He did not wish us to see how much better Raasay lived than he; so he began to object, and said he heard Lady Raasay was ill. "Oh, then," said Mr. Johnson, "we'll stay till we hear how she is." The animal answered, "Oh, no!" Mr. Johnson was struck with his desire to get rid of us.

I saw in this hut a little house-kiln for drying corn. It was about the size of a hogshead; was made of wattles, plastered with clay very firmly both on the outside and the inside. The convenience of it was that the man could dry a little at a time, as he could afford it, and instead of having one to attend in an outhouse, it could be watched by the family sitting by their fireside. The farmer here had no children, and he and his wife spoke only Erse. Adjoining to the house was another little circular room called a *keep-house*. The woman very hospitably went into it and brought us some very good milk. I went into the place. It was a kind of store-room for the few things that they had. She kept her milk in an earthen dish put within a wooden chest, which shut with a lid, so that it was very clean.

We had been met by Mr. Charles MacLeod, half-brother to Raasay, a strapping young fellow. Old Raasay had most absurdly married again after the year 1746. His widow, by whom he had several children; lives in a small comfortable house which was built for him just adjoining to the old castle of the family. She has a good farm gratis, and the interest of £400 by way of jointure. Mr. Charles took us to her house. She was a stout fresh-looking woman, very plainly dressed, and could not speak a word of English. She treated us with cream and barley-

---

[4] An inadvertent omission, supplied by the editors.

bread. It was not amiss to see the difference between her house-keeping and that of Raasay's. Folly on one side, and probably interested cunning on the other, had produced the second marriage. She was called only Mrs. MacLeod now. I know not if ever she was called *Lady*, as her husband had previously given the estate to this gentleman.

We saw the old castle,[5] then walked over to a large cave on the ———[6] coast, accompanied by Mr. Charles, who was to go to Raasay with us. From there we turned and made the best of our way back again, by somewhat a shorter road. I was much fatigued for a while, but recovered and did wonderfully. It was a fine fair day, with such a breeze as was refreshing. By the time we returned we had walked good four-and-twenty English miles. I got coffee and tea after I had dressed myself, and was most serene.

Malcolm had told us several anecdotes today of his expedition in 1745-6. He was kept prisoner in London for ———. He was carried up in Captain John Ferguson's[7] ship, where he said the prisoners were very ill maintained. But there were some soldiers on board, who lived well, and sometimes invited him to share. At London he had the good fortune to be confined in the house of one Dick, a messenger, instead of being imprisoned. To his astonishment there could but one evidence against him be found. He said he would willingly have signed his banishment. Yet he told me he would never be so ready for dying as he was then. His spirits were kept up by thinking warmly of the good cause. Lady Primrose, who took care of Miss Flora Macdonald, sent her to Scotland in a post-chaise, and bid her have any one of her friends to accompany her. She chose Malcolm. "So," said he, "I went to London to be hanged, and came down in a chaise with Miss Flora Macdonald." He said

---

[5] Brochel Castle, in the northeastern part of the island.
[6] Boswell's description, later in the text, shows that the blank should be filled by "north-western."
[7] Boswell neglected to fill in this name, which has been supplied by the editors. Ferguson was in command of H.M.S. *Furnace*.

when the Prince parted from him he insisted on his taking ten guineas out of his purse, though he was sure he had not above forty. But he said he would get enough on the mainland.

Malcolm and I became great friends. He offered to make me a present of the bottle, which was going a great length indeed. But I refused it, saying nobody should have it but himself. He had got a little pipe from the Prince, which he gave to a gentleman in England; and as he came down, he saw it at York in a silver case.

I exerted myself in an extraordinary degree in dancing to-night, drinking porter heartily at intervals, and thinking that I was fit to lead on Highlanders.

Let me gather here some gold dust, some gleanings of Mr. Johnson's conversation without regard to order of time. He said he thought very highly of Bentley; that no man now went so far in the kinds of learning that he cultivated; that the many attacks of him were owing to envy and to a desire of being known by being in competition with such a man; that it was safe to attack him because he never answered them, but let them die away. It was attacking a man who would not beat them, because his beating them would make them live the longer. And he was right not to answer, for in his hazardous method of writing he could not but be often enough wrong; so it was better to leave things to their general appearance than own himself to be wrong in particulars. He said Mallet was the prettiest-dressed poppet about town, and always kept good company.[8] That from his way of talking, he saw and always said that he had not written any of the Life of the Duke of Marlborough, though perhaps he intended to do it some time; in which case he was not culpable in taking the pension. That he imagined the Duchess was to furnish the materials

---

[8] Boswell never lost an opportunity to publish something unfavourable to David Mallet (who no doubt deserved what he got), from the time (1763) when he joined with George Dempster and Andrew Erskine in composing *Critical Strictures* upon Mallet's tragedy, *Elvira*. The authors of that abusive pamphlet were even so impolite as to call attention to the fact that Mallet had formerly been janitor in the Edinburgh High School. Note that Boswell's MS has *poppet*, not *puppet*, the reading of all the editions. *Puppet* is doubt-less to be regarded as a printer's error.

and Mallet to furnish the words and the order and all that in which the art of writing consists. That the Duchess was not a woman of superior parts, but a bold frontless woman who knew how to make the most of her opportunities in life. That Hooke got a great sum of money for writing her *Apology*; that he wondered how Hooke put in that saying that to tell another's secret to one's friend is no breach of confidence; though perhaps Hooke, who was a virtuous man, and whose *History* shows it, and did not wish her well though he wrote her *Apology*, might see its effect and yet put it in, since she desired it to be put in. He was acting only ministerially. I am afraid, though, that Hooke was bound to give his best advice. I speak as a lawyer. Though I have had clients that I did not wish well to, yet if I undertook their cause, I would not do anything to hurt it, even at their desire, without warning them first.

And now let me throw together what I can as to the Island of Raasay. It lies south and north, is about fifteen English miles long, and four broad. On the south quarter is the family seat, situated on a pleasing low spot. There is very good grass fields and corn lands about it, well-dressed. I observed, however, hardly any enclosing except a good garden well stocked with kitchen stuff, gooseberries, raspberries, currants, strawberries, apple-trees. There is a tolerable southern wall on which fruit-trees have been tried, but have been neglected. Mr. Johnson observed with how little people will do, though they may easily obtain what would be very convenient; for that the family had possessed this island 400 years and never made a landing place, when men with pickaxes might cut a stair out of the rock in a week's time.

On one of the rocks just where we landed, which are not high ones, there is rudely drawn a square with a crucifix in the middle, like this:[9] where it is said the Laird of Raasay in old

---

[9] Boswell made two attempts to draw this cross. The first sketch he blotted immediately, the second he scored out so heavily in the revision that its outlines are uncertain. For an excellent photograph from a cast, see *Proc. Soc. of Antiquaries of Scotland*, lxvii. 64.

times used to offer up his devotions. I could not but kneel upon the spot and gratefully remember the death of Christ, uttering a short prayer. This I did the morning that I left Raasay, while the family accompanied us to the shore; but nobody could imagine that I was doing anything more than attentively satisfying my curiosity.

A little off the shore westward is a kind of subterraneous house. There has been a natural fissure or separation of the rock, running towards the sea. That has been roofed over with long stones, and above them turf has been laid, till the ground gradually disappears, being lost in the beach. In that place the inhabitants used to keep their oars. About a quarter of a mile or more from the house is what is called a Danish fortification. It could not be a watch tower, for on the land side it is covered by rising ground, close to it, so could not communicate intelligence by signals. It has been a pretty high circular wall built double, so as that there was a spiral passage, like that of pipes in a hothouse, to the top, roofed[10] all along with *flag stones*, as they are called, or long pieces of freestone. In the space in the middle were the huts for the people, who were there safe, and could steal under cover to the top to explore. The middle of this was much filled up by stones having tumbled from the wall. So 'tis very imperfect. There are a tolerable number of trees near the house which grow well. Some of them are of a pretty good size. They are mostly the plane or sycamore-tree and ash. There were a few of the mountain ash or *rowan*-tree, loaded with berries and which had a rich appearance. These were between the back of the house and the garden. A little to the west of the house is an old chapel with now no roof upon it. It has never been very curious. I at first imagined it had originally two storeys, from there being holes in the wall as if joists had been there. But Mr. Johnson, who is very accurate, found that the holes were not directly opposite to each other in the two walls, and were only defects by the injury of

---

[10] Boswell wrote *roughed*, apparently an inadvertency.

time. In one of these holes we saw some human bones of an uncommon size. There was a heel-bone in particular which Dr. MacLeod said was such that if the foot was in proportion it must have been twenty-seven inches. Mr. Johnson would not look at the bones. He started back from them with a striking appearance of horror. Mr. Macqueen said it was formerly much the custom in these isles to have human bones lying above ground and in the windows of churches. This chapel appears to have been a good deal filled up with earth. On the floor of it are several gravestones, but without any legible inscriptions. A little to the east of it, I suppose about twelve feet, is a ruin of a burying-place of another tribe of the Mac-Leods (for there were several in the island), and in the space between the two were some recent graves. On the south of the chapel is the family burying-place. Above the door on the east end of it is a small bust or image of the Virgin Mary, carved upon a stone which makes part of the wall; and to the south of the family burying-place is a smaller one said to be for another tribe. All these ruins are unroofed and full of nettles and other weeds, and look like one cluster at small distance, thus:[11] and as they are now in a grove, they have somewhat of a venerable air; at least they affect the mind with pious awe to a certain degree. There is no church upon the island, which is in the parish of Portree[12] in Skye, and the minister comes and preaches there either in Raasay's house or some other house once in ———. I could not but value the family seat more for having even this ruin of a chapel so near it. There was something comfortable in the thought of being so near a piece of consecrated ground. Mr. Johnson said, "I look with reverence upon every place that has been set apart for religion," and he kept off his hat while he was within the walls of the chapel.

The eight crosses which Martin mentions as pyramids for deceased ladies have gone in a semi-circular line comprehend-

---

[11] Boswell's crude sketch is omitted.
[12] Boswell left a blank for the name of the parish, which he neglected to fill in later.

ing the chapel. They have been real crosses and have marked
out the boundaries of the sacred territory within which an
asylum was to be had. The one which we observed upon our
landing was the one which made the first point of the semi-
circle. There are ——— remaining, and they have ended at an
opposite point on the west. A good way farther north there is
a row of dry-stone buildings about four foot high and ———
yards around, twice what I could grasp and five hands. They
run along the top of a pretty high eminence and so down to
the shore on the west, in pretty much the same direction with
the crosses. Raasay took them to be the marks for the asylum.
But Malcolm thought them to be false sentinels, a common deception (of which instances occur in Martin) to make invaders
imagine the island better guarded; and Mr. Donald Macqueen,
justly in my opinion, makes the crosses which form the inner
circle to be the church's landmarks.

The south end of the island is much covered with large stones
or rocky strata. Raasay has enclosed and planted with firs one
point upon the eastern quarter of that end; and he showed me
part of a stone wall built and stones laid down for more, in
order to enclose a considerable space, which he is also to plant.

Duncaan is a mountain three computed miles from the house.
There is an ascent of the country by consecutive risings (if
that expression may be used when valleys intervene), so that
there is but a short rise at once; but it is certainly very high
from the sea. The palm of altitude is disputed for by the people of Raasay and those of Skye between Duncaan and the
mountains in Skye over against it. I take it the latter have it;
for Duncaan being not very thick, but rather like a mount
framed by the landscape, it looks to be higher than it really
is, whereas the mountains in Skye are vast lumps. We went
up the east side of Duncaan pretty easily. It is mostly rock all
around, the points of which hem the summit of it. Sailors, to
whom it is a good object as they pass along, call it Raasay's
Cap. It is more like the shape of a bonnet. Within the rocky edg-

ing at the summit there is plain green ground, though here and there a piece of rock is interspersed. Before we reached Duncaan we passed by two lakes. Of the first, Malcolm told me a strange fabulous tradition. He said there was a wild beast in it, a sea-horse which came and devoured a man's daughter. Upon which the man put on a great fire and had a sow roasted at it, the smell of which attracted the monster. The loch was in a hollow between two hills. The fire was placed on the side of the hill to the southeast, a little way down the declivity on that side away from the loch. In the fire was put a spit. The man lay concealed behind a little building of dry stones, and he had an avenue formed for the monster with two rows of large flat stones which reached from the fire over the summit of the hill, till it came on the side next to the loch. The monster came, and the man with the red-hot spit destroyed it. Malcolm showed me the little hiding-place and the rows of stones, which seemed to be artificial, though it was not certain. He did not laugh when he told this story. I recollect having seen in the *Scots Magazine* several years ago a poem upon a similar story, perhaps the same, translated from the Erse or Irish, called *Albin and the Daughter of Mey*.[13]

There is a large tract of land possessed as a common in Raasay. They have no regulations as to the number of cattle. Every man puts upon it as many as he chooses. From Duncaan northward, till you reach the other end of the island, there is a good deal of good natural pasture little hurt by stones. We passed over a spot which is appropriated for the exercising ground. In 1745, a hundred fighting men were reviewed here, as Malcolm told me, who was one of the officers that led them to the field. They returned home all but about fourteen. What a princely thing is it to be able to furnish such a band! Raasay has the true spirit of a chief. He is, without exaggeration, a

---

[13] "Albin and the Daughter of Mey: an old tale, translated from the Irish," by Jerome Stone, was published in the *Scots Magazine* for January 1756 (xviii.15–7). The story resembles Malcolm's only in that both involve a monster and a maiden.

father to his people, so far as I could learn. Not one of them has left him.

There is plenty of limestone in the island, and a great quarry of freestone. There are some pieces of natural woods, none of any age, as they cut the trees for common country uses. There are a number of lakes with trout in them. Malcolm catched one four-and-twenty pound weight in the loch next to Duncaan, which, by the by, is certainly a Danish name, as most names of places in these islands are.[14] Raasay put trout into that lake and into some of the others. On the western coast, not far from the old castle, there arose upon the sea a rock so like one of the ordinary huts in the island that everybody must mistake it for one.

The old castle is situated upon a rock very near the sea. The rock is not one mass of stone, but a concretion of pebbles and earth; but so firm that it does not appear to have mouldered. I perceived no pieces of it fallen off. The entry was by a steep stair from the quarter next the sea, of which stair only three or four steps are remaining, all at the top of it. Above them the castle projects, and there is an opening in the wall from which hot water or stones could be thrown upon an invader. Upon entering the gate or door, there was what I never saw before: a sentry box or alcove in the wall on your right hand. The man placed there could only watch in case of noise. He could see nothing. The next advance was to a court or *close* as it was called, in the centre of four towers, and open above just like any other court of an old castle in the square form. Only that this seemed extraordinary, as you came to it after ascending a stair and entering a gate; but as Mr. Johnson observed,[15] it was just an ordinary court, with the difference that the rock here was as the ground in others. The court here was very small. There was a fine well—just a spring in the rock—but it was now

---

[14] Duncaan appears to be Gaelic *dùn* (hill) plus Old Norse *kanna* (can): "the hill shaped like a can."

[15] This observation must have been made upon Boswell's description, for Johnson did not visit Brochel Castle.

filled up with rubbish. One could distinguish tolerably that there had been four towers, but time and storms had left little but ruinous fragments: pieces of wall, pieces of stairs, a part of the battlement to the sea.

There was one small room in one of the towers quite entire. It was a little confined triangular place, vaulted as in the ancient manner. In a corner of it was a square freestone in which was cut an exact circular opening such as is in every temple of Cloacina, and from it there appears a clear communication to the bottom, that is to say anything will be carried by the outside of the rock to the bottom. They call this room the *nursery*, and say the hole was for the children. But I take it to have been the necessary-house of the castle. It was much to find such a convenience in an old tower. I did not imagine that the invention had been introduced into Scotland till in very modern days, from our connexion with England. But it seems we have forgotten something of civilized life that our ancestors knew. It is strange how rare that convenience is amongst us. Mr. Johnson laughed heartily and said, "You take very good care of one end of a man, but not of the other." One should think it requires very little reflection to provide such a convenience. Raasay has none. I told him that it was a shame to see it at the old castle and not at his new house. He said it would be better. But I doubt many generations may pass before it is built.[16]

From the castle we crossed the island, or at least cut across a part of it, to a famous cave. In our way we saw a very pretty lake with two islands upon it covered with wood. Bushes, I may say. We saw the other end of Raasay, which turns in with a crook, and is as rocky or stony as the south end; and the little Isle of Fladda, belonging to Raasay, all fine green ground; and Rona, which is of so rocky a soil that it appears to be just a pavement. I was told, however, that it has a great deal of grass in the interstices. Raasay has it all in his own

---

[16] This paragraph was of course greatly condensed and modified in the published *Tour*.

hand. It keeps 160[17] cattle. His *bowman*[18] or cow-keeper resides upon it with his family. The cave which we went to see is in a striking situation. It is in a recess of a great cleft, a good way up from the sea. Before it the ocean roars, being dashed against monstrous broken rocks—grand and awful *propugnacula*.[19] On the right hand, going up to it from the sea, is a longitudinal cave, very low in the roof all[20] upon the side going in, but higher as you advance. The sea has washed it and scooped it out; I know not how it has been made more lofty as the sea went farther in. The roof of it is all covered with a kind of petrifications formed by drops which perpetually distil from it. They are like little trees. I broke off some of them. The great cave has its mouth almost built up with round pebbles. The entry is low. When you get in, it is of a good highth —no great breadth—ten paces long. It has been a place of much safety. I saw upon the floor some places for beds marked out with stones as in the cottage. I find a wretched deficiency in expressing visible objects. I must own, too, that the old castle and cave, like many other things of which one hears much, did not answer my expectations. People love to boast of the curiosities of their country, be it great or small.

This island has abundance of black cattle, sheep, and goats; a good many horses, which are used for ploughing, carrying out dung, etc. I believe the people never ride. There are indeed no roads through the island, except now and then a detached piece which use has made. Most of the houses are upon the shore, so that all the people have little boats and catch fish. There is a great plenty of potatoes here. There are blackcock in extraordinary abundance, moor-fowl, plovers, wild pigeons —just the bluish kind which we have in pigeon-houses—in the state of nature. Raasay has no pigeon-house. There are no hares nor rabbits in the island, nor there never was known to

---

[17] Boswell left a blank for this figure, which is supplied from Johnson's *Journey*.
[18] Tenant of a stock farm; see OED s.v. *bouman*.
[19] "Bulwarks."
[20] Reading somewhat doubtful.

be a fox till last year, that some malicious person landed one; which must have been the case, as a fox is a bad swimmer. He has done much mischief and they have not got him killed yet.[21] Mr. Johnson said they should set a trap for him. There is a great deal of fish caught in the sea around Raasay: rock cod, haddocks,[22]——— and in the lakes and rivers, or rather brooks, trout is taken. It is really a place where one may live in plenty, and even in luxury. There are no deer. But Raasay is to get some. Mr. Johnson said, "If one had a mind to retire for study for a summer, it would be a fine place."

I said if I had my wife and little daughter with me, I would stay here long enough. The thought of my being absent from them damped my happiness. I considered that my wife is uneasy when I am away—that it is not just, and surely not kind, to leave her for such a portion of life, when she sets such a value on my company and gives up everything else for me and my interest. And weak as it may be, I could not help having that kind of tender uneasiness which a lover has when absent from his mistress. Laugh at it who will, as not to be believed or as singular, I mark it as a fact, and rejoice at it, as it is the counterpart of more than ordinary conjugal felicity.[23]

Raasay has a barn worth remembering. The corners and a piece of wall at each door are built to the full highth of good stone and lime, to give it firmness, as a strong box is fortified in different places with brass or iron. The rest of it has a wall of the same kind about the highth of an ordinary dike, and above that is work of wattles covered on the outside with heath. It is so open that the wind gets in and the rain is kept out. And it is well thatched with heath. This is better than having slits in the walls, for the air comes more equally. In this barn he often dries his hay as well as his corn, which is a great advantage in so wet a climate, where if it stands long

---

[21] The fox had never been seen, and Johnson says in his *Journey* that he thought it imaginary.
[22] Boswell left a line blank for recording more names of fishes.
[23] This paragraph was omitted in the revision.

in the fields it may rot. They reckon nine months rain here, as it is just opposite to the western[24] coast of Skye, where the copious clouds are broken by high mountains. The hills here, and indeed all the heathy ground in general, abound with the sweet-smelling plant which the Highlanders call *gaul*,[25] and I think with dwarf juniper in many places. There is enough of turf, which is their fuel, and it is thought there is a mine of coal. I do not recollect anything more that I can put down about Raasay. I shall draw out a little account of it and get Raasay himself and his brother the doctor to revise it. They have promised to send me in writing all that they can tell of what happened in 1745.[26]

I liked to see a brother of the family a physician. He is a sensible civil man, and I am told has good skill. He was wounded at Culloden. He has had bad health of late years and has given over practice, except visiting from regard his particular friends. He has a family from Raasay upon his estate in Skye. He is married and has children. There was a son and daughter of his at Raasay. All relations are welcome there.

There has been long a league between the families of Macdonald and Raasay. Raasay has a writing concerning it, dated, as I was told, above 100 years ago, for I did not see it, as I did not hear of it till I had left the island. Whenever the head of either family dies, his sword is given to the head of the other. This Raasay has the late Sir James Macdonald's sword. But Sir Alexander, who is wrong in everything and has no generous attachment, is carrying on a lawsuit with Raasay to keep him from recovering £500 which Raasay advanced to Kingsburgh, Sir Alexander's own kinsman and tenant. Sir Alexander claims a preference as landlord. Everybody who knows the history of the families is hurt at this. I am one of Sir Alexan-

---

[24] *Sic* in the MS and all editions. Read *eastern*.
[25] Sweet gale or bog-myrtle.
[26] In the published text Boswell mentions the fact that Raasay did send him some material for his account of the '45. There is no indication, however, that the topographical notes were ever sent to Raasay for revision.

der's lawyers in the suit. But now when I have had occasion to see worthy Raasay, been so hospitably entertained by him, and have learnt the ancient alliance, I will have nothing more to do with it. The late Sir Alexander was truly friendly in 1745. "Don't be afraid, Raasay," said he. "I'll use all my interest to keep you safe; and if your estate should be taken, I'll buy it for the family." And he would have done it.

SATURDAY 11 SEPTEMBER. It was a storm of wind and rain; so we could not set out. I wrote some Journal and talked awhile with Mr. Johnson in his room, and passed the day, I cannot well say how, but very easily. Mr. Johnson was very fond of MacLeod, who is indeed a most promising youth, and with a noble spirit is to struggle with difficulties and keep his people. He has been left with £40,000 of debt and 1300 a year of annuities to pay. Mr. Johnson said, "Sir, if he gets the better of all this, he'll be a hero; and I hope he shall. He's a fine fellow, MacLeod. I have not met with a young man who had more desire to learn, or who has learnt more. I've seen nobody that I wish more to do a kindness to than MacLeod." I do not observe exact chronology in Mr. Johnson's sayings. There is no occasion.

There is neither Justice of Peace or constable in Raasay. Skye has but Ullinish, a Sheriff Depute, and no other Justice of Peace. The want of the execution of justice is much felt among the islanders. MacLeod very sensibly observed that taking away the heritable jurisdictions had not been of such service in the islands as was imagined. They had not authority enough in lieu of them. What could then have been settled at once must now either take much time and trouble or be neglected. Mr. Johnson said that a country was in a bad state which was governed only by laws; because a thousand things occur for which laws cannot provide and where authority ought to interpose. Now destroying the authority of the chiefs threw the people loose. It did not pretend to bring any positive good, but only to cure some evil; and he was not well enough acquainted with the country to know what degree of evil the jurisdictions occasioned. I maintained, hardly any, because the chiefs took care for their own sakes.

Mr. Johnson was now wishing to move. There was not enough of intellectual entertainment for him after he had satisfied his curiosity, which he did by asking questions till he had exhausted the island. And where there was such a numerous company, mostly young people, there was such a flow of familiar talk, so much noise and so much singing and dancing, that there was not much opportunity for his majestic conversation. He seemed sensible of this; for when I told him how happy they were at having him there, he said, "Yet we have not been able to entertain them much." I was apt to be fretted with irritability of nerves on account of McCruslick's loud rattling, romping, etc. I complained of it to Mr. Johnson and said we would be better if he was gone. "No, sir," said he. "He puts something into the company, and takes nothing out of it." Mr. Johnson, however, had several opportunities of instructing the company; and they were made sensible of his powers. I can recollect nothing to put down, as he run rather into general discourse upon mechanics, agriculture, and such subjects, than into science and wit. Last night Lady Raasay showed him the operation of *wawking* cloth, that is, thickening it as is done by a mill. Here it is performed by women who kneel upon the ground. The cloth is spread upon ———, and they rub it with both their hands, with ———, singing an Erse song all the time.[1] He was asking questions in the time of it, and amidst their loud and wild howl his voice was heard even in the room above.

---

[1] Boswell's incomplete description of this process can be supplemented from Pennant: "Twelve or fourteen women, divided into two equal numbers, sit down on each side of a long board, ribbed lengthways, placing the cloth on it: first they begin to work it backwards and forwards with their hands, singing at the same time, as at the quern: when they have tired their hands, every female uses her feet for the same purpose, and six or seven pair of naked feet are in the most violent agitation, working one against the other: as by this time they grow very earnest in their labours, the fury of the song rises; at length it arrives to such a pitch, that without breach of charity you would imagine a troop of female daemoniacs to have been assembled." (Thomas Pennant, *A Tour in Scotland and Voyage to the Hebrides*, 1772, ed. 1774, pp. 285–6.)

We had a ball again tonight. Miss Flora[2] is really an elegant woman (tall, genteel, a pretty face), sensible, polite, and good-humoured. I find it in vain to try to draw a portrait of a young lady. I cannot discriminate. She alone has been at Edinburgh. All the rest were never farther than Applecross, a gentleman's seat in Ross-shire on the opposite coast. Mr. Johnson said they were the best-bred children he ever saw; that he did not believe there was such another family between here[3] and London; that he had never seen a family where there was such airiness and gaiety. Not one of the family ever had the toothache. They dance every night all the year round. There seemed to be no jealousy, no discontent among them. I asked Miss Flora, "Why, you have no idea then of the unhappiness of life that we hear so much of?" "No," said she. "I have reason to be thankful." She had very good sense without any aiming at smartness more than was natural to her. The only fault Mr. Johnson could find with her was that her head was too high dressed. Can there then be no misery here? What says Mr. Johnson?—

> Yet hope not life from pain or danger free;
> Or think the doom of man revers'd for thee.

I must set him to inquire if evil has place in Raasay. They can never have the sufferings of savages by being in want of food, for they have plenty. And they have not the uneasiness which springs from refined life. They work in every way proper for young ladies. Miss —— plays on the guitar. What can disturb them? I can only say that I was disturbed by thinking how poor a chance they had to get husbands. I mused on this, in the very heat of dancing. It perhaps, though, does not occur either to them or to their father.[4]

SUNDAY 12 SEPTEMBER. It was a fine day, and although

---

[2] "She had been some time at Edinburgh, to which she again went, and was married to my worthy neighbour, Colonel Mure Campbell, now Earl of Loudoun; but she died soon afterwards, leaving one daughter."—BOSWELL. This daughter, who was born in 1780, succeeded her father in 1786 as Countess of Loudoun in her own right.

[3] Omitted inadvertently by Boswell, and supplied by the editors.

[4] Boswell need not have worried; all ten daughters made good marriages.

we do not approve of travelling on Sunday, we resolved to set
out, as we were in an island from whence we must take occasion as it serves. Besides, I had sent forward Sir Alexander's
horses to Portree against his inclination. He had most inhos-
pitably desired to have them sent back to him when we got to
the shore opposite to Raasay, and thus thought to make us shift
the best way we could after coming out of Raasay. He even
gave me a note in my almanac how to try for horses. But since
he had not proper reflection, I resolved to supply his place,[1]
upon hearing that we should hardly be able to find other
horses. Mr. Johnson said, "Don't let us part with *them* till we
get others." I said any sensible Justice of Peace would press
them for us. Mr. Donald Macqueen was clear for our keeping
them. It was accordingly done. But as he was to set out for
Edinburgh on the 15, it was necessary to send them back to
him early this week.[2] MacLeod and Talisker sailed in a boat
of Raasay's for Sconser, to take the shortest way to Dunvegan.
McCruslick went with them to Sconser, from whence he was
to go to Sleat, and so away to the mainland. We were resolved
to pay a visit at Kingsburgh and see the celebrated Miss Flora
Macdonald,[3] who is married to the present Kingsburgh; so
took the other road. All the family walked down to the shore
to see us depart. I confess I felt some pain in leaving Raasay.
But I thought I would come with my wife and daughter to
pass an autumn there. Raasay himself went with us in a large

---

[1] i.e., to do his reflecting for him.

[2] Boswell's keeping his horses was one of Lord Macdonald's chief grievances against him,
as we find in Macdonald's letter of 26 November 1785: ". . . Every consideration must
yield to the accommodation of Dr. Johnson (and yourself, of course); therefore, declin-
ing to accept the country horses, you set off with mine for Kingsburgh, about fifty miles,
where (and at other places) you detained them several days, notwithstanding you might
have been supplied at every gentleman's house upon the road; till moved, I presume, by
retrospective compunction, you returned the jaded animals, lame to the ground (without any apology), and consequently for a long time unfit for the journey which they were
originally intended to perform" (*Boswell Papers*, xvi.236).

[3] In his letter to Boswell of 26 November 1785, Lord Macdonald wrote: "At your own
behaviour every one felt some degree of resentment when you told me your only errand
into Skye was to visit the Pretender's conductress, and that you deemed every moment
as lost which was not spent in her company" (*Boswell Papers*, xvi.234).

boat with eight oars, built in his island. So did worthy Malcolm. So did Mr. Donald Macqueen, Dr. MacLeod, two of Raasay's sons, and their tutor.

Raasay said the party under the Government in 1745 destroyed a number of the very cows and horses in Raasay. A list was taken of them. But the Act of Parliament for indemnity as to those outrages prevented redress. We had a most pleasant sail between Raasay and Skye; passed by a cave where Martin says fowls were catched by lighting fire in the mouth of it. Malcolm remembers this. But 'tis not now practised, as few fowls come into it.

We spoke of death. Mr. Johnson gave us a short discourse worth any sermon, saying that the reflections of some men as to dying easily were idle talk, were partial views. I mentioned Hawthornden's *Cypress Grove*, where it is said that the world is just a show; and how unreasonable is it for a man to wish to continue in the show-room after he has seen it. Let him go cheerfully out and give place to other spectators. "Yes," said Mr. Johnson. "If he's sure he's to be well after he goes out of it. But if he is to grow blind after he goes out of the show-room, and never to see anything again; or if he does not know whither he is to go next, a man will not go cheerfully out of a show-room. No wise man will be contented to die if he thinks he is to go into a state of punishment. Nay, no wise man will be contented to die if he thinks he is to fall into annihilation. For however bad any man's existence may be, every man would rather have it than not exist at all. No, there is no rational principle by which a man can be contented, but a trust in the mercy of GOD, through the merits of Jesus Christ." All this delivered with manly eloquence in a boat on the sea, upon a fine autumn Sunday morning, while every one listened with a comfortable air of satisfaction and complacency, had a most pleasing effect upon my mind.

Mr. Johnson observed that it seemed certain that happiness could not be found in this life, because so many had tried to find it in such a variety of ways, and had not found it.

We came into the harbour of Portree, which is a large and good one. There was lying in it a vessel to carry off the emigrants. It was called the *Nestor*. It made a short settlement of the differences between a chief and his clan:

Nestor componere lites
Inter Peleiden festinat et inter Atriden.[4]

We approached her, and she hoisted her colours; at least I observed them putting them up as we came, and observed no more. Mr. Johnson and Mr. Macqueen remained in the boat. Raasay and I and the rest went on board of her. She was a very pretty vessel, we were told the largest in Clyde, being of ———— ton. Harrison, the Captain, showed us her. The cabin was commodious and even elegant. There was a little library, finely bound. I looked at nothing except a volume of the Rev. Mr. Hervey's works lying on the table. The accommodation for the emigrants was very good. A long ward I may call it, with a row of beds on each side, every one of which was the same size every way, and fit to contain four people.

We landed at Portree, which has its name from King James V having landed at it in his tour through the Western Isles, *Ree*[5] in Erse being "king," as *Re* in Italian. So it is *Kingston* or *Portroyal*. We found here a very good half-finished inn, kept by James Macdonald, who is going to America. On our landing I had a most agreeable letter from my dear wife, with the best accounts of her and Veronica; and Mr. Johnson and I had each of us letters from Lord Elibank, which were like rich cordials to us. They are state papers in this expedition. The one to Mr. Johnson was as follows:

DEAR SIR,—I was to have kissed your hands at Edinburgh the moment I heard of you, but you was gone.

I hope my friend Boswell will inform me of your motions. It will be cruel to deprive me an instant of the honour of attending you. As I value you more than any king in Christendom, I will perform that duty with infinitely greater alacrity than any courtier. I can contribute but little to your

---

[4] "Nestor hastens to allay the quarrel between Achilles and Agamemnon."—Horace, *Epist.*, I.ii.11–12.
[5] Boswell's phonetics are here, as elsewhere, English: in Gaelic spelling, *rìgh*.

entertainment, but my sincere esteem for you gives me some title to the opportunity of expressing it.

I dare say you are by this time sensible that things are pretty much the same as when Buchanan complained of being born *solo et seculo inerudito*.[6] Let me hear of you, and be persuaded that none of your admirers is more sincerely devoted to you than, dear sir, your most obedient and most humble servant,　　　　　　　　　　　　　　　　　ELIBANK.

Mine was also in an admirable style. But I need not engross it here, as I keep it.[7] Perhaps, too, I may be permitted to keep Mr. Johnson's as his *Custos Rotulorum*, but lest I should not, I have put it down; and for the same reason I shall here put down, while it is in my head to do it, his burgess-ticket of Aberdeen.

Diploma Abredonense

Pro

Samuele Johnson, LL.D.

Abredoniae, vigesimo tertio die mensis Augusti, Anno Domini millesimo septingentesimo septuagesimo tertio, in praesentia honorabilium virorum Jacobi Jopp, Armigeri, Praepositi; Adami Duff, Gulielmi Young, Georgii Marr, et Gulielmi Forbes, Ballivorum; Gulielmi Rainie, Decani Guildae; et Joannis Nicoll, Thesaurarii dicti Burgi.

Quo die vir generosus ac doctrina clarus, Samuel Johnson, LL.D., receptus et admissus fuit in municipes et fratres Guildae praefati Burgi de Aberdeen. In dediditissimi honoris et affectus ac eximiae observantiae tesseram, quibus dicti Magistratus eum amplectantur. Extractum per me,

ALEX^r CARNEGIE.[8]

At Portree, Mr. Donald Macqueen went to church and officiated in Erse, and then came to dinner. Mr. Johnson and I re-

---

[6] "On an unlettered soil in an unlettered age."

[7] In the published *Tour*, it precedes the letter to Johnson. Boswell had also promised (*ante*, p. 6) to print his own letter to Elibank, but he forgot to do so. See Appendix, where both letters are given: Boswell's from a copy in the Malahide Papers, Elibank's from the published *Tour*.

[8] "Aberdonian diploma for Samuel Johnson, LL.D. At Aberdeen, 23 August A.D. 1773, in the presence of the honourable gentlemen James Jopp, Esq., Provost; Adam Duff, William Young, George Marr, and William Forbes, Bailies; William Rainie, Dean of Guild; and John Nicoll, Treasurer of the said city. On this day Samuel Johnson, LL.D., a man of good birth and famous for his learning, was received and admitted into the number of burgesses and guild-brethren of the said city of Aberdeen. In token of the devoted esteem and affection and of the distinguished regard with which the said magistrates welcome him. Extracted by me, Alexander Carnegie." The text of this diploma which appears in the published *Tour* was not set up from Boswell's transcript, but apparently from the document itself. It differs by having in the last sentence *dedi--tissimi*, *amplectuntur*, and *amoris* (for *honoris*). *Deditissimi* and *amplectuntur* are obvious emendations, but *amoris* is not, and it is correct, as Dr. Hill's facsimile of the record at Aberdeen shows (*Footsteps of Dr. Johnson*, p. 18).

solved that we should treat; so I played the landlord, having previously ordered Joseph to pay the bill. We had a very good dinner, porter, port, and punch. We had Mrs. Macdonald, a very comely woman, James's wife, at the head of the table, and James himself sat with us. I was quite easy with him: "Come, Portroyal, your toast."

Sir James intended to have built a village here, which would have done great good. A village is like a heart to a country. It produces a perpetual circulation, and gives the country people an opportunity to make profit of eggs and many little articles which would otherwise be in a good measure lost. It was a dinner here *et praeterea nihil*. Mr. Johnson talked none. Captain Harrison dined with us. When we came to go away, behold Raasay had been beforehand and paid all, or at least concerted with James Macdonald that he should pay, as it was an inn near to his estate. This was a most uncommon degree of kindness and generosity. I would fain have contested it with him, but seeing him resolved, I declined it. I parted with cordial embraces from him and worthy Malcolm, hoping to see them again. Mr. Johnson and I set out on horseback again, accompanied by Mr. Macqueen, Dr. MacLeod, and Donald Canna. It was a very rainy afternoon. We rode what they call six miles to Dr. MacLeod's house upon Raasay's lands in Skye. On the road Mr. Johnson appeared to be somewhat out of humour. When I talked of our meeting Lord Elibank, he said, "I cannot be with him much. I long to be again in civilized life, but cannot stay long." (He meant at Edinburgh.) He said, "Let us go to Dunvegan tomorrow." "Yes," said I, "if it is not a deluge." "At any rate," said he. This showed a kind of impatience upon his spirits, and no wonder. I apprehended his giving up Mull and Icolmkill, for he said something of his fears of being detained by bad weather in going to Mull and *Iona*. However, I hoped well. We had a comfortable dish of tea at the Doctor's, a pretty good house, where was his brother, a half-pay officer. His lady was a decent well-behaved woman.

Mr. Johnson said he was glad to see her so. He had an esteem for physicians. The Doctor accompanied us to Kingsburgh, said to be but a mile farther, but the computation of Skye has no connexion whatever with the real distance.

It was fine to see Mr. Johnson light from his horse at Kingsburgh's, who received us most courteously, and after shaking hands supported Mr. Johnson into the house. He was quite the figure of a gallant Highlander—"the graceful mien and manly looks."[9] He had his tartan plaid thrown about him, a large blue bonnet with a knot of black ribbon like a cockade, a brown short coat of a kind of duffle, a tartan vest with gold buttons and gold buttonholes, a bluish filibeg, and tartan hose. He had jet-black hair tied behind and with screwed ringlets on each side, and was a large stately man, with a steady sensible countenance.

There was a comfortable parlour with a good fire, and a dram of admirable Holland's gin went round. By and by supper came, when there appeared his spouse, the celebrated Miss Flora. She was a little woman, of a mild and genteel appearance, mighty soft and well-bred. To see Mr. Samuel Johnson salute Miss Flora Macdonald was a wonderful romantic scene to me. There was a Mrs. Macdonald, wife to James, a brother of Kingsburgh's, and one of his sons. We had as genteel a supper as one would wish to see, in particular an excellent roasted turkey, porter to drink at table, and after supper claret and punch. But what I admired was the perfect ease with which everything went on. My *facility of manners*, as Adam Smith said of me, had fine play.

Miss Flora (for so I shall call her) told me she heard upon the mainland, as she was returning to Skye about a fortnight before this, that Mr. Boswell was coming to Skye, and one Mr. Johnson, a young English buck, with him. He was highly entertained with this event, and speaking of the afternoon which we passed at Anoch, he said, "I, being a *buck*, had Miss in to

---

[9] A phrase from Allan Ramsay's *Highland Laddie*.

make tea," or some such expression about Macqueen's daughter. He was rather quiescent tonight and went early to bed. I was in a cordial humour, and promoted a cheerful glass. The punch was superexcellent, and we drank three bowls of it. Honest Mr. Macqueen said of me, "His governor's gone to bed." My heart was sore to recollect that Kingsburgh had fallen sorely back in his affairs, was under a load of debt, and intended to go to America. However, nothing but what was good was present, and I pleased myself in thinking that so fine a fellow would be well everywhere. I slept in the same room with Mr. Johnson. Each had a neat clean bed in an upper chamber.

MONDAY 13 SEPTEMBER. Last night's jovial bout disturbed me somewhat, but not long. The room where we lay was a room indeed. Each bed had tartan curtains, and Mr. Johnson's was the very bed in which the Prince lay. To see Mr. Samuel Johnson lying in Prince Charles's bed, in the Isle of Skye, in the house of Miss Flora Macdonald, struck me with such a group of ideas as it is not easy for words to describe as the mind perceives them. He smiled, and said, "I have had no ambitious thoughts in it."[1] The room was decorated with a great variety of maps and prints. Among others was Hogarth's print of Wilkes grinning with the cap of liberty beside him. That, too, was a curious circumstance in the scene this morning. Such a contrast was Wilkes to the above group! It was like Sir William Chambers's idea of oriental gardening, in which all odd, strange, ugly, and even terrible objects, are to be introduced for the sake of variety, and which is so well ridiculed in an *Epistle* to him. I thought of the two lines in it,

> Here too, O King of vengeance! in thy fane,
> Tremendous Wilkes shall rattle his gold chain.

---

[1] "This, perhaps, was said in allusion to some lines ascribed to Pope, on his lying, at John Duke of Argyll's, at Adderbury, in the same bed in which Wilmot, Earl of Rochester, had slept.

> 'With no poetic ardour fir'd,
>   I press the bed where Wilmot lay;
> That here he lov'd, or here expir'd,
>   Begets no numbers, grave or gay.'"—BOSWELL.

Upon the table in our room I found a slip of paper in the morning, on which Mr. Johnson had written with his pencil these words: "Quantum cedat virtutibus aurum."[2] What he meant by writing it I could not tell.[3] He had catched cold a day or two ago, and the rain yesterday had made it worse; so he was become very deaf. At breakfast he said he would have given a good deal rather than not have lain in the bed. I said he was the lucky man; and to be sure it had been contrived between Mrs. Macdonald and him. She said, "You know young *bucks* are always favourites of the ladies." He spoke of the Prince being here, and said to Mrs. Macdonald, "*Who* was with him? We were told in England, there was one Miss Flora Macdonald with him." Said she, "They were very right." She then very obligingly told him out of her own mouth, how she had agreed to carry the Prince with her out of Lewis when it was known he was there; the country was full of troops and the coast surrounded with ships. He passed as her maid, an Irish girl, Betty Bourke. They set off in a small boat. The people on shore fired after them to bring them to. But they went forward. They landed in Skye. She got a horse and her maid walked beside her, which it seems is common in this part of the world, but Betty looked somewhat awkward in women's clothes. They came to Monkstadt. She dined at table with Lady Margaret Macdonald, where was an officer who commanded a party watching for the Prince, at whom she often laughed in good humour afterwards as having deceived him; and her maid was—I do not remember where.[4]

---

[2] "With virtue weigh'd, what worthless trash is gold!"—BOSWELL.

[3] "Since the first edition of this book, an ingenious friend has observed to me, that Dr. Johnson had probably been thinking on the reward which was offered by Government for the apprehension of the grandson of King James II, and that he meant by these words to express his admiration of the Highlanders, whose fidelity and attachment had resisted the golden temptation that had been held out to them."—BOSWELL.

[4] Flora Macdonald's later history, too, was not without romance. In August 1774 Kingsburgh and his family joined the other emigrants, as Boswell was told they planned to do, and settled in North Carolina. When the War of Independence broke out, Kingsburgh, along with his five sons and a son-in-law, joined a regiment of emigrant Highlanders serving in the royal army, and Flora herself remained with them in camp. Kingsburgh was taken prisoner, and Flora, at his request, returned to Scotland. On the sea her ship

Mr. Johnson said all this should be written down. She said Bishop Forbes at Leith had it. Mr. Johnson and I were both visibly of the *old interest* (to use the Oxford expression), kindly affectioned at least, and perhaps too openly so.

Sandie MacLeod had assured us that the Prince was in London in 1759[5] when there was a plan in agitation for him. We could hardly believe it, and Mr. Johnson said there could be no probable plan then. Dr. MacLeod said with warmth that there was. The present Royal Family were all to have been seized and put aboard a ship; he was to have been in London; a number of persons of great consequence, among which was the Lord Mayor of London, were in the plot, and James III of Britain would have been proclaimed at Charing Cross; the Prince Regent would have issued writs and called a Parliament, and all would have gone well. "But," said the Doctor, "it failed from the pusillanimity of some of those who were to have acted." Mr. Johnson said it could not have done, unless the King of Prussia had stopped the Army in Germany; for that the Army would have fought without orders, and the fleet would have fought without orders, for the king under whom they served.

I must here explain a little Mr. Johnson's political notions as well as my own. We are both *Tories*; both convinced of the utility of monarchical power, and both lovers of that reverence and affection for a sovereign which constitute loyalty, a principle which I take to be absolutely extinguished in Britain, which is one of the worst consequences of the Revolution. Mr. Johnson is not properly a *Jacobite*. He does not hold the *jus divinum* of kings. He founds their right on long possession, which ought not to be disturbed upon slight grounds. He said to me

---

was attacked by a French privateer, which was driven off, but Flora suffered a broken arm in the skirmish. She used to say that she imperilled her life in both the cause of the Stuarts and that of the House of Hanover, and that she received little from either for her pains. In 1783 her husband was released and joined her in the Highlands. She died at Kingsburgh in 1790.

[5] Dr. Hill supposed that this was either Boswell's or the printer's error for 1750. It is clearly 1759 in the MS.

once that he did not know but it was become necessary to remove the King at the time of the Revolution; and after the present family have had so long a possession, it appears to him that their right becomes the same that the Stuarts had. His difficulty is as to the right still in some measure belonging to that unfortunate family. In short, he is dubious; and he would not involve the nation in a civil war to restore the Stuarts. Nay, I have heard him say he was so dubious that if holding up his right hand would have gained the victory to the Highland army in 1745, he does not know if he would have done it. Beauclerk told me he heard him say so before he had his pension. I, again, have all that Mr. Johnson has, and something more, for my high notions of male succession make me mount up to distant times; and when I find how the Stuart family's right has been formed, it appears to me as but very casual and artificial. I find not the firm feudal hold for which I wish and which my imagination figures. I might fix my eye at the point of James IV, from whom my ancestor Thomas Boswell got the estate of Auchinleck, and look no further, had I a line of males from that Prince. But Queen Mary comes in the way; and I see the sons of Lennox on the throne. Besides, I consider that even supposing Prince Charles to have the right, it may be very generous for one to support another's right at every risk, but it is not wise, and I would not do it. Mr. Johnson's argument of right being formed by possession and acknowledgment of the people, settles my mind, and I have now no uneasiness. With all this, he and I have a kind of *liking* for Jacobitism, something that it is not easy to define. I should guard against it; for from what I have now put down, it is certain that my calm reasoning stops short at action, so that doing anything violent in support of the cause would only be following a sort of passion or warm whim. And talking much in favour of it may even in this secure and more liberal reign hurt a man in his rising in life.[6]

⁶ This very candid statement was completely revised before publication, and the refer-

Kingsburgh conducted us in his boat across one of the lochs, as they call them, or arms of the sea, which flow in upon all the coasts of Skye, to a mile beyond a place called Greshornish. Our horses had been sent round it in the morning to meet us. By this sail we saved eight miles of bad riding. Mr. Johnson said, "When we take into the computation what we have saved and what we have gained by this agreeable sail, it is a great deal." He said, "It is very disagreeable riding in Skye. The way is so narrow, one only at a time can travel, so it is quite unsocial; and you cannot indulge in meditation by yourself, because you must be always attending to the steps which your horse takes." This was a just and clear description of its inconveniences.

He said Sir Alexander would make a wilderness of his estate. While I sailed in Kingsburgh's boat and thought of the emigration, it did not hurt me. I fancied him sailing in America just as he did about Skye.

Mr. Johnson asked about the use of the dirk. He was told the Highlanders had a knife and fork besides to eat with. He asked, how did the women do? was answered, some of them had a knife and fork too. But in general the men gave to them

---

ence to Boswell's "liking for Jacobitism" suppressed. Boswell's reverence for King George had increased steadily from 1773 to 1785 until it had become almost Oriental. He was greatly worried as to the designation which he should employ for Charles Edward. "The Prince," the title he had employed throughout the journal, seemed to him risky because it implied some recognition of Stuart claims. "The Pretender" was offensive to him; it might be "a parliamentary expression, but it was not a gentlemanly expression." He finally laid his doubts before George III in a letter dated 6 June 1785; he wished the Royal permission to use the style "Prince Charles." On 15 June, having had no answer, he accosted the King at his levee. George III, after a show of displeasure which Boswell thought assumed merely to "prove" him, "with a benignant smile equal to that of any of Correggio's angels," said, "I think and I feel as you do." Boswell then asked whether the style should be "Prince Charles." When the King hesitated, Boswell suggested, "Or shall it be 'the grandson of King James the Second'?" The King assented, adding that he really thought it of no consequence what title was used. Boswell withdrew in ecstasies, but not until he had volunteered the information that he was cousin in the seventh degree to Prince Charles, which also implied cousinship to George III. In the published *Tour* (where all the anecdotes of the '45 are woven into one narrative and presented at this point in the text), Charles Edward is introduced as "the grandson of the unfortunate King James the Second" and thereafter called "Prince Charles Edward" or "Prince Charles." Boswell added a footnote of which the present note is a more explicit rendering. "I *know*," he says, "and I exult in having it in my power to tell, that THE ONLY PERSON in the world who is entitled to be offended at this delicacy, 'thinks and feels as I do.'"

and they themselves eat with their fingers. The old Tutor[7] of Macdonald always eat fish with his fingers, alleging that a knife and fork gave it a bad taste. I took the liberty to observe to Mr. Johnson that he did so. "Yes," said he; "but it is because I am short-sighted, and afraid of bones; for which reason I'm not fond of eating many kinds of fish, because I must take my fingers." Perhaps I put down too many things in this Journal. I have no fanners in my head, at least no good ones, to separate wheat from chaff. Yet for as much as I put down, what is written falls greatly short of the quantity of thought. A page of my Journal is like a cake of portable soup.[8] A little may be diffused into a considerable portion.

Mr. Johnson observed of Macpherson's *Dissertations on Scottish Antiquities*, which he had looked at when at Coirechatachan, that you might read half an hour and ask yourself what you had been reading. There were so many words to so little matter, there was no getting through the book. (I had begun by saying they were very unsatisfactory, in which he agreed.)

Kingsburgh had brought provisions for us, but we were not hungry, and after taking leave of him, rode on. We passed through a wild moor, in many places so wet that we were obliged to walk, which was hard on Mr. Johnson. Once he had advanced on horseback to a very bad step. There was a steep declivity on his left, to which he was so near that there was not room for him to dismount in the usual way. He alighted on the other side, as if he had been a *young buck* indeed. He fell at his length upon the ground, but got up immediately, and was not hurt. We were relieved by seeing several branches of the sea, that universal connexion. Our journey or ride was computed only ———— miles, but was in fact a very

---

[7] Guardian or trustee. Sir Donald Macdonald, 4th Baronet of Sleat, forfeited the estates in 1715. A friend bought them in, and William Macdonald of Aird, brother of Sir Donald, was appointed Tutor during the minority of the 7th baronet, Sir Alexander.

[8] "Portable soup, or solid broth, made from beef, veal, mutton, and chicken, is found exceedingly useful on various occasions; and has particularly recommended itself to gentlemen on journeys and at sea." (From an advertisement in the *London Chronicle* for 22 Sept. 1761.)

long and tedious expedition. We arrived at Dunvegan late in the afternoon. The great size of the castle, partly old and partly new, upon a rock on the sea, and nothing to be perceived at land but wild moorish hilly and rocky appearances, struck us —at least me. We went up a stair of twenty-two[9] steps made by the late MacLeod as a land-access, the original one having been from the sea side. I said, "This is feudal indeed." But I shall by and by describe at once all about Dunvegan as well as I can. We were received by Mr. Norman MacLeod, a young preacher, who as one of the clan did the honours of the house, MacLeod and Talisker not being yet come up. We were introduced into a large dining-room with three windows, marble tables, a screen covered with many good prints; Brodie, Lady MacLeod's father's, portrait in the dress belonging to him as Lord Lyon of Scotland, and his lady; the young Laird of Mac-Leod, father to this Laird; ———,[10] all family pictures, gave a kind of comfortable appearance, though the late Laird most gracelessly took from Dunvegan and left to his widow the family pictures, plate, etc.

In a little appeared Lady MacLeod, a sensible clever woman with whom Mr. Johnson had been acquainted at Captain Brodie's in London; and before something was ready for us to eat, the Laird and Talisker arrived. We had venison collops from Cuillin, and something else. We then went to tea, where we saw Miss MacLeod (Maria, the Laird's eldest sister), and Miss Nannie, another of his sisters. Two others were ill. We had admirable tea: ladies bred in England; everything agreeable. The drawing-room was not large. It was formerly the bedchamber of Sir Roderick MacLeod, great-great-grandfather[11] of the late Laird; and he chose it because behind it, at least on the rising ground to which its window looks, is a considerable cascade, the sound of which disposed him to sleep. Above his bed was this inscription: "Sir Rorie McLeod of Dunvegan,

---

[9] Boswell neglected to fill a blank here, but he gives the figure later.
[10] Boswell left a blank for listing more portraits.   [11] "—father" in MS.

Knight. GOD send good rest!" Perhaps some foolish painter put it on of his own accord. Perhaps Sir Rorie, who was called Rorie More ("Big Rorie"), from his size, chose it himself. There were in this room prints of the seasons by Bowles, coloured,[12] and prints of Duncan Forbes, Lord Stair, and the famous Ruins of Rome, very well copied by Lady MacLeod, a rich carpet, a good table, the tea in civilized order. Mr. Johnson became quite joyous. He laughed and said, "Boswell, we came in at the wrong end of this island." "Sir," said I, "it was best to keep this for the last." He answered, "I'd have it both first and last." In the evening there was a little repast of bread and cheese and porter and wine and punch only, as we had dined so late. I had a large old bedchamber, a large old-fashioned crimson bed, a light closet with a chest of drawers. I was quite at home.

TUESDAY 14 SEPTEMBER. Mr. Johnson said in the morning, "Is not this a fine lady?" There was not a word now of his "impatience to be in civilized life"—though indeed I should beg pardon: he found it here. We had slept well and lain long. After breakfast we surveyed the castle, walked round the rock, walked in the garden. Mr. Bethune the parish minister, Magnus MacLeod of Claggan, and Bay, another substantial man of the clan, dined. Magnus is brother to Talisker, and has children who would be next in succession to the Chief, as Talisker, the next heir, has none. We had admirable venison from Harris, good soup—in a word, all that a good table has. This was really the hall of a chief. Lady MacLeod had been much obliged to my father, who had settled by arbitration a variety of perplexed claims between her and Brodie, which made a good connexion between her and me. MacLeod started the subject of making women do penance in the church for fornication. Mr. Johnson said it was right. "Infamy," said he,

---

[12] This was later expanded to "prints of the months, published by Bowles, both in fruits and flowers, two sets coloured." There are many interlinear insertions at this point. Some of them were certainly made, and cancelled, when Boswell and Malone were revising for publication, but others may have been original.

"is attached to the crime by universal opinion so soon as it is known. I would not be the man who, knowing it alone, would discover it, as a woman may reform; nor would I commend a parson who discovers the first offence. But if mankind know it, it ought to be infamous. Consider of what importance the chastity of women is. Upon that, all the property in the world depends. We hang a thief for stealing a sheep. But the unchastity of a woman transfers sheep and farm and all from the right owner. I have much more reverence for a common prostitute than for a woman who conceals her guilt. The prostitute is known. She cannot deceive. She cannot bring a strumpet into the arms of an honest man." I said there was a great difference between the licentiousness of a single woman and that of a married woman. JOHNSON. "Yes, sir; there is a great difference between stealing a shilling and a thousand pounds; between simply taking a man's purse, and murdering him first and then taking it. But when one begins, it is easy to go on. Where single women are licentious, you rarely find faithful married women." BOSWELL. "And yet we are told that in some nations in India, the distinction is strictly observed." JOHNSON. "Nay, don't give us India. That puts me in mind of Montesquieu, who is really a fellow of genius, too, in many particulars; whenever he wants to support a strange opinion, he quotes you the practice of Japan or of ———, of which he knows nothing. To support polygamy, he tells you of the island of Formosa, where there are ten women born for one man. He had but to suppose another island, where there are ten men born for one woman, and so make marriage between 'em."[1]

At supper, Lady MacLeod mentioned Dr. Cadogan's book on the gout. Mr. Johnson said, "'Tis a good book in general, but a foolish one as to particulars. 'Tis good in general, as recommending temperance and exercise and cheerfulness. 'Tis

---

[1] "What my friend treated as so wild a supposition, has actually happened in the Western Islands of Scotland, if we may believe Martin, who tells it of the islands of Coll and Tyree, and says that it is proved by the parish registers."—BOSWELL.

only Dr. Cheyne's book told in a new way. And there should come out such a book every thirty years, dressed in the mode of the times. 'Tis foolish, as it says the gout is not hereditary, and one fit of the gout when gone is like a fever when gone." "But," said Lady MacLeod, "he does not practise what he teaches."[2] JOHNSON. "I cannot help that, madam. That does not make his book the worse. People are influenced more by what a man says, if his practice is suitable to it, because they are blockheads. The more intellectual people are, the readier will they attend to what a man tells them. If it is just, they will follow it, be his practice what it will. No man practises so well as he writes. I have, all my life long, been lying till noon. Yet I tell all young men, and tell them with great sincerity, that nobody who does not rise early will ever do any good. Only consider! You read a book; you are convinced by it; you do not know the author. Suppose you afterwards know him, and find that he does not practise what he teaches; are you to give up your former conviction? At this rate you would be kept in a state of *equilibrio* when reading every book, till you knew how the author practised." "But," said Lady MacLeod, "you would think better of Dr. Cadogan if he acted according to his principles." JOHNSON. "Why, madam, to be sure, a man who acts in the face of light is worse than a man who does not know so much. But I think there is something noble in publishing truth, though it condemns one's self." I spoke of Cadogan's recommending good-humour. Mr. Johnson said, "A man grows better-humoured as he grows older, by experience. He learns to think himself of no consequence and little things of little importance; and so he becomes more patient, and better pleased. All good-humour and complaisance is acquired. Naturally a child seizes directly what it sees, and thinks of

---

[2] "This was a general reflection against Dr. Cadogan, when his very popular book was published. It was said, that whatever precepts he might give to others, he himself indulged freely in the bottle. But I have since had the pleasure of becoming acquainted with him, and, if his own testimony may be believed (and I have never heard it impeached), his course of life has been conformable to his doctrine."—BOSWELL.

pleasing itself only. By degrees, it is taught to please others, and to prefer others; and that this will ultimately produce the greatest happiness. If a man is not convinced of that, he never will practise it. (Common language speaks the truth as to this. We say, a person is well-*bred*; as it is said that all material motion is in a right line, and is never *per circuitum*, in another form, unless by some particular cause; so it may be said intellectual motion is.") Lady MacLeod asked if no man was naturally good. JOHNSON. "No, madam, no more than a wolf." BOSWELL. "Nor no woman, sir?" JOHNSON. "No, sir." Lady MacLeod started, saying low, "This is worse than Swift."—What is within the parenthesis was said at an after time, but I bring it in here for connexion.

MacLeod of Ullinish had come in the afternoon. We were a jolly company at supper. It was fine to see the Laird surrounded by so many of his clan. They listened with wonder and pleasure while Mr. Johnson harangued. I am vexed that I cannot take down his full strain of eloquence.

WEDNESDAY 15 SEPTEMBER. The gentlemen of the clan went away early in the morning to the harbour of Loch Bracadale to take leave of some of their friends who were going to America. It was a very wet day. We looked at Rorie More's horn, which is a large cow's horn with the mouth of it ornamented with silver. It holds rather more than a bottle and a half. Every Laird of MacLeod, it is said, must as a proof of his manhood drink it off full of claret without taking it from his right arm. He holds the small end of it backwards, and so keeps it at his mouth.[1] The silver mouth to it is above an inch deep —a thin plate with such plaited carving upon it as is commonly found on the Highland dirks or forks and knives, with some other kind of figuring. And under the mouth, round the horn on the outside, are silver knobs which serve as nails to keep

---

[1] "The ceremony of quaffing claret from Rorie More's horn at the inauguration of each successive Chief of MacLeod is still [1852] continued; but an artificial bottom is inserted on these occasions in order to reduce the libation to a moderate draught."—CARRUTHERS.

the piece of silver on. From Rorie More many of the branches
of the family are descended—in particular the Talisker branch
—so that his name is much talked of. We also saw his bow,
which hardly any man now can bend, and his *claymore* which
was wielded with both hands, and is of a prodigious size.[2] We
saw some old pieces of iron armour, immensely heavy. The
broadsword which is now called the *claymore* is much smaller
than the sword used in Rorie More's time, and is of modern
invention. There is hardly a target now to be found in the Highlands. After the disarming act they made them serve as covers
to their buttermilk barrels, a kind of change like beating spears
into pruning-hooks.

Sir George Mackenzie's works were lying in a window. I
made Mr. Johnson read some of the *Characteres Advocatorum*. He
allowed power of mind, and that Sir George understood very
well what he tells, but there was too much declamation; and
that the Latin was not correct. He found fault with *appropin-
quabant* in the character of Gilmour. I tried him with the opposition between *gloria* and *palma* in the comparison between
Gilmour and Nisbet, which Lord Hailes in his Catalogue of
the Lords of Session thinks difficult to be understood. I in my
little Account of the Kirk of Scotland[3] attempted to explain
it thus: "The popular party has most eloquence; Dr. Robertson's most influence;" *penes illam gloria, penes hanc palma*. I was
very desirous to hear Mr. Johnson. He said: "I see no difficulty.
Gilmour was admired for his parts. Nisbet carried his cause by
his skill in law. *Palma* is victory." I said the character of Nich-
olson was that of Burke: *In omnes lusos et jocos se saepe resolvebat;*[4]
and *accipitris more e conspectu aliquando astantium sublimi se pro-*

---

[2] The sword was broken at some time between 1773 and 1814; for, though Boswell's later
reference to its point and his sketch of it show it to have been then entire, when Sir Walter Scott saw it on 23 August 1814 he referred to it as a "fragment of a two-handed
sword," a description which is supported by a more recent sketch and photograph of it
(*Proc. Soc. of Antiquaries of Scotland*, xxix. 271; xlvii.119).

[3] "A Sketch of the Constitution of the Church of Scotland," published in the *London
Magazine* for April and May 1772.

[4] "He often indulged himself in every species of pleasantry and wit."—BOSWELL.

trahens volatu, in praedam miro impetu descendebat.[5] "No, sir," said Mr. Johnson. "I never heard Burke make a good joke in my life." "But he's a hawk, sir," said I. Mr. Johnson, thinking that I meant this of his joking, said, "No, sir, he's not the hawk there. He's the beetle in the mire." I kept to the hawk, crying, "But he soars as the hawk." JOHNSON. "Yes, sir; but he catches nothing." MacLeod asked, "What is the particular excellence of Burke's eloquence?" JOHNSON. "Copiousness and fertility of allusion; a power of diversifying his matter by placing it in various relations. Burke has great knowledge, and great command of language; though, in my opinion, it has not in every respect the highest elegance."

Mr. Donald MacLeod, late tenant in Canna[6] but now dispossessed of it, was still with us. He was an obliging serviceable man. His father was one of MacLeod's ministers; and the late Laird educated him, and in particular had him several years at school near London. He was at present in that kind of wandering state that many a Highland younger brother is. I was sometimes angry at his appearing unanimated, speaking a few words slowly and with a weak voice, and then sitting with his mouth open. He was tall and a good sportsman. He gained me at last by saying of Mr. Johnson, "Well, it is really a happiness to be in this man's company."

Our money was now near an end. He went to Loch Bracadale today and took with him a bill of mine for £30 drawn on Sir W. Forbes & Co. to his order, for which he was to get money for me from the master of the vessel which carries away the emigrants. There is hardly any specie in Skye. Mr. Macqueen said he had the utmost difficulty to pay his servants' wages or to pay for any little thing which he has to buy. The rents are paid in bills which the drovers give; and these the Lairds

---

[5] "Like the hawk, having soared with a lofty flight to a height which the eye could not reach, he was wont to swoop upon his quarry with wonderful rapidity."—BOSWELL.

[6] For some reason—perhaps because his faithlessness, soon to be revealed, was later completely expiated—Boswell omitted all but a few references to MacLeod of Canna in the published book.

get money for at Edinburgh, and never bring it here. The people consume a great deal of snuff and tobacco, for which they must pay ready money; and pedlars who come about selling goods, as there is not a shop in the island, carry away the cash. If there were encouragement given to fishing and manufactures, and the Lairds were to stay more at home, there might be a circulation of money introduced. I got one-and-twenty shillings in silver at Portree, which was a wonderful store.

On the 65 page of the first volume of Sir George Mackenzie's folio edition, Mr. Johnson pointed out a paragraph beginning with *Aristotle*, and told me there was an error in the text which he bid me try to discover. I hit it at once. It stands that the devil answers *even* in *engines*. I corrected it to *ever* in *enigmas*. "Sir," said he, "you're a good critic. This would have been a great thing to do in the text of an ancient author."

We had a venison pasty today and most excellent roast beef. But I need say no more as to dinner or supper than that there is abundance of good things genteelly served up. Amidst the difficulties of the family, Lady MacLeod, who is a heroine for the clan, entertained us like princes. She has at the same time the greatest economy. She is butler herself, even of the porter. We had porter from the cask, as in London; claret, port, sherry, and punch. The claret we soon quitted. MacLeod and Talisker and I drank port. The rest of the men drank punch. Lady MacLeod and her daughters eat oat-bread. Mr. Johnson and I had excellent cakes of flour. She is resolved to live just as the farmers do; I should think however that the ladies might eat wheat-bread. Mr. Johnson said that it would not be above a shilling a week of odds among three.

THURSDAY 16 SEPTEMBER. Last night much care was taken of Mr. Johnson. He had hitherto most strangely slept without a night-cap. Miss MacLeod made him a large flannel one, and he was prevailed with to drink a little brandy when he was going to bed—all to do his cold good.[1] He has great

---

[1] When Dr. Hill was at Dunvegan in 1889, he was told the following anecdote by the

virtue in not drinking wine or any fermented liquor, because he could not do it in moderation. He told us[2] so on Tuesday night. Lady MacLeod would hardly believe him, and said, "I'm sure, sir, you would not carry it too far." JOHNSON. "Nay, madam, it carried me." He took the opportunity of a long illness to leave it off. It was prescribed to him then not to drink wine; and having broke off the habit, he has never returned to it. He was in high spirits this morning.

In the argument on Tuesday night about natural goodness, he denied that any child was more so than another, but by difference of instruction; though the greater attention given by one than another, and a variety of imperceptible causes (such as instruction being counteracted by servants) made it be thought that of two children equally well educated, one should be much worse than another. He owned this morning that one might have a greater aptitude to learn than another, and that we inherit dispositions from our parents. Said he, "I inherited a vile melancholy from my father, which has made me mad all my life, at least not sober." Lady MacLeod wondered he should tell this. "Madam," said I, "he knows that with that madness he is superior to other men."

I have often been astonished with what exactness and perspicuity he will explain the whole process of any art. He this

---

grand-daughter of Johnson's hostess: "One day he had scolded the maid for not getting good peats, and had gone out in the rain to the stack to fetch in some himself. He caught a bad cold. Lady MacLeod went up to his room to see how he was, and found him in bed, with his wig turned inside out and the wrong end foremost. . . . On her return to the drawing-room she said, 'I have often seen very plain people, but anything as ugly as Dr. Johnson, with his wig thus stuck on, I never have seen.'"—*Footsteps of Dr. Johnson*, p. 3. The description of Johnson's appearance may rest on fact, but the explanation of how he caught his cold can now be shown to be a mere invention resting upon a mistaken inference from Boswell's *Tour*. In the entry for 9 October, the travellers being then at Coll, Boswell recorded the fact that the peats at Dunvegan had been damp, and that Johnson had called them "a sullen fuel." So much was printed in the first edition of the *Tour*. In the Journal for 14 October he said that Johnson, at McSweyn's in Coll, had gone out on a stormy night to fetch peats. This was suppressed. At Malone's suggestion it was restored in the second edition, and connected with the "sullen fuel" of Dunvegan, simply because both passages mentioned peat. See *post*, pp. 287 and 297. Very little trust can be placed in any anecdote of the Hebridean tour not recorded by Boswell.

[2] Inadvertently omitted by Boswell; here supplied by the editors.

morning gave us all the operation of coining, and at night he gave us all the operation of brewing spirits. Mr. Macqueen said when he heard the first he thought he had been bred in the Mint. When he heard the second, that he had been bred a brewer.

It was curious to have him on this remote point of the world. Lady MacLeod was entertained with my simile, that it was like a dog who has got hold of a large piece of meat, and runs away with it to a corner, where he may devour it in peace, without any fear of others taking it from him. "In London, Reynolds, Beauclerk, and all of them are contending who shall have Mr. Johnson. We are feasting upon him undisturbed at Dunvegan."

It was still a storm of wind and rain. Mr. Johnson walked out with MacLeod, and saw Rorie More's cascade in grand fullness, by which MacLeod got such a toothache that he could not appear at supper. Every room in the house smoked but the drawing-room. We began tonight a comfortable custom of retreating to the drawing-room, where we took our glass warmly and snugly. This day we had Mr. John Bethune, minister of Harris, a young man who said little and did not seem to have much to say to such a man as Mr. Johnson. Colonel MacLeod, whom Mr. Johnson called a very pleasing man, was at present very different from what he uses to be, and I have seen him. Instead of being all life and gaiety, he was grave and low-spirited and seldom spoke. He had formerly had something of the same kind. It had returned upon him by his taking a most anxious concern in MacLeod's affairs, striving to settle with the gentlemen on the estate, and finding many of the clan, who owed much to the family, by no means disposed to act a generous or affectionate part to their chief in his distress, but bargaining with him as with a stranger. However, he was always agreeable and polite, and would at times talk very well. Mr. Johnson said he would go to Sweden with me. I said we should like to be with the King. Said Mr. Johnson, "I doubt if he would speak to us." Said the Colonel, "I'm sure Mr. Boswell would speak to him." This was a good remark as to my forwardness. He added with a genteel civility, "and with great propriety." Let me value my forwardness. It has procured me much happiness. I do not think it is impudence. It is an eagerness to share the best society, and a diligence to attain what I desire. If a man is praised for seeking knowledge though mountains and seas are in his way, is it not laudable in me to seek it at the risk of mortification from repulses? I have never yet exerted ambition in rising in the state. But sure I am, no man has made his way better to the best of company. Were my *places* to be ranged after my name, as "Member of the Club at the Turk's Head," etc., I should make as great a figure as most peers. There is a meaning in this if it were well expressed.

After the ladies were gone, we talked of the Highlanders' not having sheets; and so on we went to the advantage of wearing linen. Mr. Johnson said, "All animal substances are less cleanly than vegetable. Wool, of which flannel is made, is an animal substance; flannel therefore is not so cleanly as linen. I remember I used to think tar dirty. But when I knew it to be only a preparation of the juice of the pine, I thought so no longer. It is not disagreeable to have the gum that oozes from a plum-tree upon your fingers, because it is vegetable; but if you have any candle-grease, any tallow upon your fingers, you are uneasy till you rub it off." And then he came out with this saying: "I have often thought that if I kept a seraglio, the ladies should all wear linen gowns, or cotton; I mean stuffs made of vegetable substances. I would have no silk; you cannot tell when it is clean. It will be very nasty before it is perceived to be so. Linen detects its own dirtiness."

To hear Mr. Johnson, while sitting solemn in arm-chair, talk of his keeping a seraglio and saying too, "I have *often* thought," was truly curious.[3] Mr. Macqueen asked him if he

---

[3] Everything from this point to the end of the paragraph was heavily inked over by Boswell in a style quite different from that of his deletions for the printer. He may have suppressed the passage immediately after writing it, for fear of Johnson's displeasure, but it is more probable that the deletion was made in 1775 when he lent the MS to Mrs. Thrale.

would admit me. "Yes," said he, "if he were properly prepared; and he'd make a very good eunuch. He'd be a fine
gay[4] animal. He'd do his part well." "I take it," said I, "better
than you would do your part." Though he treats his friends
with uncommon freedom, he does not like a return. He seemed
to me to be a little angry. He got off from my joke by saying, "I
have not told you what was to be my part"—and then at once
he returned to my office as eunuch and expatiated upon it with
such fluency that it really hurt me. He made me quite contemptible for the moment. Luckily the company did not take
it so clearly as I did. Perhaps, too, I imagined him to be more
serious in this extraordinary raillery than he really was. But I
am of a firmer metal than Langton and can stand a rub better.

This morning he described Langton's house. He said the old
house of the family was burnt. A temporary building was erected;
and to this they have been always adding as the family increased. It was like a shirt made for a man when he was a child,
and enlarged always as he grew older.

We talked tonight of Luther's allowing the Landgrave of
Hesse two wives, and that it was with the consent of the wife
to whom he was first married. Mr. Johnson said there was no
harm so far as she only was concerned, because *volenti non fit
injuria*.[5] But it was an offence against the general order of society, and against the law of the Gospel, by which one man and
one woman are united. "And," said he, "no man can have
two wives but by preventing somebody else from having one."

FRIDAY 17 SEPTEMBER. After dinner yesterday, we had a
conversation upon cunning. MacLeod said that he was not
afraid of cunning people, but would let them play their tricks
about him like monkeys. "But," said I, "they'll scratch."
"And," said Mr. Macqueen, "they'll invent new tricks as soon as
you find out what they do." Mr. Johnson said that cunning had
effect from the credulity of others rather than the abilities of

---

[4] Doubtful; possibly *fat*.
[5] "No harm is done to a person who consents." MS, *voleati*.

those who are cunning. He said it required no great talents to lie and deceive. This led us to consider whether it did not require great abilities to be very wicked. Mr. Johnson instructed us nobly. Said he, "It requires great abilities to have the *power* of being very wicked; but not to *be* very wicked. A man who has the power which great abilities procure him, may use it well or ill; and it requires more abilities to use it well than to use it ill. Wickedness is always easier than virtue, for it takes the short cut to everything. It is much easier to steal a hundred pounds than to get it by labour or any other way. Consider only what piece of wickedness requires great abilities when once the person who is to be wicked has the power, for *there* is the distinction. It requires great abilities to conquer an army, but none to massacre it after it is conquered."

This day was rather better than any that we have had since we came to Dunvegan. Mr. Macqueen had often talked to me of a curious piece of antiquity near this; what he called a temple of the Goddess Anaitis. He has sent Pennant a description of it. We were every day talking of going to see it; and it would have been a shame for me to have neglected it, though I should have been wet to the skin. He and I set out after breakfast, attended by his man, a fellow quite like a savage. And I must observe here that in Skye there seems to be much idleness; for men and boys follow you as colts will follow passengers upon a road. The usual figure of a Skye boy is a *lown*[1] with bare legs, a dirty kilt, ragged coat and waistcoat, a bare head, and a stick in his hand, which I suppose is partly to help the lazy rogue to walk, partly to serve as a kind of arms to him. We walked what is called two miles, but may be four, northeast[2] from the castle, till we came to the sacred place. The country around is black dreary moor on all sides except to the seacoast, towards which there is a view through a valley, and the

---

[1] i.e., *loon*, a Scottish dialectal expression of various signification. Here, simply "boy."
[2] Left blank by Boswell; supplied from the volume to which reference is made in n. 5 below.

farm of Bay shows some good ground. The place itself is green
ground, being well drained by reason of a deep glen or valley
on each side, in each of which there runs a rivulet or brook
with a good quantity of water; for in each there are several
cascades, which make a considerable appearance and sound;
and at some places there are cascades formed by other brooks
running into these. Upon the west[3] there is one which has five
separate falls formed by different projections of rock. The first
thing we came to was an earthen mound or dike extending
from the one precipice to the other. A little farther on was a
strong stone wall, not high but very thick, extending in the
same manner. On the outside of it were the ruins of two houses,
one on each side of the entry or gate to it. The wall at the
entry is four lengths and a half of my cane.[4] The wall is built
all along of dry stone; but of stones of so large a size as to make
a very firm and durable rampart. It has been built all about
the consecrated ground except where the precipice is steep
enough to form an enclosure of itself. The sacred spot will be
more than two acres. There are within it the ruins of many
houses (none of them large), a cairn, many graves marked by
stones thus: 8o8; but what Mr. Macqueen insists on is that the
ruin of a small building standing east and west was actually
the temple of the Goddess Anaitis, where her statue was kept,
and from whence processions were made to wash it in one of
the brooks.[5] There is a hollow road really visible for a good
way from the entrance. But Mr. Macqueen walked with great
attention along what he saw to be a continuation of it, for a
good way, till there is an easy descent to the brook on the

---

[3] Blank in the MS, but the location is shown by Boswell's sketch.
[4] Boswell's cane is shown, by the dimensions which he gives for the "Temple of Anaitis,"
to have been about thirty-nine inches long.
[5] "The oldest ecclesiastical term existing in the Islands is *Annait* (*Annaid*), which is peculiar to the Celtic Church, and probably indicates in Scotland, as in Ireland, the mother-
church or monastic community of the earliest Christian settlement in the district. It is
now structurally represented only by the example in Skye." (*Ancient and Historical Monuments of Scotland. Ninth Report. The Outer Hebrides and Skye.* 1928. p. xlv. See the full description, *ibid.*, pp. 149–50.)

————. As I have often observed what looked like visible roads in moors, that is to say continued pieces of ground greener than the rest, and perhaps a little lower, I could not be sure that he was right here. All the houses, temple as well as the rest, have not more than a foot or a foot-and-a-half in height remaining of their walls. The temple is in length, within the walls, five lengths of my cane and six hands; in breadth, two lengths and a few hands, I think six too, so that it has been but a poor building. The waters on each side join at the north[6] end of the sacred ground, which is like a theatre elevated above the neighbouring ground, and then the water or river formed by them runs away due north[7] towards the sea. Whatever this place has been it has been a most striking solemn scene. The sight lost in some places on a wild moor around; the hills in some other places bounding the prospect; and then, within, the space itself, so much concentrated and closely bound in by precipices, sometimes rocky, sometimes just green steep declivities—and waters beneath. I wish I could draw. Let me try to make an awkward sketch of it.[8] It is to be supposed that when this was a place of worship, the banks or steeps on each side of the brooks were covered with wood. When that circumstance is added, I can hardly conceive a more awful rude retreat. Mr. Macqueen has collected a great deal of learning with regard to the temples of Anaitis, of which he supposes this to have been one. My sketch of it may convey some idea. But there is no exactness in it. I may truly be said to

Write about it, Goddess, and about it.[9]

When we got home, and were enjoying ourselves over admirable roasted venison, we first talked of portraits. Mr. John-

---

[6] Supplied by the editors to fill a blank in the MS.
[7] Supplied by the editors to fill a blank in the MS.
[8] See the facsimile.
[9] "For thee we dim the eyes, and stuff the head
     With all such reading as was never read:
     For thee explain a thing till all men doubt it,
     And write about it, Goddess, and about it."
                                    Pope, *Dunciad*, IV. 249–52.

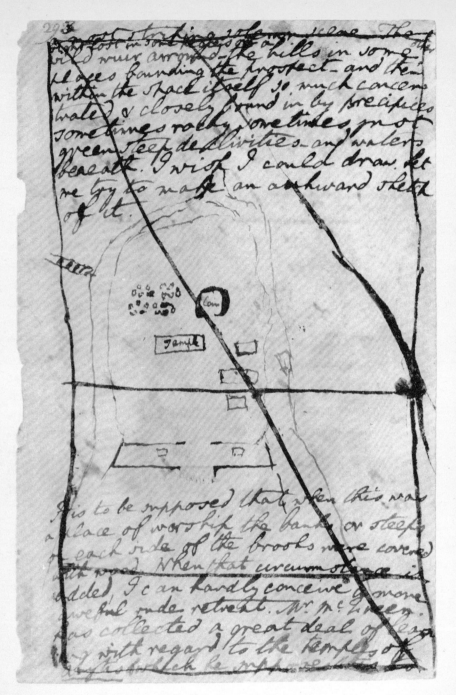

BOSWELL'S PLAN OF THE ANNAIT

have been one [?] sketch of it may convey
some idea But there is no escaping it
I may truly be said to
~~write about it head to~~ ~~on which~~ again at table
when we got home, & here ~~coming~~
~~there~~ ~~declined~~ ~~sketch~~
we first talked of portraits. ~~and we agreed~~
~~in finding them invaluable~~ in families
I asked if he would rather have ~~one~~
~~portrait~~ ~~the~~ ~~himself~~ Their
chief excellence is in being "like" ~~himself~~
"Are you of that opinion as to the portraits
of ancestors whom one has never seen" said
I ~~It then~~ becomes of more consequence
that they shall be like, that you may
~~see them~~. And I'd have them in the dress
of the times" as makes a piece of history one
should like to see how ~~Hovie~~ more looked.
Truth, Sir, is of the greatest value in
these things" Mr. McQueen observed
that if you hold that there is no
matter ~~of~~ ~~a~~ portrait ~~one~~ not life
if well painted, you may be indifferent
whether a piece of history is true or
not if well told. ~~Sir~~ I said at breakfast
today that it was but of late that
historians bestowed pains & attention
in consulting records, to attain to accuracy. Bacon in writing his history of
Henry VII. does not seem to have consulted any, but just taken what he found
in other histories, with what he learnt

son agreed in thinking them valuable in families. I asked if
he would rather have fine portraits or like ones. "Why," said
he, "their chief excellence is in being like." "But," said I, "are
you of that opinion as to the portraits of ancestors whom one
has never seen?" Said he, "It then becomes of more consequence that they should be like—that you may see them. And
I'd have them in the dress of the times, which makes a piece
of history. One should like to see how Rorie More looked. *Truth*,
sir, is of the greatest value in these things." Mr. Macqueen observed that if you hold that there is no matter though portraits
are not like if well painted, you may be indifferent whether a
piece of history is true or not, if well told.

Mr. Johnson said at breakfast today that it was but of late
that historians bestowed pains and attention in consulting
records, to attain to accuracy. Bacon in writing his History of
Henry VII does not seem to have consulted any, but just taken
what he found in other histories, with what he learnt by tradition. He agreed with me that there should be a chronicle kept
in every family.

I started Anaitis after dinner. Mr. Macqueen had laid stress
on the name given to the place by the country people, *Aunnit*;
and said he, "I knew not what to make of this piece of antiquity, till I met with the *Anaitidis delubrum*, in Asia Minor, mentioned by Pausanias and the elder Pliny."[10] Mr. Johnson, who
is wonderfully acute, examined Mr. Macqueen as to the meaning of the word *Aunnit* in Erse; and it came out to be a water-
place, or a place near a water, "which," said Mr. Macqueen,
"agrees with all the descriptions of those temples, which were
situated near rivers, that there might be water to wash the
statue."[11] "Nay," said Mr. Johnson, "the argument from the
name is gone. The name is exhausted by what we see. We have

[10] The MS reads, "mentioned by————." Malone filled in the blank.
[11] Professor Macdonald writes: "The derivation given to Boswell is obviously popular
etymology from *amhainin* + *àit*, i.e., 'river' + 'place.' There is no 'water-place' notion
about *annaid*; the sense of the popular derivation is made to fit the word as derived,
easily enough, because there is no place in the West of Scotland where water is far to
seek."

no occasion to go to a distance for what we can pick up under our feet. Had it been an accidental name, the similarity between it and Anaitis might have had something in it; but it turns out to be a mere physiological name." MacLeod said Mr. Macqueen's knowledge of etymology had destroyed his conjecture. "Yes," said Mr. Johnson, "Mr. Macqueen is like the eagle mentioned by Waller, who was shot with an arrow feathered from his own wing." Mr. Macqueen would not yield his conjecture. "Sir," said Mr. Johnson, "you have one possibility for you, and all possibilities against you. It is possible it may be the temple of Anaitis. But it is also possible that it may be a fortification. Or it may be a place of Christian worship, as the first Christians often chose remote and wild places to make an impression on the mind. Or if it was a heathen temple, there is such a multitude of divinities to whom it may have been dedicated that the chance of its being a temple of Anaitis is hardly anything. 'Tis like throwing a grain of sand upon the sea-shore today and thinking you may find it tomorrow. No, this temple, like many an ill-built edifice, tumbles down before 'tis roofed in." He had a kind of *conceit* in his discourse; for after Mr. Macqueen spoke of an altar, he said, "Mr. Macqueen is fighting *pro aris et focis*."[12]

It was wonderful how well time passed in a remote castle and in dreary weather. After supper, we talked of Pennant. It was objected that he was superficial. Mr. Johnson defended him warmly. He said, "Pennant has greater variety of inquiry than almost any man, and has told us more than perhaps one in ten thousand could have done in the time that he took. He has not said what he was to tell; so you cannot find fault with him for what he has not told. If a man comes to look for fishes, you cannot blame him if he does not attend to fowls." "But," said Col. MacLeod, "he mentions the unreasonable rise of rents in the Highlands, and says 'the gentlemen are for emptying the bag, without filling it'; for that is the phrase he uses. Why

---

[12] "For his altars and fires"—i.e., his hearth and home.

does he not tell how to fill it?" JOHNSON. "Sir, there is no end of negative criticism. He tells what he observes, and as much as he chooses. If he tells what is not true, you may find fault with him. But though he tells that the land is not well culti- vated, he is not obliged to tell how it may be well cultivated. If I tell that many of the Highlanders go barefooted, I am not obliged to tell how they may get shoes. Pennant tells a fact. He need go no farther except he pleases. He exhausts nothing. And no subject whatever has yet been exhausted. But Pennant has surely told a great deal. Here is a man six foot high, and you're angry because he is not seven." This was a capital *Oratio pro Pennantio*. But still I think he had better have given more attention to fewer things, than thrown together such a number of imperfect accounts. But I[13] think with diffidence.

SATURDAY 18 SEPTEMBER. At breakfast Lady Mac- Leod complained of the difficulties under which the family now laboured. "Madam," said Mr. Johnson, "consider what a son you have. He is as fine a young gentleman as I ever knew since I came into this world. I never knew any one who at his age had advanced his understanding so much." Before break- fast Mr. Johnson came up to my room to forbid me to mention that this was his birthday; but I told him I had done it already, at which he was displeased, I suppose from wishing to have nothing particular done on his account. MacLeod was not pres- ent when Mr. Johnson gave his mother the high character of him. But I told him of it, as I knew it would confirm him in his laudable resolutions. The lady and I got into a warm dispute. She wanted to build a house upon a farm which she has taken, about five miles from the old castle, and to make gardens and everything fine there. All of which I approved of; but insisted that the seat of the family should always be upon the rock of Dunvegan. "Ay," said Mr. Johnson, "in time we'll build all round this rock. You may make a very good house at the farm, but it must not be such as to tempt the Laird of MacLeod to

---

[13] The MS is defective. "But I" has been "with diffidence" supplied by the editors.

go thither to reside. Most of the great families of England have a secondary house, which is called a jointure-house; let this be of that kind." The lady insisted that the rock was very inconvenient. That there was no place near it where a good garden could be made; that it must always be a rude place; that it was Herculean labour to make a dinner here; that the climate was such that one might have half an hour fair now and then, though it rained in general; and therefore one should be close to where the farm is. Said Mr. Johnson, "The Laird will not mind being wet. No, we'll keep the old rock, and we'll have an armoury, though Sir Alexander Macdonald said that arms would rust." I was very keen. I was vexed to find the alloy of modern refinement in a lady who had so much old family spirit. "Madam," said I, "if once you quit this rock, this centre of gravity, there is no knowing where you may settle. You move five miles first; then to St. Andrews, as the late Laird did; then to Edinburgh; and so on till you end at Hampstead, or in France. No, no; keep to the rock. It is the very jewel of the estate. It looks as if it had been let down from heaven by the four corners, to be the residence of a chief. Have all the comforts and conveniencies of life upon it; but never leave Rorie More's cascade." "But," said she, "is it not enough if we keep it? Must we never be more convenient than Rorie More was? He had his beef brought to dinner in one basket and his bread in another. Why not as well be Rorie More all over as live upon his rock? And would not we tire of looking perpetually on this rock?" "No, madam," said I, "your eye will never wear away the old rock." Said she, "It is very well for you, who have a fine place and everything easy, to talk so, and think of chaining honest folks to a rock. You would not live upon it yourself." "Yes, madam," said I, "I would live upon it were I Laird of MacLeod, and would be unhappy if I were not upon it." Said Mr. Johnson, with a strong voice and most determined manner: "Madam, rather than quit the old rock, Boswell would live in the pit. He'd make his bedchamber

in the dungeon." I felt a degree of elation at finding my resolute feudal enthusiasm thus confirmed by such a sanction. The
lady was puzzled a little. She still returned to her pretty farm,
rich ground, fine garden. "Madam," said Mr. Johnson, "were
it in Asia, I would not leave the rock." The lady was rational
in her notions to a certain degree. But the ancient family residence must be a primary object; and if the situation is in a place
where there can be little done in farming or gardening, it has,
besides the veneration acquired by the mere lapse of time during which the family has lived here, many circumstances of
natural grandeur suited to the seat of a Highland chief. It has
the sea—islands—rocks—hills—a noble cascade. And when the
family is again in opulence, much may be done by art.

Mr. Donald Macqueen went away today, in order to preach
at Bracadale next day, as the minister there was to go and
preach for him. We were so comfortably placed at Dunvegan
that Mr. Johnson could hardly be moved from it. I proposed
to him that we should leave it on Monday. "No, sir," said he.
"I'll not go before Wednesday. I'll have some more of this
good." However, as the weather was at this season so bad and
so very uncertain, and we had a good deal to do yet, Mr.
Macqueen and I prevailed with him to agree to set out on Monday if the day should be good. Mr. Macqueen, though it was
inconvenient for him to be away from his harvest, engaged to
wait on Monday at Ullinish for us. When he was going away,
Mr. Johnson said, "I shall ever retain a great regard for you."
Then asked him if he had the *Rambler*. Mr. Macqueen said no,
but his brother had it. JOHNSON. "Have you the *Idler*?" "No,
sir." JOHNSON. "Then I'll order one for you at Edinburgh, which
you will keep in remembrance of me." Mr. Macqueen was
much pleased with this. He expressed himself in the strongest
terms as to his admiration of Mr. Johnson's wonderful knowledge, and every other quality for which he is distinguished.
I asked Mr. Macqueen if he was satisfied to be a minister in
Skye. He said he was. But he owned that his forefathers hav-

ing been so long there, and he himself being born there, made a chief ingredient in his contentment. I should have mentioned that, on our left hand, between Portree and Dr. MacLeod's, Mr. Macqueen told me there had been a college of the Knights Templars; that tradition said so, and that there was a ruin remaining of their church, which had been burnt. I must get him to explain this better. Mr. Johnson has weakened my belief in remote tradition. In the dispute about Anaitis, Mr. Macqueen said Asia Minor was peopled by Scythians, and as they were the ancestors of the Celts, the same religion might be in Asia Minor and Skye. Said Mr. Johnson, "What can a nation that has not letters tell of its original? I have always difficulty to be patient when I hear authors gravely quoted as giving accounts of savage nations, which accounts they had from the savages themselves. What can the Macraes tell about themselves a thousand years ago? There is no tracing ancient nations but by language, and therefore I'm always sorry when language is lost, because languages are the pedigree of nations. If you find the same language in distant countries, you may be sure that the inhabitants of each have been the same people; that is to say, if you find the languages a good deal the same; for finding a word here and there will not do; as *Hudibras*, by way of ridicule, finds the word *penguin* in the Straits of Magellan, signifying a bird with a white head; and that word has the signification in Wales of a whiteheaded wench: *pen*, head, *guin*, white; therefore the people near the Straits of Magellan are Welsh."

A young gentleman of the name of Maclean, nephew to the Laird of the Isle of Muck, came this morning; and just as we sat down to dinner, came the Laird of the Isle of Muck himself; his lady, sister to Talisker; a Miss Maclean, his niece; a Miss Macqueen, a relation (both of them young girls); and a Miss Mally MacLeod, daughter of the late Hammer, who wrote a treatise on the second sight, etc., under the designation of Theophilus Insulanus. She was, as I was told, past sixty; but affected[1] youthfulness. It was curious to hear the Laird called by his title. "Muck" would not do well, but he was called "Isle of Muck," which went off with great readiness. His lady was called Mrs. Maclean. He was a hearty High-lander, and his lady a cheerful woman as could be. We were immediately quite easy with them; and Mr. Johnson, hearing that their island lay between Skye and Mull, cried, "We'll go to the Isle of Muck." They offered us a hearty welcome, but as we found out that it would be inconvenient for them to go home so soon as our time required, we laid aside the scheme. The name is ugly, though it is worse as now written; the Erse is *Mouack*,[2] the sow's island, and Buchanan calls it *Insula Porcorum*. It is so called from its form. Some call it Isle of *Monk*. The Laird insists on this. It was formerly church lands belonging to Icolmkill, and a hermit lived in it. It is two miles long, and about three-quarters of a mile broad. The Laird said he had sevenscore of souls upon it. Last year he had fourscore children inoculated; some of them indeed were eighteen years of age. He agreed with a surgeon to come and do it at half-a-crown a head. It is very fertile in corn. They export some; and its coasts abound in fish. A tailor comes there six times in a year. They get a good blacksmith from the isle of Eigg when they want him. It was after supper before these particulars were told us. This addition to our society had just landed from the Long Island.[3] In the evening we had an excellent dance, but Mr. Johnson did not come to it. Neither did he come to supper for these two last nights, but only joined us after supper. Tonight he supped.

SUNDAY 19 SEPTEMBER. It was rather worse weather than any that we have had yet. At breakfast Mr. Johnson said that some cunning men chose fools for their wives, thinking to

---

[1] Conjectural; defect in the MS.

[2] Gaelic *muc*. Boswell means that "Island of the Pigs" is ugly to those who understand the Gaelic, but that the name would not be so ugly to English-speaking people if it were not assimilated by its spelling to an ugly English word.

[3] Not a single island, but another name for the Outer Hebrides

manage them; but they always failed. "There is a spaniel fool and a mule fool. The spaniel fool may be made to do by beating. The mule fool will neither do by words nor blows; and suppose a fool to be made do pretty well, you must have the continual trouble of making her do. Depend upon it, no woman is the worse for sense and knowledge." Whether he meant merely to say a polite thing, or to give his opinion, I could not be sure; but he said men knew that women were an overmatch for them; and therefore they chose the weakest or most ignorant. If they did not think so, they never could be afraid of women knowing as much as themselves. I must have this more amply discussed with him.

He came to my room this morning before breakfast to read my Journal, which he has done all along. He often before said, "I take great delight in reading it." Today he said, "You improve. It grows better and better." I said there was a danger of my getting a habit of writing in a slovenly manner. "Sir," said he, "it is not written in a slovenly manner. It might be printed, were the subject fit for printing."[1] He sat in his room with a volume of Lord Bacon's works, the *Decay of Christian Piety*, Monboddo's *Origin of Language*, and Sterne's sermons beside him, while Mr. Bethune preached in the dining-room. We had some of the neighbours assembled. There was just an ordinary Presbyterian forenoon's service, which was very decent, and which is always here when the family cannot go to church. He asked me today how we were so little together. I told him my Journal took up so much time. But at the same time, it is curious that although I will run from one end of London to another to have an hour with him, I should omit to seize any spare time to be in his company when I am in the house with him. But my Journal is really a task of much time and labour, and Mr. Johnson forbids me to contract it.

I omitted to mention that Mr. Johnson told Mr. Macqueen

---

[1] "As I have faithfully recorded so many minute particulars, I hope I shall be pardoned for inserting so flattering an encomium on what is now offered to the public."—BOSWELL.

that he had found the belief of the second sight universal in Skye, except among the clergy, who seemed determined against it. I took the liberty to say to Mr. Macqueen that the clergy were actuated by a kind of vanity. Say they, "The world takes us to be credulous men in a remote corner. We'll show them that we are more enlightened than they think." The worthy man said that his disbelief of it was from his not finding sufficient evidence. But I could perceive that he was prejudiced against it.

After dinner today we talked of the extraordinary fact of Lady Grange's being sent to St. Kilda.[2] Mr. Johnson said, "If MacLeod would let it be known that he had such a place for naughty ladies, he might make it a very profitable island." We had in the course of our tour heard of St. Kilda poetry. Mr. Johnson said, "It must be very poor, because they have very few images." "But," said I, "there may be a poetical genius to combine these, and in short to make poetry of them." "But, sir," said he, "a man cannot make fire but in proportion as he has wood. He cannot coin guineas but in proportion as he has gold." He came the length this day of contracting Monboddo and calling him "Mony." This was a piece of kindness, for he does so to all his friends. At tea he talked of his intending to go to Italy in 1775. MacLeod said he would like Paris better.[3] Mr. Johnson said there was none of the *literati* now alive to see

[2] "The true story of this lady, which happened in this century, is as frightfully romantic as if it had been the fiction of a gloomy fancy. She was the wife of one of the Lords of Session in Scotland, a man of the very first blood of his country. For some mysterious reasons, which have never been discovered, she was seized and carried off in the dark, she knew not by whom, and by nightly journeys was conveyed to the Highland shores, from whence she was transported by sea to the remote rock of St. Kilda, where she remained, amongst its few wild inhabitants, a forlorn prisoner, but had a constant supply of provisions, and a woman to wait on her. No inquiry was made after her, till she at last found means to convey a letter to a confidential friend, by the daughter of a Catechist, who concealed it in a clew of yarn. Information being thus obtained at Edinburgh, a ship was sent to bring her off; but intelligence of this being received, she was conveyed to MacLeod's island of Harris, where she died."—BOSWELL. The latter part of this note is omitted in this edition. St. Kilda, an island in the Outer Hebrides, is now entirely abandoned, the Government having brought the remaining inhabitants to the mainland in 1930.

[3] As readers of the *Life of Johnson* know, he visited Paris in the autumn of 1775; but his trip to Italy with the Thrales, planned for the spring of 1776, was postponed because of the death of the Thrales' son, and was never realized.

whom he would cross a sea. He said he could find in Buffon's book all that he could say.[4]

After supper he said he was sorry that prize-fighting was gone out; that every art should be preserved, and the art of defence was important; that it was absurd that our soldiers should have swords and not be taught the use of them; that prize-fighting made people accustomed not to be alarmed at seeing their own blood, or feeling a little pain from a wound. He said the heavy claymore was an ill-contrived weapon. A man could only strike once with it. It employed both his hands, and he must of course be soon fatigued with wielding it; so that if his antagonist can only keep playing awhile, he is sure of him. He said, "I'd fight with a dirk against Rorie More's sword. I could ward off a blow with a dirk, and then run in upon my enemy. When within that heavy sword, I have him. He's quite helpless, and I could stab him at my leisure, like a calf." He said it was thought by sensible military people that the English did not enough avail themselves of their superior strength of body against the French; for that must always have a great advantage in pushing with bayonets; that he had heard an officer say that if women could be made to stand, they'd do as well as men in a mere interchange of bullets from a distance; but if a body of men should come close up to 'em, then, to be sure, they must be overcome. "Now," said he, "in the same manner the weaker-bodied French must be overcome by our strong soldiers."

He said as to duelling that there is no case in England where one or other *must* die; that if you have overcome your adversary either by killing him or disarming him, your honour, or the honour of your family, is restored, as much as it can be by a duel. That it would be cowardly to make a man renew the combat when you know that you have the advantage of him.

---

[4] "I doubt the justice of my fellow-traveller's remark concerning the French literati, many of whom, I am told, have considerable merit in conversation, as well as in their writings. That of Monsieur de Buffon, in particular, I am well assured is highly instructive and entertaining."—BOSWELL.

You might just as well go and cut his throat while he's asleep in his bed. That when a duel begins, it is supposed there may be an equality; because it is not always skill that prevails. "It depends much on presence of mind; nay, on accidents. The wind may be in a man's face—he may fall—many such things may decide the superiority. A man is punished by being called out and subjected to the risk that is in a duel." But as I suggested that the injured person is equally subjected to risk, Mr. Johnson owned he could not explain the rationality of duelling.

I was under the greatest apprehensions for fear of the itch, which is really very common in these parts (especially among the young people), and very little minded. I this day perceived several pimples or rather blisters on the palm of my right hand, which were hot, painful, and itchy; but I was assured it never began so. I was, however, uneasy. The horror of having so vile a distemper and carrying it home made me shudder. I may appear to talk in too strong terms of a *minor* disease. But I feel what I write. As yet in the Highlands I was only bit with fleas at Anoch and Glenelg, and when changing my shirt at Armadale I found what I thought a *bug* sticking fast on my left arm. Perhaps it was some other sucking animal.[5]

MONDAY 20 SEPTEMBER. When I awaked, the storm was higher still. I read some of Pennant's *Tour* in bed, and was very well pleased. I have read little here. Indeed I have been always writing. I found in my closet a large Prayer-Book and Bible and Apocrypha with prints, all in one volume. I read in it daily. The storm abated about nine, and the sun shone; but it rained again soon, and it was not a day for travelling. At breakfast, Mr. Johnson told us that there was once a pretty good tavern in Catherine Street, where very good company met in an evening, and each man called for his own half-pint of wine, or gill, if he pleased; they were frugal men, and no-

---

[5] This paragraph was omitted in the published *Tour*. The prevalence of vermin in the Eighteenth Century has certainly been exaggerated. This passage shows that Boswell, at the age of thirty-three, had never had scabies and was familiar neither with the habits nor the appearance of "bugs."

body paid but for what he himself drank. The house furnished no supper, but a woman attended with mutton pies, which anybody might have. Mr. Johnson was introduced to this company by Cumming the Quaker, and used to go there sometimes when he drank wine. He said that in the last age, when his mother lived in London, there were two sets of people, those who gave the wall and those who took it; the peaceable and the quarrelsome. When he returned to Lichfield after having been in London, his mother asked him whether he was one of those who gave the wall, or those who took it. Now it is fixed that every man keeps to the right; or, if one is taking the wall, another yields it, and it is never a dispute. He was very severe on Lady Macdonald; he said he would have her sent to St. Kilda. She was as bad as negative badness could be, and stood in the way of what was good. That insipid beauty would not go a great way, and that such a woman might be cut out of a cabbage, if there was a skilful artificer.

MacLeod was too late in coming to breakfast. Mr. Johnson said laziness was worse than the toothache. "No," said I, "a basin of cold water or a horse-whip will cure laziness." "No," said Mr. Johnson, "it will only put off the fit; it will not cure the disease. I have been trying to cure laziness all my life, and could not do it." "But," said I, "if a man does in a shorter time what might be the labour of a life, there is nothing to be said." JOHNSON. "Suppose that flattery to be true, the world has nothing to say to a man; but that will not justify him to himself."

After breakfast he said a Highland chief should now endeavour to do everything to raise his rents by means of the industry of his people; that formerly it was right to have his house full of idle people—they were his defenders, his servants, his dependants, his friends. "Now they may be better employed. The system of things is now so much altered that the family cannot have influence but by riches, because it has no longer the power. An individual of a family may have it; but it cannot now belong to the family unless you could have a perpetuity of men with the same views. One man like Sir Alexander destroys what twenty ancestors have gained. MacLeod has four times the land that the Duke of Bedford has. I think with his views he may in time make himself the greatest man in the King's dominions, for land may always be improved to a certain degree. And," said he, "don't sell land to throw money into the funds, as is done, or to try any other species of trade. Depend upon it, this rage of trade will destroy itself. You and I shall not see it, but the time will come when there will be an end on't. Trade is like gaming. If a whole company are gamesters, it must cease, for there is nothing to be won. When all nations are traders, there is nothing to be gained by trade. And it will stop the soonest where it is brought to the greatest perfection. Then, only the proprietors of land will be the great men." I said it was hard for MacLeod to find ingratitude in so many of his people. "Sir," said he, "gratitude is a fruit of great cultivation. You do not find it among gross people." I should doubt of this. Nature seems to have implanted it. The lion mentioned by Valerius Maximus[1] had it. I should think culture, which brings luxury and selfishness with it, may weaken the principle or passion of gratitude. This too must be discussed.

Mr. Johnson said this morning, when talking of our setting out, that he was in the state that Lord Bacon represents kings. He desired the end but did not like the means. He wished much to get home, but was unwilling to travel in Skye. "And," said I, "you are like kings too in this, that you must act under the direction of others."

This day (half an hour past three) I have brought up my Journal to a minute, at least to this very forenoon. We had at dinner Ullinish and ———. I must observe that Mr. Johnson read all my Journal to the foot of the preceding page, and said to me, "It is a very pretty Journal." It has therefore his sanction, and I am encouraged to go on. After dinner he let me

---

[1] *Sic* in the first edition, but changed to Aulus Gellius in the third, with a reference in a footnote: Aul. Gellius, Lib. v., c. xiv.

copy his *Ode on Skye*. There was a dance at night; but I kept out of the way, and danced only one reel before supper. We were more jovial than ordinary tonight, and sat up till two in the morning. But there was no excess. The weather had changed, and it was to be our last night here.

TUESDAY 21 SEPTEMBER. Never was I so long of hearing from my dear wife as I have been now. Her last letter was dated the 1st of this month. She could write but once a week, and her letter of the 8th instant had not been sent on to Dunvegan. I could not help being uneasy. Mr. Johnson has the advantage of me, in having no wife or child to occasion anxious apprehensions in his mind. It was a good morning, so we resolved to set out.

We have truly had a very comfortable residence at Dunvegan. The castle is upon a rock just upon the sea-shore. It was inaccessible every way but by a stair on the side near the sea, till the late Laird built a stair of two-and-twenty steps on the land side. On the right hand after you come up this stair is an old tower, to which is joined a large building four storeys high, which it is said was here when Leod, the first of this family, came from the Isle of Man and married the heiress of the MacCrails, the ancient possessors, and conquered as much as married.[1] He was *felix* both *bella gerere* et *nubere*. He was like the heroes mentioned by John Home in his *Agis*:

> "They sack'd the cities," etc.[2]

---

[1] Leod lived in the 13th century; but archaeological investigation has shown that the portion of the castle which Boswell here describes does not antedate the 14th century. (See *Proc. Soc. of Antiquaries of Scotland*, xxix.255–6.)

[2] "This facile temper of the beauteous sex
Great Agamemnon, brave Pelides, proved:
They sack'd the cities, and they slew the sires,
The brothers, and the lovers of the fair,
Who weep'd awhile, then wiped their wat'ry eyes,
And lost their sorrows in the hero's arms."
                                                    —*Agis*, Act IV.

"*Felix* both *bella gerere* et *nubere*" (fortunate both in war and marriage) is adapted from a famous epigram on the policy of Austria: "Let others wage wars; do thou, O fortunate Austria, give thyself in marriage. For the kingdoms which Mars gives to others, Venus gives to thee." Wittenberg, Boswell's German translator, was shocked by Boswell's Latin; *nubere*, as he points out, can properly be applied only to females.

John Breck, the grandfather of the late Laird, began to repair it or rather complete it. He, like some of those who had their epitaphs written before they died, had an inscription cut upon a large stone above one of the lower windows, of which I have a copy. It was composed by Mr. Dugald Macpherson,[3] the parish minister. On the left hand after you come up this stair is a large building along the top of the rock with a —— and a row of false cannon of stone.[4] This was one of the oldest parts of what was built upon the rock that was ever inhabited. Adjoining to it is a square tower in which is the drawing-room. There has been a wall here along the edge of the rock. Part of it remains and is covered with ivy. On the opposite corner is the remains of another tower, which was formed by the late Laird into a pigeon-house above and a little-house below. These towers are said to be the oldest buildings here. A square is formed along the rock by buildings of different kinds, by the late Laird: lodging rooms, kitchen, servants' apartments. But all of them are in sad disrepair. The court or close, clear of the buildings—that is to say, within them—is thirty canes long and thirteen broad. I shall have my cane measured, which will ascertain the number of feet.[5] Rorie More's horn is ten inches in circumference at the root. In length, following the curves, two feet; black for about three inches next the top, and sharp there. Mr. Johnson laid me half-a-crown I should not show him so large a horn in the Lothians. I was wrong in my description of the carving on the silver mouth of it. It has alternate circles filled up with plaited work and a beast which I took to be a griffin with a ribbon or —— between, thus:[6] This scratch will serve to help out the idea. The bow is five feet eight inches. The claymore, from the knob to the guard,

---

[3] The name has been filled in by the editors. Mr. Macpherson was minister of Duirinish from 1684 until 1717.

[4] These false cannon serve as gargoyles. Boswell's blank should perhaps be filled with *parapet*.

[5] See p. 179, n. 4.

[6] Boswell's crude sketch of the decoration of the horn is omitted. See the photograph and drawing, *Proc. Soc. of Antiquaries of Scotland*, xlvii.110, 115.

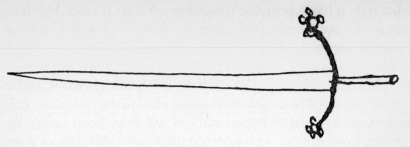

thirteen inches and a half; from the guard to the point, full three feet. Rorie More was not denominated "More" from his size, but from his great spirit. I had the true ancient spirit in this castle. There is, under the shade of the rock on the———, two rows of sycamores planted by the late Laird, which grow pretty well; and from the drawing-room window you see a few ashes and other trees also planted by him. Before the castle on the land side, nothing is to be seen but wild hills interspersed with humps of whin-rock. The gradation of them begins directly. The cascade is grand; and on the——— and ——— there are some good spots of ground which might be cultivated. The sea before the castle is curiously broken with islands and necks of land. The late Laird planted the Island of ———. But it was neglected in his absence, and cattle destroyed the trees. There is a well in the court of the castle. There is an inn at Dunvegan, as it is a convenient port for the Long Island. There is a blind man here who has been thirty years in the house. He was blind since he was three years of age, and he carries china and everything else quite safely. I cannot enough praise the genteel hospitality with which we were treated. The lady had sense and most meritorious resolution. She told me she believed she never would leave Dunvegan, so heroically resolved is she to retrieve the family. Miss Bell, the youngest daughter, appeared a few times. But Miss MacLeod and Miss Nanny were always with us. They had lived much in Hampshire, and had the agreeable language and manners of English girls. As I left Dunvegan, I warmly wished for the prosperity of the family. In the state in which it now is, it is like Corsica in miniature; at least it resembles it in struggling to emerge from distress, and in having a chief of singular merit.

MacLeod and Talisker set out with us. We passed by the parish church, Duirinish. The churchyard is not enclosed, but a pretty murmuring brook runs along one quarter of it. In it is a pyramid erected to the memory of Thomas, Lord Lovat, by his son Lord Simon, who suffered on Tower Hill. It is of freestone, and I suppose about thirty feet high. There is upon it a square piece of marble with the arms of Lovat, and on the base a larger piece with an inscription on it, which I am persuaded was the composition of Lord Lovat himself, being quite his style—full of vainglory as to his own family and flattery of the MacLeods. I took a copy of it, which is to be found on the last page of this volume.[7] Mr. Johnson said it was poor stuff, such as[8] Lord Lovat's butler might have written; and he justly stigmatized Lovat's character, and repeated some good verses from one of the magazines on the several personages who suffered in 1745. (This he did at Ullinish. I shall look for the verses.)[9]

I saw a strange thing in this churchyard: a parcel of people assembled at a funeral before the grave was dug; and there was the coffin with the corpse in it lying on the grass, while the people alternately lent a hand in making a grave. One man at a little distance was busy cutting a turf for it with the crooked spade which is used in Skye, a very awkward instrument. The iron part of it is like a plough coulter. It has just a rude tree for a handle, and a good way up a pin is placed for the foot to press upon. It is somewhat in this form:[10] I was told, however, that the usual way is to have a grave previously dug by the kirk officer. I could not help having a fallacious feeling for the corpse which was kept so long waiting.

---

[7] This does not appear in the MS as we have it, but is given in the published *Tour*.

[8] Inadvertently omitted.

[9] Boswell found them in the *Gentleman's Magazine* for April 1747. They are given in the *Life of Johnson*, i. 180–1.

[10] Boswell's sketch is omitted.

I observed today that the usual way of carrying home their grain here is in loads on horseback. They have also a few sledges, or *cars* as they are called in Ayrshire, clumsily made and rarely used. They are made of two crooked trees. Two ends drag on the ground; two lean on a horse, one on each side, like the ————[11] of a cart or chaise; and for a good way there are cross bars between them and a back of sticks. It is hardly worth while to draw it, but I shall scratch a little:[12]

We went a mile off the road to Ullinish and viewed Mac-Leod's farm, which is a very large and beautiful one upon the sea-coast, a peninsula or great neck of land. Mr. Johnson said it was quite an English farm. We got to Ullinish about six; found a very good farm-house of two storeys. Ullinish himself, a plain honest man in brown, much like an English Justice. His daughter, who was never out of Skye, a very well-bred girl.

We talked of Phipps's voyage to the North Pole. Mr. Johnson said it was conjectured that our former navigators have kept too near land, and so have found the sea frozen far north, because the land hinders the free motion of the tides; but, in the wide ocean, where the waves tumble at their full convenience, it is imagined that the frost does not take effect.

Though we came so late, we had dinner, tea, and supper. I had a good room at night. Several books lay on the head of an escritoire. The *Scots Acts*, Bankton's *Institutions*, Milton's *Poems*, *Fingal*, some of the works of Dryden, etc. Mr. Donald Macqueen slept in a closet by me.

WEDNESDAY 22 SEPTEMBER. Donald MacLeod, who had gone to Bracadale to get us £30 for my bill, had not yet returned. This looked odd. An express was sent last night for him, but word came that he was gone to Portree. We were also informed that he had been mortally drunk, had been throwing away money, and had some stolen from him. This was offensive, as Mr. Johnson said. I was vexed at first, thinking

[11] Blank in the MS. The word Boswell could not recall was no doubt *thills*.
[12] Boswell's sketch is omitted.

myself to blame for having trusted such a man. But when I considered that I did not know of his failings, and saw him received everywhere, I found that I might make myself easy in what concerned the imputation of folly. Talisker dispatched a baron-officer with a letter to him and another to James Macdonald at Portree, that if any money remained, it might be had for us. All however despaired of our recovering any; not because the man was dishonest, for he was never suspected of that, but because when he drank he became quite extravagant.

In the morning I walked out and saw the ship, the *Margaret of Clyde*, fairly pass by with a number of emigrants on board. It was a kind of melancholy sight. After breakfast we walked to see a subterraneous house about a short mile off. Mr. Johnson and Ullinish rode to it. It was upon the side of a rising ground. It was discovered by a fox's having taken up his abode in it, and in chasing him they dug into it. It was ten sticks long, following a very gentle curve till we reached the upper end, where it was choked up by the digging. However, it seemed to have been not much longer, for we got a man with a crooked spade to dig a little beyond that, and he did not find the appearance of its continuance. Besides, just adjoining to where they had dug for the fox at that end (for they had dug at both ends), we found the foundations of little stone houses, which seemed to be four feet wide, and three feet high. Ullinish's servant went in with a candle, and we followed. Mr. Johnson crept into it wonderfully. It has been fairly dug in the earth; the sides of it are faced with pebbles or whinstones of the ordinary size. The roof is formed of flagstones laid across, as in the subterraneous place at Raasay. Mr. Macqueen, who is always for making everything as ancient as possible, boasted that it was the habitation of some of the first inhabitants of the island, and what a curiosity it was to find a specimen of the houses of the aborigines here, which he believed could be found nowhere else. Mr. Johnson well observed that they who made this were not in the rudest state, for that it was more difficult to make it than to make a house; therefore, to be sure, those who made it had houses, and had this only as a hiding-place. This seems clear. It appeared to me that the vestiges of houses just by it confirmed Mr. Johnson's opinion.

We then proceeded a little way farther, to the top of a rising ground on which are the remains of what is said to have been the first residence of Leod, the ancestor of the MacLeods. We found a circular wall of ten feet in thickness, built without mortar, of very large whinstones, for raising which it seems certain that machinery had been employed. The wall is admirably built, and the stone is everlasting. Some of it seemed to be almost iron. One of the stones, which composed one side of the door or entry, had the very look almost of solid iron, and when I struck it, it sounded like a smith's anvil. I saw on each side of the entry an opening in which the bolt of this fortress had run. It was found some years ago sunk in the ground. It was of iron, very thick and long. A coulter for a plough and several spades were made of it. It was a pity to destroy it. The diameter of the circle within the walls is forty feet. (When I am precise in dimensions, it is from actual measurement.) Mr. Johnson believed it to be only a temporary retreat. Indeed, we could not perceive a well, but that may be filled up. We saw, however, the vestiges of five different houses or apartments within it. Mr. Macqueen conjectures that these were inhabited, and that the circular wall defended them. From this old tower, or dun or whatever it shall be called, is a grand view of the mouth of Loch Bracadale, and at a distance, Barra and South Uist; and on the land side, the Cuillin, a prodigious range of mountains, capped with rocks like pinnacles in a strange variety of shapes, somewhat thus:[1] They resemble the mountains near Corte, of which I have a print. They make part of a great forest for deer. Martin erroneously writes the name *Quillin*.

Many heavy showers fell when we were out. When we got

---

[1] Sketch omitted. There is a fine plate showing these mountains in Dr. Hill's *Footsteps of Dr. Johnson*, facing p. 204.

home, dinner was on the table; so instead of setting out for Talisker, as we intended, without dining, we took a good meal, after which we were going to take boat to depart; but it was reconsidered, and found too late. Upon which we determined to employ the afternoon in seeing what we could here. Ullinish carried us in his boat down to the shore of an island[2] possessed by him, but to which there is access by land when the sea is out. The coast is an exceeding high rock. But there is first a stratum of rocky substance, not very high. We scrambled up that and went into an immense cave, an *antrum immane* indeed, much more so than that of the Sibyl to which that description is annexed by Virgil. It is one hundred and eighty feet long, thirty feet broad where it is broadest, and from twenty to thirty in other places. Mr. Johnson thought it only twenty feet high, but most of us thought it thirty; some, forty. By throwing stones to the roof of it, I guessed it to be at least thirty. Near to it is another large cave, parallel with the sea and open at both ends; and nearer Ullinish, another in the same direction with the immense one, very near a circle, but not high in the roof. I forget its size, but it was considerable. The immense cave, we were told, had a remarkable echo, but we found none. They said it was owing to the great rains having made it damp. There were several continued droppings, or rather runnings, from the roof. We sailed a little farther down the shore, and saw a singular appearance: a piece of rock standing by itself like the front wall of an old castle, with an opening like a window quite through it, which has been made by the beating of wind and rain within these seven years; for Ullinish and his son both remember when it was not there.

Mr. Johnson had never catched any fish in the sea. Two little girls were fishing from a rock. We borrowed their lines, and Mr. Johnson drew one or two cuddies, but he let them go again.[3] I saw as we walked from the shore a mineral spring,

---

[2] The Island of Wiay.
[3] Johnson's fishing, with much else in this part of the MS, was omitted from the printed *Tour*.

very strong of steel, or rather iron. There is a plentiful garden at Ullinish, and several trees; and just above the house is a hill, called ———, "the hill of strife," where Mr. Macqueen says justice was of old administered. It is like the *mons placiti*, the Moots hill of Scone, or those *laws*, as we call them on the south of Tay, such as North Berwick Law and several others. It is curious that it should happen now to be just by the sheriff's residence.

While we were at dinner, snow had fallen on Cuillin, so that the mountainous parts were white; and there was a good deal of hail while we were on the sea. I was glad to get safe home, for some of the boatmen, whether in earnest or not I cannot tell, said, before we took boat, that they heard an English ghost cry; and my superstition and fear are both easily excited.

The sheriff had excellent peats, and the evening went on admirably. Mr. Johnson said the Lords Orrery, till this, have been writers. The first wrote several plays. The second[4] was Bentley's antagonist; the third[5] wrote the Life of Swift, and several other pieces. His son Hamilton, Earl of Orrery, wrote several papers in the *Adventurer* and *World*. He said he knew well Swift's Lord Orrery. He was a feeble-minded man. He was much hurt by the counter-Life written by Delany. Mr. Johnson comforted him by saying they were both right. He had seen most of the good side of Swift, my lord of the bad. MacLeod asked if it was not wrong in Orrery to expose the defects of a man with whom he lived in intimacy. MR. JOHNSON. "Why no, sir, after the man is dead, and it is done historically." He said if Lord Orrery had been rich, he would have been a very liberal patron. That his conversation was like his writing, neat and elegant, but without strength. That he grasped at more than his abilities could reach. Tried to pass for a better talker, and a better writer, and a better thinker than he was. He said there was a quarrel between him and his son Hamilton, in which my lord was criminal, because it arose

---

[4] Actually the fourth earl; Boswell or Johnson was mistaken.
[5] Actually the fifth earl.

from Hamilton's not allowing his wife to keep company with my lord's mistress. My lord showed his resentment in his will[6] —leaving his library by his son, because he could not make use of it, or something to that purpose.[7]

I mentioned my lord's affectation of ending all his letters about Swift in different ways, and never "I am, etc.," (an observation which I have heard Sheridan make); and that a foreign lady said to me that this was peculiar to, or at least most frequent among, the English. I took up a volume of Dryden, containing *The Conquest of Granada*, *Amboyna*, *The Assignation*, etc., and all of the dedications had such conclusions. Mr. Johnson said it was more elegant than "I am." He said when addressing the Duke of York, the mode Dryden used was more respectful. I agreed that *there* it was better. It was making his escape from the royal presence with a genteel sudden timidity, in place of having the resolution to stand still and make a formal bow.

Orrery's attack on his son in his will led us to talk of the dispositions a man should have when dying. I said I did not see why a man should alter his behaviour to those whom he thought ill of when well, merely because he was dying. Mr. Johnson said, "I should not scruple to speak against a party when dying; but not against an individual." He said it was told of Sixtus Quintus that on his death-bed, in the intervals of his last pangs, he signed death-warrants. Mr. Macqueen said he should not do so. He would have more tenderness of heart. Said Mr. Johnson, "I believe I should not either; but Mr. Macqueen and I are cowards. It would not be from tenderness of heart, for the heart

---

[6] There is an error here, corrected in the printed *Tour*, which reads: "There was a quarrel between him and his father, in which his father was to blame; because it arose from the son's not allowing his wife to keep company with his father's mistress. The old lord showed his resentment in his will," etc.

[7] Croker quotes the relevant section of the will: "Having never observed that my son hath showed much taste or inclination, either for the entertainment or knowledge which study and learning afford, I give and bequeath all my books and mathematical instruments . . . to Christ Church College in Oxford, &c.: my said son, within two years next after my decease, taking thereout, and which I do hereby give him for his sole use and benefit, such books relating to the English constitution and parliamentary affairs, as he shall think fit to make choice of."

is as tender when a man is in health as when sick, though his resolution may be stronger. Sixtus Quintus was a sovereign as well as a priest, and if the criminals deserved death, he was doing his duty to the last. You would not think a judge died ill who should be carried off by an apoplectic fit while pronouncing sentence of death. Consider a class of men whose business it is to distribute death—soldiers, who die scattering bullets. Nobody thinks they die ill on that account."

Talking of biography, he said he did not know any literary man's life in England well-written. It should tell us his studies, his manner of life, the means by which he attained to excellence, his opinion of his own works, and such particulars. He said he had sent Derrick to Dryden's relations, and he believed Derrick had got all he should have got, but it was nothing. He said he had a kindness for Derrick, and was sorry he was dead.

His notion as to the poems given by Macpherson as the works of Ossian, was confirmed here. Mr. Macqueen always evaded the point, saying that Mr. Macpherson's pieces fell far short of what he knew in Erse, and were said to be Ossian's. Said Mr. Johnson, "I hope they do. I am not disputing that you may have poetry of great merit, but that Macpherson's is not a translation from ancient poetry. You do not believe it. I say before you, you do not believe it, though you are very willing that the world should believe it." Mr. Macqueen could not answer to this. Said Mr. Johnson, "I look upon Macpherson's *Fingal* to be as gross an imposition as ever the world was troubled with. Had it been really an ancient work, a true specimen how men thought at that time, it would have been a curiosity of the first rate. As a modern production, it is nothing."

Mr. Johnson said he could never get the meaning of an Erse song. They told him the chorus was generally unmeaning. "I take it," said he, "they are like a song which I remember. It was composed in Queen Elizabeth's time on the Earl of Essex, and the burthen was

Radaratwo, radarati, radaratadara tandore."

"But," said Mr. Macqueen, "there would be words to it which had meaning." Said Mr. Johnson, "I recollect one stanza:

> O then bespoke the prentices all,
> Living in London both proper and tall,
> For Essex's sake they would fight all.
> Radaratwo, radarati, etc."[8]

When Mr. Macqueen began again upon the beauty of Ossian's poetry, Mr. Johnson cried, "Ay, radaratwo, radarati." Mr. Rorie MacLeod, son to the sheriff, said he believed Macpherson's book to be a forgery; for that the Erse songs of Ossian which he had heard had no resemblance to Macpherson's English. Mr. Macqueen is the most obstinate man I ever found. He has not firmness of mind sufficient to break. He is like a supple willow. No sooner is he pressed down than he rises again, just where he was. He always harped on this: "Macpherson's translations are far inferior to Ossian's originals." "Yes," said I, "because they are not the same. They are inferior as a shilling is to a guinea, because they are not the same." It was really disagreeable to see how Macqueen shuffled about the matter.

THURSDAY 23 SEPTEMBER. I took Ossian down to the parlour in the morning and tried a test proposed by Mr. Rorie. Mr. Macqueen had said he had some of him in the original. I made him read what he had, which was a passage on page 50, quarto edition, and Rorie looked on with me on the English, and said it was pretty like. But when Mr. Macqueen read a description of Cuchullin's[1] sword, with a verse translation by Sir James Foulis, Rorie said that was much liker than Macpher-

---

[8] "This droll quotation, I have since found, was from a song in honour of the Earl of Essex, called *Queen Elizabeth's Champion*, which is preserved in a collection of Old Ballads, in three volumes, published in London in different years between 1720 and 1730. The full verse is as follows:

> 'Oh! then bespoke the prentices all,
> Living in London, both proper and tall,
> In a kind letter sent straight to the Queen,
> For Essex's sake they would fight all,
>> Raderer too, tandaro te,
>> Raderer, tandorer, tan do re.' "
>> —BOSWELL.

[1] Inserted later in the MS.

son's. Mr. Macqueen repeated in Erse a description of one of the horses in Cuchullin's car. Rorie said Macpherson's English was nothing like it.

When Mr. Johnson came down, I told him that Mr. Macqueen had repeated a passage pretty like; and that he himself had required Macpherson's Ossian to be no liker than Pope's Homer. "Well," said he, "this is just what I always said. He has found names, and stories, and phrases—nay passages in old songs—and with them has compounded his own compositions, and so made what he gives to the world as the translation of an ancient poem." "But," said I, "it was wrong in him to pretend that there was a poem in six books." JOHNSON. "Yes, sir. At a time too when the Highlanders knew nothing of *books* and nothing of *six*—or perhaps were got the length of counting six. We have been told, by Condamine, of a nation that could count no more than four. I'd tell Monboddo that. It would help him. There's as much charity in helping a man downhill as in helping him uphill." BOSWELL. "I don't think there's as much charity." JOHNSON. "Yes sir, if his *tendency* be downwards. Till he's at the bottom, he flounders. Get him to it, and he's quiet. Swift tells that Stella had a trick, which she learnt from Addison, to encourage a very absurd man in absurdity, rather than strive to pull him out of it."

Mr. Macqueen evaded our questions about Ossian in so strange a manner that I said if Macpherson was capitally tried for forgery, two such witnesses would hang him; because the truth that comes from an unwilling witness makes the strongest impression, gives the fullest conviction. Mr. Johnson said, "I should like to see Mr. Macqueen examined in one of our courts of justice about Ossian." Said I, "Were he to evade as he has done now, in one of our courts, he would be committed." JOHNSON. "I hope he would. Sir, he has told Blair a little more than he believes, which is published; and he sticks to it. Sir, he is so much at the head of things here that he has never been accustomed to be closely examined; and so he goes on quite smoothly." BOSWELL. "He has never had anybody to work him." JOHNSON. "No, sir. And a man is seldom disposed to work himself; though he ought to work himself, to be sure." Mr. Macqueen stood patiently by while all this passed.[2]

Mr. Johnson told us that Garrick, though accustomed to face multitudes, was so disconcerted by a new mode of appearance —as a witness in Westminster Hall—that he could not understand what was asked. It was a cause where a man claimed a *free benefit*; that is to say, a benefit without paying the expense of the house; but the meaning of it was disputed. Garrick was asked, "Sir, have you a free benefit?" "Yes." "Upon what terms have you it?" "Upon—the—terms—of—a free benefit." He was dismissed for stupidity. Mr. Johnson is often too hard on Garrick. When I asked him, going from Forres to Nairn, why he did not mention him in the Preface to Shakespeare, he said, "I would not disgrace my page with a player. Garrick has been liberally paid for mouthing Shakespeare. If I should praise him, I should much more praise the nation who paid him. He has not made Shakespeare better known.[3] He cannot illustrate Shakespeare. He does not understand him. Besides, Garrick got me no subscriptions. He did not furnish me with his old plays. I asked to have them, and I think he sent me one. It was not worth while to ask again.[4] So I have reasons enough

---

[2] "I think it but justice to say, that I believe Dr. Johnson meant to ascribe Mr. Macqueen's conduct to inaccuracy and enthusiasm, and did not mean any severe imputation against him."—BOSWELL.

[3] "It has been triumphantly asked, 'Had not the plays of Shakespeare lain dormant for many years before the appearance of Mr. Garrick? Did he not exhibit the most excellent of them frequently for thirty years together, and render them extremely popular by his own inimitable performance?' He undoubtedly did. But Dr. Johnson's assertion has been misunderstood. Knowing as well as the objectors what has been just stated, he must necessarily have meant, that Mr. Garrick did not as *a critic* make Shakespeare better known; he did not *illustrate* any one *passage* in any of his plays by acuteness of disquisition, or sagacity of conjecture: and what had been done with any degree of excellence in *that* way was the proper and immediate subject of his preface. I may add in support of this explanation the following anecdote, related to me by one of the ablest commentators [Malone] on Shakespeare, who knew much of Dr. Johnson: 'Now I have quitted the theatre,' cries Garrick, 'I will sit down and read Shakespeare.' ''Tis time you should,' exclaimed Johnson, 'for I much doubt if you ever examined one of his plays from the first scene to the last.'"—BOSWELL.

[4] Johnson's complaint was suppressed in the published *Tour*, but reappeared in the *Life*

against mentioning him, were reasons necessary. There should be reasons *for* it." I mentioned Mrs. Montagu's high praises of Garrick. JOHNSON. "It is fit she should say so much, and I should say nothing." He said Reynolds was fond of her book, and he wondered at it; for neither he nor Mrs. Thrale nor Beauclerk could get through it.[5]

Last night Mr. Johnson gave us an account of the whole process of tanning, and of the nature of milk and the various operations upon it, as making whey, etc. His variety of knowledge is quite amazing, and it gives one much satisfaction to find such a genius bestowing his attention on the useful arts. Ullinish was much struck with his knowledge; "and," said he, "he is a great orator, sir. It is music to hear this man speak." A strange thought struck me: to try if he knew anything of an art (or invention, or whatever it should be called), which is no doubt very useful in life, but which certainly lies far out of the way of a philosopher and poet—I mean the trade of a butcher. I began with observing that Banks tells us the art was not known in Otaheite; for instead of bleeding their dogs to death, they strangle them. This he told me himself; and I supposed that their hogs would certainly be slaughtered in the same way. Mr. Johnson said, "This would be owing to their not having knives, though they have sharp stones with which they can

---

of Johnson. Boswell says that Garrick assured him that he had made Johnson welcome to his library at any time; but evidently Johnson wanted to have the plays sent to him. Upon this, Boswell remarks aptly: "But indeed, considering the slovenly and careless manner in which books were treated by Johnson, it could not be expected that scarce and valuable editions should have been lent to him" (*Life*, ii.192).

[5] Boswell's long note in his third edition, in reply to Mrs. Thrale's observation on this passage in her *Anecdotes of Dr. Johnson*, is here omitted. She had maintained that, on the contrary, she had always commended Mrs. Montagu's *Essay on Shakespeare*. Boswell pointed out, first, that the remark was Dr. Johnson's, not his own; secondly, that Dr. Johnson had read the Journal, and had pointed out no inaccuracy in the paragraph in question; and thirdly, that Mrs. Thrale herself had read the Journal and had at that time made no comment. He added that he cancelled her name in the proofs for the first edition, but restored it on the advice of a friend (probably Malone) who said he should not deprive Mrs. Thrale of the honour of having her opinion mentioned with that of Johnson and Beauclerk. As a matter of fact, Mrs. Thrale's name is cancelled in the MS. Boswell either forgot where he made the cancellation, or else he restored the name in the first proofs and cancelled it in the revises.

cut a carcass in pieces tolerably." By degrees, he showed that he knew something even of butchery. He said an ox was knocked down and a calf stunned, but a sheep had its throat cut without anything done to stupefy it. That the butchers had no view to the ease of the animals, but only to make them quiet, which they did not mind with sheep.[6] He said Hales was of opinion that every animal should be blooded without having any blow given to it, because it bleeds better. I said it would be cruel. Mr. Johnson said, "No, sir. There is not much pain if the jugular vein be properly cut." He said the kennels of Southwark run with blood two or three days in the week. That he was afraid there were slaughter-houses in more streets in London than one thinks—speaking with a kind of horror of butchering. And yet he said that any of us would kill a cow rather than not have beef. I said we *could* not. "Yes," said he, "any one may. The business of a butcher is a trade indeed; that is to say, there is an apprenticeship served to it. But it may be learnt in a month."

I mentioned a club in London at the Boar's Head in Eastcheap, the very tavern where Falstaff and his joyous companions met;[7] and the members of it all assume Shakespeare's characters. One is Falstaff, another Prince Henry, another Bardolph, and so on. Mr. Johnson said, "Don't be of it. Now that you have a name, you must be careful to avoid many things not bad in themselves, but which will lessen your character.[8] This," said he, "every man who has a name must observe. A man who is not publicly known may live in London as he pleases without any notice being taken of him. But it is wonderful how a person of any consequence is watched. There was a Member of Parliament[9] who wanted to prepare himself

---

[6] The MS is defective, and the last two words have been supplied by the editors.

[7] Boswell is mistaken here; the original tavern was burned down in the great fire, but was rebuilt in 1668.

[8] "I do not see why I might not have been of this club without lessening my character. But Dr. Johnson's caution against supposing one's self concealed in London, may be very useful to prevent some people from doing many things, not only foolish, but criminal."—BOSWELL.

[9] Possibly W. G. ("Single-Speech") Hamilton, as Croker conjectured.

to speak on a question that was to come on in the House, and he and I were to talk it over together. He did not wish it should be known that he talked with me; so he would not let me come to his house, but came to me. Some time after he made his speech in the House, Mrs. Cholmondeley, a very airy lady, told me, 'Well, you could make nothing of him,'—naming the gentleman, which was a proof that he was watched. I had once some business to do for Government,[10] and I went to Lord North's. It was dark before I went. Yet a few days after, I was told, 'Well, you have been with Lord North.' That the door of the Prime Minister should be watched is not so wonderful; but that a Member of Parliament should be watched, or my door should be watched, is wonderful."

We set out this morning in Ullinish's boat, having taken leave of him and his family. There was an ease in his house, an appearance as if everything went on daily just as we saw it, that was very agreeable. It made one quite free of the idea that our company was any burden. As we sailed along, Mr. Johnson got into one of his fits of railing at the Scots. He owned that we were a very learned nation for about 100 years, from about 1550 to about 1650. But that we lost our learning during the Civil War and had never recovered it. He said we afforded the only instance of a people among whom the arts of civil life did not advance in proportion with learning; that we had hardly any trade, any money, or any elegance before the Union. That it was strange how with all the advantages that other nations have, we had not any of those arts which are the fruit of industry, till we came in contact with a civilized nation. "We have taught you," said he; "and we'll do the same in time to all barbarous nations—to the Cherokees—and at last to the orang-outangs"—laughing as if Monboddo had been present. I said we had wine before the Union. "No sir," said he; "you had some weak stuff, the refuse of France, which would not make

---

[10] Croker guessed that this had to do with Johnson's pamphlet about the Falkland Islands.

you drunk." BOSWELL. "I assure you, sir, there was a great deal of drunkenness." JOHNSON. "No, sir; there were people who died of dropsies which they contracted in trying to get drunk."

I must here glean some of his conversation at Ullinish, which I have omitted. He said for five years of his life he made him a bowl of punch every night. He repeated his remark that a man in a ship was worse than a man in a jail. "The man in a jail," said he, "has more room, better food, and commonly better company, and is in safety." "Ay, but," said Mr. Macqueen, "the man in the ship has the pleasing hope of getting to shore." JOHNSON. "Sir, I am not talking of a man's getting to shore, but of a man while he is in a ship; and then, I say, he is worse than a man while he is in a jail. A man in a jail *may* have the pleasing hope of getting out. A man confined for a certain time *has* it." MacLeod mentioned his schemes for carrying on fisheries, with spirit, and how he would wish to understand well the construction of boats. I said he might go to a dockyard and work, as Peter the Great did. "Nay," said Mr. Johnson, "he need not work. Peter the Great had not the sense to see that the mere mechanical work may be done by anybody, and that there is the same art in constructing a vessel whether the boards are well or ill wrought. Sir Christopher Wren might as well have served his time to a bricklayer, and first indeed to a brickmaker."

There is a beautiful little island in the Loch of Dunvegan, called Isay. MacLeod said he would give it to Mr. Johnson, on condition of his residing on it three months in the year, nay, one month. Mr. Johnson was highly pleased with the fancy. I have seen him please himself with little things, even with mere ideas, as this was. He talked a great deal of this island—how he would build a house, how he would fortify it, how he would have cannon, how he would plant, how he would sally out and *take* the Isle of Muck; and then he laughed with a glee that was astonishing, and could hardly leave off. I have seen him do so at a small matter that struck him, and was a

sport to no one else. Langton told me that one night at the
Club he did so while the company were all grave around him;
only Garrick in his smart manner addressed him, "Mighty pleasant, sir; mighty pleasant, sir." Poor Langton's Will was a sport
of this kind; but there I own Mr. Johnson carried me along
with him, as he made it really most ludicrous; and perhaps
the contrast of Chambers's gravity, who had helped Langton
to make the Will, gave additional keenness to our risibility.
MacLeod humoured Mr. Johnson finely as to his island; told
him that as it was the practice in this country to name every
man by his lands, he begged leave to drink him in that manner: "*Island Isay*, your health!" Ullinish, Talisker, and Mr.
Macqueen all joined in their different manners, while Mr.
Johnson bowed to each in excellent good humour.

We had a fine sail this day. There cannot be a finer harbour
than the basin which we saw sheltered from every wind. Mac-
Leod showed us an arm of the sea which runs up with very
deep water for a mile, upon which he intends to build a town.
We sailed up another arm. The shore was varied with hills and
rocks and cornfields, and natural wood or bushes. We landed
near to the house of Fernilea. He himself was waiting on the
shore, with a horse for Mr. Johnson. The rest of us walked up.
We found at Fernilea a very comfortable house. His wife is
daughter to Bernera. When I took off my *scalck*, with hearty
readiness he said, "Fare fa' you!"[11] His parlour was paved with
flagstones, not in squares, but just in the shapes which they
naturally had in the quarry. I liked this better. It had more
variety. I preferred it by the same rule that Mr. Johnson pre-
fers the variety of the English conclusions of letters to the common style, "I am, etc." We had here an excellent dinner, in
particular a remarkable leg of boiled mutton with turnips and
carrots. MacLeod has really shown us a chief and his clan. We

---

[11] i.e., "Fair fall you." Burns, *To a Haggis*: "Fair fa' your honest, sonsie face." In *fare*,
Boswell may be attempting to reproduce a Hebridean pronunciation, or he may have
confused the word with the first syllable of *farewell*.

saw some of them with him at Dunvegan. We now saw him with some of them. On both sides there was the most agreeable kindness. I expressed to MacLeod the joy which I had in seeing this. Said he, "Government has deprived us of our ancient power, but it cannot deprive us of our domestic satisfactions. I would rather drink a bottle of punch in one of their houses" (meaning his people) "than a bottle of claret in my own." Here he said at once what every chieftain should think. All that he can get by raising his rents is more luxury in his own house. Is it not far better to share the profits of his estate to a certain degree with his kinsmen, and so have both social intercourse and patriarchal influence? Fernilea seemed to be a worthy, sensible, kind man.

We had a very good ride for about three miles to Talisker, though we had showers from time to time. At Talisker, we found Mrs. MacLeod, the Colonel's lady, a civil genteel woman. She had some resemblance of Tom Davies's "mighty pretty wife";[12] at least she put me in mind of her. We found here too Donald Maclean, the young Laird of Coll (nephew to Talisker). I had a letter to him from his uncle, Professor MacLeod at Aberdeen. Mr. Johnson said he was a fine fellow. He was a little brisk young man, had been a good deal in England studying farming, and was resolved to improve his father's lands without hurting the people or losing the ancient Highland fashions. He had seen[13] Donald MacLeod at Loch Bracadale, who had been paying some small debts which he owed to some of the emigrants, but had £21 of our money remaining, and was trying to muster up what he had given away of it. This was so far good news.

Talisker is really a fine place. It is situated in a rich bottom, containing ——— acres. Before it is a wide expanse of sea, on

---

[12] "With him came mighty Davies.—On my life,
　　That Davies hath a very pretty wife!
　　Statesman all over!—In plots famous grown!—
　　He mouths a sentence, as curs mouth a bone."—Churchill's *Rosciad*.
[13] The MS is defective; "had seen" is supplied by the editors.

each hand of which are immense rocks. On the left there is a rock of considerable size, quite detached, standing in the sea.[14] A good way to the —— are three columnal rocks rising to sharp points, also detached from the main rock, and advanced before each other into the sea, thus:[15] the outermost being the lowest; the middle one the next lowest; and the innermost of an immense height, and (what is remarkable) higher than the main rock. They are called "MacLeod's Maidens." On the upper end of the valley or bottom is a large black rock —— feet from the level of the bottom. Mr. Johnson said it was like a haystack, which is indeed the appearance which it has from Talisker. The end of it there is quite round; but it goes backward a good way and has a considerable body to its head, as Arthur's Seat has. Mr. Pennant took a drawing off it.[16] The billows break with prodigious force and noise on the coast of Talisker. There are here a good many trees, mostly planted by the late Talisker, and some of them by this gentleman. They are very well grown. Talisker is an extensive farm. The possessor of it has for these —— generations been the next heir to MacLeod, as there has been but one son always in the family; and no rent ever was paid for Talisker till the distress of the family obliged this gentleman to pay £100 a year. The court before the house is most injudiciously paved with the round bluish-grey pebbles which are found upon the seashore, so that you walk as if upon cannon-bullets driven into the ground. The house is a very bad one. However we found a comfortable parlour, paved like the one at Fernilea; and the bedrooms, though small, were furnished with so much contrivance of convenience and neatness that we did very well. Mr. Johnson had a room to himself, MacLeod and I one between us. I had a very

---

[14] Probably the "lofty insulated rock," "pyramidal and inclining," which **Pennant** calls *Stach in nuchidar*.

[15] Boswell's sketch is omitted. See the fine plate in Dr. Hill's *Footsteps of Dr. Johnson*, facing p. 206.

[16] Not reproduced in his *Tour*; but the hill (Preshal) is fully described there. He compares its structure to that of the Giant's Causeway.

clever bed raised some feet from the ground, that a large chest might be kept under it, and MacLeod had a cradle.[17] Our tea was in good order, and we had a genteel supper. The Colonel had claret, port, sherry, and punch, with porter in abundance. Though he was depressed by lowness of spirits, he disturbed nobody with his complaints. He was attentive and polite. Only I missed that vivacity which I found about him at Edinburgh.

We talked of the assiduity of the Scotch clergy in visiting and privately instructing their people, and how in this they excelled the English clergy. Mr. Johnson would not let this pass. He tried to turn it off by saying, "There are different ways of instructing. Our clergy pray and preach." MacLeod and I pushed the subject, upon which he grew warm, and broke forth, "I do not believe your people are better instructed. If they are, it is the blind leading the blind, for your clergy are not instructed themselves. There is Macaulay—the most ignorant booby and the grossest bastard."[18] (Coll says Mr. Johnson said Macaulay was as obstinate as a mule and as ignorant as a bull, but I do not recollect this.) Mr. Johnson took himself[19] well, and said, "When I talk of the ignorance of your clergy, I speak of them as a body. I do not mean that there are not individuals who are learned" (looking at Mr. Macqueen). "I suppose there are in Muscovy. The clergy of England have produced the most valuable books in support of religion, both in theory and practice. What have your clergy done since you sunk into Presbyterianism? Can you name one book of any value in religion written by them?" We could not. Said he, "I'll help you. Forbes wrote very well, but I believe he wrote before Episcopacy was quite extinguished"; and then

---

[17] Boswell probably means a cot-bed; possibly a hammock. This portion of the MS was omitted in the published *Tour*.

[18] Since the reader will naturally be somewhat incredulous at finding such language assigned to Johnson, it seems incumbent upon the editors to testify that the reading rests upon no conjecture. The MS at this point is as legible as a printed book. It must also be remembered that Johnson read the Journal and did not request a correction.

[19] "Checked himself"—a dialectal usage common in Boswell's letters and journals.

pausing a little, he said, "Yes, you have Wishart AGAINST re-pentance."[20] "But, sir," said I, "we are not contending for the superior learning of our clergy, but for their superior assidu-ity." He bore us down again with thundering against their ig-norance, and said, "I see you have not been well taught, for you have not charity." He had been in a manner forced into this, for when he began, he said, "Since you *will* drive the nail." He again thought of good Mr. Macqueen, and taking him by the hand, said, "Sir, I did not mean any disrespect to you."

Here I must observe that he conquered by leaving the argu-ment, which was just where I put it. The assiduity of the Scot-tish clergy is certainly greater than that of the English. His taking up the topic of their not having so much learning, was, though most ingenious, yet a fallacy in logic. It was as if there should be a dispute whether a man's hair is well dressed, and Mr. Johnson should say, "Sir, his hair cannot be well dressed, for he has a dirty shirt. No man who has not clean linen has his hair well dressed."

He used tonight an argument against the Scottish clergy being learned which I doubt was not just. Said he, "As we believe a man dead till we know that he is alive, so we believe men ignorant till we know that they are learned." Now our maxim in law is to believe a man alive till we know he is dead. However, indeed, it may be answered that we must first know that he is alive, and that we have never known the learning of the Scottish clergy. Mr. Macqueen, though he was of opinion[21] that Dr. Johnson had deserted the point really in

---

[20] "This was a dexterous mode of description, for the purpose of his argument; for what he alluded to was a sermon published by the learned Dr. William Wishart, formerly Principal of the college at Edinburgh, to warn men *against* confiding in a death-bed *re-pentance*, of the inefficacy of which he entertained notions very different from those of Dr. Johnson."—BOSWELL.

[21] At this point four pages (357–60) are missing from the MS, and the text is supplied from the first edition. Two paragraphs of this material are omitted, because they appear elsewhere in the MS. What is peculiar to the printed text by no means fills enough space to account for all that must have been in the missing pages. The lost portion, however, may have been no more than Boswell's expatiation on the "luxury of the little-house at Talisker." See the beginning of the entry for 3 October.

dispute, was much pleased with what he said, and owned to me he thought it very just; and Mrs. MacLeod was so much captivated by his eloquence that she told me I was a good advocate for a bad cause.

FRIDAY 24 SEPTEMBER. This was a good day. Dr. Johnson told us at breakfast that he rode harder at a fox chase than anybody. "The English," said he, "are the only nation who ride hard a-hunting. A Frenchman goes out upon a managed horse, and capers in the field, and no more thinks of leaping a hedge than of mounting a breach. Lord Powerscourt laid a wager, in France, that he would ride a great many miles in a certain short time. The French academicians set to work, and calculated that, from the resistance of the air, it was impossible. His lordship, however, performed it."

Talisker, Mr. Macqueen, and I, walked out, and looked at no less than fifteen different waterfalls near the house, in the space of about a quarter of a mile. We also saw Cuchullin's well, said to have been the favourite spring of that ancient hero. I drank of it. The water is admirable. On the shore are many stones full of crystallizations in the heart.

Though our obliging friend, Mr. Maclean, was but the young laird, he had the title of "Coll" constantly given him. After dinner he and I walked to the top of Preshal, a very high rocky hill, from whence there is a view of Barra, the Long Island, Bernera, the Loch of Dunvegan, part of Rum, part of Raasay, and a vast deal of the Isle of Skye. Coll, though he had come into Skye with intention to be at Dunvegan and pass a considerable time in the island, most politely resolved first to conduct us to Mull and then to return to Skye. This was a very fortunate circumstance, for he planned an expedition for us of more variety than merely going to Mull. He proposed we should see the islands of Eigg, Muck, Coll, and Tyree. In all of these islands he could show us everything worth seeing; and in Mull he said he should be as if at home, his father having lands there, and he a farm.

SATURDAY 25 SEPTEMBER. It was resolved that we should set out, in order to return to Sleat, to be in readiness to take boat whenever there should be a fair wind. Talisker, having been bred to physic, had a tincture of scholarship in his conversation which pleased Dr. Johnson, and he had some very good books; and he had introduced the ease and politeness of the Continent into this rude region, in consequence of[1] his and Mrs. MacLeod's having been abroad and improved in the art of living. Mr. Johnson wrote a letter today; and it was long before we could get him roused to depart. He did not come to breakfast, but had it sent to him. When he had finished, it was twelve o'clock, and we should have been away by ten. He said to me, "Do you remember a song which begins,

> Ev'ry island is a prison
> Strongly guarded by the sea.
> Kings and princes, for that reason,
> Pris'ners are as well as we?"

I suppose he had been thinking of our situation. He would fain have had a boat from this, in place of riding back to Sleat. A scheme for it was proposed. He said, "We'll not be driven tamely from it." But it proved impracticable.

Last night we talked of Dr. Birch. Mr. Johnson said he knew more small particulars than anybody. I said Percy knew a great many; that he flowed with them, like one of the brooks here. But said he, "If Percy is like one of the brooks here, Birch was like the River Thames. Birch excelled Percy in that, as much as Percy excels Goldsmith." He was not pleased with Lord Hailes for publishing only such memorials and letters as were unfavourable for the Stuart family. He said, "If a man fairly warns you, 'I am to give all the ill, do you find the good,' he may. But if he publishes to give a view of a reign, let him tell all the truth. I would tell truth of the two Georges, or of that scoundrel King William." He said Granger's Biographical

---

[1] The entry for 25 September, up to this point, is taken from the printed Tour, but has been modified by the editors to connect with the MS, which now begins again.

Dictionary might have been better done. He said, "The dog is a Whig. I do not like much to see a Whig in any dress. But I hate to see a Whig in a parson's gown."

We took leave of MacLeod and the family of Talisker, and set forward. Young Coll was now our leader. Mr. Macqueen was to go with us half a day more. We stopped at a little hut where we saw one old woman grinding with the quern, the ancient Highland implement which it is said was introduced by the Romans. It consists of two circular whinstones like iron plates, roughened by having holes made in them by a pickaxe. These stones are placed one above another. In the centre of the upper one is an opening in which a frame of wood, which serves as the hopper, is fixed, and into which the grain is thrown. There are four holes in the upper stone by way of uniformity, but only one is necessary, *viz.*, that into which a stick is fixed by which the stone is turned about. The upper end of the stick is supported by being placed in a little semi-circular opening formed of straw-rope, fixed to the wattling of the roof. The woman turned about the stick, and the upper stone had a pin of wood near the middle fixed in the under one, on which pin it moved as on an axis. The upper stone is convex, and the under concave, by which the meal falls down on all sides of it from the centre. I cannot draw it. But young Coll has promised to send me one from Mull, as he has set up a mill on his estate there, and is abolishing the quern, which is a very poor and tedious implement. I must try if Mr. Johnson can describe it. Generally two women work at it. They can grind a boll in a day, as young Coll told me.

The cottages in Skye are frequently built by having two stone walls at several feet distance filled up with earth, by which a thick and very warm wall is formed. The roof is generally bad. The couples, such as they are, do not reach to the extremity of the wall, but only rise from the inner side of it; so that the circumference of the roof is a good deal less than that of the walls of the house, which has an odd appearance to strangers; and the storm finds a passage between the roof and the wall, as the roof does not advance so as to project over the wall. They are thatched sometimes with straw, sometimes with heath, sometimes with ferns. The thatch is fixed on by ropes of straw or of heath; and to fix the ropes there is a stone tied in the end of each. These stones hang round the bottom of the roof, and make it look like a lady's head in papers; but I should think that when there is wind they would come down and knock people on the head. I observed a good many kind of enclosures in Skye, by earthen dikes or mounds of a great thickness, the making of which must have cost much labour. When a road passes through them, there is a little rude gate, thus:[2] A tree is fixed in a hole in the ground, so as to turn about as on an axis, and it is loosely fixed both above and below to the dike by ropes of heath.[3] From it issue horizontally several smaller trees with unequal ends just as they grow, and across them are some small bars or branches interwoven. They open very easily, by the slightest pull at one of the trees, and fall back again to their former situation. I find I can do nothing in the way of description of any visible object whatever. Whether it is owing to my not seeing with accuracy, or to my not having the use of words fitted to such sort of description, I cannot say.

We had some pretty good natural road for —––––— miles, till we got to Sligachan, within a mile of Sconser, which was steep and rocky. We had a full view of Raasay, just opposite to us. It was pleasing to see it again. At Sconser I received a letter from my dear wife, of date the 8th current. I can hardly express the comfort which it gave me. But it made me impatient to be home, when I found that she was under continual apprehensions. I wrote to her from Sconser.[4] We had here an inn in a poor state, James Macdonald the landlord being about

---

[2] Sketch omitted.
[3] The MS is defective; *to turn about* and *both above and* have been supplied by the editors. Boswell's sketch indicates the general sense.
[4] "Her letter told that Joseph's wife had got a son, which was joyful news to him, and as we all liked him, we were all glad." (Interlinear addition made by Boswell in the MS, apparently at the time of revising for the printer, later struck out.)

to emigrate. Our landlady was Mr. Macqueen's daughter. We sent our horses round a point of land, that we might shun some very bad road, and go by boat. We here took leave of Mr. Macqueen. Mr. Johnson said, "Dear sir, do not forget me." I promised to write to him from time to time letters full of questions concerning the Isle of Skye, which he promised to answer, and so by degrees he would write an account of it. Mr. Johnson wished he would, and I thought this the best way to lead him on insensibly. Mr. Johnson promised to look over the papers. He said Mr. Macqueen should tell all that he could, distinguishing what he knows, what is traditional, and what is conjectural.

It was seven when we took our boat. We had many showers, and it soon grew pretty dark. Mr. Johnson sat silent and patient. Once he said, as he looked on the black coast of Skye—black as being composed of rocks seen in the dusk—"This is very solemn." Our boatmen were bad singers. It was like hearing wild Indians when they sung. A very little imagination was necessary to give one the impression of being upon an American river. We landed at Strollamus, from whence we got a guide to walk before us two miles to Coirechatachan. We could get no horse for our baggage. So I took one portmanteau before me, and Joseph another. We had just one star that seemed to afford us light. It was about eleven when we arrived. We were most hospitably received by the master and mistress, who were just going to bed, but with unaffected ready kindness got a good fire on, and at twelve o'clock at night had supper[5] on the table.

James Macdonald, of Knockhoe, Kingsburgh's brother, whom we had seen at Kingsburgh, was there. He showed me a bond granted by the late Sir James Macdonald, to old Kingsburgh, the preamble of which does so much honour to the feelings of that much-lamented gentleman that I thought it worth transcribing. It was as follows:

---

[5] Six pages (367–72) are here missing from the MS. The text is supplied from the first edition.

"I, Sir James Macdonald of Macdonald, Baronet, now, after arriving at my perfect age, from the friendship I bear to Alexander Macdonald of Kingsburgh, and in return for the long and faithful services done and performed by him to my deceased father, and to myself during my minority, when he was one of my tutors and curators; being resolved, now that the said Alexander Macdonald is advanced in years, to contribute my endeavours for making his old age placid and comfortable"—therefore he grants him an annuity of fifty pounds sterling.

Dr. Johnson went to bed soon. When one bowl of punch was finished, I rose, and was near the door, in my way upstairs to bed; but Coirechatachan said it was the first time Coll had been in his house, and he should have his bowl; and would not I join in drinking it? The heartiness of my honest landlord, and the desire of doing social honour to our very obliging conductor, induced me to sit down again. Coll's bowl was finished; and by that time we were well warmed. A third bowl was soon made, and that too was finished. We were cordial, and merry to a high degree; but of what passed I have no recollection with any accuracy. I remember calling Coirechatachan by the familiar appellation of "Corry," which his friends do. A fourth bowl was made, by which time Coll and young Mackinnon, Coirechatachan's son, slipped away to bed. I continued a little with Corry and Knockhoe, but at last I left them. It was near five in the morning when I got to bed.

SUNDAY 26 SEPTEMBER. I awaked at noon with a severe headache. I was much vexed that I should have been guilty of such a riot, and afraid of a reproof from Dr. Johnson. I thought it very inconsistent with that conduct which I ought to maintain while the companion of the Rambler. About one he came into my room, and accosted me, "What, drunk yet?" His tone of voice was not that of severe upbraiding; so I was relieved a little. "Sir," said I, "they kept me up." He answered "No, you kept them up, you drunken dog." This he said with good-humoured English pleasantry. Soon afterwards, Coirechatachan, Coll, and other friends assembled round my bed. Corry had a brandy bottle and glass with him, and insisted I should take a dram. "Ay," said Dr. Johnson, "fill him drunk again. Do it in the morning, that we may laugh at him all day. It is a poor thing for a fellow to get drunk at night, and skulk to bed, and let his friends have no sport." Finding him thus jocular, I became quite easy; and when I offered to get up, he very good-naturedly said, "You need be in no such hurry now."[1] I took my host's advice and drank some brandy, which I found an effectual cure for my headache. When I rose, I went into Dr. Johnson's room, and taking up Mrs. Mackinnon's prayer-book, I opened it at the twentieth Sunday after Trinity, in the epistle for which I read, "And be not drunk with wine, wherein there is excess." Some would have taken this as a divine interposition.

Mrs. Mackinnon told us at dinner that old Kingsburgh, her father, was examined at Monkstadt by General Campbell as to the particulars of the dress of the person who had come to his house in woman's clothes, along with Miss Flora Macdonald, as by this time the General had received intelligence of that disguise. The particulars were taken down in writing, that it might be seen how far they agreed with the dress of the Irish girl who went with Miss Flora from the Long Island.

---

[1] "My ingenuously relating this occasional instance of intemperance has I find been made the subject both of serious criticism and ludicrous banter. With the banterers I shall not trouble myself, but I wonder that those who pretend to the appellation of serious critics should not have had sagacity enough to perceive that here, as in every other part of the present work, my principal object was to delineate Dr. Johnson's manners and character. In justice to him I would not omit an anecdote, which, though in some degree to my own disadvantage, exhibits in so strong a light the indulgence and good humour with which he could treat those excesses in his friends, of which he highly disapproved.

"In some other instances, the critics have been equally wrong as to the true motive of my recording particulars, the objections to which I saw as clearly as they. But it would be an endless task for an author to point out upon every occasion the precise object he has in view. Contenting himself with the approbation of readers of discernment and taste, he ought not to complain that some are found who cannot or will not understand him."—Boswell. Boswell has principally in mind Dr. Wolcot ("Peter Pindar"), whose *Bozzy and Piozzi* treats this episode with a good deal of wit:

"'Alas!' says I, 'the sinner that I am!'
And having made my speech, I took a dram."

Kingsburgh, she said, had but one song, which he always sung when he was merry over a glass. She dictated the words to me, which are foolish enough:

> Green sleeves and pudding pies,
> Tell me where my mistress lies,
> And I'll be with her before she rise,
> Fiddle and aw' together.
>
> May our affairs abroad succeed,
> And may our king come home with speed,
> And all pretenders shake for dread,
> And let *his* health go round.
>
> To all our injured friends in need,
> This side and beyond the Tweed!—
> Let all pretenders shake for dread,
> And let *his* health go round.
>   Green sleeves, etc.

While the examination was going on, this Talisker, who was there as one of MacLeod's militia, could not resist the pleasantry of asking Kingsburgh, in allusion to his only song, "Had she *green sleeves*?" Kingsburgh gave him no answer. Lady Margaret Macdonald was very angry at Talisker for joking on such a serious occasion, as Kingsburgh was really in danger of his life. Mrs. Mackinnon added that Lady Margaret was quite adored in Skye. That when she rode through the island, the people ran in crowds before her, and took the stones off the road, lest her horse should stumble and she be hurt. Her husband, Sir Alexander, is also remembered with great regard. We were told that every week a hogshead of claret was drunk at his table.

This was another day of wind and rain, but good cheer and good society helped to beguile the time. I felt myself comfortable enough in the afternoon. I then thought that my last night's riot was no more than such a social excess as may happen without much moral blame; and recollected that some physicians maintained that a fever produced by it was, upon the whole, good for health: so different are our reflections on the same subject at different periods, and such the excuses with which we palliate what we know to be wrong.

MONDAY 27 SEPTEMBER. Donald MacLeod arrived this morning. He looked miserably[1] both from distress of mind and from the great fatigues of riding over the country in quest of money and us. He brought with him two-and-twenty pounds, which I was glad to get. He said he had given eight in payment of debt to a poor family of emigrants, and he expected to get some money which was owing to him. The difference between losing eight pounds and thirty was such as made me easy, though he should not get the eight which he said he would.

The plenty at Coirechatachan was wonderful, and the neatness with which things were set down. Yet I had still some squeamishness when I thought of the dirtiness of the lower Highlanders. My immediate fears of the itch were now off, for the pimples on the palm of my hand had almost disappeared. Besides, Mr. Johnson treated the distemper lightly, as a thing that might pass off in a few days. I saw a closet here, with a good many more books than what were lying about. Mr. Johnson told me he found a library in his room at Talisker, and observed that it was one of the remarkable things of Skye that there were so many books in it.

One thing is strange. Coirechatachan, with all his abundance, has no garden at all, not even a turnip or carrot or cabbage—in short, literally no garden. At dinner they talked of the crooked spade, and maintained that it was better than the usual garden spade, and that there was an art in tossing it, by which those used to it could work very easily with it. "Nay," said Mr. Johnson, "it may be useful in land where there are many stones to raise, but it certainly is not a good instrument for good land. A man may toss it, to be sure, but he will toss a light spade much better. Its weight makes it an encumbrance. A man *may* dig any land with it, but he has no occasion for such a weight in digging good land. You may

---

[1] The preceding sentence and these three words are supplied by the editors (with some help from the printed *Tour*) to make a transition to the MS, which begins again at this point.

take a field-piece to shoot sparrows. But all the sparrows you can bring home will not be worth the charge."

I had a good cup of coffee this afternoon. Dr. Macdonald's wife, "Mrs. Dr. Roy" (i.e., red Doctor), as Malcolm MacLeod toasted her, was a neat, pretty little girl. She sat down upon Mr. Johnson's knee, and upon being bid by some of the company, put her hands round his neck and kissed him. "Do it again," said he, "and let us see who will tire first." He kept her on his knee some time, while he and she drank tea. He was now like a *buck* indeed. All the company laughed in great glee, and they were all pleased to see him have so much good humour. To me it was a very high scene. To see the grave philosopher—the Rambler—toying with a little Highland wench![2] There was a coincidence of opposed ideas. But what could he do? He must have been surly, and weak too, had he not behaved as he did. He would have been laughed at, and not more respected, though less loved.

He read tonight, as he sat in the company, a great deal of this volume of my Journal, and said to me, "The more I read of this, I think the more highly of you." "Are you in earnest?" said I. Said he, "It is true, whether I am in earnest or no." I went to bed at two in the morning, but the rest of the company sat still. They drank on and sung Erse songs till near five. I lay in great uneasiness. I was quite sombre in the dark, and could get no rest. I tried to think how long I had been free now, but all the gloomy chances that imagination can figure disturbed me. I had the utmost impatience to get home. I was tormented for some time, till at last those who lay in the same room with me came up. Unluckily Coll found a bottle of punch standing; upon which in tumbled all the company, and they drank it, and another which Coirechatachan brought.

[2] Margaret M. Williamson, great-great-grand-niece of Macdonald of Kingsburgh, gives the following version of this story: "Mrs. Mackinnon's daughter, Margaret Macalister, then a young bride of sixteen, having just married Dr. Macdonald of Gillen, took a bet with some sprightly young ladies that she would sit on Dr. Johnson's knee in the drawing-room and kiss him. These young ladies had dared her to do it, saying he was too ugly for any woman to kiss" (*Notes and Queries*, ser. 10, vol. x.147).

They made many apologies for disturbing me. I said I once thought of rising and going down to them. Honest Corry said that to have had me do that, he would have given a cow. I thought I suffered so much tonight that the scene would make a figure in my Journal, but it makes but a wretched one.[3]

TUESDAY 28 SEPTEMBER. The weather was worse than yesterday. I felt as if imprisoned. Mr. Johnson said it was irksome to be detained thus. Yet he seemed to have less uneasiness or more patience than I had. What made our situation worse here was that we had no rooms that we could command, for the good people here had no notion that a man could have any occasion but for a mere sleeping place; so, during the day, the bedrooms were common to all the house. Servants eat in Mr. Johnson's, and mine was a kind of general rendezvous for all under the roof, children and dogs not excepted. The ladies indeed had no place during the day but Mr. Johnson's room, except the parlour. I had always some good quiet time to write in it, before Mr. Johnson was up; and by degrees I accustomed the ladies to let me sit at my Journal, and not mind me.

Mr. Johnson was this morning for going to see as many islands as we could, never minding the uncertainty of the season, which might detain us in one place for many weeks. He said to me, "I have more the spirit of adventure than you." For my part I was anxious to get to Mull, from whence we might almost any day reach the mainland.

It was between eleven and twelve before we breakfasted today. This was certainly very disorderly living in a farmer's family; and I . . . t the table, which was kept . . . constantly full. Yet it . . .[1] She offered me even the Paris-plaster medallion

---

[3] Boswell has written in the margin, "Insert the ludicrous scene of Joseph and the . . ." The MS being defective, we shall never know what the "ludicrous scene" was. He later decided against putting it into the printed *Tour*.

[1] Both lower corners of this page are defective. The next leaf (pp. 377–8) is missing altogether, and the printed text contains nothing corresponding to it. After *mainland*, above, Boswell directed the printer to "go to 379." The sentence with which p. 379 begins shows that Boswell had been talking with Mrs. Mackinnon about Prince Charles. Per-

of the Prince. She told me the print of Mrs. Brooks was bought by her husband at the sale of one of the emigrants.

Happily the weather cleared up between one and two, and we got ready to depart. But they would not let us go without a *snatch*, as they called it, which was in truth a very plentiful dinner.

I must not forget that in the morning Mr. Johnson told us that the few ancient Irish gentlemen who remain have the highest pride of family. Mr. Sandford, a friend of his, whose mother was Irish, told him that O'Hara, who was true Irish both by father and mother, and he, and Mr. Ponsonby, son to the Earl of Bessborough, the greatest man of the three, but of an English family, went to see one of those ancient Irish; and that he distinguished them thus: "O'Hara, you are welcome. Mr. Sandford, your mother's son is welcome. Mr. Ponsonby, you may sit down."

He talked both of threshing and thatching. He said it was very difficult to determine how to agree with a thresher. "If you pay him by day's wages, he'll thresh no more than he pleases, though to be sure the negligence of a thresher is more easily detected than that of most labourers, because he must always make a sound while he works. If you pay him by the piece, by the quantity of grain which he produces, he will thresh only while the grain comes freely, and though he leaves a good deal in the ear, it is not worth while to thresh the straw over again; nor can you fix him to do it sufficiently, because it is so difficult to prove how much less a man threshes than he ought to do. Here then is a dilemma. But for my part, I'd engage him by the day. I'd rather trust his idleness than his fraud." He said a roof thatched with Lincolnshire reeds would last seventy years, as he was informed. He told it to a great thatcher in London, who said he believed it might be true. This showed that Mr. Johnson is at pains to get the best information on every subject.

haps the missing leaf contained some of the material from which he constructed his narrative of the Prince's escape.

He said it was difficult for a farmer in England to find day-labourers, because the lowest manufacturers can always get more than a day-labourer. "There is no matter," said he, "how high the wages of manufacturers are, but it would be of very bad consequence to raise the wages of those who procure the immediate necessaries of life, because that would raise the price of provisions. Here, then, is a problem for politicians. It is not reasonable that the most useful body of men should be the worst paid, yet it does not appear how it can be ordered otherwise. It were to be wished that a mode for its being otherwise were found out. In the mean time, it is better to give temporary assistance to poor labourers, at times when provisions are high, than to raise their wages; because if wages are once raised, they'll never get down again."

While we were at dinner, Mr. Johnson kept a close whispering conference with Mrs. Mackinnon about the particulars that she knew of the Prince's escape. The company were entertained and pleased to observe it. Upon that subject there was a warm union between the soul of Mr. Samuel Johnson and that of an Isle of Skye farmer's wife. It is curious to see people, though ever so much removed from each other in the general system of their lives, come close together on a particular point which is common to each. (I could illustrate this by a variety of instances from the ancient and modern world, but must be sparing of my paper, my own two books being now exhausted, and this small one which Mr. Johnson gave me being all that remains.) We were merry with Coirechatachan on Mr. Johnson's whispering with his wife. She cried, "I'm in love with him. What is it to live and not love?" So she humoured our merriment. At the same time, she was really most heartily taken with his conversation. Upon her saying something, which I did not hear or cannot recollect, he seized her hand keenly and kissed it. Here was loyalty strongly exemplified.

She told us a very extraordinary dream which she had during her first marriage. She saw the late Sir Alexander Macdonald; but recollecting that he was dead, she asked him if it was not so. "No," said he, "I am not dead. I am alive." Said she, "You mean, sir, that you are alive in another state—in heaven" (or "happiness"). "Yes," said he; "and I'll tell you anything that you'll ask me." "Why, then," said she, "sir, will you tell me if this unfortunate man will ever be restored to the throne of Britain?" "Yes," said he. "He certainly will." There was something so generous in her making this her first question—in her loyalty going before her concern for her family and everything else—that I was touched in a most sensible manner, and took hold of her hand across the table, shook it eagerly, and made her health go round. She had then nine children, and the smallpox of a very fatal kind was raging in Skye. She asked how her children would come off. He said she would lose but two; and those that survived would be a great comfort to her. This has exactly happened. She asked if Lady Margaret would marry again. He said, "No." She asked what kind of man Sir James would be. He said, "He'll be the best man you ever had, while you have him"; which meant that they would not have him long. She said that everything else which Sir Alexander told her in this dream has turned out so exactly that she had a firm faith in the restoration which was also told. Mr. Johnson said to me afterwards that he did not believe this dream; "for," said he, "she has dreamt something, and has always added to it, as she told it."

Last night I showed Coirechatachan in Baker's *Chronicle* two passages of King James VI's (or rather I's, as it is an English book) character that apply to Mr. Johnson: his method of riding, and the accuracy of his extemporaneous discourse.[2]

As we were going, the Scottish phrase of "honest man," which signifies kindness and regard, was often and often re-

---

[2] Boswell prefixed the second of these passages (somewhat inaccurately transcribed) to the printed *Tour*, as a sort of motto. See p. 2 of this volume. The reference to James's riding immediately precedes: "It is said he had such a fashion in riding that it could not so properly be said he rode, as that his horse carried him; for he made but little use of his bridle; and would say, 'A horse never stumbled but when he was reined.'"

peated by many of Mr. Johnson. I myself was shown as much
kindness and regard as I could desire; and I must take some
merit from my assiduous attention to him, and the happy art
which I have of contriving that he shall be easy wherever he
goes, that he shall not be asked twice to eat or drink anything
(which always disgusts him), that he shall be provided with
water at his meals, and many such little things, which, if not
attended to, would fret him. I have also an admirable talent
of leading the conversation; I do not mean leading as in an
orchestra, by playing the first fiddle, but leading as one does in
examining a witness: starting topics, and making the company
pursue them. Mr. Johnson appeared to me like a great mill,
into which a subject is thrown to be ground. That is the test
of a subject. But indeed it requires fertile minds to furnish materials for this mill. It vexes me when I see it unemployed, but
sometimes I feel myself quite barren, and have nothing to
throw in. I know not if this mill be a good figure; Pope makes
his mind a mill for turning verses.[3] It is fine to see how the nonsense is thrown off from Mr. Johnson's mill, or specious error
crushed.

We set out about four. Young Coirechatachan went with us.
We had as fine an evening as I ever saw, and arrived at Ostaig,
the house of Mr. Martin Macpherson, minister of Sleat. It is a
pretty good house, built by his father upon a farm near the
church . . .[4] as I ever saw anywhere. Coll went to pay a visit at
Camascross, and was not to come up till next day. We had here
Mr. and Mrs. Macpherson and Miss Mackinnon, all of whom
we had seen at Coirechatachan. Mr. Johnson and I and young
Mr. Mackinnon and James Macdonald, the factor or bailie,
made up the company. Miss Macpherson sung lively Erse songs

---

[3] "This subtle thief of life, this paltry time,
    What will it leave me if it snatch my rhyme?
    If ev'ry wheel of that unwearied mill
    That turn'd ten thousand verses, now stands still?"
                    Second Epistle of the Second Book of Horace, 76–9.
[4] Two lines, or about fourteen words, are lost here. There is nothing corresponding in
the printed *Tour*.

to us.[5] Mr. Johnson had a good room to himself with a press stored with books, Greek, Latin, and French and English, most of which had belonged to the learned Dr. Macpherson. The Bailie and young Mackinnon in one bed, and I in another, had the room opposite to Mr. Johnson's.

WEDNESDAY 29 SEPTEMBER. After a very good sleep, I rose more refreshed than I had been for some nights. We were now nearer the shore, and saw the sea from the windows, which made our voyage seem nearer, and there was more convenience for us here than at Coirechatachan. I altered my opinion of Mr. Macpherson. I saw that what I have censured in him at Coirechatachan was only mistake or inaccuracy. He said there was an Erse Bible, confounding Erse with Irish. He said there were Erse manuscripts, thinking modern writings were understood. At least I viewed him now with a most favourable eye, because I saw real goodness of character in him. He was a young man with his own hair cut short and round, with a pleasing countenance and most unaffected kindness. He said Mr. Johnson was an honour to mankind, and if the expression might be used, was an honour to religion.

Coll and Donald MacLeod got up to us at breakfast, after which the Bailie went home. The day was windy and rainy; so that we had just seized a happy interval last night. We had very good entertainment here, and time enough to ourselves. The day slipped along imperceptibly. We talked of Shenstone. Mr. Johnson said he was a good layer out of land, but would not allow him excellence as a poet. He said he had, he believed, tried to read all his Love Pastorals, but did not get through them. I repeated the stanza,

> She gazed as I slowly withdrew.

He said, "That seems to be pretty." I said he seemed to have had thought, from his short maxims in prose. Mr. Johnson would not allow him that merit. Mr. Macpherson said Garrick had

---

[5] This passage is expanded in the printed *Tour*: "Miss Macpherson . . . pleased Dr. Johnson much. . . . He afterwards sent her a present of his *Rasselas*."

written a very pretty epitaph for him.[1] Mr. Johnson here was too severe, as usual, on Garrick, for he said, "Then if he could get up, he should pull it down. He was above having an epitaph upon him by Garrick." When I defended Garrick, Mr. Johnson said, "The next subject you talk to him of, 'tis two to one he is wrong."[2] He agreed however with Shenstone, that it was wrong in the brother of one of his correspondents to burn his letters;[3] "for," said he, "Shenstone was a man whose correspondence was an honour." He said Hammond's *Elegies* were poor things. He called Hanbury Williams a wretched scribbler, and said he had no fame but from boys who drank with him.

He looked at a Latin paraphrase of the Song of Moses in the *Scots Magazine*, by Dr. Macpherson, and said it did him honour; that he had a great deal of Latin, and good Latin. I mentioned to him a droll Scottish poem which I had just seen on occasion of his being entertained by the professors at St. Andrews. He desired to hear it. I read it all but two lines about *skait* which were rather indecent, and explained it.[4] He laughed, but said nothing. I asked him if he had never been accustomed to wear a night-cap. He said, "No." I asked if it was best not to do it. He said he had that custom by chance; "and perhaps no man shall ever know whether 'tis best to sleep with or without a night-cap." Something occurred where he was laughing at some deficiency, I fancy in the Highlands, and said, "One might

---

[1] This epitaph, inscribed on an urn erected in Halesowen churchyard, in memory of Shenstone, was erroneously attributed in the newspapers to Garrick. It was composed, and the urn was erected, by Richard Graves. It begins:
> "Whoe'er thou art, with rev'rence tread
> The sacred mansions of the dead. . . ."

[2] This petulant remark was omitted in the published *Tour*.

[3] Shenstone's correspondent was Anthony Whistler of Whitchurch; the brother was John Whistler.

[4] This poem, by Robert Fergusson, "To the Principal and Professors of the University of St. Andrews, on their superb treat to Dr. Samuel Johnson," Boswell found in the *Weekly Magazine* (Edinburgh) for 2 September 1773 (xxi.305–6). The author refers with scorn to the dainty dishes with which Johnson was probably regaled; and then recommends a homelier bill of fare as more appropriate, including a haggis and sheep's head and trotters. The lines to which Boswell refers are as follows:
> "Then neist whan Samy's heart was faintin',
> He'd lang'd for scate to mak him wanton."

Skate was apparently considered to have aphrodisiac properties.

as well go without——" (I forget what), "or without shoes and stockings." I, thinking to have a little hit at his own deficiency, ventured to say, "or without a *night-cap*." But I had as well have let it alone, for he was at me directly. "I do not see the connexion there" (laughing), and then, "Nobody before was ever foolish enough to ask whether it was best to wear a night-cap or not. This comes of being a little wrong-headed" —and he carried the company along with him. And yet the truth is that if he had always worn a night-cap, as is the common practice in England, and found the Highlanders not doing it, he would have had a sally at their barbarity; so that I had him fair enough.

THURSDAY 30 SEPTEMBER. There was as great a storm of wind and rain as I have almost ever seen. Mr. Johnson said he did not grudge Burke's being the first man in the House of Commons, for he was the first man everywhere; but he grudged that a fellow who makes no figure in company, and has a mind as narrow as the neck of a vinegar cruet, should make a figure in the House of Commons merely by having the knowledge of a few forms, and being furnished with a little occasional information.[1] He said the first time he saw Dr. Young was at Mr. Richardson's (*Clarissa*). He was sent for to come to him, that the Doctor might read to him his *Conjectures on Original Composition*, which he did, and Mr. Johnson made his remarks; and he was surprised to find the Doctor receive as novelties what Mr. Johnson thought very common thoughts. He said he believed Young was not a great scholar, nor had studied regularly the art of writing. He said there were very fine things in his *Night Thoughts*, though you could not find twenty lines together without some extravagance.[2] He repeated two

---

[1] "He did not mention the name of any particular person; but those who are conversant with the political world will probably recollect more persons than one to whom this observation may be applied."—BOSWELL.

[2] Boswell could not recall the exact word and left a blank. Filled in by Malone at the time of revision.

passages from his *Love of Fame*—the characters of[3] Brunetta and
Stella. He said Young pressed him much to come to Welwyn.
He always intended it, but never went. He was sorry when he
died. He said the cause of quarrel between Young and his son
was that his son insisted that Young should turn away a clergyman's widow who lived with him, and who, having great influence over the father, was saucy to the son. Mr. Johnson said
she could not conceal her resentment at him for saying to
Young that an old man should not resign himself to the management of anybody. I asked him if there was any improper
connexion between them. "No sir, no more than between two
statues. He was past fourscore, and she, a very coarse woman,
I suppose made his coffee and frothed his chocolate, and did
such things as an old man wishes to have done for him." This
is another proof that Wilson, the barber at Stevenage, who pretended to know Dr. Young well, and told me he kept a mistress,
which I have mentioned in my Journal, spring 1772, was a
lie.[4] I once spoke of it to Percy, who said there was no more
foundation for such a suspicion than between Mr. Johnson and
Mrs. Williams.

Mr. Johnson said Dr. Doddridge was author of one of the
finest epigrams in the English language. It is in Orton's Life of
him. He repeated it. The subject is his family motto, *Dum vivi-
mus vivamus*. I shall copy it.[5]

I should have mentioned that we had MacLeod's horses all
the way to this place. We sent them back yesterday. Each of us

---

[3] Eight or nine words have been cancelled here so heavily as to be partially indecipher-
able. Brunetta was a lady who neglected trifles, Stella a beauty who nevertheless had sense.
[4] Such anacolutha occasionally appear in Boswell's journals, especially where (as here)
a sentence is carried over to a second page. They result from his habit of interrupting
his writing at the foot of a page rather than at the end of a sentence.
[5] "Live, while you live, the *epicure* would say,
And seize the pleasures of the present day.
Live, while you live, the sacred *preacher* cries,
And give to God each moment as it flies.
Lord, in my views let both united be;
I live in *pleasure*, when I live to *thee*."

wrote him a letter. I have transcribed a paragraph of mine on the last leaf of the second volume of this Journal.[6]

I asked if it was not strange that Government should permit so many infidel writings to pass without censure. Mr. Johnson said, "Sir, it is mighty foolish. It is for want of knowing their own power. The present family on the throne came to the crown against the will of nine-tenths of the people. Whether these nine-tenths were right or wrong is not our business now to inquire. But such being the situation of the Royal Family, they were glad to encourage all who would be their friends. Now you know every bad man is a Whig; every man who has loose notions. The Church was against this family. They were, as I say, glad to encourage any friends; and therefore, since the accession of this family, there is no instance of any man being kept back on account of his bad principles—and hence this inundation of impiety."

There was something not quite serene in his humour to-night after supper, for he spoke of hastening away to London without stopping much at Edinburgh. I said he had General Oughton and many others to see. "Nay," said he; "I shall neither go in jest, nor stay in jest. I shall do what is fit." "Ay, but," said I, "all I desire is that you will let me tell you when it is fit." JOHNSON. "Sir, I shall not consult you." Yet he was very good company upon the whole. Donald MacLeod insisted to have an extraordinary bowl of punch tonight. I humoured him. He gave a very good gradation as to Mr. Johnson. "First, when you see him," said he, "you are struck with awful reverence; then you admire him; and then you love him cordially." Poor fellow, I thought this merited my sitting up a little longer with him than was quite agreeable to me, and made up for the £8 of our money which he had failed to bring us.

I read a very pretty ode by Dr. Macpherson, written from

---

[6] Not preserved in the MS as we have it. The leaves were removed from their bindings at the time of revision for the printer, and are now all loose. Johnson's letter is still preserved at Dunvegan. See Dr. Hill's edition of Johnson's Letters, i.260–1.

Barra, when he was minister there.[7] I looked a little at Voltaire's *War, 1741*, read Lord Kames against hereditary indefeasible right, and some of Congreve. If a man would keep an exact account of everything that he reads, it would much illustrate the history of his mind. I would have every minute circumstance marked: what a man reads, how much, at what times, and how often the same things. Mr. Johnson told me that from twenty-one to fifty-six he had read no Greek; at least not above five chapters of the New Testament. He saw a Xenophon's *Cyropaedia*[8] in Mr. Thrale's library, and took it down; and he was not sensible that he had lost anything of it. He read all the New Testament that year, and has since read a good deal of Greek. Coll and Mr. Mackinnon slept in my room, and Donald MacLeod on a bed on the floor.[9]

FRIDAY 1 OCTOBER. There was pretty good weather. The Bailie came up, and asked us to go to Armadale, which we agreed to do. I was very placid at Ostaig. The green hills and the brooks of Sleat had a kind of superior value when I recollected Sir James Macdonald.

I showed to Mr. Johnson verses in a magazine on his Dictionary, composed of uncommon words taken from it:

Little of *Anthropopathy* has he,[1] etc.

He read a few of them, and said, "I'm not answerable for all

---

[7] In the printed *Tour* Boswell quotes four stanzas, with a commentary, at the end of the entry for 28 September.

[8] "Xenophon's *Cyropaedia*" was inserted later.

[9] The last sentence was added later.

[1] Boswell found these lines, which were written by his friend John Maclaurin, later Lord Dreghorn, in the *Weekly Magazine* (Edinburgh) for 14 January 1773 (vol. xix.81–2). They ran, in part, as follows: *On Johnson's Dictionary.*

> In love with a pedantic jargon,
> Our poets now-a-days are far gone;
> So that a man can't read their songs,
> Unless he has the gift of tongues.

(He proceeds with a warning to young poets to use Johnson with care, distinguishing Greek and Latin words from English, and using only English, or the result may be such as this specimen:)　Little of *anthropopathy* has he,

> Who in yon fulgid *curricle* reclines
> Alone; while I, *depauperated* bard!
> The streets *pedestrious* scour; why, with bland voice,
> Bids he me not his *vectitation* share? etc.

the words in my dictionary." I told him how Garrick kept a book of all who had either praised or abused him. Mr. Johnson, on the subject of his own reputation, said, "Now that it has been so current a topic, I wish I had done so too." But he said it could not well be done now, as so many things are scattered in newspapers. I told him I would try to collect all. He said he was angry at the boy of Oxford[2] who wrote in his defence against Kenrick; because it was doing him hurt to answer Kenrick. He said the boy was to come to him to ask a favour. He first thought to treat him rudely on that account. But then he considered, he had meant to do him all the service in his power; and he took another resolution, told him he would do what he could for him in the affair, and did so; and the boy was satisfied. He said he did not know how his pamphlet was done, as he had read very little of it. The boy made a good figure at Oxford, but died. He said attacks on authors did them much service. "A man who tells me my play is very bad, is less my enemy than he who lets it die in silence. A man whose business it is to be talked of, is much helped by being attacked." Garrick, I said, had been so helped. "Yes," said he; "though Garrick has more opportunities than almost any man to keep the public in mind of him, by exhibiting himself to such numbers, he would not have had more reputation than others, had he not been so much attacked. Every attack produces a defence; and so attention is engaged. There is no sport in mere praise when people are all of a mind." "Then," said I, "Hume is not the worse for Beattie's attack." "Yes," said he, "because Beattie has confuted him. I do not say but that there may be some attacks which will hurt an author. Hume was the better of other attacks." (He certainly could not include those of his old preceptor Dr. Adams, and Tytler.) Talking of loose men being all Whigs, I mentioned Hume as a Tory. "Sir," said he, "Hume

---

[2] James Barclay, of Balliol College, who took the degree of B.A. in 1768. Kenrick had written a slashing review of Johnson's *Shakespeare*.

is a Tory by chance,[3] as being a Scotsman, but not upon principle of duty; for he has no principle. If he is anything, he is a Hobbist." I said Goldsmith was the better of attacks. "Yes," said he; "but he does not think so yet." He said the *Critical* reviewers, on occasion of he and Goldsmith doing something together (i.e., publishing each a book at the same time, Mr. Johnson the *Idler*),[4] let them know that they might review each other. Goldsmith was for accepting. He said, "No. Set them at defiance." He told me he said to old Bentley, upon the attacks against him, "Why, they'll write you down." "No, sir," said he. "Depend upon it, no man was ever written down, but by himself." Mr. Johnson observed to me that the advantage of attacks to authors was in matters of taste, where you cannot confute, as so much may be said on either side. He told us he did not know who was the author of the *Adventures of a Guinea*;[5] but that the bookseller had sent the first volume to him in manuscript to have his opinion if it should be printed, and he thought it should.

Mr. Johnson had a horse to carry him to Armadale, and Mr. Macpherson and Donald MacLeod and I walked at his foot. Coll and the Bailie attended the ladies, who were all to be with us. When we got to it, we found Mr. Archibald Macdonald, who had taken a lease of it, and a Mr. Simson from Islay, who had a vessel along with him of twelve tons, and readily agreed to land us in Mull. This was a much better opportunity for us than going in Sir Alexander's open boat. Miss Katie, the Bailie's sister, and Captain MacLeod, whom we

---

[3] In his last interview with Hume "when he knew himself to be dying," Boswell became nettled at Hume's imperturbable scepticism, and repeated this remark of Johnson. "I am sorry that I mentioned this at such a time. I was off my guard."

[4] The passage in parentheses was inserted later. But Boswell revised it once more for the printed text, omitting there the title of the *Idler*, either because he was not sure that he was quoting Johnson exactly, or else because he had neglected to ascertain what it was that Goldsmith published. The first collected edition of the *Idler* was published in October 1761. The last letter in Goldsmith's "Citizen of the World" series was published in the *Public Ledger* on 14 August 1761. The collected edition was published in May 1762.

[5] *Chrysal, or the Adventures of a Guinea* (1760–5), was written by Charles Johnstone.

formerly saw, were here. The house had quite a different air from what it had in Sir Alexander's time. We made a company of fourteen. We had a good dinner, excellent strong beer got on purpose for me, tea in good order, and a fiddler and a dance at night; then a good supper; and both at dinner and supper, excellent punch. At night both brandy punch and rum punch. The Bailie had much of my friend Hallglenmuir's manner. He was most attentive and obliging. He had a chest of books carried up to Mr. Johnson's room, who observed it would have been long before Sir Sawney would have thought of it. His factor's hospitality disgraced the knight. We had many Erse songs. Mr. Johnson had always been merry with Miss Macpherson; asked her to go to London, and said many little jocular complimentary things to her which afforded us amusement. Her brother discovered veins of pleasantry. He imitated Mr. Johnson's method of talking surprisingly well. He even said a thing a little in his way tonight. He had a dispute with Coll. Said Coll, "I'll bet a guinea." Said Macpherson, "But, sir, till you win your bet, we shall not be convinced." Macpherson danced freely. I saw in Skye that clergymen may without offence live much as other people do, who live innocently cheerful. At Dunvegan Mr. Bethune danced very well on Saturday night, and next morning preached very well; and there did not seem to be any incongruity. Mr. Johnson was now in good humour at Armadale, and I was very much so.

SATURDAY 2 OCTOBER. I was quite as I could wish here. I had my former room, with Joseph to sleep in a bed by me; so that I had a home, while all but Mr. Johnson were crowded into common rooms. I had now got the habit of taking a *scalck* or dram every morning. It really pleased me to take it. They are a very sober people, the Highlanders, though they have this practice. I always loved strong liquors. I was glad to be in a country where fashion justified tasting them. But I resolved to guard against continuing it after leaving the isles. It would become an article of happiness to me. I thought with satisfac-

tion when I got up that it waited me, as one thinks of his breakfast; so much is a man formed by habit.[1]

I told Mr. Johnson this morning that Sir Alexander said to
me once that he left Skye with the blessings of his people. Said
Mr. Johnson, "You'll observe this was when he *left* it. It is only
the back of him that they bless." He said Sir Alexander should
have come and lived among them, and made his house the
court of Skye, had he and his lady been fit for it. They should
have had so many of the gentlemen's daughters to receive their
education in the family, to learn pastry and such things from
the housekeeper, and manners from my lady. That was the
way in the great families in Wales—at Lady Salusbury's, Mrs.
Thrale's grandmother's, and at Lady Philipps's. He designed
the families by the ladies, as he spoke of what was properly
their province. There were always six young ladies at Sir John
Philipps's. When one was married, her place was filled up. There
was a large school room where they learned needlework, etc.
I observed that at the courts in Germany young people were
educated. There is an academy for the pages. Mr. Johnson said
that manners were best learnt at these courts. "You are admitted with great facility to the Prince's company, and yet
must treat him with great respect. At a great court, you are
at such a distance that you get no good." I said, "Very true.
A man sees the court of Versailles, as if he saw it in a theatre."
He said the best book that ever was written upon good breeding grew up at the little court of Urbino—*Il Cortegiano* by Cas-
tiglione. He said I should read it, which I shall do. I am glad
always to have his opinion of books. At Macpherson's, he read
some of Whitby's Commentary, which he commended; said he
had heard him called rather lax, but he did not perceive it.
He had looked at a novel called *The Man of the World* at Raasay,
but thought there was nothing in it. He said today while reading my Journal, "This will be a great treasure to us some years
hence." He told me before that he was to copy part of it about

---

[1] This paragraph was omitted in the published *Tour*.

Raasay, which he had not. I said I wished he would translate it. "How?" said he. BOSWELL. "Into good English." JOHNSON. "Sir, it is very good English."

He said today that Sir Alexander exceeded *L'Avare* in a farce. I said he was quite a character for a play. Foote would take him finely. The best way to make him do it would be to bring Foote to be entertained at his house for a week, and then it would be *facit indignatio*.[2] Said Mr. Johnson, "I wish he had him. I, who have eat his bread, will not give him him; but I should be glad he came honestly by him. Nay," said he; "they are both characters." And then he took off my lady: "Thomson, some wine and water," with her mouth full; adding, "People are generally taught to empty their mouths of meat before they call for drink. She wants to be whipped in a nursery."

He said he was angry at Thrale for sitting at General Ogle-thorpe's without speaking. He censured a man for degrading himself to nonentity. I observed that Goldsmith was on the other extreme, for he spoke at all ventures. "Yes," said he; "Goldsmith, rather than not speak will talk of what he knows himself to be ignorant, which can only end in exposing him. I wonder if he feels that he exposes himself."[3] "If," said I, "he was with two tailors—" and was going on. Mr. Johnson took it up—"Or with two founders, he'd fall a-talking on the method of making cannon, though both of them would soon see that he did not know what metal a cannon was made of." We were very social and merry in his room this forenoon. We had again a good dinner, and in the evening a great dance. We made out five country squares without sitting down; and then we per-formed with much activity a dance which I suppose the emi-gration from Skye has occasioned. They call it "America." A brisk reel is played. The first couple begin, and each sets to one —then each to another—then as they set to the next couple, the

---

[2] ". . . facit indignatio versum," i.e., Foote's anger would furnish the inspiration. Juve-nal, *Satires*, I.79.

[3] In the MS this sentence was originally ascribed to Johnson, but in revision was trans-ferred to Boswell.

second and third couples are setting; and so it goes on till all are set a-going, setting and wheeling round each other, while each is making the tour of all in the dance. It shows how emigration catches till all are set afloat. Mrs. Mackinnon told me that last year when the ship sailed from Portree for America, the people on shore were almost distracted when they saw their relations go off; they lay down on the ground and tumbled, and tore the grass with their teeth. This year there was not a tear shed. The people on shore seemed to think that they would soon follow. This is a mortal sign.

I recollect another anecdote, which Dr. Donald Macqueen told me he had from the late Sir Alexander Macdonald. When Lord Lovat came in sight as a prisoner, Sir Everard Fawkener said to Sir Alexander, "*Raro antecedentem scelestum deseruit poena pede claudo.*"[4] This happened at Fort Augustus.

I had written letters all forenoon. It was a very bad day, and at night there was a great deal of lightning. I was really fatigued with violent dancing. I do not like dancing. But I force myself to it, when it promotes social happiness, as in the country, where it is as much one of the means towards that end as dinner; so I danced a reel tonight to the music of the bagpipe, which I never did before. It made us beat the ground with prodigious force. I thought it was better that I should engage the people of Skye by taking a cheerful glass and dancing with them rather than play the abstract scholar. I looked on this tour to the Hebrides as a co-partnery between Mr. Johnson and me. Each was to do all he could to promote its success; and I am certain that my gayer exertions were of much service to us. Mr. Johnson's immense fund of knowledge and wit was a wonderful source of admiration and delight to them. But they had it only at times; and they required to have interstices agreeably filled up, and even little elucidations of his grand text. Besides, they observed that it was I who always "set

---

[4] Horace, *Odes*, III.ii.31–2. "Rarely does punishment, though she seems to halt, fail to overtake a scoundrel."

him a-going." The fountain was locked up till I interfered. (I want a word here, as Macklin used to say when lecturing on oratory.) It was curious to hear them, when any dispute happened when Mr. Johnson was out of the room, saying, "Stay till Mr. Johnson comes. Say that to *him*." Had they been barbarians, he was an Orpheus to them. But I cannot give them that character with any justice.

I should mention that on Sunday last, Raasay sent his boat to Sconser for us, begging to have us again in his island, and if it was not convenient, he would come over and spend the evening with us. So Mr. Donald MacLeod informed me.

Yesterday Mr. Johnson said, "I cannot but laugh to think of myself roving among the Hebrides at sixty. I wonder where I shall rove at fourscore." This evening he disputed the truth of what is said as to the people of St. Kilda catching cold whenever strangers come. He said, "How can there be a physical effect without a physical cause?" He laughed and said that the arrival of a ship full of strangers would kill them; "for," said he, "if one stranger gives them one cold, two strangers must give them two colds; and so in proportion." I wondered to hear him ridicule this, as he had praised Macaulay for putting it in his book. He said the evidence was not adequate to the improbability of the fact. That if a physician, rather disposed to be incredulous, should go to St. Kilda and report the fact, he would begin to look about him. They said it was annually proved by MacLeod's steward. He turned jocular then and said, "The steward always comes to seek something from them, and so they fall a-coughing. I suppose the people in Skye all take a cold when Sir Alexander comes." They said Sir Alexander came only in summer. JOHNSON. "That is out of tenderness to you. Bad weather and he, at the same time, would be too much."

SUNDAY 3 OCTOBER. Mr. Johnson told me there were two faults in my Journal: one was expatiating too much on the luxury of the little-house at Talisker.[1] This fault, however, he

---

[1] This passage has unfortunately disappeared from the MS. See *ante*, p. 216, n. 21.

mentioned as if he liked it—as if my expatiating had been congenial with his own feelings. The other fault was in my representation of the dispute about the Scottish clergy (*vid. supra*[2]); "for," said he, "I did not say the man's hair could not be well dressed because he had not a clean shirt, but because he was bald."

We did not get up till ten o'clock. Joseph said the wind was still against us. Mr. Johnson said, "A wind, or not a wind? that is the question," for he can amuse himself at times with a little play of words, or rather of sentences. I remember when he turned his cup at Aberbrothock, he muttered, "*Claudite jam rivos, pueri.*" I added, "*Sat prata biberunt.*"[3] I am most scrupulously exact in this Journal. Mr. Johnson said it was a very exact picture of his life.

While we were chatting in the indolent style of men who were to stay here all day at least, we were suddenly roused with being told that the wind was fair, that a little fleet of herring vessels was passing by for Mull, and that Mr. Simson's vessel was lying off the shore for us. Hugh Macdonald, the skipper, came to us, and we were hurried to get ready, which we soon did. I just wrote a few lines to my wife. I felt my heart light at the thoughts of getting away. Breakfast was got ready for us. Mr. Johnson with composure and solemnity repeated the observation of Epictetus, that, "As man has the voyage of death before him, whatever he does, he should always be ready at the Master's call; and an old man should never be far from the shore, lest he should not be able to be in readiness." He had a horse, and I and the other gentlemen walked about an English mile to the shore, where the vessel was. Donald MacLeod, poor man, gave me a good bill upon Mr. MacLeod of Ose for the deficient £8. Mr. Johnson said he should never forget Skye, and returned thanks for all civilities. We were carried to the vessel in a small boat which she had, and we set sail very briskly

---

[2] p. 216.
[3] "Dam up the ditches, boys; the meadows have drunk enough." Virgil, *Eclogues*, III. 111.

about one o'clock. I was much pleased with the motion for
many hours. Mr. Johnson grew sick, and retired under cover,
as it rained a good deal. I kept above, that I might have fresh
air. I eat bread and cheese, and drank whisky and rum and
brandy. The worthy Bailie had sent with us half a sheep and
biscuits and apples and beer and brandy. There was a little
room or den at the forecastle, with two beds, and a fire in it.
Dinner was dressed, and I was persuaded to go down. I eat
boiled mutton and boiled salt herring, and drank beer and
punch.⁴ I exulted in being a stout seaman, while Mr. Johnson
was quite in a state of annihilation. But I soon had a change;
for after imagining that I could go with ease to America or the
East Indies, I turned woefully sick, and was obliged to get
above board, though it rained hard.

I regretted that we passed the island of Eigg, where there is
a very large cave in which all the inhabitants were smoked to
death by the MacLeods. They had murdered some MacLeods
who were sailing near their coast. MacLeod and a number of
the clan came to revenge the murder. The people of Eigg saw
them coming, and all retired into this cave, which has a low
and narrow entry, so that but one man can get in it at a time,
but afterwards becomes spacious and lofty like a church. Mac-
Leod and his people landed, and could not find a soul. They
might perhaps have gone away. But one of the Eigg people,
after waiting a long time in the cave, grew impatient, and
went out to see what was become of the enemy. Perceiving
them not gone, he returned. There was a deep snow upon the
ground, by which means he was tracked by the print of his
feet. The MacLeods came to the mouth of the cave. Nothing
could be done in the way of fighting, because but one man at
a time could either go out or in, and would be killed directly.
MacLeod called in to them that if they would give up the
murderers, he would be satisfied. This they refused to do. Upon

⁴ Boswell's illness is mentioned in the published *Tour*, but the account gains more point
when we learn what he had eaten and drunk.

which he ordered a quantity of peats to be laid in the mouth of the cave and to be set on fire, and thus the people of Eigg, man, woman and child, were smoked to death. Young Coll told us he has been in the cave, and seen great quantities of bones in it; and he said one can still observe where families have died, as big bones and small, those of a man and wife and children, are found lying together. This happened in —————— time.[5]

I was also sorry that we passed by the Isle of Muck. But Mr. Simson wanted to get forward; and besides, we knew that the Laird could not be yet at home, on account of contrary winds. I saw on the southeast as we sailed along, Morar, the present Laird of which had Prince Charles delivered to his care by Mackinnon. I wished much to have seen him, because it is said he owns that he has the second sight, which is hereditary in his family.

On the same quarter I saw Loch Moidart, into which the Prince entered on his first arrival, and within which is a lesser loch called Lochninua,[6] where the Prince actually landed. The hills around, or rather mountains, are black and wild in an uncommon degree. I gazed upon them with much feeling. There was a rude grandeur that seemed like a consciousness of the royal enterprise, and a solemn dreariness as if a melancholy remembrance of its events had remained.

Mr. Simson was brisk in his hopes for a while, for the wind was for a while for us. He said if it continued so, he would land us at "I" (i.e., Icolmkill) that night. But when the wind failed, it was resolved we should make for the Sound of Mull, and land in the harbour of Tobermory. We got up with the five herring vessels for a while. But four of them got before us, and one little wherry fell behind us. When we got in full view

---

[5] The massacre took place probably in 1577, in the time of Norman, 11th Chief of MacLeod. It is said that 395 people died in the cave. In the following year a band of the Macdonalds of Clan Ranald, to which the Macdonalds of Eigg belonged, landed on Skye at Waternish, seeking vengeance. They set fire to a church at the time of worship and made other depredations, but were finally captured and slaughtered by the MacLeods.
[6] Loch nan Uamh. It is not where Boswell says it is, however, but opens from the Sound of Arisaig, several miles north of Loch Moidart.

of the point of Ardnamurchan, the wind changed, and was full against our getting to the Sound. We were then obliged to tack, and get forward in that tedious manner. As we advanced, the storm grew greater, and the sea very rough. Coll then began to talk of making for Eigg or Canna or Coll. Macdonald, our skipper, said he would get us into the Sound. We struggled a good while for this. Then he said he would push forward till we were near the land of Mull, where we might cast anchor till the morning; for although before this there had been a good moon, and I had pretty distinctly seen not only the land of Mull, but up the Sound, and the country of Morvern as at one end of it, the night was now grown very dark. Our crew consisted of old Macdonald our skipper, a man with one eye, and another sailor. Mr. Simson himself, Coll, and Hugh Macdonald his servant, all helped. Simson said he would willingly go for Coll if young Coll or his servant would undertake to pilot us to a harbour, but as the island is low land, it was dangerous to run upon it in the dark. Coll and his servant seemed a little dubious. The scheme of running for Canna seemed then to be embraced, but Canna was ten leagues off, all out of our way; and they were afraid to attempt the harbour of Eigg. All these different plans being in agitation, I was much frightened. The old skipper still tried to make for the land of Mull; but then it was considered that there was no place there where we could anchor in safety. Much time was lost in striving against the storm. At last it became so rough, and threatened to be so much worse, that Coll and his servant took more courage, and said they would undertake to hit one of the harbours in Coll. "Then," said the skipper, "let us run for it, in GOD's name," and instantly we turned towards it. The little wherry which had fallen behind us had hard work. The master begged that, if we made for Coll, we should put out a light to him. Accordingly one of the sailors waved a glowing peat for some time. I had a short relief when I found we were to run for a harbour before the wind. But it was very short, for I soon heard that our sails were very bad, and were in danger of being torn in pieces, in which case we would be driven upon the rocky shore of Coll. It was very dark indeed, and there was a very heavy rain almost incessantly. The sparks of the peat-fire in the boat flew terribly about. I dreaded that the vessel might take fire. Then, as Coll was a sportsman, and had powder on board, I figured that we might be blown up. Simson and he both appeared a little frightened, which made me more so; and the perpetual talking, or rather shouting, which was carried on in Erse, alarmed me. A man is always suspicious of what is saying in an unknown tongue; and if fear be his passion at the time, he grows more afraid. The boat often lay so much to a side that I trembled lest she should be overset; and indeed they told me afterwards that they had run her sometimes to within an inch of the water, so anxious were they to make what haste they could before the night should be worse. I saw tonight what I never saw before, a prodigious sea with immense billows coming upon a vessel, so as that it seemed hardly possible to escape. There was something grandly horrible in the sight. I am glad I have seen it once. Amidst all these terrifying circumstances, I endeavoured to compose my mind. It was not easy to do it, for all the stories that I had heard of the dangerous sailing among the Hebrides, which is proverbial, or at least often mentioned, came full upon my recollection. It distressed me to think how much my dearest wife would suffer should I now be lost, and in what a destitute, or at least wretchedly dependent, state she would be left. I upbraided myself as not having a sufficient cause for putting myself in such danger. Piety afforded me a good deal of comfort. I prayed fervently to GOD, but I was confused, for I remember I used a strange expression: that if it should please him to preserve me, *I would behave myself ten times better*. Be the expression what it may, I shall never forget —at least I hope so—the good resolutions which I then formed. While I prayed, I was disturbed by the objections against a particular providence and against hoping that the petitions of an individual would have any influence with the Divinity; objections which have been often made, and which Dr. Hawkesworth has lately revived in his preface to the *Voyages to the South Seas*; but Dr. Ogden's excellent doctrine on the efficacy of intercession prevailed. I was really in very great fear this night.

It was half an hour after eleven before we set ourselves in the course for Coll. As I saw them all busy doing something, I asked Coll with much earnestness what I could do. He with a lucky readiness put into my hand a rope which was fixed to the top of one of the masts, and bid me hold it fast till he bid me pull. This could not be of the least service; but by employing me, he kept me out of their way, who were busy working the ship; and at the same time diverted my fear to a certain degree, by making me think I was occupied. There did I stand firm to my post while the wind and rain beat upon me, always expecting a call to pull my rope.

The man with one eye steered. Old Macdonald and Coll and his servant lay upon the forecastle looking sharp out for the harbour. It was necessary to carry much *cloth*, as they termed it, that is to say, much sail, in order to keep the vessel off the shore of Coll. This made terrible plunging in a rough sea. At last they spied the harbour of Lochiern,[7] and Coll cried, "Thank God, we're safe!" We run up till we were opposite to it, and then were wafted, I may say, though not gently, into it, where we cast anchor. The comfort which I felt may easily be imagined.

Mr. Johnson had all this time been quiet and unconcerned. He had lain down on one of the beds, and having got free of sickness, was quite satisfied.[8] Once during the doubtful consultations he asked whither we were going; and upon being told that it was not certain whether to Mull or Coll, he cried, "Coll for my money." I now went down, with Coll and Simson, be-

---

[7] Probably Loch Eatharna.
[8] At this point in the published *Tour* Boswell adds: "The truth is, he knew nothing of the danger we were in." Boswell had been dissatisfied with Johnson's account of this storm in his *Journey*. In his "Remarks" on that book, which he sent to Johnson, he said, "You treat the storm too lightly. Coll and all the islanders thought we were really in danger."

side him. He was lying in philosophic tranquillity, with a grey-hound of Coll's at his back keeping him warm. Coll is quite the *juvenis qui gaudet canibus*. He had when we left Talisker two greyhounds, two terriers, a pointer and a large Newfoundland water-dog. He lost one of his terriers by the road, but had five dogs still with him. I was miserably sick and very desirous to get to shore. When I was told that I could not get ashore that night, as the storm had now increased, I looked woefully, as Coll informed me. Shakespeare's phrase, which he puts into the Frenchman's mouth, of the English soldiers when starved: "Piteous they will look, like drowned mice,"[9] might have been applied to me. There was in the harbour before us a Campbel-town vessel, the *Betty*, Kenneth Morison master. She was tak-ing in kelp at Coll, and was bound for Ireland. This was a lucky opportunity for us to get across to Mull in a strong ship after seeing Coll, which we could do while she took in the rest of her loading, part of which she was to get just at Coll's house. She was about twenty yards from us. Coll and Simson sent our boat to beg beds in her for two gentlemen, and that she would send her boat, which was larger.[10] They were to go and leave me with Mr. Johnson in our vessel. I was so very uneasy that I imagined I should be better in the other vessel; so went with them, and flattered myself with finding a spacious cabin. But behold, there was only a little confined place. I wished to re-turn to the former vessel, but was ashamed to give more trou-ble. I began to think it was wrong for me to leave Mr. John-son. But I considered that he was quite well; that I had left Joseph to take care of him; that the crew would have more room to warm themselves by my being away; and that my ex-treme sickness was a sufficient excuse for my trying everything I could for relief. Morison very genteelly yielded his bed to Simson. Coll and I had the other, for the cabin held just two. It was a very small one, and we were squeezed into it in a very

---

[9] *I Henry VI*, I.ii.
[10] The remainder of this entry was omitted in the published *Tour*.

uneasy manner. I was soaked to the skin all this time, for I had
a short greatcoat which defended me little. I threw off tonight
only my boots and greatcoat.[11] I lay in considerable pain, for
though the ship was at anchor, there was a great rolling, which
made my sickness continue; and as the storm grew much worse
and beat furiously upon the ship, I could not help being frightened that she might be set to sea again. I recollected reading in
the newspapers of ships being driven from their moorings. I got
some broken slumbers. My head was very cold, as having only
my wig for a night-cap. In the morning I fell upon the expedient
of wrapping my coat around it, which made me warm enough.

MONDAY 4 OCTOBER. Between eight and nine I got up
and went above deck. By this time, Mr. ——— Macdonald from
Campbeltown, another of the owners of the ship (she belonged
to Morison and him jointly) was come on board from the shore,
where he had been all night. We soon got ready, and were carried in the ship's boat alongside of Simson's vessel. We saw nothing of the poor wherry and were afraid. We took in Mr. Johnson
and Joseph, and Simson's boat carried Coll's servant, the dogs,
and the baggage. Mr. Johnson was quite well, though he had
not tasted victuals, except a dish of tea without bread, since
Saturday night. I was happy that he was not angry at my leaving him. I may here mention that when he lived in the Temple,
and had no regular system of living, he has fasted for two days,
that is to say from Sunday night till Wednesday morning. He
went about and visited, though not at meal-times. He drank
tea during that time, but ate no bread. This was not intentional
fasting, but happened just in the course of a studious life or a
literary life.

There was a little poor public house close upon the shore,
to which we would have gone had we landed last night. But
this morning Coll resolved to take us directly to the house of

---

[11] A corner of a leaf is missing, and several words in the preceding three sentences have
been supplied by conjecture. Those which are doubtful are "into it," "soaked," "a
short," "little," and "boots and great—." Instead of "a short" we should perhaps read
"only a."

Captain Lauchlan Maclean, a descendant of his family, who had made money in the East Indies, and come home and taken a farm in Coll. We had about an English mile to go to it. Coll and Joseph and some other men, I forget whether part of the crew or people of the island, ran to some little horses that were going on a field, and catched one of them. We had a saddle with us which was clapped upon it, and a straw halter was put on his head. Mr. Johnson was then mounted, and Joseph very slowly and gravely led the horse. I said to Mr. Johnson I wished the Club saw him in this attitude.[1]

It was a prodigious rain, and I was wet to the skin, both at the neck and legs. Captain Maclean had but a poor temporary house, or rather hut, just a little larger than the common country house. However, it was a very good haven to us. He gave me a dry shirt and dry stockings directly. There was a blazing peat-fire, and Mrs. Maclean, daughter of the minister of the parish, got us tea. I felt still the motion of the sea. Mr. Johnson said it was not imagination, but a continuation of motion in the fluids, like that of the sea itself after the storm is over.

There were some books on the board which served as a chimney-piece. Mr. Johnson took up Burnet's *History of His Own Times*. He said the first part of it was quite dramatic: while he went about everywhere, saw everywhere, and heard everywhere. He said by the first part he meant so far as it appeared that Burnet himself was actually engaged in what he narrated; and this he said one might easily distinguish. The Captain censured him for his high praise of Lauderdale in a

---

[1] "This curious exhibition may perhaps remind some of my readers of the ludicrous lines, made, during Sir Robert Walpole's administration, on Mr. George (afterwards Lord) Lyttelton, though the figures of the two personages must be allowed to be very different:

'But who is this astride the pony;
So long, so lean, so lank, so bony?
Dat be de great orator, Lytteltony.'"—BOSWELL.

"Here I first mounted a little Highland steed; and if there had been many spectators, should have been somewhat ashamed of my figure in the march. The horses of the Islands, as of other barren countries, are very low: they are indeed muscular and strong, beyond what their size gives reason for expecting; but a bulky man upon one of their backs makes a very disproportionate appearance" (Johnson's *Journey*).

dedication, when he shows him in his history to have been so bad a man. Mr. Johnson said, "I do not think myself that a man should say in a dedication what he could not say in a history. But there is a great difference; for the known style of a dedication is flattery. It professes to flatter. There is the same difference between what a man says in a dedication and a history, as between a lawyer pleading a cause and reporting it."

Mr. Macdonald from the ship was now with us. He had been here last night. The day slipped along easily enough. We had a very good dinner: the best shortbread just baked by Mrs. Maclean, and pleasant rum punch soured with lemon shrub. I had not tasted lemon for more than a month. The wind turned fair for Mull in the evening, and Mr. Simson resolved to sail next morning. It was so fair that I began to waver whether we should not go with him; and Mr. Johnson said to me, "I'll do what you please." However, I considered that it would be weak just to land on Coll, and run away from it without seeing the old castle or anything else; and as we had the Campbeltown vessel to take us to Mull in a day or two, I determined to stay.

At night I was a little disconcerted. There were but three rooms or divisions in the house. The Captain and Mrs. Maclean had one. Mr. Johnson had another, with Joseph on a straw-bed beside him. And in the room where we sat all day were two beds. Simson and Macdonald had the one. The other was for young Coll and me. I have a mortal aversion at sleeping in the same bed with a man; and a young Highlander was always somewhat suspicious as to scorbutic symptoms. I once thought of sleeping on chairs; but this would have been uncivil and disobliging to a young gentleman who was very civil and obliging to us. Upon inspection, as much as could be without his observing it, he seemed to be quite clean, and the bed was very broad. So I lay down peaceably, kept myself separated from him, and reposed tolerably.[2]

TUESDAY 5 OCTOBER. Simson went off about seven. I

---

[2] This paragraph was omitted in the published *Tour*.

rose and wrote my Journal till about nine, and then went to Mr. Johnson, who sat up in bed and talked and laughed. I said it was curious to look back ten years to the time when we first talked of visiting the Hebrides. How distant and improbable the scheme then appeared! Yet here we were actually among them. "Sir," said he, "people may do anything almost by talking of it. I really believe I could talk myself into building a house upon island Isay, though I'd probably never come back again to see it. I could easily persuade Reynolds to do it. There would be no great sin in persuading him to do it. Sir, he'd reason thus: 'What will it cost me to be there once in two or three summers? Why, perhaps £500, that is, £150 a year; and what is that in comparison of having a fine retreat to which a man can go, or to which he may send a friend?'—and he'd never find out that he may have this within twenty miles of London. Then I'd tell him that he may marry one of the Miss Mac-Leods, a lady of great family. Sir, it is surprising how people will go to a distance for what they may have at home. Mrs. Langton came up to Knightsbridge with one of her daughters, and gave five guineas a week for a lodging and having a warm bath, that is, mere warm water. *That*, you know, could not be had in Lincolnshire. They said it was made either too hot or too cold there."

The house here was built of stone without mortar, and had no plaster or finishing at all. It was as cold as a stable. The Captain is going to build. Before the house where he now lives, there is like a rampart of whinstone upon the ridge of a rising ground running to the sea. We were here about four miles from the east end of the island.

After breakfast Mr. Johnson and I and Joseph mounted horses, and Coll and the Captain walked with us about a short mile across the island. We called for Mr. Hector Maclean, the minister.[1] His parish consists of Coll and Tyree. He was about

---

[1] A note on the margin of this page (421) of the MS reads, "Mem: the ministers named by their Christian names, Mr. Donald, Mr. Martin, etc." More than once in his journals Boswell refers to the Rev. Mr. George Reid, Lord Auchinleck's old tutor, as "Mass George."

seventy-seven, a decent old man in a full suit of black and a
black wig. He was like a Dutch minister or one of the assembly
of divines at Westminster. Mr. Johnson said he was a fine old
man—was as well dressed and had as much dignity in his appearance as the dean of a cathedral. We saw his wife and another daughter. A glass of whisky and cheese and barley-bread
were served about by Miss, who was dressed in a clean printed
linen gown. The old gentleman, we were told, has a valuable
library, though he has but poor accommodation for it. He has
no manse, only a small farm-house; and his books are kept in
large chests. Coll says he is determined to purchase the library
when the old man dies. It was curious to see him and Mr. Johnson. Neither of them heard very quickly; so each of them talked
in his own way, and at the same time. Mr. Hector said he had
a confutation of Bayle by Leibnitz. Said Mr. Johnson, "What
part of Bayle do you mean? The greatest part of his writing is
not confutable. It is historical and critical." Mr. Hector said,
"The irreligious part," and proceeded to talk of Leibnitz's controversy with Clarke, calling him a great man. Mr. Johnson said
that Leibnitz persisted in affirming that Newton called space
the *sensorium numinis*, notwithstanding he was corrected and desired to observe that Newton said *quasi sensorium numinis*. "No,"
said he, "Leibnitz was as paltry a fellow as I know. As he was
patronized by Queen Caroline, Clarke treated him too well."

During the time that Mr. Johnson was thus going on, old
Mr. Hector was standing with his back to the fire, cresting up
erect, pulling down the front of his periwig, and talking what
a great man Leibnitz was. To give an idea of the scene would
require a page with two columns; but it could not be quite well
represented but by two players. The old gentleman said Clarke
was very wicked for going so much into the Arian system. "I
will not say he was wicked," said Mr. Johnson; "he might be
mistaken." Said Mr. Hector, "He was wicked to shut his eyes
against the Scriptures;" adding, "worthy men since, in Eng-

land, have confuted him to all intents and purposes." "I know not," said Mr. Johnson, "*who* has confuted him *to all intents and purposes*." Here again there was a double talking.

I regretted that Mr. Johnson did not practise the art of accommodating himself to different sorts of people. Had he been softer with this venerable old man, we might have had more conversation. But Mr. Johnson's forcible spirit and impetuosity of manner may be said to spare neither sex nor age. I have seen even Mrs. Thrale stunned. But I have often maintained that it is better so. Pliability of address I take to be inconsistent with that majestic power which he has, and which produces such noble effects. A bar of iron nor a lofty oak will not bend like a supple willow, or like many plants between those. What though he presses down feeble beings in his course? They get up again like stalks of ripe grass.

He told me afterwards he liked firmness in an old man, and was pleased to see Mr. Hector so orthodox. "At his age," said he, "it is too late for a man to be asking himself questions as to his belief."[2]

Mr. Hector said he had taken up a list of his parishioners between seven and seventy by order of the General Assembly, and found nine hundred. According to this there must be about 1,200 souls in Coll. There must be two hundred under seven, and I should think fifty may be reckoned above seventy. The island is computed to be twelve English miles long, and three broad at an average. It is very populous. The inhabitants live mostly in little rural villages, for so I may call a number of houses close to each other, almost; at least with but small interstices. I saw at one place near the west end of the island, a village where I counted above thirty houses, and saw they would exceed forty. Fifty-eight families lived in it. Their stacks of corn were not much unlike their thatched houses. The village looked at a little distance like a very full barn-yard.

---

[2] From this point forward, the account of Coll was greatly cut in the published *Tour*.

The people in Coll live more comfortably than those in Skye; for each has a little garden—a kale-yard, which few have in Skye; and the people here appeared to be better dressed.

It was very agreeable, as we went along, to see all the people come from their work and shake hands with the young laird. Mr. Johnson wished that he had more conversation than that of a mere farmer; and indeed he seemed to be just a young country lad who had been a while in England. He had worked there with his own hands, while he lived at farmers' houses in Hertfordshire, in[3] order to learn to improve his paternal acres, or rather *miles*. Mr. Johnson said that was like the Czar of Muscovy. By this, however, his manners were not those of a chieftain in point of dignity. But if he had not reverence from his people, he had their affection. I could find no traces of learning about him; though he had been educated under the care of his uncle, the professor at Aberdeen. But he had a constant good humour, and readiness of conversation upon common things. Then he had a clear sharp voice, and was not afraid to talk to Mr. Johnson; informed him as to many particulars, and stuck to his point when Mr. Johnson opposed what he said, until very handsomely driven off. With all this he had as much civility as could be wished, and very great attention to have everything right about Mr. Johnson.

We rode near to the shore opposite to the Captain's on the north of the island. There we saw the ruins of a church or chapel. The place is called Kilymaik or the Kirktown. It has not been large; the wall remains for about the highth of four feet all along, without any gap. The inside was covered with water. Beside it was a place of graves. There were two stones over lairds of Coll, and not many other stones. The family has never had any built burial place; and this place here has never been so much as enclosed. I could see no vestige that it has. We returned to near the minister's. The Captain walked a little farther with us, and then turned back.

---

[3] Preceded by a blank in the MS, probably for a place-name or an indication of time.

We went on about two miles till we came to Grishipoll, or the rough pool. It is just on the seaside, and the waves beat very high. It is about the middle of the island on the north side. On the beach here there is a singular variety of globular stones. I picked up one, which I called a Siberian turkey's egg, and another which was very like a small cucumber. By the by, Mr. Johnson told me that Gay's phrase, "as men should serve a cucumber," in the *Beggar's Opera*, has no waggish meaning with reference to men flinging away cucumbers as too *cooling*, which some have thought; for it has been a common saying in England of every great physician, that he prescribed that a cucumber should be well sliced and dressed with vinegar, and then thrown out, as good for nothing. So the phrase is just a . . . beauty as people should always serve a cucumber—in conformity with the ordinary prejudice. This is my commentary.[4]

I saw here growing in the sand on the sea-shore and among small pebbles, a large green plant very like to kale or coleworts. It has a salt taste. It is purgative. The cattle will not eat it. Indeed it has rather a harshness on the palate.

We found at Grishipoll an excellent slated house of two storeys. It was built by the present Coll while his eldest brother was alive; and just as it was finished he succeeded to the estate. The tenant, with whom we dined, was Mr. McSweyn. His predecessors had been in Skye from a very remote period, upon the estate belonging to MacLeod; but probably before the MacLeods had it, as the name is certainly Norwegian, from Sueno, King of Norway. This Mr. McSweyn left Skye upon MacLeod's raising his rents. He then got this farm from Coll, whom he had *fostered*. I must explain what is meant by fostering. It has been a custom in the Highlands and isles for substantial farmers or tacksmen to take the children of the lairds into

---

[4] Polly Peachum's mother, on discovering her secret marriage to Macheath, remarks that after all the pains they have taken to dress her "with care and cost, all tempting, fine, and gay, As men should serve a cucumber, she flings herself away." This passage in Boswell, which was written in a cramped hand at the very bottom of a page, has been rendered more difficult by being heavily scored out in the revision. The undeciphered portion may contain eight or nine letters.

their houses, a little after they are weaned, and keep them till they are fit for education; and then they gave them by way of portion a number of cattle, which were called *mackalive*[5] cattle. The custom I fancy may still prevail; at least it did lately. This same young Coll was fostered by a Campbell in the island of Tyree, and got forty mackalive cattle. It seems it has not been required that the fosterers should be of the same clan with the children. Young Coll should be a hero, for he may be said to have been fostered by a wolf, as Romulus and Remus were nursed. The Macleans have suffered so much from the ravages of the Campbells that his being fostered by a Campbell may be compared to the Roman emblem. Girls were given to be fostered as well as boys. The present Lady Coll, sister to Talisker, was also fostered by Mr. McSweyn. It is a strange custom.

McSweyn was now about seventy-seven, but looked as fresh and was as stout as a man of fifty. His son Hugh really looked older, and as Mr. Johnson observed, had more the manners of an old man than he. I had often heard of such instances, but never saw one before. Mrs. McSweyn was a decent old gentle-woman, not much failed, though she had been above fifty years married. She was dressed in tartan, and could speak nothing but Erse. She said she had taught Sir James Macdonald Erse, and would teach me soon. I could now sing a verse of the words to *Hatyin foam eri*,[6] upon Allan, the famous captain of Clanranald, who fell at Sheriffmuir, and of whom his servant who lay on the field watching his dead body, being asked next day who that was, answered, "He was a man yesterday"; and I had picked up I suppose thirty words.

We had here the best goose that I ever eat. Mr. Johnson was much pleased with it; and we had whisky in a clam-shell, ac-

---

[5] Properly *mackallow*, from Gaelic *macaladh*, "fostering."

[6] Boswell's phonetics are English, and would be less ambiguous if written *Ha cheen foam airy*. The Gaelic spelling is *Tha tighinn fodham èiridh*. These words constitute a refrain, frequently repeated, the meaning being, "It comes upon me to arise"—i.e., for the Jacobite cause.

cording to the ancient Highland custom. Mr. Johnson drank a little water out of it.

In the forenoon Mr. Johnson said that it would require great resignation to live in one of these islands. "I don't know," said I; "I have felt myself at times in a state of almost physical existence, satisfied to eat, drink and sleep, and walk about and enjoy my own thoughts; and I can figure a continuation of this." "Ay, sir," said he; "but if you were shut up here, your own thoughts would torment you; you would think of Edinburgh or London, and that you could not be there."

We were entertained at McSweyn's with a primitive heartiness. He and Coll got a horse; and McSweyn, Junior, walked before us to Breacacha, the family seat, where his wife was waiting to be landlady to us. It is called Breacacha, or the spotted field, because in summer it is enamelled with clover and daisies, as young Coll told me. I should have mentioned that at Grishipoll the hearths were formed of the round sea-pebbles, such as those with which the court at Talisker was paved, but as it was most inconvenient at the latter, it was very rational at Grishipoll; because, as Mr. Johnson observed, it kept the fire, which is always made in these islands upon the hearth, from moving, and so served both as hearth and fender. As we rode along in the forenoon, we saw a wonderful plenty of whinstone upon the surface of the earth. Mr. Johnson said, "I see a plain of stone." There are however innumerable spots of earth between them, on which corn grows; and when it is cut, they set it up on the stony places to dry. I observed that the corn in Coll is very short, so that there is less straw produced than I ever saw anywhere else. We rode from Grishipoll aslant the island to the southwest. We passed by a place where there is a large lump of whinstone, I may call it a rock—"a vast weight for Ajax." The tradition is that a giant threw such a lump at his mistress up to a hill or little mountain at a small distance to the southwest, and that she in return threw this lump down to him. It was all in sport:

Malo me petit lasciva puella.[7]

The hill is called Ben Hogh, the hill of Hogh, a neighbouring farm. Coll said that each of these stones is supported by a number of small ones. I got off my horse and inspected the one below. I did perceive stones under it, but I could not be sure but they were pieces of itself. I could however put my cane a great way under it. Mr. Johnson said there was no matter whether there were stones under it or not. It could hardly fall anywhere here that it would not rest upon stones. The question was, had it a root in the earth? I really thought not. Coll said the one on the hill was much more plainly detached. How this has happened it is difficult to say. There is no large rock near of which it could have been a part. Perhaps some violence of nature has burst or pounded a large rock originally here, and so scattered its fragments around. At present the appearance is like the pieces of a broken loaf of sugar. No loaf is to be seen, only bits of sugar of different sizes. A little farther on, we came to two triangular flagstones △ △ placed I imagine about ten yards from each other. (I afterwards measured: fourteen of my paces.) They have probably been a Druidical temple. Of latter times they are used for putting a trick on any stranger who is passing that way. He is desired to lie down behind the easternmost one (or westernmost, according to the route he is on) and told that he will hear everything that is said by the company, who stand at the other stone; and while he is lying in patient attention, the company get off and leave him; and when he at last gets up, he finds himself all alone. The stones are called Sgeulachdan, that is to say, "Long tales." Coll said if it had not been too late, he would have made me go through the ceremony.

There is a curious custom at Coll. On the last night of the old year, a man puts upon him a cow's skin and runs round the house, while a number of people make a noise chasing him and beating upon the skin, which sounds like a drum. This

7 "The wanton girl throws an apple at me."—Virgil, *Eclogues*, III.64.

brings out the strangers who are in the house to see what is the matter; and most of the family go out to decoy strangers, or for their diversion. Then the door is shut, and nobody gets in without repeating a verse of their own composition. It need not be extemporary. Some will be preparing for it all the year. When they are all got in, the evening is spent in great merriment, and the verses of each are criticized with emulation. Mr. Johnson, who is for all old customs, said he would keep up this.

About ten days at Christmas time the people in Coll make merry. All the men in the island are divided into two parties. Each party is headed by a gentleman. The Laird perhaps heads one, and Captain Maclean another; or other two gentlemen of the family are leaders. There is a ball thrown down in the middle of a space above the house, or on a strand near it; and each party strives to beat it first to one end of the ground with clubs or crooked sticks. The club is called the *shinny*. It is used in the low-country of Scotland. The name is from the danger that the shins run. We corrupt it to *shinty*. The leader of the party which prevails receives the bet which the opposite leader has lost to him, and gives it to the people to drink.

As we advanced, we came to a large extent of plain ground. I had not seen such a place for a long time. Coll and I took a gallop upon it by way of race. It was very refreshing to me, after having been so long taking short steps in hilly countries. It was like stretching a man's legs after being cramped in a short bed. We also passed close by a large extent of sand hills, I dare say near two miles square. Mr. Johnson was like to be angry with me for being pleased with them. I said I saw only dryness and cleanliness. He said he never had had the image before. It was horrible, if barrenness and danger could be so. I heard him, after we were in the house of Breacacha, repeating to himself as he walked about the room,

> "And smother'd in the dusty whirlwind, dies."

I suppose he had been repeating the whole of the simile in *Cato*, as the sandy desert had struck him strongly. The sand has blown of late over a good deal of meadow. But it is not so thick but that grass grows in summer. It is very alarming. People in the island tell that their fathers told them they saw ploughed land over most of the space which is now covered with sand. Coll's house is situated on a bay called Breacacha Bay, from the place where the family residence has always been. We found here a neat gentleman's house with four rooms on a floor, three storeys and garrets. The dining-room and the other three rooms on that floor were well wainscoted with good fir, and were very snug in dry weather. The storm, which beats on the front of the house and on one end, from the south-west, has hurt the timber of the windows much, so that they let in rain. There are two neat wings or pavilions to the house. On our arrival here, we felt ourselves very comfortable. There was in the dining-room a map of the world and many tables, one large, one covered with wax-cloth. We had not been in so good a house since we were in Lord Erroll's. Mr. Johnson rel-ished it much at first, but soon remarked that there was noth-ing becoming a chief about it. It was quite a tradesman's box. It was at present a kind of waste[8] house. However, young Coll did very well. McSweyn, Junior, and his wife were busy to get things right; and a very clever girl, a Maclean, a native of the island, who had been five years a servant-maid at Glasgow and was come home on a visit to her relations, was got to officiate. Mr. Johnson seemed quite at home. He told me he could easily enough say "Lady Raasay," but could not bring his tongue to pronounce readily the address to a laird by his title alone, as "MacLeod," "Raasay." By this time he had improved, for he called, "Now, Coll, if you could get us a dish of tea." We had it directly, and we had a very good supper served on china. We had a bold tune from the piper, a decent comely fellow with a green cloth waistcoat with silver lace; and then he helped to serve at table. His name was Neill Rankin. These Rankins have been pipers to the family of Maclean for many genera-

---

[8] Unoccupied.

tions. They used to have a college in Mull for teaching the bagpipe, but it has not been in practice now for sixteen years. I forgot to mention that there was a college for the bagpipe in Skye kept by the MacCrimmons, the hereditary pipers of the Laird of MacLeod. It subsisted in a certain degree till last year, that an admirable piper went to America. MacLeod's present piper, whom we heard every day, is yet no professor, though he has a good ear, and plays very well.[9]

Mr. Johnson and I had each an excellent bedroom on the dining-room floor. We had a dispute which of us had the best curtains. He rather had, as his were linen. But I insisted that I had the best posts, which was undeniable. Said he, "If you have the best posts, we'll have you tied to 'em and whipped" —and so he got the better of me. As he did in this mere trifle, he will do at times in disputes of serious import. I can never forget Goldsmith's lively saying, the fruit of many a severe defeat which he has suffered. Said he one day when we dined at Colman's, "There's no arguing with Johnson, for if his pistol misses fire, he knocks you down with the butt-end of it."

WEDNESDAY 6 OCTOBER. After a sufficiency of sleep, we assembled at breakfast. We were just as if in barracks. Everybody was master.[1] We went and viewed the old castle of Coll, which is about two gun-shots from the present house, very near to the shore, and founded on a rocky bottom. The late Coll, brother to the present laird, lived in it till within ——

---

[9] "MacLeod's *hereditary* piper is called MacCrimmon, but the present holder of the office has risen above his profession. He is an old man, a lieutenant in the army, and a most capital piper, possessing about 200 tunes and pibrochs, most of which will probably die with him, as he declines to have any of his sons instructed in his art. He plays to MacLeod and his lady, but only in the same room, and maintains his minstrel privilege by putting on his bonnet so soon as he begins to play. These MacCrimmons formerly kept a college in Skye for teaching the pipe-music. MacLeod's present piper is of the name, but scarcely as yet a deacon of the craft. He played every day at dinner."—Sir Walter Scott, in Lockhart's *Memoirs*, 24 August 1814.

[1] The emendation *muster'd* has been suggested, but the MS shows that *master* is correct. Boswell means that Coll's manner was not that of a host, but of a companion, and that nobody paid him any particular deference. Boswell has the same comparison in his Journal for 9 March 1777, where, speaking of Treesbank, he says, "It was a picture of desolation to find both Master and Mistress gone; yet I know not how, there was a sort of feeling of ease, as in barracks."

years of his death. He died in 1754. There were thirty cows killed for his funeral, and about fifty sheep. There were gentlemen at it from the mainland as well as the neighbouring islands. We surveyed the old castle very minutely. It was more entire than any that I ever saw. It has never been a large feudal residence, Coll being but a second son of the Maclean family. There was a wall had gone all round; and one square tower was plainly very ancient, as was also a round tower which had an arched roof, and a parapet wall around the top. It served as a spying place towards the sea. There were battlements towards the east. There were two doors or gates to the castle on the ground. Above each was a place for throwing stones down in case of an attack. On the second storey we saw a vault which was, and still is, the family prison. There was a woman put into it by the Laird for stealing peats, within these ten years; and any offender would be put in yet, for from the necessity of the thing, as the island is remote from any power established by law, the Laird must exercise his jurisdiction to a certain degree. There were several other pieces of building within the walls, I know not of what age. All the roofs of all the different buildings here were covered with slates of an uncommon size. One of them was as long as my cane, and they were also uncommonly broad and thick. The walls, as in all old castles, were of an immense thickness. There was a bedroom, as it was called, and indeed it was used as such, in the thickness of the wall. It had two slits by way of windows. Mr. Johnson examined all this remaining specimen of ancient life with wonderful eagerness. It was very inconveniently arranged. There was one narrow passage which he tried to get through, but found it would not do. He persisted however; opened his waistcoat and pressed through. There was in the thickness of the walls on the southwest what Coll called a closet. It was a narrow passage or stripe to the southwest corner, and then it run at a right angle to the north for a little way. Mr. Johnson had first looked at it from the entry into it. I went in and reported that it was a

circular closet. I was mistaken, to be sure, in every sense; for
the line which it formed had nothing of the circle. Coll agreed
with me. This incited Mr. Johnson's curiosity to a keener pitch,
as he was almost positive we were wrong, from the cursory
view he had taken. "How the plague is it circular?" said he;
and back he went, and proceeded into it, and confuted us.
This old castle exemplified Gray's verses on one:

> Huge windows that exclude the light
> And passages that lead to nothing.

Besides the two doors on the ground, there was one to the
square tower from the battlements.

In the prison, which is a good large vault, we were shown
in a corner a hole into which Coll said greater criminals used
to be put. It was now filled up with rubbish of different kinds,
particularly broken bottles. Coll said it was of a great depth.
"Ay," said Mr. Johnson. "All such places *that are filled up* were
of a great depth." He is very quick in showing why he does
not give credit to what he is told, when that is the case. Since
we came into Coll, somebody told him of 10,000 somethings,
I do not recollect what. He said to me, "Why, sir, you know
10,000 is an even number." He made a similar observation
on the number of people in the parish of Sleat being given
him without any small fractions, as I may say (such as 1555),
but in round hundreds. I think this was one of his instances
of shrewd correction, and to be sure it is hardly to be believed
that exact regular numbers will happen; so, when a man mentions such, it is probable he has not been exact. Mr. Macpherson at Sleat told us there had not been above 1000[2] Highlanders engaged abroad in the last war. He must be mistaken, I
should imagine. After seeing the castle, we looked at a small
house, just a hut, built to the north of it, touching the wall.
It is called *Teigh Franchich*,[3] i.e., the Frenchman's house. Coll
could not tell what was the history of it. A poor man with a

---

[2] The first digit is somewhat doubtful: perhaps 4.
[3] Better, *taigh an Fhrangaich*.

wife and ——— children now lived in it. Mr. Johnson walked into it and we followed. He gave some charity. There was one bed for all the family. It was very smoky. When he came out, he said to me, "*Et hoc secundum sententiam philosophorum est esse beatus.*"[4] I said the philosophers, when they placed happiness in a cottage, supposed cleanliness and no smoke. He said they did not think about either.

We walked a little in the garden, a piece of ground enclosed with a stone dike, and well stored with garden stuff. But not a tree is to be found in Coll. They have tried many in the garden, but as soon as they got higher than the dike, they died. We saw a few very young fruit-trees on the southwest wall, and a nursery of firs. Mr. Johnson prescribed sowing the seeds of hardy trees, such as birch. Coll showed us four very good rooms on the ground floor. One of them was a charter-room. The papers were confusedly kept. He without scruple opened both a little trunk and a cabinet where they lay, and let me look. I shall afterwards mention some of them.

He and I went and took a ride, I upon a black stoned-horse,[5] he on a bay mare followed by a foal which sucked her when there was any halt. We saw a very pretty turnip-field near the house, which young Coll hoed all with his own hand. He had one last year. These have been the first in the Western Isles. We rode along a fine strand on the south, or rather southwest, side of the island, for it lies southeast and northwest. The strand may be a mile and a half, admirable airing ground. Young Coll has tried to make roads in the island. We saw two pieces very well executed. The day was clear and only a little windy. We saw Mull, Icolmkill, Fladda, the Dutchman's Cap (the two last small islands between Coll and Mull), as also Cairnbulg, a rock in the sea on which was a fortification of old.

We came to a farm called Crossapoll, i.e., the pool of the

---

[4] "And that, according to the opinion of philosophers, is happiness." The last three words were added at the time of revision for publication.
[5] i.e., a stallion.

Cross. The tenant, Maclean, is a most industrious man. He has ten children. He gives a college education at Aberdeen to his eldest son, who in the vacation keeps a school here, having so much paid him by the gentlemen of the island. We were now within about a mile and a half of the west end of the island. We crossed over to the north side and looked at an appearance of lead, which seemed very promising. It has been long known, for I found in Coll's cabinet letters to the late laird from Sir John Erskine and Sir Alexander Murray, respecting lead—Sir John's directly so, and Sir Alexander's so as mentioning it in such a way as I understood it—and I fancy Coll never had any other view of lead but this. We passed along through a great extent of ground blown over with sand, till we came to another very good airing strand on the north side of the island; then turned to the right by the village of Foill, where I counted so many houses, and so got home.

After dinner came Mr. Maclean of Cornaig, brother to Isle of Muck, who is a cadet of the family of Coll. He possesses the two ends of Coll, which belong to the Duke of Argyll, as part of the estate of Maclean, which the Duke has, but which is now contested at law by Sir Allan Maclean. The two ends of Coll were church lands belonging to Icolmkill. At the Reformation Maclean got them back. Coll used to have a lease of the two ends. The last rent was £45. Upon the Duke's demanding a high rent, Coll would no longer be tenant; so this gentleman, Cornaig (which is the name of the principal place on the lands), took them in 1771 for nineteen years at £105. His brother, Isle of Muck, has a share with him. Cornaig told me they were resolved to *go the length of their tether* rather than let a Campbell into Coll; and the Campbells had offered near as much. Mr. Johnson well observed that landlords err much when they calculate merely what their land *may* yield. "The rent must be in a proportionate ratio of what the land may yield, and of the power of the tenant to make it yield. A tenant cannot make by his land but according to the corn and cattle which he has.

Suppose you should give him twice as much land as he has, it does him no good unless he gets also more stock. It is clear then," said he, "that the Highland landlords who let their substantial tenants go, are infatuated; for the poor small tenants cannot give them good rents, from the very nature of things. They have not the means of raising more from their farms." Cornaig was a tall stout man with grey hair, tied, but he was but middle-aged. Mr. Johnson found him the most distinct man that he had met with in these isles. He said he did not shut his eyes or put his fingers in his ears, which he seemed to think, with justice too, was a good deal the mode with most of the people whom we have seen of late. At night came Crossapoll and his eldest son, really an ingenious lad. He had taken a pretty good view of Staffa. We were jovial tonight. Cornaig sung Erse songs. We had no liquor but whisky punch without souring. The cellars of Coll were quite empty. I came to like it well enough. I sat till after three in the morning with them, and then left them to finish a new bowl. This day was fair but windy.

THURSDAY 7 OCTOBER. Captain Maclean came to breakfast. Crossapoll and his son had set out early. There came on a dreadful storm of wind and rain, which continued all day, and rather increased at night. The windows of the dining-room let in a deal of rain; and as[1] the wind was from the southwest, it was directly against our getting to Mull. We were in a strange state of abstraction from the world. We could neither hear from our friends, nor write to them. It gave me much uneasiness to think of the anxiety which my dear wife must suffer. Coll had brought Lucas *On Happiness*, Daillé *On the Fathers*, and More's *Dialogues*, from the minister's, and Burnet's *Own Times* with Salmon's *Remarks*, from the Captain's; and he had of his own some books of farming and Gregory's Geometry. Mr. Johnson read a good deal of Burnet and of the latter, and he even made notes in the end of his journal about geometry. I read a little of

---

[1] Omitted inadvertently.

Young's *Six Weeks' Tour through the Southern Counties*. I wrote a deal of journal today.

We got up late, and the day moved on without my being at all splenetic. I am grown a hard-minded fellow. Mr. Johnson when we were at Captain Maclean's, on my talking of Garrick's having rye-bread on his table at breakfast, said he had probably seen it at some great man's; and he observed how strangely people are swayed by what others tell them, and how few have the resolution to say plainly that they like wheat-bread best. "I could undertake," said he, "to make Langton eat all the kinds of grain in bread, and think each best."... ise to us; for he ... t which he grate[2] ... and so made it more palatable.

We were to have gone with Mr. Johnson this morning to the mine. He said, when the storm was raging, "We may be glad we are not *damnati ad metalla*."[3] This book which he gave me will soon be done. But he bid me not contract my Journal, and rather beg some paper.[4]

FRIDAY 8 OCTOBER. The Campbeltown ship was to come down to the harbour here to take in nine tuns of kelp, but could not get forward. Coll was of opinion that Mr. Johnson and I had better freight[1] her to set us down in Mull, which might be done with a wind that would not bring her hither. And supposing her here, she must wait a day for her ladening, and then the wind might come contrary again; so that by taking her directly from Lochiern, we had several more chances to get away. Morison and Macdonald, the two Masters, came here today. Mr. Johnson was clear for freighting them. He felt today the weight of this barren way of passing time. He said, "I

---

[2] Both lower corners of this leaf are defective, the *lacunae* (which involve perhaps fifteen or sixteen words) being too extensive to permit restoration with any degree of confidence. The editors' guess is that Johnson was having difficulty with the island fare, and was furnished something "which he grated over his food, and so made it more palatable."

[3] "Condemned to the mines."

[4] Johnson, in his *Journey*, says that Boswell was able to purchase paper at a shop in Coll.

[1] i.e., hire.

want to be on the mainland, and go on with existence. This is a waste of life." He has talked little here.

I shall here insert, without regard to chronology, some of his sayings. He told us that a man had been well received for two years among the gentlemen of Northamptonshire by calling himself his brother. At last he grew so impudent as by his influence to get tenants turned out of their farms. Allen the printer, who is of that county, came to Mr. Johnson, asking him with much appearance of doubtfulness if he had a brother; and upon being assured he had none alive, he told Mr. Johnson of the imposition, and immediately wrote to the country and the fellow was dismissed. Mr. Johnson said it pleased him that so much was got by using his name. Said he, "It is not every name that can carry double; do both for a man's self and his brother" (laughing). "I should be glad to see the fellow." He said a man could have no redress for his name being used, or ridiculous stories told of him in the newspapers, except he could show he had suffered damage. Some years ago some foolish piece was published "by S. Johnson." Some of Mr. Johnson's friends wanted him to be very angry about this. He said it would be in vain, for the answer would be, "'S. Johnson' may be Simon Johnson, or Simeon Johnson, or Solomon Johnson; and even if it had been full Samuel Johnson, it might be said, 'It is not you. It is a much cleverer fellow.'"

He and Beauclerk and Langton, and Lady Sydney Beauclerk, mother to our friend, were one day driving in a coach by Cuper's Gardens, which were then let to nobody. Mr. Johnson for a joke proposed he and Beauclerk and Langton should take them; and they amused themselves scheming how they would all do. Lady Sydney grew angry, and said an old man should not put such things in young people's heads. Mr. Johnson said she had no notion of a joke; had come late into life, and had a mighty unpliable understanding.

He said Carte's *Life of the Duke of Ormonde* was considered as a book of authority, but it was ill-written; the matter diffused in too many words; no animation, no compression, no vigour; that two good volumes in duodecimo might be made out of the two in folio.

Joseph informed us that he found several lice upon our shirts when we threw them off. This was very disagreeable. Mr. Johnson made himself merry with the Scots. "I remember," said he, "a song against them, I think in James 1st's time:

> Your waistcoats and doublets were but thin,
> Where many a louse was shelter'd in."

But he owned that this poet did not know the meaning of a doublet, which is the same with waistcoat.

I observed of our confinement here that this was just what Seneca complains so grievously of while in Corsica. "Yes," said Mr. Johnson, "and he was not farther from home than we are. The truth is, he was much nearer."[2]

Captain Maclean went home today. It rained at times, and the wind was still contrary. Cornaig attended me while I rummaged through the cabinet and looked at all the papers. I shall now put down some anecdotes of the family and introduce some curious things which I found in the cabinet. The first laird of Coll was a younger son of the family of Maclean. His father gave him the middle part of Coll for his patrimony, but made it the jointure lands of Lady Maclean. MacNeil of Barra married her, and came and lived in Coll. Young Coll was so impatient to get possession that he got some of the clan to assist him against MacNeil. They killed him at Grishipoll, and then Coll took the estate. Some generations after, Maclean wanted to resume Coll, and there was a bloody battle, or skirmish rather, in which Coll prevailed; and since that time his chief never disturbed him.

Coll had the £20 land of Lochiel. He was living there. The Camerons came upon him and killed him. His lady was with

---

[2] In the published text, the last sentence is not included in the quotation. But in the MS, the quotation marks, added in revising for the printer, do enclose it. The punctuation of the published text is probably correct.

child. She was put under the care of Cameron, called Maclonich, with orders that if she bore a son, he should be put to death; if a daughter, she might be allowed to live. Maclonich's wife and Lady Maclean were brought to bed at the same time, the former of a daughter, the latter of a son. Maclonich generously made the children be exchanged; so that young Coll was saved. Thus the young laird of Coll had the same good fortune with Cyrus. Perhaps both the stories are fables. There is, however, for Coll's story all that tradition can go.[3] When young Coll grew up, he came home to this island and was joyfully received by his people. Ever since that time there has been the greatest kindness shown by Coll's family to all the Maclonichs. Poor boys of that tribe from Lochaber would beg their way to Coll and be brought up about the kitchen till able to work for themselves. The chief of the tribe has always been educated by Coll. The present chief was with Coll at Aberdeen getting education. He would be a soldier. Coll could not get him a commission, so he is a sergeant in the train of artillery. I saw above the door upon the battlements of the old castle a vacant place where was a square stone, with an inscription in Erse bearing that if a Maclonich should come there at midnight with a man's head in his hand, he should be protected. The meaning was, if he should even be a murderer. So late as the year 1737 this privilege was demanded. I found the following letter:

To The Laird of Coll

DR SIR,—The long standing tract of firm affectionate friendship 'twixt your worthy predecessors and ours affords us such assurance as that we may have full relyance on your favour and undoubted friendship in recommending the bearer, Ewen Cameron, our Cousin, son to the deceast Dugall McConnill of Innermaillie, sometime in Glenpean, to your favour and conduct; who is a man of undoubted honesty and discretion, only that he has the misfortune of being alledged to have been accessory to the killing of one of McMartin's family about fourteen years ago, upon which alledgeance the McMartins are now so sanguine on revenging that they are fully resolved for the deprivation of his life, to the preventing of which you are relyed on by us, as the only fit instrument and a most capable person.

---

[3] i.e., "can attain to." Boswell probably became confused between two constructions.

Therefore your favour and protection is expected and intreated during his good behaviour, and failing of which behaviour you'll please use him as a most insignificant person deserves.

Sir, he had upon the alledgeance foresaid been transported at Lochiel's desire to France to gratify the Macmartins; and, upon his return home about five years ago, married. But now he is so much threatened by the Macmartins that he is not secure enough to stay where he is, being Ardmurchan, which occasions this trouble to you. Wishing prosperity and happiness to attend still yourself, worthy Lady, and good family, we are in the most affectionate manner, Dr Sir, your most obliged, affectionate, and most humble servants,

> Duigall Cameron of Strone.
> Dugall Cameron of Barr.
> Dwgall Cameron of Inviriskvoulline.
> Dugall Cameron of Invinvalie.

Strone, 11 March 1737

Ewen Cameron was protected, and his son has now a farm from the Laird of Coll, in Mull.

I take the oldest charter of Coll which the family has, to be one granted by James V at Edinburgh, 1 December 1528:

Jacobus, Dei gratia Rex Scotorum, omnibus probis hominibus totius terre sue, clericis et laicis, salutem. Sciatis quia quondam Johannes Makclane, avus predilecti nostri Johannis Makclane de Coill, terras subscriptas sibi pertinentes habuit ipsi per quondam nobilissimum progenitorem nostrum Jacobum secundum Scotorum Regem bone memorie, cuius anime propitietur Deus, concessas; et quod sue litere et evidentie————terrarum per suos inimicos destruuntur et earundem registrum combustum . . .[4]

The family of Coll was very loyal in the time of the great Montrose, from whom I found two letters in his own handwriting. The first is as follows.

> *For my very loving friend the Laird of Coall*
>
> Strethearne 20 Jañ 1646

Sir,—I must heartily thank you for all your willingness and good affection to his Majesty's service, and particularly the sending along of your

---

[4] A leaf (pp. 453–54) is missing from the MS at this point. Boswell did not include this charter in the published *Tour*. What follows down to the point indicated by the next footnote is supplied from the printed text. The fragment of the charter may be translated as follows: "James, by the grace of God King of Scots, to all good men of all his realm, clerks and laymen, greeting. Know ye, that because the late John Maclean, grandfather of our beloved John Maclean of Coll, held as his property the lands below mentioned, which were granted to him by our late most noble ancestor, James the Second, King of Scots, of good memory (whose soul God rest), and because his papers and his proofs to the title of the lands are destroyed by his enemies and the register of the same burned" [therefore the King grants John Maclean a new charter].

sons, to who I will heave ane particular respect, hopeing also that you will still continue ane[5] goode instrument for the advanceing ther of the King's service, for which, and all your former loyal carriages, be confident you shall fynd the effects of his Mās favour, as they can be witnessed you by your very faithfull freinde,

MONTROSE.

The other is

For the Laird off Coall

Petty, 17 April 1646

SIR,—Having occasion to write to your fields, I cannot be forgetful of your willingness and good affection to his Majesty's service. I acknowledge to you, and thank you heartily for it; assuring, that in what lies in my power, you shall find the good. Meanwhile I shall expect that you will continue your loyal endeavours, in wishing those slack people that are about you to appear more obedient than they do, and loyal in their Prince's service, whereby I assure you you shall find me ever your faithful friend,

MONTROSE.

These are honourable documents, and should be carefully preserved. I have written the first just after the original. From the second letter it would seem that Coll's zeal had rather failed a little, for the style is not so warm as that of the first. It gently hints complaints.

I found a contract of marriage in 1649 between Sir Lachlan MacLain of Dowart, as taking burden for his sister Finvoll (it should be Finvola, which they say is the same with Flora) and John MacLain, Laird of Coll. The knight gives with her nine score head of *keye* (cows); and she is to have as her jointure eighteen score, and (as I read it) the half of the house—thus,[6]— and the half of all future conquests, i.e., what should be gained.

I found a curious piece on the death of the present laird's father: "Nature's Elegy upon the death of Donald Maclean of Coll."[7] Mr. Johnson read the whole of this curious piece, and he wondered who wrote it. I suppose it has been some country schoolmaster. He said the epitaph was not so very bad.[8]

---

[5] Here the MS begins again.

[6] Boswell here traces the letters of the doubtful word.

[7] Again at this point there is at least one leaf of MS missing, on which Boswell transcribed the "curious piece."

[8] "Nature's minion, Virtue's wonder,
Art's corrective here lies under."

(From printed *Tour*.)

I asked what "art's corrective" meant. "Why," said Mr. Johnson, "that he was so exquisite that he set art right when she was wrong."

I found among the Coll papers a copy of a letter from the late MacLeod to the late Kingsburgh, in which he tells him that the Young Pretender will probably pay him a visit in expectation of his protection; that he knows the danger of assisting him, and the reward offered by Government, by which he may aggrandize his family beyond many in Scotland; and hopes he will do his duty to himself, family, and country. What a shocking exhortation! He also uses the name of Sir Alexander Macdonald, and says he can assure Kingsburgh his sentiments are the same with his (MacLeod's). I cannot justly convict him of writing this infamous letter, as I have not seen the original; but I take it to be genuine, since I do not see that a forgery would have been laid up by the late laird of Coll, to whom I found many original letters from MacLeod. I also found a copy of a letter from Lochiel and Keppoch to Invernochiel, dated Glenivask,[9] 20 March 1746, desiring to communicate their sentiments to the leading men among the Campbells; upbraiding them for their cruelty in burning houses, and attacking women, children, and cattle. But I shall transcribe it.

Yesternight we had a letter from Clunie, Younger, giving an account of the success of the party sent by his R. H.[10] under the command of Lord George Murray. A part of that letter we thought proper to send you enclosed, as you happen for the present to be stationed contiguous to the Campbells. It is our general desire that you instantly communicate to Airds, the Sheriff, and other leading men amongst them, our sentiments (which, GOD willing, we are determined to execute) by transmitting this our letter and the copy enclosed, to any most convenient to you.

It is our opinion that, of all men in Scotland, the Campbells had the least reason of any to engage in the present war against his R. H.'s interest, considering that they had always appeared in opposition to his royal family since the reign of King James the 6th, and have been guilty of so many acts

---

[9] i.e., Glennevis.

[10] It must be remembered that this letter was written by a Cameron and a Macdonald, who were Jacobites, and that the Campbells always supported the line of Hanover. Therefore "his royal highness" is Prince Charles Edward (the "Young Pretender"), and "his present majesty" is his father James (the Chevalier de St. George or the "Old Pretender").

of rebellion and barbarity during that time that no injured prince but would endeavour to resent it when GOD was pleased to put the power in his hand. Yet his present Majesty and his R. H. the Prince R. are graciously pleased by their respective declarations to forgive all past miscarriages to the most virulent and inveterate enemy, and even bury them in oblivion, provided they returned to their allegiance. And though they should not appear personally in arms in support of the royal cause, yet their standing neuter would entitle them to the good graces of their injured sovereign. But in spite of all the lenity and clemency that a prince could show or promise, the Campbells have openly appeared with their wonted zeal for rebellion and usurpation, in a most officious manner.

Nor could we ever form a thought to ourselves that any men endowed with reason and common sense could use their fellow creatures with such inhumanity and barbarity as they do; and of which we have daily proof by their burning of houses and stripping of women and children and exposing to the open field and severity of the weather, burning of corns (i.e., corn or grain), houghing of cattle, and killing of horses. To enumerate the which would be too tedious at this time. They must naturally reflect that we cannot but look on such cruelty with horror and detestation and hearts full of revenge. Will certainly endeavour to make reprisals, and are determined to apply to his R. H. for leave and orders to enter their country with full power that we are to act at discretion; and if we are so lucky as to obtain it, we shall show them that we are not to make war against brute creatures, but against men. But as GOD was pleased to put so many of their people in our custody, we hope to prevail with his R. H. to hang a Campbell for every house that shall hereafter be burnt by them.

Notwithstanding the scandalous and malicious aspersions contrived by our enemy against us, they have never, since the commencement of the war, charged us with any act of hostility, or with the least tendency to cruelty as they exercised against us, though we had it in our power. It's barbarous enough to exert it, when courage fails, against men. It betrays cowardice to a degree to vent their spleen against brutes, houses, women, and children, who cannot resist. We are not ignorant of this villainous intention, by the intercepted letter from Airds to the Sheriff, which plainly discovers that it was by application that their General Cumberland granted orders for burning, which he could not be answerable for to the British Parliament; it being most certain that such barbarity could never be countenanced by any Christian senate. We are, sir, your most humble servants,

DONALD CAMERON of Lochiel.
ALEX. MACDONALD of Keppoch.

P. S. I cannot omit taking notice that my people have been the first that have felt the cowardly barbarity of my pretended Campbell friends. I shall only desire to have an opportunity of thanking them for it in the open field.

DONALD CAMERON.

I read this letter to Mr. Johnson and called it a good one. Said he, "It is a very good one, upon their principles." Since I mentioned MacLeod's letter to Kingsburgh, Hugh McSweyn (i.e., the younger McSweyn) told me that he was present when MacLeod wrote a letter to Kingsburgh, but whether it was the same with the copy, he could not tell. He said the Duke of Cumberland was by while MacLeod wrote, so that the letter was quite under his direction. This MacLeod alleged as his excuse.

In the year 1745 the Laird of Coll assisted Government by sending sixty militia to Inveraray, which he raised at his own expense. They were sent home, as the Argyllshire battalion was made up before they arrived. Coll never had the least acknowledgment from Government for his service and expense. I found a copy of a letter from him to General Campbell, explaining how arms from the Prince's party had been brought into Coll. He tells the General that a brother of his, Lauchlan, whom he describes as of a very idle, odd character, and whom indeed he disinherited, had got these arms from an Irish officer; "This *blade*," says he, "got them from the *League*." Young Coll told me that Lauchlan was a pretty fellow, and a poet, though very wild. All the boats in Coll were destroyed, except one for the laird's use, lest the Prince should escape in one.

I found many excellent letters to Coll from Mr. John MacLeod of Muiravonside, who had a pension of £40 Scots as lawyer for the family. I found the bond of pension discharged. There was one very religious letter on the death of Coll's lady. He talks in his letters with great affection of his son,[11] whom he calls "my dear absent friend," and says he must be supplied at any rate; and he mentions his hope as to *the good cause* —he plainly means so, with much faith. It would seem from these letters that though the laird sent sixty men, he was in his heart of the principles which warmed the breast of his an-

---

[11] Alexander MacLeod—"McCruslick."

cestor, Montrose's correspondent. I found some letters from the present Lord Justice-Clerk when at the bar, exceedingly full and accurate with respect to some of Coll's family settlements.

I found a copy or scroll of an agreement among the inhabitants of Tyree, mentioning that they were oppressed by strangers coming among them, from a belief that their island was more fertile than others, and begging grain from them; by giving away quantities of which, they were impoverished, and were also burdened with the maintenance of the strangers, as they were often stopped by storms; and therefore they resolved to give nothing to strangers, under a penalty which I forget. This agreement, I was told, never took place. Mr. Johnson said he was glad of it.

Young Coll, whom I called "Rum," as Raasay's eldest son is called "Rona," said that he intended to make the inhabitants of Rum enter into such an agreement; for strangers impoverish them by coming and getting wool in gifts, and live long upon them at times. I found a letter from President Duncan Forbes—nothing in it but something about the two ends of Coll, which the laird and he understood. It is a pity that the Duke of Argyll has them. He would exchange them for some of Coll's lands in Mull; but Coll will not do that, because the lands in Mull are some of the best and . . .[12]

I found several letters to the late Coll from my father's old companion at Paris, Sir Hector Maclean, one of which was written at the time of settling the colony in Georgia. It dissuades Coll from letting people go there, and assures him there will soon be an opportunity of employing them better at home. Hence it appears that emigration from the Highlands, though not in such numbers at a time as of late, has always been practised. Dr. Johnson observed that instead of improving their country, they diminished their people.

There are several districts of sandy desert in Coll. There are

---

[12] Here again a leaf or more is missing from the MS, and the text is taken from the published *Tour*.

forty-eight lochs of fresh water, but many of them are very small, mere pools. About one-half of them, however, have trout and eel. There is a great number of horses in the island, mostly of a small size. Being overstocked, they sell some in Tyree, and on the mainland. Their black cattle, which are chiefly rough-haired, are reckoned remarkably good. The climate being very mild in winter, they never put their beasts in any house. The lakes are never frozen so as to bear a man, and snow never lies above a few hours. They have a good many sheep, which they eat mostly themselves, and sell but a few. They have goats in several places. There are no foxes; no serpents, toads, or frogs, nor any venomous creature. They have otters and mice here, but had no rats till lately that an American vessel brought them. There is a rabbit-warren on the northeast of the island, belonging to the Duke of Argyll. Young Coll intends to get some hares, of which there are none at present. There are no black cock, moor-fowl, nor partridges; but there are snipe, wild duck, wild geese, and swans, in winter; wild pigeons, plover, and great numbers of starlings, of which I shot some, and found them pretty good eating. Woodcocks come hither, though there is not a tree upon the island. There are no rivers in Coll, but only some brooks, in which there is a great variety of fish. In the whole isle there are but three hills, and none of them considerable for a Highland country.

The people are very industrious. Every man can tan. They get oak and birch bark and lime from the mainland. Some have pits, but they commonly use tubs. I saw brogues very well tanned, and every man can make them. They all make candles of the tallow of their beasts, both moulded and dipped; and they all make oil of[13] fish. The little fish called cuddies produce a great deal. They boil their livers to make it. They sell some oil out of the island, and they use it much for light in their houses, in little iron (or unpainted black metal) lamps, most of which they have from England; but of late their own

---

[14] Here the text is resumed from the MS.

blacksmith makes them. He is a good workman; but he has
no employment in shoeing horses, for they all go barefooted
here, except some better ones of young Coll's, which were now
in Mull. There are two carpenters in Coll; but most of the
inhabitants can do something as boat-carpenters. They can
all dye. They use heath for yellow; and for red, a moss which
grows on stones. They make broadcloth, and tartan and linen,
of their own wool and flax, enough for themselves, as also stockings. Their bonnets come from the mainland. There is a man
goes every year with a boat to Greenock and brings home a
quantity of hardware, ribbons, and other small things; and
keeps a little shop at the small village, where is the house in
which public worship is held, as there is no church. It is a
wretched hut, pretty long, with four little windows one way
and two another, glass in none of 'em; only a bunch of straw
is used to stop them in case of rain. There are also two people
in the island who occasionally act as pedlars. In these particulars they are more improved than the Skye people; for
there the pedlars are strangers, and I could hear of no shop
except that of a glover at Portree, who, as Ullinish told me,
makes very good gloves remarkably cheap. I did not think the
luxury of gloves had been in Skye till he informed me. They
have much need of them when they are to shake hands with
strangers. In Coll it is a practice to have cottars who are obliged
to furnish two horses each for work, as also a third of the seed-
corn; and for this and their work through the year, they have a
third of the crop and three milk-cows grazed. This is a good
method to make servants have a common interest with their
masters. The plough is a good deal used here, but they have
also a spade for digging corn land upon steep places and among
rocks. It is different from the Skye crooked spade, being much
straighter:[14] I have drawn it the wrong way, and too straight.
The Skye one is: I have seen many as crooked.[15] The ——— is
made of one piece of wood, both in Skye and Coll.

[14] Boswell's sketches are omitted.   [15] i.e., as the sketch.

The inhabitants of Coll have increased considerably within these thirty years; for I find that when application was made to the Lords for disuniting it and Tyree, which were then one parish, Coll was said to contain between seven and eight hundred examinable persons; and the highest number would be given upon that occasion. Now, the minister told us, there are nine hundred examinable persons. There are but three considerable tacksmen[16] on Coll's property here: McSweyn, Captain Maclean, and Mr. Maclean of Knock; and they only have cottars, as above. The rest is let to small tenants, who pay four, three, or even two guineas. Crossapoll has the highest rented farm of any of them. His rent is £7. Upon this he has always lived creditably for one of his station. He has seven daughters and three sons, and his wife is with child. His eldest son (Donald) he has educated for the Church of Scotland. He was taught by the tutor of Coll's sons. (Coll has eight sons and a daughter.) He then went to Aberdeen, where he gained a burse in King's College, upon a competition. Coll has now procured him a burse for four years as a student of divinity. He goes to Aberdeen from the opposite mainland, and returns on foot; and when at home, teaches his sisters and brothers to read and write. Mr. Johnson said there was something noble in a young man's walking two hundred miles and back again, every year, for the sake of learning. He said he would send him his small Dictionary. He did not know his merit when he was with us, or he would have talked to him. I talked a little to him. He teaches a few other children besides his father's. He told me he taught them first to read English, and then Erse was easily learnt. He can read the Irish character too. His father is like a judge among his neighbours.

Cornaig left us after dinner. I saw in the morning a good number of people who had come to Coll with complaints of each other's trespasses. Cornaig told them, "If you do not agree,

---

[16] A middleman who leases directly from the proprietor of an estate a large piece of land which he sublets in small farms.

we have the lawyer here from Edinburgh, who will take you to task" (or some such phrase). They said they were never used to take that way. They hoped Coll would settle matters himself.

SATURDAY 9 OCTOBER. We had agreed with the Campbeltown ship to put us in Mull for three guineas. The wind was still unfavourable, but it was a fine morning. Coll and I rode out first as far as our horses could go up the hill where the stone thrown up by the giant lies. Mr. Johnson sat down on the ground with a whin-rock at his back, and his hat tied down with his handkerchief, and read old Gataker on Lots and on the Christian Watch, a very learned book of the age of ———[1] which Coll found in the garret. Mr. Johnson said it was a treasure here. He had a most eremitical appearance. He sat there while Coll and I walked up to the stone. It is really a curious sight. It is of a triangular form, or rather like a huge coffin. I measured it with my handkerchief, and marked with a pencil how many lengths of that, and to a knot which I made on it. I put down the measurement with a lead pencil, and when we got home reduced it to feet by a foot-rule. It lies east and west. It is on the south side above nine feet long. Breadth, west end, about five feet; breadth, east end, four hands and a half. In circumference, tracing all its turns, about twenty-two feet. Highth, about four feet. It is clearly detached from the earth or any rock. The top of the hill is rocky, but it is supported upon three stones of no great size. I saw two others lying loosely under it. Perhaps they have also been supports, but it does very well without them. There is all the appearance that it has been set up artificially; yet it is difficult to conceive how it has been done. It is a very hard granite, and has over much of it a crust of crystallized substance, as many of the stones in Coll; and it has a great deal of the two kinds of moss with which Coll abounds growing upon it. I pulled a little of the moss and picked off a little of the crust, and put them up. The other

---

[1] These were two books by Thomas Gataker, *Of the Nature and Use of Lots* and *The Spirituall Watch*, both published in 1619, and here evidently bound together.

stone lying below, which I have mentioned already, is much larger. I have now measured it with my cane, which gives me a rough computation. It is three canes and more than one in highth (for I could not reach the top)—four broad—six long. It really seems to be as much detached as the one on the hill, and to have stones for supporters; but as it rests upon earth, it has sunk; while the other has kept up, as it rests on rock. Coll says tradition is not clear which of them was thrown by the giant, which by his mistress. When a compound ratio is taken of the smaller one being thrown up, and the larger thrown down, the difficulty of performing either will be pretty equal. Mr. Johnson was so much engaged with Gataker that he said he did not miss us.

We returned by the house, where I refreshed myself with a glass of whisky and a bit of bread. Mr. Johnson two days ago very justly reproved me for taking the *scalck* or dram every morning. He said, "For shame!" and that it was now really become serious. It was lucky that he corrected me. I refrained from it since, as a regular morning mode; but this forenoon I was fatigued with walking up the hill, and it was a reasonable indulgence.[2]

We resolved at last to go and see the lead mine in company. It was curious to see Mr. Johnson mounted on the large bay mare, without shoes and followed by a foal. He and I had a good gallop on the south strand. When we came to Crossapoll, I alighted and viewed the burying place. Coll had told me that there never was a church or chapel there. I was going to write on a very singular thing which I had found in Coll— a burying ground not at all connected with the sanctity of a religious edifice, which seemed to be a token of uncommon coldness of mind, of a deficiency in a principle or prejudice which all nations have had. But before I had time to write down this piece of curiosity, young Maclean of Crossapoll told me that there were vestiges of what was said to have been an

[2] This paragraph was omitted in the published *Tour*.

old chapel. He showed me today the roots of the walls of the chapel, and also of a wall which had enclosed the consecrated ground. I fancy the place has its name from a cross having been there: Crossapoll, the Pool of the Cross. There has been a very ancient burying place here; I saw some very ancient tombstones, one with a broadsword engraven upon it with a kind of foliage:[3] It was of a blue slate. I saw also many very recent ones, and graves without stones. It serves for a burying place equally with the one beside the ruins of the chapel near the minister's.

I forgot to mention that at the minister's, Mr. Johnson asked if the people here had any superstitions. The minister said, "No." Their not choosing to cut peats at the increase of the moon was mentioned by somebody. "There," said Mr. Johnson, "is a superstition." Said the minister, "It's not a superstition. It's a whim." The correction I thought not amiss. However, Mr. Johnson maintained that there are superstitions not connected with religion.

We went to the mine. The sea rose very high in foaming waves on the shore. Mr. Johnson contemplated it intensely. He looked at the mine, and young Maclean and I dug some pieces of ore with a pickaxe, which were very heavy. We rode with Mr. Johnson through a long tract of sand-hills. Coll and Maclean said there were vestiges of houses which had been blown over with sand. Mr. Johnson would not believe it. I desired we might be shown them. This led us a strange zigzag journey among the sand-hills. There was a good deal of wind, and good deal of sand was blown in our faces. I cried, "This is quite Arabian." It was easy riding; for our horses could trot down apparent precipices without danger, the sand always sliding away from their feet. Mr. Johnson observed that if the sand had been dry, it would have been impossible to ride here. We came at last to what they said was a house blown over. Mr. Johnson said it was a house abandoned and the stones

---

[3] Boswell's sketch is omitted.

taken away for other purposes. He bid me observe the large stones, which form the foundations of the houses here, were still standing higher than the sand; and that if they were not blown over, it was clear nothing higher than they could be blown over. This was quite convincing to me. But it made not the least impression on Coll, young Maclean, and another man. The sky overcast and threatened a storm. We hastened home by the north strand, turning at Foill.

We did not sit down to dinner till between six and seven. We really lived plentifully here, and had true welcome; as Mr. Johnson said, we were in nobody's way. We had a *spring* from the piper at breakfast, at dinner, and at supper. The peats were good and made a cheerful fire. Those at Dunvegan, which were damp, Mr. Johnson called "a sullen fuel."[4] I slept admirably here; and my room came to be like a home, from being accustomed to pass time comfortably in it. We had wheat bread, both loaf and biscuit, from Captain Maclean's. There was abundance of cream both at dinner and supper. I said young Coll's want of dignity made him seem rather a favourite servant of the laird's than the young laird himself. He was quite companionable with all the people. But I observed they all kept themselves uncovered when they spoke with him. Perhaps he is right to be thus easy. He is of a very diminutive figure, and better adapted for being liked than reverenced. We had to serve us at table, the piper, Allan Maclean the gardener, a very decent-looking man, and Hugh Macdonald, his own servant. Joseph also attended. Everybody seemed happy.

Mr. Johnson told me he had never seen Blenheim. He had not gone formerly; and he would not go now just as a common spectator for his money. He would not put it in the power of some man about the Duke of Marlborough to say, "Johnson was here. I knew him, but I took no notice of him." This is a very proper pride in one who has arrived at his consequence. He said he would be very glad to see Blenheim if prop-

---

[4] See *ante*, p. 173, n. 1.

erly invited, which in all probability would never be the case, as it was not worth his while to seek for it. He had a prudent and delicate resolution against asking Beauclerk[5] to carry him there, which I should not have thought of, but have asked him slapdash. "I doubt," said he, "if Beauclerk be on that footing with the Duke as to carry anybody there; and I would not give him the uneasiness to see that I knew it, or even to put himself in mind of it."[6] I must study to have more of this kind of delicacy. It is the same to many men with regard to the mind as to the body. I would not strip myself naked before every one, and would be shocked to occasion another being so exposed. Mental nakedness should be avoided with equal scrupulousness.

The sky predicted well. There came on a very extraordinary storm. I went to bed snug, as being in a good warm place; was quite well as to immediate existence, and had no uneasiness but the recollection that my wife would be in impatience and fear. I had Ovid's Epistles with me, which I bought at Inverness, and sometimes looked at, particularly those of Penelope and Ulysses.

SUNDAY 10 OCTOBER. We had one of the most terrible storms of wind and rain that I ever remember. There was a kind of dismal quietness in the house. When Mr. Johnson wondered who had written the "Elegy on Coll," he said it was the Ghost of Ossian. I said Ossian would have had grander images; for that it could not be denied that there were some in *Fingal*. But I said there was a certain sameness[1] in *Fingal*, though every one is not sensible of it. That it was like the paper with which a room is finished, where you have a number of birds and a number of figures and a number of trees and a number of flowers; and as there is a variety of objects, one does not at once perceive that the finishing is composed of pieces all ex-

[5] Beauclerk was the Duke's brother-in-law.

[6] The remainder of this entry is omitted in the published *Tour*.

[1] "A certain sameness" is a conjecture of the editors', the MS being defective at this point.

actly the same. By the time your eye has made the round of
the pattern, you forget what you first looked at. So is it with
Ossian's poetry to a considerable degree. I said this from a very
imperfect recollection of them. But I take it to be just. I shall
try at some idle time ———²

The day was passed without much conversation; only, upon
my observing that there must be something bad in a man's
mind who does not like to give leases to his tenants, but to keep
them in a perpetual wretched dependence on his will, Mr.
Johnson said I was right. "It is a man's duty," said he, "to extend comfort and security among as many people as he can.
He should not wish to have his tenants mere ephemerae—
mere beings of an hour." I objected that they might grow insolent, which was very disagreeable; and I put him in mind
that he had said that an English tenant would *throw* his rent
at his landlord. "Depend upon it," said he, "it is the landlord's own fault if it is thrown at him. A man may always keep
his tenants under dependence enough, though they have leases.
He must be a good tenant, indeed, who will not fall behind in
his rent, if his landlord will let him; and if he does fall behind,
his landlord has him at his mercy. Indeed," said he, "the poor
man is always much at the mercy of the rich, no matter whether
master or tenant. If the tenant lets his landlord have a little
rent beforehand, or has lent him money, then the landlord is
in his power. There cannot be a greater man than a tenant
who has lent money to his landlord; for he has under subjec-
tion the very man to whom he should be subjected."³

I had lain awake a good while last night, and had thought
much of my long absence from home. Imagination suggested
a variety of gloomy ideas. It was really heavy, it was distressing, to consider that I might be shut up here for another week
or even a fortnight; and that after I got to Mull and Icolmkill
I might be detained by storms in either of those places, I knew

---

² Boswell forgot to complete this sentence.
³ The remainder of this entry is omitted in the published *Tour*.

not how long. I grew quite impatient, and resolved to make for the mainland directly. All this day I ruminated on my nocturnal uneasiness. I found the enamel of philosophy which I had upon my mind, broke, worn off, or worn very thin, and fretfulness corroding it.

I talked with Coll, and found by his calculation that going to Icolmkill would probably consume ten days. I considered that in that case we should not reach Auchinleck before the sitting down of the Session; so that I should lose having Mr. Johnson at the romantic seat of our family, and with my father, and upon my own land of Dalblair, all which was of much more value than our being at Icolmkill. But I was against mentioning my objections to Mr. Johnson, for fear he should fix me down; for I still had a great desire to be at Icolmkill. It had been in my mind from the first time that Mr. Johnson and I talked of visiting the Hebrides. I had mentioned too to many people that we were to see "that ancient seat of religion and learning." I read Martin's account of it over again, and was in doubt how to determine. Then I had heard Coll talk of our visiting Sir Allan Maclean, his chief, in a pretty island in our way to Icolmkill; and Lochbuie, a curious laird who has a large old castle, in our way from it. At last the arguments against going preponderated, and I fairly tabled my intention for the mainland to Mr. Johnson. He said, "But don't say that I would not go with you to Icolmkill." This piqued my spirit, and set me up again. "Poor Iona!" said I. "It is lucky that though sometimes the one is against going thither, sometimes the other, we are never both at a time against it." I now thought I would keep my mind in a sort of indecision whether to go or not, just as I found it agreeable after we were loose from Coll.

I had with me on this jaunt a Bible which I had in a present from Lord Mountstuart when we were in Italy together.[4] I value it highly, and always have it with me. I read in it frequently. I also read this day Dr. Ogden's fourth sermon.

---

[4] See p. 38, n. 2.

MONDAY 11 OCTOBER. The morning was fine and the wind fair and moderate. My mind was sound as ever, and the enamel of philosophy entire. It had not been broke, I take it, for it is not easily repaired. Coll was in a hurry to get us down to the harbour where the ship lay. But he was too late of beginning. We did not get away till about eleven. It seems young McSweyn and his wife live in the house here to take care of it. She was one of the hardest-favoured women that I ever saw, swarthy and marked with the smallpox, and of very ungainly manners.

She had never been upon the mainland. Mr. Johnson said of her and before her, "That is rather being behindhand with life. I'd go and see Glenelg," and he laughed. "Why," said I, "you have never seen, till now, anything but your native island." "But," said he, "by seeing London I have seen as much of life as the world can show." "You have not seen Pekin," said I. "Sir," said he in a sort of anger, "what is Pekin? Ten thousand Londoners would *drive* all the people of Pekin. They'd drive them like deer."[1]

I should have mentioned that in the old castle here is a little-house. I rebuked Coll, as I did Raasay, by observing that his ancestors were more civilized than the family now is in that very essential particular; for there is not one at the new house. Coll promised to me that he would erect one soon. Mr. Johnson and I talked of it. I called it now *Domus Taliskeriana*. Mr. Johnson said I had that much at heart. He said if ever a man thinks at all, it is there. He generally thinks then with great intenseness. He sets himself down as quite alone, in the first place. I said a man was always happy there, too. Mr. Johnson said he did not know that. I told him of an elegant one at the Dutch ambassador's,[2] when I was at Paris—quilted seats, etc. "Sir," said he, "that is Dutch; quilted seats retain

[1] The next two paragraphs were omitted in the published *Tour*. Part of the first sentence has been restored by conjecture, the MS being defective. "Is a little-house" may not have been Boswell's words, but there is no doubt as to his meaning.
[2] Mattheus Lestevenon, Heer van Berkenrode.

a bad smell. No, sir, there is nothing so good as the plain board." I was for having books and prints. He did not insist for that. He told me he knew a gentleman who had a set of the *Spectator* in that place.

I find myself insensibly acquiring some of Mr. Johnson's expressions, such as beginning a sentence with "Why, sir." Lord Hailes and I had once a serious dispute whether I should introduce that expression in quoting Mr. Johnson in my *Tour to Corsica*. I have the letters by me upon it. I have even learnt a more curious expression, which is to resume a subject with "No, sir," though there is no negation in the case. As thus he will say, after having talked of Langton and praised him, "No, sir, I know no better man than Langton." It . . .[3]

We set out about eleven for the harbour; but before we reached it, so violent a storm came on that we were obliged again to take shelter in the house of Captain Maclean, where we dined and passed the night.

TUESDAY 12 OCTOBER. After breakfast, we made a second attempt to get to the harbour; but another storm soon forced us[1] to turn. Coll and I had walked down before. We met Mr. Johnson and the baggage and Joseph, and turned them. Coll had said to me that if we were stopped, we should go up to McSweyn's and wait. I insisted on doing it directly. When we returned to the Captain's, of whom we had taken leave, it was not a very cordial meeting on either side.[2] I was wet to the skin, and resolved to have one drying for all. So Coll and I walked, and Mr. Johnson followed us on horseback.

---

[3] Eight or ten letters are missing at the end of this page, and then an entire leaf (pp. 475–6) of the MS is gone. The published *Tour* gives only the briefest of summaries for the remainder of the entry, but under date of 12 October it preserves a little of the conversation at Captain Maclean's: "On Monday we had a dispute at the Captain's, whether sand-hills could be fixed down by art. Dr. Johnson said, 'How *the devil* can you do it?' but instantly corrected himself, 'How can you do it?' I never before heard him use a phrase of that nature."

[1] Here the text is resumed in the MS. "Forced us" has been supplied by the editors, as the whole sentence was revised in publication.

[2] In the published *Tour* he says that Captain Maclean's house was "in some confusion, on account of Mrs. Maclean's being expected to lie-in."

By the road, I fell into a brook and wet myself to the middle very much. My boots were almost filled with water. I stood in two lochs, as they would say here, where a loch is used to denote pieces of water of any size. Mr. Johnson said in England they have several gradations: pits, pools, meres, lakes. When we reached Grishipoll, I got myself all shifted—got on waistcoat and breeches of Joseph's, and a good Highland coat of old McSweyn's, of black cloth with hollow silver buttons, which had lasted him fifty years, and which pass from generation to generation in the Highlands. It was a short coat. Mr. Johnson said I looked much better in it, and if I were to go a-courting, should wear such a coat. I had taken hardly any breakfast, for fear of being sick at sea; so was keenly hungry. I had some barley bread and cheese, on which I feasted. A strange resolution was taken in the family that we should have no dinner till late in the evening, and tea in the mean time. Mr. Johnson opposed the tea *till after dinner*; but they persisted, and he took it very readily. He said to me afterwards, "You must consider, sir, a dinner here is a matter of great consequence. It is a thing to be first planned and then executed. I suppose the mutton was brought some miles off, from some place where they knew there was a sheep killed." His minute observation strikes me with wonder.

He said life had not got at all forward by a generation in McSweyn's family; "for," said he, "the son is exactly formed upon the father. What the father says, the son says; and what the father looks, the son looks." He was disgusted with the coarse manners here. He said to me, "I know not how it is, but I cannot bear low life. And I find others, who have as good a right as I to be disgusted, bear it better, by having mixed more with different sorts of men. You would think that I have mixed pretty well, too."

He read a good deal of my Journal in the little book which I had from him, and was pleased; for he said, "I wish thy books were twice as big." He helped me to supply blanks which

I had left in first writing it, when I was not quite sure of what he had said; and he corrected any mistakes that I had made. He said, "They call me a scholar. And yet how very little literature is there in my conversation." "Sir," said I, "that must be according to your company. You would not give literature to Coll and McSweyn. Stay till we meet Lord Elibank."

We had a tolerable little chat by ourselves this evening. Old Mrs. McSweyn did not appear till supper. Mr. Johnson said when he thought that she could not read, it was strange. There was something shocking in it. We had a very decent supper, after which a glass of whisky punch, while Mr. Johnson and old Mrs. McSweyn drank tea. I have not seen him drink tea at night since he left Edinburgh. By Coll's advice, Mary Macdonald, a comely black girl who had been three years at Glasgow, washed my feet with warm water, which was Asiatic enough; and then I lay down in clean sheets upon a bed of straw, which I preferred to one of their feather-beds. Coll had a bed in the room with me. I soon fell asleep.

WEDNESDAY 13 OCTOBER. Coll called me up, with intelligence that it was a good day for a passage to Mull; and just as we rose, a sailor from the vessel arrived for us. We got all ready with dispatch. Mr. Johnson was displeased at my bustling and walking quickly up and down. He said it did not hasten us a bit. It was getting on horseback in the ship. "All boys do it," said he; "and you are longer a boy than others." He himself has no alertness, or whatever it may be called; so he may dislike it, as *Oderunt hilarem tristes.*[1]

Let me here mark a few detached things. There are what may be called rivers which run into Loch Eirach.[2] One upon the left, as you enter it, comes in quite fresh. The one upon the right, which runs by Captain Maclean's house, is met by a loch, or arm of the sea, so that salmon go up it a little way.

---

[1] HORACE—"Gloomy people hate a merry fellow."
[2] This must be Loch Eatharna again, though it is hard to explain how Boswell, whose ear was uncommonly accurate, could have gone so far wrong. Perhaps he confused for the moment Loch Eatharna with Loch Airidh, a small inland lake in the vicinity.

Neither are rivers of any size, comparatively speaking. I saw at Grishipoll a fir tree which had been thrown ashore. There adhered to it a number of shells in clusters, with kind of stalks or branches of sea-ware connecting them to the timber. They say a bird is hatched in each of these shells. I put up two or three of them. There are many wrecks or things thrown ashore in Coll. There was lately some excellent mahogany, and some years ago there were some casks of Malaga. The country people, finding it sweet and mild, drank of it without fear of intoxication, till they were mortally drunk. There is here the bird called a curlew. It is a sucking bird, like a woodcock, but as large as a wild duck. We had two to dinner one day. They eat pretty well, and had no fishy taste. There is in the sand on the seashore a plant which they call sea holly. Young Maclean said it was eringo. It has prickly leaves, and they are at different places formed into roses. Solan geese fly about Coll, but do not breed here. The seamaws or gulls are very numerous. So are the cormorants or scarts. The island has a good many small birds, but I cannot be exact as to them. I saw larks enough. There is a deal of the aromatic plant called gaul. There is no tree whatever but dwarf juniper and short willows. There is a kind of plant grows on the hills and rocks, somewhat like ivy till you come near it, when it is rather like willow.

Before we reached the harbour, the wind grew high again. However, the small boat was waiting, and took us on board. We waited for some time in a kind of uncertainty what to do. At last it was determined that, as a good part of the day was over, and it was dangerous to be at sea at night, we should not sail till the morning, when the wind would probably be gentler with the first of the tide. We resolved not to go ashore again, but lie here in readiness. Mr. Johnson and I had each a bed in the cabin. Coll sat at the fire in the forecastle, with the two captains and Joseph and his servant and the two sailors. They eat mutton and potatoes and drank whisky. I licked some oatmeal, of which I found a barrel in the cabin. I had not done this since I was a boy. Mr. Johnson told me he used to be fond of it when a boy. I note this because I can tell him that *he* too had somewhat of an oatmeal education. He and I eat some roasted potatoes at night. He indeed eat only one. Captain Macdonald pressed him much to eat mutton or butter or cheese —in short, pressed him to all that was on board. He made Mr. Johnson grow surly. Mr. Johnson said to me, "I know not whether a man should blame himself for not making a proper return to awkward civility. Here now is this man who thinks he is doing the best he can to me, and I can hardly use him well." I got some of Ovid's Epistle from Penelope to Ulysses by heart, which served well to divert the tedious hours; and there was a Belfast newspaper in the ship, of no very old date, which was to my hungry mind as Irish meal is to a town when meal is scarce.

THURSDAY 14 OCTOBER. I had slept pretty well. Mr. Johnson had been up twice. Between six and seven the day was just as we could wish. We hauled in our anchors, which was a tedious operation, and at last set sail from Coll. We had a fine breeze. Mr. Johnson was very uneasy for a while. He got up, and looked out of the cabin hatchway, and was pale as death. He then went to bed again, and was quiet all the time.

We descried off Rum a vessel making fine sail towards us. She came up quickly. It was cheerful to see her approach. At first our captains took her to be one of the desperate armed Irish smuggling vessels, which they called *buckers*. But she proved to be a king's cutter commanded by Mr. Craufurd. She came close up to us, after having first hailed us with a speaking trumpet. She asked, "From whence?" "From Coll." "Where are you bound for?" "Larne." "With what are you loaded?" "Kelp." "What news in Coll?" "None." Her strength and the excellence of her rigging gave one a feeling of security; and seeing about twenty men above deck was a more lively scene than I had seen for some time. She soon left us, and run before us for . . .[1]

---

[1] A leaf of the MS (pp. 485–6) is here missing. A portion of the text is supplied from the printed *Tour*, with slight re-arrangement.

When Dr. Johnson awaked this morning, he called, *"Lanky!"* having, I suppose, been thinking of Langton, but corrected himself instantly, and cried, *"Bozzy!"* He has a way of contracting the names of his friends. Goldsmith feels himself so important now as to be displeased at it. I remember one day when Tom Davies was telling that Dr. Johnson said, "We are all in labour for a name to *Goldy's* play," Goldsmith cried, "I have often desired him not to call me *Goldy*."

I must endeavour to recollect what I may have omitted on former occasions.—When I boasted at Raasay of my independency of spirit, and that I could not be bribed, he said, "Yes, you may be bribed by flattery."—He has particularities which it is impossible to explain. He never wears a night-cap, as I have already mentioned; but he puts a handkerchief on his head in the night.—The day that we left Talisker, he bade us ride on. He then turned the head of his horse back towards Talisker, stopped for some time; then wheeled round to the same direction with ours, and then came briskly after us.— He sets open a window in the coldest day or night, and stands before it. It may do with his constitution; but most people, amongst whom[2] I am one, must say, with the frogs in the fable, "This may be sport to you, but it is death to us."—It is curious to hear the Highlanders always calling him *honest man.* By honest, they, as the Scotch in general, mean good or worthy in general. Old McSweyn used it in another sense; for when his son told that he saw Mr. Johnson with his handkerchief tied on his head, bringing peats to himself in a stormy night, the old man said that was *main honest.*—It is in vain to try to find a meaning in every one of Mr. Johnson's particularities, which I suppose are mere habits contracted by chance; of which every man has some which are more or less remarkable. His speaking to himself, or rather repeating, is a common habit with studious men accustomed to deep thinking; and of course they will laugh by themselves if the subject which

---

[2] Here the text is resumed from the MS.

they are musing on is a merry one. Smith the moral theorist has this habit much. Mr. Johnson is often uttering pious ejaculations when he appears to be talking to himself; for sometimes his voice grows stronger, and parts of the Lord's Prayer are heard. I have sat beside him with more than ordinary reverence on such occasions.[3] Last night, when I told him I was going to sleep, he said, "GOD bless you, for Christ's sake."

We got safely and agreeably into the harbour of Tobermory, before the wind, which for some days has always risen about noon, came onward.[4] Tobermory is really a noble harbour. An island[5] lies before it; and it is surrounded by a hilly theatre. The island is too low; otherwise this would be quite a secure port. But as the island is not high enough, some storms blow very hard here. Not long ago, fifteen sail of vessels were blown from their moorings. There will sometimes be sixty or seventy sail here. There was today twelve or fourteen vessels. To see such a fleet was the next thing to seeing a town. The vessels were from different places: Clyde, Campbeltown, Newcastle, etc. One was returning to Lancaster from Hamburg. After having been shut up in Coll, the sight of such an assemblage of moving habitations, containing such a variety of people engaged in different pursuits, gave me much gaiety of spirit. Mr. Johnson said, "Boswell is now all alive. He is like Antaeus; he gets new vigour whenever he touches land." I went to the top of a hill fronting the harbour, and took a good view of it. We had here a tolerable inn, kept by a Mr. McArthur. Mr. Johnson had owned to me this morning that he was out of humour. Indeed, he showed it a good deal in the ship; for when I was expressing joy on being landed in Mull, he said he had no joy when he thought it would be five days before he should get to the mainland. I was afraid he would now take a sudden

---

[3] "It is remarkable that Dr. Johnson should have read this account of some of his own peculiar habits, without saying anything on the subject, which I hoped he would have done."—BOSWELL.

[4] The bottom of the leaf on which this sentence begins is missing, and fourteen words have been adapted from the published *Tour* to fill the gap.

[5] Calve.

resolution to give up seeing Icolmkill. A dish of tea, some good wheaten cakes (scones) and fresh butter did him service, and his bad humour went off. I told him that I was diverted to hear all the people with whom we were as we travelled, say, "Honest man! he's pleased with everything. He's always content!" "Little do they know," said I. He laughed and said, "You rogue."

We sent to find horses to carry us forward for Sir Allan Maclean's. Dr. Maclean, who is married to Coll's aunt, was not at home, or we were to have gone to his house at Erray, which is but a mile off. Coll went and drank punch with the two captains and Joseph and one Nisbet, master of a Newcastle ship.

Mr. Johnson and I sat and talked a good deal. I told him how I had seen in Leandro Alberti's *Tour of Italy* a good deal of what Addison says. Mr. Johnson said that the collection of passages from the classics had been made by another man than he. "But," said he, "it is impossible to detect a man as a plagiary in such a case, because all who set about making such a collection must find the same; but," said he, "if you find the remarks in another, then Addison's learning in that book tumbles down." He said it was a tedious book, and if it were not attached to Addison's previous reputation, one would not think much of it. Had he written nothing else, his name would not have lived. He said, "Addison does not seem to have gone deep in Italian literature. He shows nothing of it in his subsequent writings. He shows a great deal of French learning." Mr. Johnson said, "There is perhaps more knowledge circulated in the French language than in any other. There is more original knowledge in English." "But the French," said I, "have the art of accommodating literature." "Sir," said he, "we have no such book as Moréri's Dictionary." "Their *Ana*," said I, "are good." He said few of them were; and we have one book of that kind better than any of them: Selden's *Table Talk*. "As to original literature," said he, "the French have a couple of tragic poets who go round the world, Racine and Corneille;

one comic poet, Molière." I mentioned Fénelon. "Why," said
he, "*Telemachus* is pretty well." I mentioned Voltaire. Said he,
"He has not stood his trial yet. And what makes Voltaire
chiefly circulate is collection—as his *Universal History*." I mentioned the Bishop of Meaux. He said, "Nobody reads him."[6]
He would not allow Massillon and Bourdaloue to go round
the world. He praised the French industry.

He asked me if he had mentioned in the *Rambler* the description in Virgil of the entrance into hell, and applied it to the
press; "for," said he, "I do not much remember them" (i.e.,
the papers in the *Rambler*). I told him no. Upon which he repeated it. "Now," said he, "almost all these apply exactly. All
these are about a printing-house." I would have had him to dictate an essay on it, and I would write. He would not then, but
said perhaps he would write a paper on it.

The Sunday evening that we sat by ourselves at Aberdeen,
I asked him several particulars of his life from his early years,
which he readily told me, and I marked down before him.
This day I proceeded in my inquiries, also marking before him.
I have them on separate leaves of paper. I shall lay up au-
thentic materials for THE LIFE OF SAMUEL JOHNSON, LL.D.,
and if I survive him, I shall be one who shall most faithfully do
honour to his memory. I have now a vast treasure of his conversation at different times since the year 1762[7] when I first
obtained his acquaintance; and by assiduous inquiry I can
make up for not knowing him sooner.[8]

Nisbet, the Newcastle man, would be in to sit a while with
us. He was much in liquor, and spoke nonsense about his being
a man for "Wilkes and Liberty," and against the ministry. Mr.

---

[6] "I take leave to enter my strongest protest against this judgment. Bossuet I hold to be
one of the first luminaries of religion and literature. If there are who do not read him,
it is full time they should begin."—BOSWELL.

[7] It is strange that Boswell here wrote 1762 for 1763, and never corrected it.

[8] "It is no small satisfaction to me to reflect that Dr. Johnson read this, and, after being
apprised of my intention, communicated to me, at subsequent periods, many particulars of his life, which probably could not otherwise have been preserved."—BOSWELL.

Johnson was angry that a fellow should come into *our* company who was fit for *no* company. He left us soon.

Coll had gone up to see his aunt, and she insisted that we should come to her house that night, and horses were sent. Mr. Campbell, the Duke of Argyll's factor in Tyree, came. He was a genteel agreeable man. He was going to Inveraray, and promised to put letters in the post office for us. Mr. Johnson now showed that anxiety to have an opportunity to write made him so impatient to get to the mainland. We had tongue and fowls and greens to dinner about seven o'clock, and a little brandy punch, and then we set out for Dr. Hector Maclean's.

Mr. Johnson was mounted on a little strong Mull sheltie, and another sheltie carried the baggage. Coll and I and the servants walked. A Highlander led Mr. Johnson's horse, and Coll's servant walked, holding a candle which burned till we saw the light of a candle at Dr. Maclean's. It was a curious procession for about a mile. We arrived at a strange confused house built by Mackinnon the proprietor about sixty years ago. We had been refreshed by the sight of two or three trees near the inn. We perceived several here. We were conducted through a large unfinished cold kitchen to a narrow timber stair, and then along a passage to a large bedroom with a coach roof, ornamented with some bad portraits, prints of several eminent physicians and others, and a piece of shell-work made by Miss Maclean, the Doctor's daughter. We were received by Mrs. Maclean, a little brisk old woman in a bedgown with a brown wig, and Miss Maclean, a little plump elderly young[9] lady in some dress which I do not recollect farther than that she had a smart beaver hat with a white feather. Dr. Maclean had been above thirty years at Glasgow, so that his wife and daughter were not mere Highland ladies. We had here too Mr. Angus Maclean, a third cousin of the Doctor's, a fine old gen-

---

[9] *Sic.* If, as Carruthers says, she lived until 1826, the "elderly" should be deleted. Or did Boswell mean that her manners were those of an elderly woman?

tleman of seventy-nine with little or no failure. He had been at the battle of Sheriffmuir. He was a tall comely man, a widower; had been unlucky in the world and now lived among his relations, chiefly with Dr. Maclean. Mr. Johnson observed when he heard his history that he had not now long to struggle with difficulties. Though dressed in a shabby kilt with shabby tartan hose, a coat and waistcoat of coarse dark brown cloth grown old, a wig too little for his head, with no curls, also aged, and a coloured handkerchief about his neck, he had the air of a gentleman. One could not but have a respect for him. Mr. Johnson was taken with the appearance of the room. He cried to me, "You're not observing. This is the prettiest room we have seen since we came to the Highlands." We had beef collops, potatoes, sowans and cream for supper. Mr. Johnson took sowans and cream heartily. We had a bowl of rum punch. After supper when we were by ourselves, Mr. Johnson asked me to give him paper to write letters. I begged he would write short ones and not *expatiate*, as we should set off early. He turned in bad humour; said, "What must be done, must be done; the thing is past a joke." "Nay, sir," said I, "write as much as you please; but do not blame me if we are kept six days before we get to the mainland. You was very impatient in the morning, but no sooner do you find a good room with a few prints than you do not think of moving." I got him paper enough, and we parted quietly.

Let me bring up all with me. In the morning I said to him before we landed, "At Tobermory we shall see Dr. Maclean, who has written the history of the Macleans." JOHNSON. "I have no great patience to stay to hear the history of the Macleans. I'd rather hear the history of the Thrales." When on Mull I said, "Well, sir, this is the fourth of the Hebrides that we have been upon." JOHNSON. "Nay, we cannot boast of the number we have seen. We thought we should see many more. We thought of sailing about easily from island to island; and so we should, had we come at a better season; but we, being wise men, thought it should be summer all the year where we were. However, sir, we have seen enough to give us a pretty good notion of the system of insular life."

Coll and I had each a bed in a room at the other end of the passage. There was a parrot in it which Mrs. Maclean had had for sixteen years. She said it could speak very well in Glasgow, but it had rusted in Mull, where the family had now been for seven years. Mr. Johnson had his favourite coach-roofed room. Let me not forget that at Capt. Maclean's he read a good deal in *The Charmer*, a collection of songs. I read some in it too. When I was going to bed, Joseph perceived that the sheets were not clean.[10] I looked at them, and was shocked at their dirtiness. I threw off only my boots and coat and waistcoat, and put on my greatcoat as a night-gown, and so lay down. The mixture of brandy punch at the inn and rum punch here, joined with the comfortless bed, made me rest very poorly.

FRIDAY 15 OCTOBER. After I had tossed long in weariness, Joseph came and called me and let in light. I would have risen, but was afraid to put my hand anywhere in the dark, for fear of spiders, or some uncleanly circumstance of sloth. I was not well at all, but I got up, sat down to my Journal, and soon was better. Another damp to my gay prospect of advancing with celerity occurred. There was a violent storm of wind and rain. We should have been wet to the skin immediately had we set out; but it was absolutely impossible for us to get forward, because the rivers were swelled. There was no help for it. We were doomed to stay here all this day. I could hardly keep from repining indecently. Mr. Johnson said, "Now that I have had an opportunity to write to the mainland, I'm in no such haste." I wrote to my dear wife. It was a relief to me to think that she would hear of me, though I could not hear of her till I got to Inveraray. I also wrote to my father. I told him that, having been now for some time in countries where great attention is paid to dreams, I had been gloomy from having

---

[10] This, and a great deal more from this entry, was omitted in the published *Tour*.

dreamt that I had lost him.[1] I hoped in GOD he was well, and longed much to see him. It gives me pain to consider that there is much doubt if he has now that warm affection for me which he once had, and which I really have for him. I have now made up to him for all the uneasiness which my follies gave him. The satisfaction which I feel on his living till that was the case, is very great. I shall do my part now as well as I can; and shall never check my sincere affection for him (an affection which has much of the tenderness of a child) though he should appear cold.

At breakfast we had currant jelly,[2] which led Coll to talk of Sir Alexander Macdonald's having treacle to breakfast as a sweetmeat, which I told him, as I was witness to it. Mr. Johnson said, "We had it not at Armadale. We had nothing there but the *animated* looks of his lady. The difference between that woman when alive, and when she shall be dead, is only this. When alive she calls for beer. When dead she'll call for beer no longer."

I wrote journal a good part of the forenoon, and looked at a manuscript history of the Macleans by the Doctor, Tytler's *Queen Mary*, and the Account of Montrose's Funeral. Mr. Johnson looked into the manuscript. We had a roasted turkey and some other things for dinner, by candlelight. When I spoke of having great resolution in going forward, Mr. . . .[3]

Dr. Johnson asked in the evening to see Dr. Maclean's books.

---

[1] No such dream is recorded in the Journal as now preserved, but it may well have been in one of the missing portions.

[2] Boswell was so fond of currant jelly that he once published some verses on it, of which the following are a specimen:

"Long ere the cups were fill'd, I'd eager rise,
(The love of jelly flaming in my eyes),
A slice of nicest cut, and spoon, would seize,
And, with my usual much-becoming ease,
Would the ambrosia plentifully spread
In mode genteel upon the wheaten bread."

Alexander Donaldson's *Collection of Original Poems by Scotch Gentlemen*, ii.89.

[3] Here occurs a great gap in the MS (pp. 507–64), only about a third of which can be supplied from the printed *Tour*.

He took down Willis *De Anima Brutorum* and pored over it a good deal.

Miss Maclean produced some Erse poems by John Maclean, who was a famous bard in Mull, and had died only a few years ago. He could neither read nor write. She read and translated two of them: one, a kind of elegy on Sir John Maclean's being obliged to fly his country in 1715; another, a dialogue between two Roman Catholic young ladies, sisters, whether it was better to be a nun or to marry. I could not perceive much poetical imagery in the translation. Yet all of our company who understood Erse seemed charmed with the original. There may perhaps be some choice of expression and some excellence of arrangement that cannot be shown in translation.

After we had exhausted the Erse poems, of which Dr. Johnson said nothing, Miss Maclean gave us several tunes on a spinet, which, though made so long ago as in 1667, was still very well toned. She sung along with it. Dr. Johnson seemed pleased with the music, though he owns he neither likes it nor has hardly any perception of it. At Mr. Macpherson's, in Sleat, he told us that he knew a drum from a trumpet, and a bagpipe from a guitar, which was about the extent of his knowledge of music. Tonight he said that if he had learnt music he should have been afraid he would have done nothing else than play. It was a method of employing the mind, without the labour of thinking at all, and with some applause from a man's self.

We had the music of the bagpipe every day at Armadale, Dunvegan, and Coll. Dr. Johnson appeared fond of it, and used often to stand for some time with his ear close to the great drone.

The penurious gentleman[4] of our acquaintance, formerly alluded to, afforded us a topic of conversation tonight. Dr. Johnson said I ought to write down a collection of the instances of his narrowness, as they almost exceeded belief. Coll told us that O'Kane, the famous Irish harper, was once at that gen-

---

[4] Sir Alexander Macdonald.

tleman's house. He could not find in his heart to give him any money, but gave him a key for a harp, which was finely ornamented with gold and silver and with a precious stone, and was worth eighty or a hundred guineas. He did not know the value of it; and when he came to know it, he would fain have had it back, but O'Kane took care that he should not. JOHNSON. "They exaggerate the value; everybody is so desirous that he should be fleeced. I am very willing it should be worth eighty or a hundred guineas, but I do not believe it." BOSWELL. "I do not think O'Kane was obliged to give it back." JOHNSON. "No, sir. If a man with his eyes open, and without any means used to deceive him, gives me a thing, I am not to let him have it again when he grows wiser. I like to see how avarice defeats itself; how, when avoiding to part with money, the miser gives something more valuable." Coll said the gentleman's relations were angry at his giving away the harp-key, for it had been long in the family. JOHNSON. "Sir, he values a new guinea more than an old friend."[5]

Coll also told us that the same person having come up with a sergeant and twenty men working on the high road, he entered into discourse with the sergeant, and then gave him sixpence for the men to drink. The sergeant asked, "Who is this fellow?" Upon being informed, he said, "If I had known who he was, I should have thrown it in his face." JOHNSON. "There is much want of sense in all this. He had no business to speak with the sergeant. He might have been in haste and trotted on. He has not learnt to be a miser; I believe we must take him apprentice." BOSWELL. "He would grudge giving half a guinea

---

[5] Lord Macdonald's own version of this story, related in his letter to Boswell of 26 November 1785, differs considerably from Coll's: ". . . O'Kane, the drunken blind harper, . . . after having slurred over some tunes for a week at my house under the inordinate influence of Bacchus, was dismissed with two guineas in his pocket and a key which he valued more than one hundred guineas, made of common agate. His reason for putting so extraordinary a value upon it was because he said it belonged to Roderick O'Kane, a famous harper in King Charles II's time; being apprehensive of losing what he deemed a precious relic during his drunken vagaries, I am informed he deposited it afterwards in the hands of a relation of mine, who I am confident would restore it to me if I thought it of importance to claim it."

to be taught." JOHNSON. "Nay, sir, you must teach him gratis.
You must give him an opportunity to practise your precepts."

Let me now go back and glean Johnsoniana. The Saturday
before we sailed from Sleat, I sat awhile in the afternoon with
Dr. Johnson in his room, in a quiet serious frame. I observed
that hardly any man was accurately prepared for dying, but
almost every one left something undone, something in confusion; that my father, indeed, told me he knew one man (Carlisle of Limekilns), after whose death all his papers were found
in exact order, and nothing was omitted in his will. JOHNSON.
"Sir, I had an uncle[6] who died so, but such attention requires
great leisure and great firmness of mind. If one was to think
constantly of death, the business of life would stand still. I am
no friend to making religion appear too hard. Many good people have done harm by giving severe notions of it. In the same
way as to learning: I never frighten young people with difficulties; on the contrary, I tell them that they may very easily get
as much as will do very well. I do not indeed tell them that they
will be Bentleys."

The night we rode to Coll's house, I said, "Lord Elibank is
probably wondering what is become of us." JOHNSON. "No, no;
he is not thinking of us." BOSWELL. "But recollect the warmth
with which he wrote. Are we not to believe a man when he
says that he has a great desire to see another? Don't you believe
that I was very impatient for your coming to Scotland?" JOHN-
SON. "Yes, sir, I believe you was; and I was impatient to come
to you. A young man feels so, but seldom an old man." I however convinced him that Lord Elibank, who has much of the
spirit of a young man, might feel so.—He asked me if our jaunt
had answered expectation. I said it had much exceeded it. I
expected much difficulty with him, and had not found it. "And,"
he added, "wherever we have come, we have been received
like princes in their progress."

He said he would not wish not to be disgusted in the High-

[6] Dr. Joseph Ford.

lands, for that would be to lose the power of distinguishing, and a man might then lie down in the middle of them. He wished only to conceal his disgust.

At Captain Maclean's, I mentioned Pope's friend Spence. JOHNSON. "He was a weak conceited man."[7] BOSWELL. "A good scholar, sir?" JOHNSON. "Why, no, sir." BOSWELL. "He was a pretty scholar." JOHNSON. "You have about reached him."

Last night at the inn, when the factor in Tyree spoke of his having heard that a roof was put on some part of the buildings at Icolmkill, I unluckily said, "It will be fortunate if we find a cathedral with a roof on it." I said this from a foolish anxiety to engage Dr. Johnson's curiosity more. He took me short at once. "What, sir? How can you talk so? If we shall *find* a cathedral roofed! As if we were going to a *terra incognita*: when everything that is at Icolmkill is so well known. You are like some New England men who came to the mouth of the Thames. 'Come,' said they, 'let us go up and see what sort of inhabitants there are here.' They talked, sir, as if they had been to go up the Susquehanna, or any other American river."

SATURDAY 16 OCTOBER. This day there was a new moon, and the weather changed for the better. Dr. Johnson said of Miss Maclean, "She is the most accomplished lady that I have found in the Highlands. She knows French, music, and drawing, sews neatly, makes shell-work, and can milk cows; in short, she can do everything. She talks sensibly, and is the first person whom I have found that can translate Erse poetry literally."—We set out, mounted on little Mull horses. Mull corresponded exactly with the idea which I had always had of it: a hilly country, diversified with heath and grass, and many rivulets. Dr. Johnson was not in very good humour. He said it

---

[7] "Mr. Langton thinks this must have been the hasty expression of a splenetic moment, as he has heard Dr. Johnson speak of Mr. Spence's judgment in criticism with so high a degree of respect as to show that this was not his settled opinion of him. Let me add that, in the preface to the *Preceptor*, he recommends Spence's *Essay on Pope's Odyssey*, and that his admirable Lives of the English Poets are much enriched by Spence's anecdotes of Pope."—BOSWELL.

was a dreary country, much worse than Skye. I differed from him. "Oh, sir," said he, "a most dolorous country!"

We had a very hard journey today. I had no bridle for my sheltie, but only a halter; and Joseph rode without a saddle. At one place, a loch having swelled over the road, we were obliged to plunge through pretty deep water. Dr. Johnson observed, how helpless a man would be were he travelling here alone and should meet with any accident, and said he longed to get to "a country of saddles and bridles." He was more out of humour today than he has been in the course of our tour, being fretted to find that his little horse could scarcely support his weight; and having suffered a loss, which, though small in itself, was of some consequence to him while travelling the rugged steeps of Mull, where he was at times obliged to walk. The loss that I allude to was that of the large oak-stick, which, as I formerly mentioned, he had brought with him from London. It was of great use to him in our wild peregrination; for, ever since his last illness in 1766, he has had a weakness in his knees, and has[1] not been able to walk easily. It had too the properties of a measure, for one nail was driven into it at the length of a foot, another at that of a yard. In return for the services it had done him, he said this morning he would make a present of it to some museum, but he little thought he was so soon to lose it. As he preferred riding with a switch, it was entrusted to a fellow to be delivered to our baggage-man, who followed us at some distance; but we never saw it more. I could not persuade him out of a suspicion that it had been stolen. "No, no, my friend," said he, "it is not to be expected that any man in Mull who has got it will part with it. Consider, sir, the value of such a *piece of timber* here!"

As we travelled this forenoon, we met Dr. Maclean, who expressed much regret at his having been so unfortunate as to be absent while we were at his house.

We were in hopes to get to Sir Allan Maclean's at Inchken-

---

[1] Inadvertently omitted in the first edition; supplied in the second.

neth tonight; but the eight miles of which our road was said to consist were so very long that we did not reach the opposite coast of Mull till seven at night, though we had set out about eleven in the forenoon; and when we did arrive there, we found the wind strong against us. Coll determined that we should pass the night at MacGuarie's, in the island of Ulva, which lies between Mull and Inchkenneth, and a servant was sent forward to the ferry to secure the boat for us; but the boat was gone to the Ulva side, and the wind was so high that the people could not hear him call, and the night so dark that they could not see a signal. We should have been in a very bad situation had there not fortunately been lying in the little sound of Ulva an Irish vessel, the *Bonetta*, of Londonderry, Captain Mc-Clure, master. He himself was at MacGuarie's, but his men obligingly came with their long-boat and ferried us over.

MacGuarie's house was mean, but we were agreeably surprised with the appearance of the master, whom we found to be intelligent, polite, and much a man of the world. Though his clan is not numerous, he is a very ancient chief, and has a burial place at Icolmkill. He told us his family had possessed Ulva for nine hundred years; but I was distressed to hear that it was soon to be sold for payment of his debts.[2]

Captain McClure, whom we found here, was of Scotch extraction, and properly a MacLeod, being descended of some of the MacLeods who went with Sir Norman of Bernera to the battle of Worcester, and after the defeat of the royalists, fled to Ireland, and, to conceal themselves, took a different name. He told me there was a great number of them about Londonderry, some of good property. I said they should now resume their real name. The Laird of MacLeod should go over and assemble them, and make them all drink the large horn full, and from that time they should be MacLeods. The Captain in-

---

[2] Carruthers says that MacGuarie sold Ulva in 1777. Though he was then sixty-two years of age, he entered the Army, served with distinction for many years, and died in 1818, at the great age of 103. The first purchaser of Ulva was a Campbell. In 1835 it was sold to a Lowlander, F. W. Clark.

formed us he had named his ship the *Bonetta* out of gratitude
to Providence; for once, when he was sailing to America with
a good number of passengers, the ship in which he then sailed
was becalmed for five weeks, and during all that time, numbers of the fish bonetta³ swam close to her and were catched
for food; he resolved therefore that the ship he should next get
should be called the *Bonetta*.

MacGuarie told us a strong instance of the second sight. He
had gone to Edinburgh and taken a man-servant along with
him. An old woman who was in the house said one day, "Mac-
Guarie will be at home tomorrow and will bring two gentlemen with him"; and she said she saw his servant return in red
and green. He did come home next day. He had two gentlemen with him; and his servant had a new red and green livery,
which MacGuarie had bought for him at Edinburgh upon a
sudden thought, not having the least intention when he left
home to put his servant in livery; so that the old woman could
not have heard any previous mention of it. This, he assured
us, was a true story.

MacGuarie insisted that the *Mercheta Mulierum*, mentioned
in our old charters, did really mean the privilege which a lord
of a manor or a baron had to have the first night of all his
vassals' wives. Dr. Johnson said the belief of such a custom
having existed was also held in England, where there is a tenure
called *Borough-English*, by which the eldest child does not inherit, from a doubt of his being the son of the tenant.⁴ Mac-
Guarie told us that still, on the marriage of each of his tenants, a
sheep is due to him, for which the composition is fixed at five shillings. I suppose Ulva is the only place where this custom remains.

Talking of the sale of an estate of an ancient family, which
was said to have been purchased much under its value by the
confidential lawyer of that family, and it being mentioned

---

³ The bonito or striped tunny, a fish common in tropical seas.
⁴ "Sir William Blackstone says in his Commentaries that he cannot find that ever this
custom prevailed in *England*; and therefore he is of opinion that it could not have given
rise to *Borough-English*."—BOSWELL.

that the sale would probably be set aside by a suit in equity, Dr. Johnson said, "I am very willing that this sale should be set aside, but I doubt much whether the suit will be successful, for the argument for avoiding the sale is founded on vague and indeterminate principles: as that the price was too low, and that there was a great degree of confidence placed by the seller in the person who became the purchaser. Now, how low should a price be? or what degree of confidence should there be to make a bargain be set aside? a bargain, which is a wager of skill between man and man. If, indeed, any fraud can be proved, that will do."

When Dr. Johnson and I were by ourselves at night, I observed of our host, "*Aspectum generosum habet.*" "*Et generosum animum,*" he added. For fear of being overheard in the small Highland houses, I often talked to him in such Latin as I could speak, and with as much of the English accent as I could assume, so as not to be understood in case our conversation should be too loud for the space.

We had each an elegant bed in the same room; and here it was that a circumstance occurred, as to which he has been strangely misunderstood. From his description of his chamber,[5] it has erroneously been supposed that his bed being too short for him, his feet, during the night, were in the mire; whereas he has only said that when he undressed he felt his feet in the mire: that is, the clay floor of the room, on which he stood before he went into bed, was wet, in consequence of the windows being broken, which let in the rain.

SUNDAY 17 OCTOBER. Being informed that there was nothing worthy of observation in Ulva, we took boat and proceeded to Inchkenneth, where we were introduced by our friend Coll to Sir Allan Maclean, the chief of his clan, and to

---

[5] "The house and the furniture are not always nicely suited. We were driven once, by missing a passage, to the hut of a gentleman, where, after a very liberal supper, when I was conducted to my chamber, I found an elegant bed of Indian cotton, spread with fine sheets. The accommodation was flattering; I undressed myself, and felt my feet in the mire."—Johnson's *Journey.*

two young ladies, his daughters. Inchkenneth is a pretty little island, a mile long and about half a mile broad, all good land.

As we walked up from the shore, Dr. Johnson's heart was cheered by the sight of a road marked with cart-wheels, as on the mainland; a thing we had not seen for a long time. It gave us a pleasure similar to that which a traveller feels when, whilst wandering on what he fears is a desert island, he perceives the print of human feet.

Military men acquire excellent habits of having all conveniencies about them. Sir Allan Maclean, who had been long in the Army, and had now a lease of this island, had formed a commodious habitation, though it consisted but of a few small buildings, only one storey high. He had, in his little apartments, more things than I could enumerate in a page or two.[1]

Among other agreeable circumstances it was not the least to find here a parcel of the *Caledonian Mercury*, published since we left Edinburgh, which I read with that pleasure which every man feels who has been for some time secluded from the animated scenes of the busy world.

Dr. Johnson found books here. He bade me buy Bishop Gastrell's *Christian Institutes*, which was lying in the room. He said, "I do not like to read anything on a Sunday but what is theological; not that I would scrupulously refuse to look at anything which a friend should show me in a newspaper, but in general, I would read only what is theological. I read just now some of Drummond's *Travels*, before I perceived what books were here. I then took up Derham's *Physico-Theology*."

Every particular concerning this island having been so well described by Dr. Johnson, it would be superfluous in me to present the public with the observations that I made upon it in my Journal.[2]

Dr. Johnson here showed so much of the spirit of a High-

---

[1] The enumeration no doubt *did* occupy some of the missing pages of the MS.
[2] This undoubtedly accounts for the greater part of what was in the missing pages of the MS. Boswell's description of Coll was similarly shortened, as a comparison with the published text will show.

lander that he won Sir Allan's heart; indeed, he has shown it during the whole of our tour. One night in Coll he strutted about the room with a broadsword and target, and made a formidable appearance; and another night I took the liberty to put a large blue bonnet on his head. His age, his size, and his bushy grey wig with this covering on it, presented the image of a venerable *sennachie*; and, however unfavourable to the Lowland Scots, he seemed much pleased to assume the appearance of an ancient Caledonian. We only regretted that he could not be prevailed with to partake of the social glass. One of his arguments against drinking appears to me not convincing. He urged that in proportion as drinking makes a man different from what he is before he has drunk, it is bad, because it has so far affected his reason. But may it not be answered that a man may be altered by it *for the better*; that his spirits may be exhilarated without his reason being affected? On the general subject of drinking, however, I do not mean positively to take the other side. I am *dubius, non improbus*.

Some days earlier I had been in great indecision as to the trip to Icolmkill. Mr. Johnson, however, appeared to be placidly indifferent. I had attempted to rouse him to a decision by stating the case for both sides. "Sir," said I, "if we include Icolmkill in our tour, it will take us a week[3] to go to it, and we may perhaps not be able to get to Auchinleck before the Session, which would be losing something more valuable to me—seeing you upon our old castle. But, on the other hand, I have always had Icolmkill as a capital object in my mind, since we first talked of visiting the Hebrides. We should think our tour imperfect, and have a regret, if we did not see it. I may go at another time, but then I should not see it with you. Come, what do you say?" JOHNSON. "Sir, you have put it very well on both sides. I can only say, '*Non nostrum est tantas componere*

---

[3] At this point the text is resumed from the MS. The preceding portion of this paragraph has been supplied by the editors to make a transition.

lites."[4] "But," said I, "give your opinion. Be my council. I shall be king, and determine after I have heard you." He said, "Do as you will." This day what had appeared so difficult and dubious seemed easy and clear. Sir Allan said if the weather was good he would conduct us by sea, if bad, by land; that was to say, he would either take us all the way by sea, or cross over to Mull, ride along to the Point of Ross, and from thence cross over to Iona. MacGuarie made a kind of promise of coming with his boat and going with us, but Sir Allan was the man on whom we depended.

I was quite easy with Sir Allan almost instantaneously. He knew the great intimacy that had been between my father and his predecessor, Sir Hector, and I suppose knew my character. He talked with a strange unaccountable sort of hesitation whether he was to go with us or not; though he observed at the same time that we should be very ill off without him. Said I, "Is it not curious to hear him express uncertainty, when he knows it is certain he is to go with us? You had better do it with a good grace."

I love little peculiar circumstances about any place. When I mentioned the track of cart-wheels, I should have marked that one of the young ladies had been overturned on the road a day or two before. It seems they rode in a cart, as the only carriage that they could get to take an airing in. Mr. Johnson marked in his journal that in the islands they call a gentleman's boat his *carriage*. He did this because Mr. Donald Macqueen, in his card to me, called Raasay's boat so; but upon inquiry I found that it was not a common mode of speech, and set Mr. Johnson right. It was just a *conceit* of Mr. Macqueen's, and Mr. Johnson took it to be a general phrase. Thus it is that travellers generalize both as to phrases and customs.

Sir Allan said he had got Dr. Campbell about a hundred subscribers to his *Britannia Elucidata*, of whom he believed

---

[4] "It is not for me to settle a controversy of such importance" (Virgil, *Eclogues*, III.108).

twenty were dead. Mr. Johnson said he believed the delay of publication was owing to this: that after publication there would be no more subscribers, and few would send the additional guinea to get their books; in which they would be wrong, for there would be a great deal of instruction in the book. He said he thought highly of Campbell. "In the first place, he has very good parts. In the second place, he has very extensive reading; not, perhaps, what is properly called learning, but history, politics, and in short that popular knowledge which makes a man very useful. In the third place, he has learnt much by what is called the *vox viva*. He talks with a great many people."

Mr. Johnson told us at Raasay a good story of Dr. Campbell and him. He called on Dr. Campbell, and they talked of Tull's *Husbandry*. Dr. Campbell said something. Mr. Johnson began to dispute it. "Come," said Dr. Campbell, "we do not want to get the better of one another. We want to increase each other's ideas." Mr. Johnson took it in good part, and the conversation then went on coolly and instructively.

I was agreeably disappointed in Sir Allan. I had heard of him only as an officer in Lord Eglinton's Highland regiment, and as a great companion of the Earl's, so I apprehended that I should find a riotous bottle companion and be pressed to drink; in place of which, the Knight was as sober after dinner as I could wish, and let me do as I pleased. And what surprised me still more agreeably, though he swore, as Dr. Campbell does, he was a man of religion like Dr. Campbell. He said he always made his daughters read prayers every Sunday evening, as he thought it of great consequence that they should keep in mind their duty to GOD. He spoke warmly in favour of the Episcopal Church—said that his father had a chaplain of the Church of England, and that the people chose to attend worship with him rather than go to the Presbyterian kirk. Mr. Johnson said they would all do so in the isles if they had an opportunity. Sir Allan agreed they would; and he said if he prevailed in his cause, he would build several chapels. We had our tea comfortably; and at night prayer-books were brought. Miss Maclean read the evening service with a beautiful decency. We read the responses and other parts that congregations read. When she came to the prayer for the royal family, she stopped. I bid her go to the prayer for the clergy. She did so. Mr. Johnson pointed out to her some prayers, which she read. After all, she and her sister sung the Hymn on the Nativity of our Saviour. It was the 19th[5] Sunday after Trinity. I shall ever remember it. Mr. Johnson said it was the most agreeable Sunday evening that he had ever passed in his life. We were all in a good frame. I was truly pious.[6]

I walked out in the dark to the cross, knelt before it, and holding it with both my hands, I prayed with strong devotion, while I had before me the image of that on which my Saviour died for the sins of the world. The sanctity of venerable Columbus[7] filled my imagination. I considered that to ask the intercession of a departed saint was at least innocent, and might be of service. I indulged my inclination to what is called superstitious prayer. I said, "*Sancte Columbe, ora pro me*. O Columbus, thou venerable Saint, as we have all the reason that can be to believe that thou art in heaven, I beseech thee to pray GOD that I may attain to everlasting felicity." I cannot be sure of the exact words (I am now writing at Glasgow, October 28). But what I said was to the above purpose. I felt a kind of pleasing awful confusion. I was for going into the chapel; but a tremor seized me for ghosts, and I hastened back to the house.[8] It was exceedingly dark, and in my timorous hurry I stepped suddenly into a hollow place, and strained a sinew on my right foot. It was painful a while; but rubbing it with rum and vinegar cured it by next day at breakfast.

I should have mentioned that after prayers I read to the

---

[5] Boswell neglected to fill a blank here.
[6] Everything that follows in this entry was omitted in the published *Tour*.
[7] i.e., Columba. Martin had used this spelling of the name.
[8] "Boswell, who is very pious, went into it [the chapel] at night to perform his devotions, but came back in haste, for fear of spectres" (Johnson to Mrs. Thrale, 23 October 1773).

company Dr. Ogden's 2d and 9th Sermons. I promised to send a copy of them to Miss Maclean.

Sir Allan had made an apology at dinner that he had neither red wine nor biscuits, but that he expected both. Luckily the boat arrived with them this very afternoon. We had a couple of bottles of port and hard biscuits at night, after some roasted potatoes, which is Sir Allan's simple fare by way of supper.

Sir Allan and Coll had each a bed in the room where I dressed. Mr. Johnson and I had each one in the room where we passed the day. Mine was the camp-bed of the Hon. Roger Townshend, who was killed in America,[9] and whose monument is in Westminster Abbey. Sir Allan's camp equipage was destroyed by a bomb. General Amherst desired him to take Colonel Townshend's, as he had been intimate with him, and settle as to the value of it with Lord Townshend, when he went to England. Sir Allan, when in London, begged my lord to accept of a £100 bank bill, but my lord would by no means have anything. There was something curious in sleeping in a camp-bed which had actually been in service in America. My old soldierly inclinations revived.[10]

MONDAY 18 OCTOBER. We had agreed to pass this day with Sir Allan; and he engaged to have everything in order for our journey tomorrow.[1] Before breakfast, I repaired to the chapel, knelt at the ruined altar, and prayed in a pleasing holy frame, "with sense of gratitude and joy," as Parnell says. I thought I had so steady, so certain a prospect of celestial felicity that I should never again be vicious and could die with perfect peace. LORD, grant that when the period of my disso-

---

[9] At Ticonderoga, 25 July 1759.

[10] Boswell's trip to London at the end of 1762 was made ostensibly for the purpose of seeking a commission in the Guards, but he admitted later in his memoirs that he was motivated chiefly by a love of the metropolis. His memoranda for that period, however, which are preserved among the Malahide papers, show that for a time at least he did make a serious though futile attempt to ingratiate himself with such people as he thought could assist him in his quest: the Countess of Northumberland, Lord Adam Gordon, the Duke of Queensberry, etc.

[1] The remainder of this paragraph was omitted in the printed *Tour*.

lution arrives, I may be in the same state! "Thou wilt keep him in perfect peace, whose mind is stayed on thee," etc.

The night we were at Ulva, I told how Coll prescribed to me to have my feet washed and take a warm drink immediately, by which the cold which I contracted by being wet lasted only a quarter of an hour. Said Mr. Johnson, "Coll does everything for us. We'll erect a statue to Coll." "Yes," said I, "and we'll have him with his various attributes and characters, like Mercury or any other of the heathen gods. We'll have him as a pilot. We'll have him as a physician—and so on."

I this morning got a spade and dug a little grave in the floor of the chapel, in which I carefully buried what loose bones were there. I said, "Rest in peace, so far as I can contribute to it." I said I hoped somebody would do as much for me. JOHNSON. "Well said." He praised me for what I had done, though he said he would not do it. He showed, in the chapel at Raasay, his horror at dead men's bones. He showed it again at Coll's house. In the charter-room there was a remarkably large shinbone of a man, which was said to have been a bone of John Garve,[2] one of the lairds. The present Coll, with a strange unnaturality, took it home from the family burial-place, and now it is just a show, which is using an ancestor oddly. I desired young Coll to have it put back to its place. Mr. Johnson would not look at it, but started away from us. I lifted the bones today with my bare hands quite easily, conscious that I was doing a kind of pious office.

At breakfast I asked, "What is the reason that we are angry at a trader's having opulence?" "Why, sir," said Mr. Johnson, "the reason is (though I don't undertake to prove that there is a reason), we see no qualities in trade that should entitle a man to superiority. We are not angry at a soldier's getting riches, because we see that he possesses qualities which we have not. If a man returns from a battle, having lost one hand and with the other full of gold, we feel that he deserves the

[2] i.e., John Garve Maclean, the first Laird of Coll.

gold; but we cannot think that a fellow, by sitting all day at a desk, is entitled to get above us." "But," said I, "may we not suppose a merchant to be a man of an enlarged mind, as the *Spectator* makes Sir Andrew Freeport?" JOHNSON. "Why, sir, we may suppose any fictitious character. We may suppose a philosophical day-labourer, who is happy in reflecting that by his labour he contributed to the fertility of the earth and to the support of his fellow-creatures; but we find no such philosophical day-labourer. A merchant may, perhaps, be a man of an enlarged mind; but there is nothing in trade connected with an enlarged mind."

I was very much taken with Inchkenneth. I said I was resolved to have it for an elegant retreat for our family during a month or two in summer. Sir Allan said, if he recovered it from the Duke of Argyll, I should have it on my own terms. I really indulged serious thoughts of buying it. My brother David always talked of purchasing an island. "Sir," said Mr. Johnson, "so does almost every man, till he knows what it is." Sir Allan and he and I walked awhile on the shore under the houses. We looked at a cave or cleft or recess of a rock, in which Sir Allan keeps his peats dry. We looked at a bed of oysters, which I had never seen anywhere before. I took up one, broke it between two stones, and eat it, by way of having a proof how I could live if I were thrown upon a coast where I could get only raw shell-fish; and I thought I could do. Mr. Johnson and I were also occupied in gathering little yellow shells like a more elegant species of whelks. Mr. Johnson gathered for little Miss Thrale, I for my father.

I mentioned that I had heard Solander say he was a Swedish Laplander. JOHNSON. "Sir, I don't believe he's a Laplander. The Laplanders are not much above five[3] feet high. He is as tall as you; and he has not the copper colour of a Laplander." BOSWELL. "But what motive could he have to make himself a Laplander?" JOHNSON. "Why, sir, he must either mean the

[3]Inserted by Malone at the time of revision. The published text reads *four*.

word Laplander in a very extensive sense; or may mean a voluntary degradation of himself: 'For all my being the great man that you see me now, I was originally a barbarian'; as if Burke should say, 'I came over a wild Irishman,' which he might say in his present state of exaltation."

Coll and his dogs and Joseph were busy seeking for otters, of which this island has many. Sir Allan, Mr. Johnson and I sailed in a little boat with two oars to a small island called Sannaland or Sandyland,[4] very near Inchkenneth, in order to be on another isle, and to look for more shells. We found a great many of the small yellow whelks, and a good many small silver buckies, of which there are some on the coast of Inchkenneth. Mr. Johnson lay down and gathered, as he is short-sighted. Sannaland is a small spot. It has, as Mr. Johnson said, three parts: sand, rock, and rock covered with a little earth and grass upon it. It feeds a riding horse[5] in summer. It is an appendage to Inchkenneth, so I am to have it; and I am also to have a right of game over all Sir Allan's lands in Mull. In summer I can have goats for milk, as there is a variety of fine herbage upon it. It is a kind of objection to Inchkenneth that sometimes the sea between it and Mull is at one place so shallow that people may wade over. This breaks the natural security of being surrounded by the sea. But it is a very rare thing to have so shallow a sea; and even then there are none can pass but people particularly well-acquainted with the place, as there are quicksands. I can have a battery of cannon on that quarter.

Mr. Johnson said I should build me a fortification, if I came to live on Inchkenneth; "for," said he, "if you have it not, what should hinder a parcel of ruffians to land in the night and carry off what things you have in the house, which in a remote country would be more valuable than some of your cows and sheep; and this besides the danger of having your throat cut." I said I would have a large dog. "So you may,"

---

[4] i.e., Sandland.
[5] There is a blank in the manuscript after this word.

said he. "But a large dog is of no use but to alarm." He however, I apprehend, thinks too lightly of the power of that animal. I have heard him say he would be afraid of no dog. He
would take him up by the hinder legs, which would render him
quite helpless, and then knock his head against a stone and
beat out his brains. Beauclerk told me that at his house in
the country two large dogs were fighting. Mr. Johnson looked
steadily at them for a little, and then, as one would separate
two little boys who are foolishly hurting each other, he ran up
to them and cuffed their heads till he had them asunder from
one another. But few men have his intrepidity, Herculean
strength, or contrivance. Most thieves or robbers would be afraid
to encounter a mastiff.

Mr. Johnson takes a kind of pleasure in laughing at his friends
in trifles. There was a mere black barren rock in our view today as we sailed. He called to me, "This shall be your island,
and it shall be called Inch Boswell"; and then he laughed,
with a strange appearance of triumph.

Coll was busy digging for rabbits after he could not find otters, being desirous to have rabbits in his lands of Quinish in
Mull. I say *his* lands; for he always says "my," and not "my
father's" lands; and indeed the old gentleman gives him full
scope. There has been a custom in this family that the laird
resigns the estate to his eldest son when he comes of age, reserving to himself only a certain life-rent. So young Coll told
me. He said it was a voluntary custom. But I think I found an
instance in the charter-room that there was such a resignation
in consequence of a contract of marriage. I must get a copy of
the clause, as I neglected to attend to it exactly. If the custom
was voluntary, it was only curious; but if by any obligation, it
was dangerous; for Banks told me that in Otaheite, whenever
a child is born (a son, I think) the father loses his right to the
estate and honours, and this unnatural, or rather absurd, custom—as property is not natural either in one way or another—
occasions the murder of many children.

Young Coll told us he could run down a greyhound; "for," said he, "the dog runs himself out of breath by going too quick, and then I get up with him and beat him at speed." Mr. Johnson observed that *I* explained the cause of this, by remarking that Coll had reason, and knew to moderate his pace, which the dog had not sense to know. Indeed, Coll is not a philosopher. Mr. Johnson said, "He is a noble animal. He is as complete an islander as mortality can figure. He is a farmer, a sailor, a hunter, a fisher; he will run you down a dog. If any man has a tail, it is Coll. He is hospitable; and he has an intrepidity of talk, whether he understands the subject or not."

Mr. Johnson observed that there was nothing of which he would not undertake to persuade a Frenchman in a foreign country. Said he, "I'll carry a Frenchman to St. Paul's Churchyard, and I'll tell him, 'Sir, by our law you may walk half round the church, but if you walk round the whole, you will be punished capitally'; and he'll believe me at once. Now, no Englishman would readily swallow such a thing. He'd go and inquire at somebody else." I said the Frenchman's credulity must be owing to his being accustomed to implicit submission; whereas every Englishman reasons upon the laws of his country, and instructs his representatives who compose the legislature.

Mr. Johnson sailed near to the house to avoid walking. Sir Allan and I took a walk. I went to the beach where we landed yesterday, and looked for transparent white stones, but found hardly any pure ones. The gloss of being wet makes them all look transparent. Gathering pebbles is a gentle, pleasing amusement. I thought a pretty poem might be made upon it. We dined cheerfully and drank tea, after which Miss Maclean played several tunes on the harpsichord very well. I proposed a reel; so Miss Sibby[6] and Coll and I danced, while Miss Maclean played, which was making the most of it. As I have formerly observed, my exertions as a dancer are all forced by a reflex desire to promote lively good humour.

---

[6] Sir Allan's second daughter was named Sibella.

TUESDAY 19 OCTOBER. It was this day, and not yesterday, that I buried the bones.[1] The day was charming for a voyage to Icolmkill. When I went out, I met Miss Maclean, who
said, "I have been employed for you this morning. I have been
scrambling among the rocks to get petrifications for you." She
gave me a few, but none of them were curious. I once more
paid my devotions to GOD in the old chapel.

After breakfast we took leave of the young ladies, and of our
excellent companion Coll, to whom we had been so much
obliged. He had now put us under the care of his chief, and
was to hasten back to Skye. There was a kindly regret at part-
ing with him which was both proper and pleasing. He had been
a kind of banker to me, in supplying me with silver. There
remained six-and-sixpence due by me to him on settling our
accounts today. He desired that I should purchase with it a
cap to Joseph's young son. A small circumstance shows benevolence. He and Joseph had been often companions.[2]

Sir Allan had a good boat with four stout rowers. One of
them, Lauchlan Dow———,[3] was a remarkably strong and
clever fellow, either at sea or at land. All of them, and he in
particular, took a great liking for me before we parted, as Sir
Allan told me by interpretation. We coasted along Mull till we
reached Gribon, where is what is called Mackinnon's Cave,
an *antrum immane* indeed, to which the one at Ullinish is nothing. It is in a rock of a great highth just upon the sea. Upon
the left of its entrance there is a cascade, almost perpendicular
from top to bottom of the rock, of no great size, but very
pretty. There is a tradition that it was conducted thither arti-

---

[1] In the printed *Tour*, however, the account occurs in the same place as in the MS.

[2] The following passage occurs here in the printed *Tour*: "We parted from him with
very strong feelings of kindness and gratitude, and we hoped to have had some future
opportunity of proving to him the sincerity of what we felt; but in the following year he
was unfortunately lost in the Sound between Ulva and Mull; and this imperfect memorial, joined to the high honour of being tenderly and respectfully mentioned by Dr.
Johnson, is the only return which the uncertainty of human events has permitted us to
make to this deserving young man."

[3] Boswell did not catch the man's family name. *Dow* is his spelling for Gaelic *dubh*,
"black," better known to English readers in the form adopted by Sir Walter Scott—"Dhu."

ficially, to supply the inhabitants of the cave with water. Mr.
Johnson gave no credit to this tradition. As his faith in the
Christian religion is firm upon good grounds, he is incredulous
when there is no sufficient reason for belief, being in this just
the reverse of modern infidels. Lord Hailes said that somebody
should write an "*Essai sur la crédulité des incrédules.*"

The highth of this cave I cannot tell with any tolerable exactness, but it seemed to be very lofty, and to be a pretty regular arch. After advancing a little, we found it to be forty-five
feet broad. Afterwards we found a passage or gallery about
four or five feet broad—for we did not measure it. Then we
came to a place fifteen feet broad. There we found a large stone
table lying on the floor. Sir Allan said it had stood on supporters or pillars, and we saw some broken stones near it, but
Mr. Johnson was of opinion that machinery sufficient to raise
it could not be erected in the cave; so that there was a mistake as to the pillars. Sir Allan said there were stone benches,
too, around the table. I think I saw some stones which may be
called such. Where the table is, the floor of the cave is a good
deal elevated above the floor of the entrance, by gradual pro-
gression. The floor is sometimes of loose pebbles; sometimes of
a fine dry sand; sometimes embarrassed with large stones, I
suppose fragments of the rock. As we advanced, the arch of
the roof became less regular, the rock filling up a considerable
part of the space on the left, but so as a man could clamber up
it. A yard or two beyond the table, we found another heap of
fragments, beyond which I could perceive that I might go;
but as we had but one candle with us, to be a proof when the
air should grow bad, and to give us light, we did not choose to
risk its going out. Tradition says that a piper and twelve men
advanced into the cave, nobody knows how far, but never returned. At the heap to which we went, which was 485 feet
from the entrance of the cave, the air was quite good, for the
candle burnt freely without the least appearance of the flame's
growing globular; and there was as much light from the large

mouth, though distant, as that a man would not find himself quite in a dismal state, and would find his way out tolerably well. Mr. Johnson said this was the greatest natural curiosity he had ever seen.

We saw the Island of Staffa, at no very great distance, but could not land upon it, the surge was so high on its rocky coast. We sailed close to a point called Ardtun, on the Mull coast, where we saw a miniature specimen of the Giant's Causeway, and some of the same kind of natural pilasters on rock as are described to be at Staffa. Sir Allan said people who had seen both were of opinion that the appearances at Ardtun were better than those at Staffa; prettier or finer, he said. If so, there must have been wondrous puffing about Staffa. He said if we had seen it, we should have had a controversy.

Sir Allan, anxious for the honour of Mull, was always talking of *woods* that he said were upon the hills of that island, which appeared at a distance as we sailed along. Said Mr. Johnson, "I saw at Tobermory what they called a wood, which I unluckily took for *heath*. If you show me what I shall take for *furze*, it will be something."

Our rowers sung Erse songs, or rather howls. Sir Allan said the Indians in America sung in the same manner when rowing. We passed by the mouth of a large basin, arm of the sea, or loch, called Loch Scridain, upon the shore of which Mr. Neil MacLeod, minister of Kilfinichen, lives. I had a letter to him from Kenneth Macaulay; and he was the best man we could get to show us Icolmkill with knowledge. But we were not sure of finding him at home, and thought it at any rate imprudent to go out of our way much, as we might lose a good day, which was very valuable. I however insisted that we should land upon the shore of Loch ———,[4] which we came to a little after, but which, not being very far back into the country, cost us but a little deviation. My reason for insisting to land was to get some whisky or rum for our boatmen. The fellows

---

[4] Left blank in the MS. Probably Loch na Lathaich.

were rather for pushing straight for Iona. But I could not be easy unless they had a *scalck*. Besides, the nearest public house was kept by Lauchlan Maclean,[5] lately servant to Sir Allan; and we proposed to take him with us both as an additional rower and as quartermaster at Icolmkill, for which he was well fitted, having been with Sir Allan not only in the best parts of Scotland, but in many parts of England.

Sir Allan, like all other officers, who, though by their profession obliged to endure fatigues and inconveniencies, are peculiarly luxurious, expatiated in prospect on the expertness with which Lauchlan would get on a good fire in a snug barn, and get us clean straw for beds, and dress us, along with Joseph, an Austrian campaigner, a tolerable supper. I take it the suffering, or at least the contemplating of hardships, to which officers are accustomed (for from Sir Allan's account even of the American expeditions, it appeared that though the poor common soldiers are often wretchedly off, the officers suffer little, having their commodious camp equipage, and their chocolate, and other comforts carried along in little room, and prepared by their men, who are most subservient beings), makes them fonder of all indulgences.

We went ashore upon a little rising ground, which is an island at high water. We sat down upon a seat of rock, and took a repast of cold mutton, bread and cheese and apples, and punch. Lauchlan Dow in the mean time ran to Lauchlan Maclean's house. When he returned with Lauchlan Maclean, we had the disappointment of finding that no spirits of any kind were to be found. A burial some days before had exhausted them. Mr. Campbell of ———, a tacksman of the Duke of Argyll's, lived not far off. Sir Allan sent the two Lauchlans thither, begging the loan of two bottles of rum. We got them, with a message that Mr. Campbell had expected us to dinner, having heard that we were to pass; that he was sorry he had not then seen us, and hoped we would be with him next day.

---

[5] Boswell left a blank for Lauchlan's family name at every occurrence except that on p. 332.

We refreshed our crew. The weather grew coldish. I proposed an expedient to keep our feet warm, which was to strew the boat plentifully with heath, the chief production of the island where we dined. Accordingly I fell to work and pulled, as did some of our men, and Mr. Johnson pulled very assiduously. Sir Allan, who had been used to command men, and had no doubt superintended soldiers making roads or throwing up ramparts or doing some other kind of work, never stopped, but stood by *grieving* us (the Scottish expressive term for overseeing as a taskmaster, an overseer being called a *grieve*; as my lord Loudoun tells, a countryman said to him, Mr. Dun our minister was *grieving* my father, who was busy gathering stones to mend a road). We made ourselves very comfortable with the heath. The wind was now against us, but we had very little of it.

We coasted along Mull, which was on our left. On our right was the Atlantic, with Staffa and other islands in it for some part of the way. Then we came to a large black rock in the sea; then to Nun's Island,[6] which it is said belonged to the nuns of Icolmkill, and that from it the stone for the buildings of Icolmkill was taken; as the rocks still there are of the same kind of stone, and there is none such in Icolmkill. It became very dusky, or rather dark, about seven; for our voyage, by going along the turnings of the coast, would be, Sir Allan said, forty miles from Inchkenneth to Iona; so that we were benighted. Mr. Johnson said, as we were going up the narrow sound between Mull and Nun's Island, with solemn-like rocks on each side of us, and the waves rising and falling, and our boat proceeding with a dancing motion, "This is roving among the Hebrides, or nothing is." A man has a pleasure in applying things to words, and comparing the reality with the picture of fancy. We had long talked of "roving among the Hebrides." It was curious to repeat the words previously used, and which had impressed our imaginations by frequent use; and then to feel how the immediate impression from actually rov-

---

[6] i.e., Eilean nam Ban, "isle of women."

ing differed from the one in fancy, or agreed with it. It will be curious too, to perceive how the impression made by reading this my Journal some years after our roving will affect the mind, when compared with the recollection of what was felt at the time. Mr. Johnson said I should read my Journal about every three years. Joseph made a very good observation. "Your journey," said he, "will always be more agreeable to you."

I often do not observe chronology, for fear of losing a thing by waiting till I can put it in its exact place. Joseph said this one night as I was going to bed, and was resuming to him with much complacency some of our past scenes on this expedition. He meant what I have often experienced: that scenes through which a man has gone improve by lying in the memory. They grow mellow. It is said, "*Acti labores sunt jucundi.*"[7] This may be owing to comparing them with present ease. But I also think that even harsh scenes acquire a softness by length of time;[8] and many scenes are like very loud sounds, which do not please till you are at a distance from them, or at least do not please so much; or like strong coarse pictures, which must be viewed at a distance. And I don't know how it is, but even pleasing scenes improve by time, and seem more exquisite in recollection than when they were present, if they have not faded to dimness in the memory. Perhaps there is so much evil in every human enjoyment when present, so much dross mixed with it, that it requires to be refined by time; and yet I do not see why time should not melt away the good and the evil in equal proportions, why the shade should decay and the light remain in preservation. I must hear Mr. Johnson upon this subject.

The boat had so much motion tonight that I had a renewal of the uneasiness of fear at sea; and I wondered how I could so soon totally forget what I had endured when driven to Coll.

---

[7] "Past labours are sweet" (Cicero's *De Finibus*).
[8] "I have lately observed that this thought has been elegantly expressed by Cowley:
　　'Things which offend when present, and affright,
　　In memory, well painted, move delight.'"—BOSWELL.

People accustomed to sail give every little direction with so loud a tone that a fresh-water man is alarmed. Sir William Temple's observation on the boisterous manners of seamen, from their being used to contend with a boisterous element, will apply in some degree to all "who go down into the sea"— at least while they are upon it. Coll talks loud at sea, and Sir Allan talks loud at sea. I asked if we should not be quieter when we were in the Sound between Mull and Icolmkill. Sir Allan said no. We should have a rougher sea, as we should then have a stronger current against us, and have the Atlantic quite open from each end of the Sound. I yielded so much to fear as to ask if it would not be better that we should go ashore for that night on Mull, and cross the Sound in the morning with daylight. Sir Allan was for going on. Mr. Johnson said, "I suppose Sir Allan, who knows, thinks there is no danger." "No, sir," said Sir Allan. Mr. Johnson was satisfied. I therefore had nothing to say, but kept myself calm. I am so much a disciple of Dr. Ogden's that I venture to pray even upon small occasions if I feel myself much concerned. Perhaps when a man is much concerned, the occasions ought not to be called small. I put up a petition to GOD to make the waves more still. I know not if I ought to draw a conclusion from what happened; but so it was, that after we had turned the point of Nun's Island and got into the Sound of Icolmkill, the tide was for us, and we went along with perfect smoothness, which made me feel a most pleasing tranquillity.[9]

In a little, I saw a light shining in the village at Icolmkill. All the inhabitants of the island, except perhaps a few shepherds or rather cowherds, live close to where the ancient buildings stood. I then saw the tower of the cathedral just discernible in the air. As we were landing, I said to Mr. Johnson, "Well, I am glad we are now at last at this venerable place, which I have so long thought that you and I should visit. I

---

[9] Boswell's petition—and a great deal besides in this entry—was omitted in the published *Tour*.

could have gone and seen it by myself. But you would not have been with me; and the great thing is to bring objects together." "It is so," said he, with a more than ordinary kind complacency. Indeed, the seeing of Mr. Samuel Johnson at Icolmkill was what I had often imaged as a very venerable scene. A landscape or view of any kind is defective, in my opinion, without some human figures to give it animation. What an addition was it to Icolmkill to have the Rambler upon the spot! After we landed, I shook hands with him cordially.

Upon hearing that Sir Allan Maclean was arrived, which was announced by his late servant Lauchlan whom we dispatched into the village, which is very near to the shore, the inhabitants—who still consider themselves as the people of Maclean, though the Duke of Argyll has at present possession of the ancient estate—ran eagerly to him. We went first to the house of —— Macdonald, the most substantial man among them. Sir Allan called him the Provost. He had a tolerable hut with higher walls than common, and pretty well built with dry stone. The fire was in the middle of the room. A number of people assembled. What remained of our snuff was distributed among them. Sir Allan had a little tobacco, of which he gave several of them a little bit each. We regretted that there was not a drop of spirits upon the island, for we wished to have given them a hearty cup on occasion of a visit from Sir Allan, who had not been there for fourteen years, and in the interval had served four years in America. The people seemed to be more decently dressed than one usually finds those of their station in the isles.

Icolmkill pays £150 of rent. They sell about forty cattle and more than 150 bolls of barley; and what is remarkable, they brew a good deal of beer, which I could not find was done in any of the other isles. I was told that they imported nothing but salt and iron. Salt they might soon make. It is a very fertile island, and the people are industrious. They make their own woollen and linen webs, and indeed I suppose everything else, except any hardware for which they may have occasion. They have no shoes for their horses.

After warming ourselves in Mr. Macdonald's, we were informed that our barn was ready, and we repaired to it. There was a fire in the middle of the floor, but the smoke was ceased before we went into the barn. We had cuddies and some oysters boiled in butter, that we might say we had fish and oyster sauce. Mr. Johnson eat none of that dish. We had roasted potatoes, of which I think he eat one; and he drank a mug of sweet milk. The fire was then carefully removed, and good hay was strewed at one end of the barn. Mr. Johnson lay down with all his clothes and his greatcoat on. Sir Allan and I took off our coats and had them laid upon our feet. But we had also a pair of clean sheets which Miss Maclean had put up, and some very good blankets from the village; so that we had a tolerably comfortable bed. Each had a portmanteau for a pillow. Mr. Johnson lay next the one wall, I next the other, Sir Allan in the middle. I could not help thinking in the night how curious it was to see the chief of the Macleans, Mr. Samuel Johnson, and James Boswell, Esq. lying thus. Our boatmen were lodged somewhere in the village. Joseph, Lauchlan Maclean, and Donald MacDougal, a fine smart little boy-servant to Sir Allan, lay across the barn, at a little distance from our feet. It was just an encampment. There was a good deal of wind blew through the barn, so that it was rather too cool.

WEDNESDAY 20 OCTOBER. Between seven and eight we rose and went to see the ruins. We had for our cicerone ———, who calls himself the descendant of St. Columbus's cousin. It is said their family has from time immemorial had ten acres of land in Icolmkill rent free, till it was lately taken from them by the Duke of Argyll. Sir Allan said if he recovered the island, they should be restored to their old possession. We had also a number of men following us. Our cicerone was a stupid fellow.

We first viewed the monastery of the nuns. The church has been a pretty building. Mr. Johnson took a very accurate inspection of all the ruins, and will give a very enlarged account of them in the *Tour*, or whatever he shall call it, which the world will gain by this expedition, to which I have had the merit of persuading him. I shall therefore only mention such circumstances as struck me on a cursory view.

It shocked one to observe that the nuns' chapel was made a fold for cattle, and was covered a foot deep with cow-dung. They cleared it off for us at one place and showed us the grave-stone of a lady abbess. It was of that bluish stone or slate which is frequent in Highland churchyards. At one end was carved the abbess with her crosier at her side,[1] and hands folded on her breast. At another, with the heads in an opposite direction, a Virgin and babe.[2] I think the figures at each end were entire, whole lengths. Round the stone was an inscription telling who the lady was.—But I am, I find, growing minute when I write, though for the reason which I have mentioned it is unnecessary; and besides, I did not give exact attention to the nuns, as I considered that so many people had examined them: Dr. Pococke, Dr. Walker, Mr. Banks, Mr. Pennant; and when I saw Mr. Johnson setting himself heartily to examine them, my mind was quiescent, and I resolved to stroll among them at my ease, take no trouble to investigate, and only receive the general impression of solemn antiquity and the particular ideas of such objects as should of themselves strike my attention.

We walked from the monastery of nuns to the great church or cathedral, as they call it, along an old pavement or causeway. They say that this was a street, and that there were good houses built on each side. Mr. Johnson doubted if it was anything more than a paved road for the nuns. Some small houses now stand at various distances on each side of it. Mr. Johnson said if there were houses there formerly, he did not imagine

---

[1] Boswell (who was writing from memory) was mistaken about the crosier, which he shows also in his crude sketch. The grave-slab commemorates the Prioress Anna, daughter of Donald McTearlach. She died in 1543. Some time after Boswell's visit the slab was broken.
[2] Sketch omitted.

they were better. Indeed, when we saw how small a house the bishop had, it was not probable that inferior houses were better than what we now think poor cottages. Indeed, the houses here are all built of stone, as the inhabitants have without scruple made quarries of the walls of the religious buildings. The convent of monks, the great church, Oran's Chapel, and four more, are still to be discerned. Of some, more remains; of some, less. I restrain myself from saying anything in particular of them. I was struck with a noble long cross called St. Martin's[3] Cross. But I must own that Icolmkill did not come up to my expectations, as they were high, from what I had read of it, and still more from what I had heard of it and thought of it, from my earliest years. Mr. Johnson said it came up to his, because he had taken his impression from an account of it subjoined to Sacheverell's *History of the Isle of Man*, where it is said there is not much to be seen. Both he and I were disappointed when we were shown what are called the monuments of the kings of Scotland, Ireland, and Denmark, and of a king of France.[4] There are only some gravestones flat on the earth; and we could see no inscriptions. How far short was this of marble monuments, like those in Westminster Abbey, and which I had imaged here! The gravestones of Sir Allan Maclean's family, and of that of MacGuarie, had as good an appearance as the royal ones; if they were royal, which Mr. Johnson doubted.

We were shown St. Columbus's well. I drank out of it. Mr. Johnson had his drink from it last night. We were told that here, as at Inchkenneth, the water was conveyed in leaden pipes. All that I could observe was that at the well the water came out of a flat freestone with a springing motion, as if conducted to the orifice by a pipe. But whether there was a lead

---

[3] "Martin's" is supplied by the editors to fill a blank in the MS. For a photograph and description of this cross, see R. Jaffray's *Iona* (1907), pp. 13–14.
[4] According to Martin, there were forty-eight kings of Scotland, eight kings of Norway, and four kings of Ireland buried in Iona.

pipe or not is a moot point. We also looked at the —— house, which has been inconsiderable.

We walked down again to our barn, where breakfast was prepared—milk, cheese, eggs, bread and butter. I slipped away and returned to the cathedral and its environs to perform some pleasing serious exercises of piety. I knelt before St. Martin's[5] Cross and said a short prayer. I went to the black stone on which the islanders of old used to swear. I had been shown a greyish piece of freestone, which they said was it; and I adopted their inaccurate information. I put my knees to this greyish freestone and said, "I here swear with all the solemnity that any honest, honourable, and brave man ever swore upon this stone, that I will stand by Sir Allan Maclean and his family." I had told Sir Allan that I would swear a covenant with him upon the black stone. I could not easily get him with me privately; so I went alone, and told him what I had done, which pleased him mightily; and I hope I shall have it in my power to convince him of my sincerity and steadiness.[6]

My easiness to receive information in the isles was too great. Had not Mr. Johnson been with me, I might have brought home loads of fiction or of gross mistakes. No wonder that he is in a passion at the people, as they tell him with such readiness and confidence what he finds, upon questioning them a little more, is not true. Sir Allan told me plainly that the greyish freestone which stood like a stone at the end of a grave, near the wall of the monastery,[7] was the famous black stone. I, either not attending to the striking objection that it was not black, or thinking that the epithet "black" might have been given to it from its solemn purposes and not from its colour (for I do not

---

[5] Supplied by the editors to fill a blank in the MS.
[6] This paragraph was omitted in the published *Tour*. Boswell's professions of fidelity were not a meaningless whim. He was Sir Allan's lawyer in the case against the Duke of Argyll.
[7] Boswell left a blank here. Pennant describes the black stone (he says "stones") as being in a corner of the ruins of the monastery, by which he means the house of the monks —distinguishing that of the nuns by the term "nunnery."

clearly remember how I believed implicitly), very gravely thought myself kneeling on that stone where so many chiefs and warriors had knelt. Sir Allan told me afterwards, of his own accord, that the black stone was quite sunk into the earth. However, I found (if Sir Allan could be credited as an antiquary a second time) that the black stone was sunk quite close to where the greyish stands; so that I really was upon the black stone while I swore to stand by Maclean.

I then went into the cathedral, which is really grand enough when one thinks of its antiquity and of the remoteness of the place; and at the end, I offered up my adorations to God. I again addressed a few words to Saint Columbus; and I warmed my soul with religious resolutions. I felt a kind of exultation in thinking that the solemn scenes of piety ever remain the same, though the cares and follies of life may prevent us from visiting them, or may even make us fancy that their effects were only "as yesterday when it is past," and never again to be perceived. I hoped that ever after having been in this holy place, I should maintain an exemplary conduct. One has a strange propensity to fix upon some point from whence a better course of life may be said to begin. I read with an audible voice the fifth chapter of St. James, and Dr. Ogden's tenth sermon. I suppose there has not been a sermon preached in this church since the Reformation. I had a serious joy in hearing my voice, while it was filled with Ogden's admirable eloquence, resounding in the ancient cathedral of Icolmkill.[8]

I had promised to write to my worthy old friend Grange[9] from Icolmkill. I therefore wrote a short solemn letter to him here. While I was writing it, Mr. Johnson entered, that he

---

[8] The prayer to St. Columba and the readings from St. James and Ogden were reduced in the published *Tour* to a bare reference to "devout meditation." This paragraph is perhaps the most amusing, and at the same time the most touching passage recovered from the MS.
[9] i.e., John Johnston of Grange, an Edinburgh attorney, one of Boswell's two closest friends, the other being the Rev. W. J. Temple. It was a whim of Boswell's to write letters to his friends from solemn or sacred places. At Wittenberg in 1764 he wrote a letter to Johnson using the tomb of Melanchthon as a table; but it was not until 1777 that he found the courage to send it.

might attentively view and even measure the ruins. I left him there, as I was to take a ride to the shore where Columbus landed, as it is said, and where the green pebbles called Icolmkill stones are found. I eat some eggs for breakfast, while Sir Allan sat by me. —— MacGinnis, whose horse I was to ride, came in. Sir Allan had been told that he had refused to send him some rum which he had; at which Sir Allan was in great indignation. "You rascal," said he, "don't you know that I can hang you if I please?" I, not adverting to the chieftain's veneration from his clan, was supposing that Sir Allan had known of some capital crime that the fellow had committed, which he could discover and so get him condemned; and I said, "How so?" "Why," said Sir Allan, "are they not all my people?" Sensible of my inadvertency, and most willing to contribute what I could towards the continuation of feudal authority, "Very true," said I. Sir Allan went on: "Refuse to send rum to me, you rascal! Don't you know that if I ordered you to go and cut a man's throat, you are to do it?" "Yes, an't please your honour," said MacGinnis; "and my own too, and hang myself too." The poor fellow denied that he had refused to send the rum. His making these professions was not merely a pretence in presence of Sir Allan. After he and I were out of Sir Allan's reach, he told me, "Had he sent his dog for the rum, I would have given it. I would cut my bones for him." It was something very remarkable to find such an attachment to a chief, though he had then no connexion with the island. I was highly pleased with it, and so was Mr. Johnson when I told him of it. Sir Allan, by way of upbraiding the fellow, said, "I believe you are a *Campbell*." MacGinnis is the name of a tribe of the Macleans.

I had a pleasant ride over some fertile land, while Mac-Ginnis run before me. I saw on the right three rocks on the shore, which looked like haystacks, as the mountain at Talisker does; till upon getting to the —— of them, they were seen not to be of a round form on all quarters. The shore is about

two miles from the village. They call it *Portawherry*,[10] from the
wherry in which Columbus came, as I suppose; though when
you are shown the length of a vessel as marked on the beach by
a heap of stones at each end of the space, they say, "Here is the
length of the *curach*,"—using the Erse word.

I had from my earliest years been shown by my father an
Icolmkill stone, and then been told of the venerable antiquities of that place. So I was curious to gather some of the stones
myself. I did so, and was in a fine placid humour. I knelt on
the beach and offered up a short prayer, supposing it to be
actually the place where the holy man landed. It was far in
the forenoon when I got back to the village. But Sir Allan and
Mr. Johnson did not scold much. I put up a stone of the wall
of the cathedral, to be preserved as a memento for devotion,
and a stone for the convent of monks, as a talisman for chastity. The former was red; the latter, black. It seems there is no
peculiar words in English to signify the distinction between a
sacred society of females and one of males. I thought a convent had been appropriated to monks, a monastery to nuns.
Mr. Johnson said no; for a monastery signified a segregation
from the world of a society of either sex.

We had a goodly number of the people to launch our boat;
and when we sailed, or rather rowed, off, they took off their
bonnets and huzza'd. I should have observed a striking circumstance: that in this island which once enlightened us all
there is not now one man that can read, and but two that can
speak English. There is not a school in it. There is, near the
village, a hill upon which St. Columbus took his seat and
meditated and surveyed the sea. Icolmkill struck me as not
so remote as I had imagined, there being so small a sound between it and the large island of Mull. But on the quarter
where Columbus landed, it seems far enough in the western
ocean; and besides, being near Mull in old times was being near

[10] Port na Curaich. Boswell mistook the pronunciation, and was thus led into unnecessary etymologizing.

a very rude country, and is so to a certain degree to this day.

We had a fine passage upon the sea today. We set Lauchlan Maclean ashore at Ardtun. It has its name from two holes, which are called tuns. They are from the top of a rock of moderate highth, down to the sea. If a stone is thrown into one of them, it makes its way downwards till it bursts or plunges out upon the sea with a great noise; or I should rather say a considerable noise, for the account of it appeared exaggerated, after Lauchlan made the experiment.

We wished to have called on Mr. Campbell, who was so polite to us yesterday, but found it would make us too late; so we pulled away along Loch Scridain till we landed near to Mr. Neil MacLeod's, to whose house we walked. He met us, having heard of our landing from Donald, whom we sent forward. He came to meet us. His first appearance was taking. He had a black wig and a smart air, like an English parson; and he had his hat covered with wax-cloth, which showed an attention to convenience. With him was a Lieutenant Hugh Maclean. His house was a good farm-house of one storey, dry and well furnished. His wife a very well-behaved woman. She was the daughter of the former minister; so, as Mr. Johnson said, she knew how to live in the minister's house. We had tea first, and then an excellent supper. Mr. MacLeod talked sensibly and distinctly. Mr. Johnson said he was the cleanest[11]-headed man he had met in the islands. He said to Mr. Johnson, "Sir, I have been often obliged to you, though I never had the pleasure of seeing you." Our evening went on well. Sir Allan, Mr. Johnson, and I had each a good clean bed in the room where we supped. There were some good books here, and good pens and ink, which was no small rarity.

Mr. MacLeod told us he had lived for some time in St.

---

[11] It has been suspected that *cleanest* in the published *Tour* should have been *clearest*. Since Boswell's "n's" and "r's" are generally identical, the MS is incapable of settling the question. We have preferred to read *cleanest*, because Boswell allowed that reading to pass through three editions. As Carruthers points out, one of Johnson's definitions of *clean* is "elegant, not unwieldy; not encumbered with anything useless, or disproportioned."

Kilda, under the tuition of the minister or catechist there, and had there first read Horace and Virgil. Their scenes would be strongly contrasted with what was around him.

THURSDAY 21 OCTOBER. Mr. Johnson said the saying *Nitimur in vetitum*[1] was not true; for that forbidding a thing did not make us have a greater liking for it. He said, "Pulteney was as paltry a fellow as could be. He was a Whig who pretended to be honest; and you know it is ridiculous for a Whig to pretend to be honest. He cannot hold it out." He called Pitt a meteor; Sir Robert Walpole, a fixed star. He said, "It required all the force of Government to prevent Wilkes from being chosen the Chief Magistrate of London, though the liverymen know he'd rob their shops, know he'd debauch their daughters."[2]

I said the history of England was so strange that if we had it not so well vouched as it is, it would hardly be credible. "Sir," said Mr. Johnson, "if it were told as shortly, and with as little preparation for introducing the different events, as the history of the Jewish kings, it would be equally liable to objections of improbability." Mr. MacLeod was pleased with the justice and novelty of the thought. Mr. Johnson illustrated what he had said by mentioning Charles the First's concessions to his Parliament, in proportion as they grew more insolent and less deserving of trust.

---

[1] Ovid, *Amores*, III.iv.17. "We strive for what is forbidden us."

[2] "I think it incumbent on me to make some observation on this strong satirical sally on my classical companion, Mr. Wilkes. Reporting it lately from memory in his presence, I expressed it thus:—'They knew he would rob their shops, *if he durst*; they knew he would debauch their daughters, *if he could*'; which, according to the French phrase, may be said *renchérir* on Dr. Johnson; but on looking into my Journal, I found it as above, and would by no means make any addition. Mr. Wilkes received both readings with a good humour that I cannot enough admire. Indeed both he and I (as, with respect to myself, the reader has more than once had occasion to observe in the course of this Journal) are too fond of a *bon mot* not to relish it, though we should be ourselves the object of it.

"Let me add, in justice to the gentleman here mentioned, that at a subsequent period, he *was* elected Chief Magistrate of London, and discharged the duties of that high office with great honour to himself, and advantage to the city.—Some years before Dr. Johnson died, I was fortunate enough to bring him and Mr. Wilkes together; the consequence of which was, that they were ever afterwards on easy and not unfriendly terms. The particulars I shall have great pleasure in relating at large in my LIFE OF DR. JOHNSON."—BOSWELL.

Sir Allan began to brag that Scotland had the advantage of England, by its having more water. "Sir," said Mr. Johnson, "we would not have your water, to take the vile bogs which produce it. You have too much. A man who is drowned has more water than either of us"—and then he laughed. (But this was surely robust sophistry; for the people of taste in England who have seen Scotland, own that its variety of rivers and brooks makes it naturally prettier than England in that respect.) "Sir," said Mr. Johnson, pursuing his victory over Sir Allan, "your country consists of two things: stone and water. There is indeed a little earth above the stone in some places, but a very little; and the stone is always appearing. It is like a man in rags; the naked skin is always peeping out."

He took leave of Mr. MacLeod, saying, "Sir, I thank you for your entertainment and your conversation."

Mr. Campbell, who had been so polite yesterday, came up this morning on purpose to breakfast with us. He was a civil, jolly-looking man. Mr. MacLeod thought as Mr. Johnson did of Icolmkill. Mr. Campbell had with him a manuscript account of it, by Mr. Campbell, the schoolmaster of the parish. Mr. MacLeod promised that a copy of it should be sent to me for Mr. Johnson. Mr. Johnson said, "If I shall find that I can make any use of it in case I publish anything about Icolmkill, may I do it? Or," said he, "I shall try to get Mr. Campbell something for it from a bookseller, and let it be published as it is; and then I may make what use I please of it in the way of extract, as all the world may do." This was approved of by Mr. MacLeod. Mr. Johnson said, "I dare say I may get him five guineas for it; perhaps ten."[3] This was the first indication that Mr. Johnson gave of a design to give the world an account of his tour with me. I rejoiced at the thought.

We were furnished with horses here by Mr. MacLeod and Mr. Campbell; and I had a very pretty bay galloway belong-

---

[3] The account seems never to have been published. Johnson does not refer to it in his *Journey*.

ing to Dr. Alexander Maclean, another physician in Mull. We advanced well, till we came to this other physician's. He was one of the stoutest and most hearty men that I have seen, more of the farmer than of the doctor. He had a dinner prepared for us, so we could not refuse to stay and eat it. His wife did very well. We had a very good dinner.

Mr. Johnson said of the *Turkish Spy*, which lay in the room, that it told nothing but what everybody might have known at the time; and that what was good in it did not pay you for the trouble of reading to find it. He said it was written in London by ——— and ———.[4] Dr. Maclean said, "This man is just a hogshead of sense." He and I took much to one another.

We had travelled on tolerably plain road in the forenoon, along the northern[5] shore, at least in view of it. After dinner, we struck away to the southeast, and ascended a high mountain, from whence, had the weather been clear, Sir Allan said I might have seen Islay and Jura, besides many more smaller islands. We proceeded till we descended a sloping pathless moor or marshy meadow, and then came to a glen wilder in my mind than either Glenmoriston or Glen Shiel. It must be an excellent place for deer. It is part of Lochbuie's territory. We had sent on Donald to Moy, his seat, which is in a good plain on a branch of the sea called Loch Buy. As *buy* signifies yellow, I conjectured ingeniously that "the Yellow Loch" might be said as well as "the Red Sea" for it seemed not easy to explain how a loch came to be called yellow. But Sir Allan told me that a hill above the plain in which the house stands is called Ben[6] Buy from its being of a yellowish hue, and from it the loch has been named.

We arrived between seven and eight. We had heard a great

---

[4] It is unfortunate that Boswell neglected to fill these blanks, for the authorship of the *Turkish Spy*, a collection of pseudo-foreign letters first published late in the Seventeenth Century, remains unknown. It has been attributed to William Bradshaw.

[5] i.e., of the Ross of Mull. This word, and "southeast" below, have been supplied by the editors to fill blanks in the MS.

[6] Boswell left a blank for this word. Ben Buy (2352 ft.) is more than a "hill," but must be the elevation to which Boswell refers.

deal of Lochbuie's being a great roaring braggadocio, a kind of Sir John Falstaff both in size and manners. But it appeared that they had swelled him up to a fictitious size and clothed him with imaginary qualities. Coll said he was quite a Don Quixote, and that he would give a great deal to see him and Mr. Johnson together. But the truth was that Lochbuie proved to be only a bluff, hearty, rosy old gentleman, of a strong voice and no great depth of understanding. He was not taller than the common size. He was a good deal like Craigengillan, but had a longer face. His wife, Sir Allan's sister but much older than him, was a strange being to be a lady at the head of a family which I was told has £1000 a year. She had on a mean bed-gown, and behaved like the landlady of an ale-house. Sir Allan said they were just antediluvians. Their daughter was as wild as any filly in Mull, at least had as little notion of good-breeding. Mr. Johnson tried to talk with her. But it would not do. The poor thing knew nothing. Though about seventeen, she had never read a play. Mr. Johnson said my comparing of her to a filly was not just, for she had not the friskiness of a wild animal. Lochbuie has spent a great deal of money in lawsuits. It was strange to see a man of his fortune, and one whose guineas have been liberally distributed to counsel, have a poor house, though of two storeys indeed. The dining-room, where we sat, had a bed in it; and neither the ceiling nor the walls were plastered, though they were prepared for it. We had tea, which was an immediate comfort. Lochbuie bawled out to Mr. Johnson, "Are you of the Johnstons of Glen Croe, or of Ardnamurchan?" Mr. Johnson gave a curious look. Sir Allan and I told Lochbuie that Mr. Johnson was not Johns*ton*, but John*son*, and that he was an Englishman.

Lochbuie tried not long ago to prove himself a fool, or what we call a facile man, in order to set aside a lease which he had granted to Gillean Maclean, his natural son; but it did not do, though I suppose there were foolish things enough proved. Mr. Johnson told me that in England they will not allow a man to stultify himself,[7] as they term it. Lochbuie some years ago was fined in 500[8] merks, or paid that sum by way of damages to some gentlemen whom he imprisoned in the dungeon of his old castle. Sir Allan said he still imagines that he has an heritable jurisdiction. I must do Lochbuie the justice to mention that he was very hospitable. Our supper was indeed but a poor one. I think a sort of stewed mutton was the principal dish. I was afterwards told that he has no spit, and but one pot, in which everything is stewed. It is probable enough.

He had admirable port. Sir Allan and he and I drank each a bottle of it. Then we drank a bowl of punch. I was seized with an avidity for drinking, and Lochbuie and I became mighty social. Another bowl was made. Mr. Johnson had gone to bed as the first was finished, and had admonished me, "Don't drink any more *poonch*."[9] I must own that I was resolved to drink more, for I was by this time a good deal intoxicated; and I gave no answer, but slunk away from him, with a consciousness of my being brutish and yet a determination to go somewhat deeper. What I might have done I know not. But luckily before I had tasted the second bowl, I grew very sick, and was forced to perform the operation that Antony did in the Senate house, if Cicero is to be credited; so that Mr. Johnson's admonition to drink no more punch had its effect, though not from any merit of mine. I went to bed in the dining-room, which was my chamber; and my stomach being clear, I fell asleep immediately, while Sir Allan and Lochbuie finished the bowl beside me.[10]

FRIDAY 22 OCTOBER. It humbled me to find that my

---

[7] "This maxim, however, has been controverted. See Blackstone's *Commentaries*, Vol. II, p. 292; and the authorities there quoted."—BOSWELL.

[8] Boswell neglected to fill in this figure. Besides the fine of 500 marks Scots, equivalent to less than thirty pounds sterling, Lochbuie had to pay £180 of damages and expenses. The gentlemen whom he imprisoned were Hector Maclean of Killean and Allan Maclean of Kilmory (J. P. MacLean, *Hist. of the Clan MacLean*, pp. 244–5).

[9] Boswell always delighted in pointing out this relic of Staffordshire pronunciation in Johnson's speech.

[10] Lochbuie's one pot and Boswell's bout of drinking were denied admittance to the published *Tour*.

holy resolutions at Icolmkill had been so ineffectual that the very day after having been there I had drank too much. I went to Mr. Johnson before he was up. He first said none of our Club would get drunk, but then, taking himself, he said Burke would get drunk and be ashamed of it; Goldsmith would get drunk and boast of it, if it had been with a little whore or so, who had allowed him to go in a coach with her.[1]

Before Mr. Johnson came to breakfast, Lady Lochbuie said he was a "dungeon of wit," a very common phrase in Scotland, though Mr. Johnson told me he had never heard it. She proposed that he should have some cold sheep-head for breakfast. Sir Allan was very angry at her vulgarity. "I think," said I, "it is but fair to give him an offer of it. If he does not choose it, he may let it alone." "I think so," said the lady. When Mr. Johnson came in, she called to him, "Do you choose any cold sheep-head, sir?" "No, madam," said he, with a tone of surprise and anger. "It's here, sir," said she, as if he had refused it to save the trouble of bringing it. He confirmed his refusal sufficiently; and I was entertained to see the ludicrous crosspurposes.

We walked in the garden after breakfast. Sir Allan anxiously called the attention of Mr. Johnson to some trees growing in it. Ashes, I think. We walked down to the old castle, which is very near the present house, and surveyed it attentively. Lochbuie roared out, what excellent cellars he had in the vaults! Mr. Johnson was offended at being disturbed in his antiquarian researches, or rather meditations, and said, "I don't care about cellars." We viewed the *pit* for which Lochbuie had been fined by the Court of Justiciary. He said to me, "Your father has heard of this" (or "knows this").

We then set out for the ferry, by which we were to cross to the mainland of Argyllshire. Lochbuie and Sir Allan accom-

---

[1] The references to Burke and Goldsmith were deleted. At this point Boswell interrupted the writing of the Journal, and did not resume it until 1779, as a note in the MS shows. He wrote less than a page at that time, however, for at the top of the next page (642) he noted that he was writing on 23 August 1780.

panied us. We were told much of a war-saddle on which Lochbuie used to be mounted. But we did not see it, for the young
laird had it at one of the fairs for black cattle, Falkirk, I think.
(I am glad to find that I remember so many particulars after
the lapse of almost seven years. My Journal cannot have the
same freshness and fullness when written now as when written
recently after the scenes recorded. But I hope I shall preserve
some valuable remains or fragments.)

We bid adieu to Lochbuie and to our kind conductor Sir Allan
Maclean on the shore of Mull, and then got into the ferry-
boat, the bottom of which was strewed with branches of trees
or bushes, upon which we sat. We saw the old Castle of Duart
at a distance, while we sailed. I do not recollect distinctly any
other objects. We landed at Oban, having had a good day
and a fine passage. Sir Allan had given us a card to introduce
us to the Laird of MacDougall. But as we understood from
his way of speaking, whether rightly or not, that the Laird
would not be very willing to entertain us, we did not go to
his castle, though very near. Sir Allan had recommended us
to an inn at Oban, where we would get the best entertainment. But I think it was full, for we could not be accommodated. It was a thatched house of one storey. We went to
another inn in this small village, if a very few houses should
be so called. It was a slated house of two storeys, and we were
well enough entertained; at least we were satisfied, though we
had nothing like what is to be found in good inns upon a frequented road.

Here we found a newspaper, in which I read an account of
the death of Alexander, Earl of Galloway, which affected me in
a pretty sensible manner, as I had from my early years viewed
him as a Great Man who had seen much of the world; and
when I came to be well acquainted with him, had found him
to be remarkably knowing in the affairs of life, lively, and like a
man of fashion. There is a pleasure in being to a certain degree
agitated by events. This I experienced on the present occasion.

discovered

‡ [Here we found that from the conjectures which were formed they the people on the main land were entirely ignorant of our motions; ~~premise believe~~ for in a Glascow newspaper we found ~~the following~~ a paragraph, which as it contains as just and well-turned compliment to my illustrious friend, I shall transcribe

[Here take in the par. marked A.]

Saturday 23 October

After a good night's
we

SUBSTITUTE PARAGRAPH IN MALONE'S HAND

had from my early ye—
him as a great Man who had
seen much of the World, and
when I came to be better acquainted with him had found him
to be remarkably knowing in
the Affairs of Life lively, and
likely Man of _____ him. There
is a pleasure in _____ to a
certain degree _____ by
_____. This I experienced
on the present occasion.
It was comfortable to _____
_____ time after so
many States of uncertain
confinement _____
to be now on the Main land
and sure, if in health to
get to any place in Scot-
land or England in so many
days. I remember _____
the conversation this night.
Saturday 23 October
_____ on 20 August
After a good night to rest we

It was comfortable to Mr. Johnson and me, after so many states of uncertain confinement in islands, to be now on the mainland, and *sure*, if in health, to get to any place in Scotland or England in so many days. I remember none of the conversation this night.

SATURDAY 23 OCTOBER. (Writing on 23 August 1782.) After a good night's rest, we breakfasted at our leisure. We talked of Goldsmith's *Traveller*, of which Mr. Johnson said, I think, he had not written more than twenty lines.[1] He spoke highly in praise of it; and while I was helping him on with his greatcoat, he began to repeat from it the character of the English,[2] which he did with great energy.

We could get but one bridle here, which, according to the maxim *detur digniori*, was, to be sure, appropriated to Mr. Johnson's sheltie. My servant and I rode with halters. I ought to have put myself before my servant in this narrative. But I am not sure but he rode before me in the march. We had a fourth sheltie for the baggage. There came on a heavy rain. I recollect nothing of the country through which we passed. We crossed, I think, Loch Awe, a pretty wide lake, in a ferry-boat; and on this side of it, just on the shore, found a hut for our inn. We were much wet. I changed my clothes in part, and was at pains to get myself well dried. Mr. Johnson resolutely kept on all his clothes, wet as they were, letting them steam before the smoky turf fire. I thought him in the wrong. But his firmness was a species of heroism.

I remember but little of our conversation. I mentioned Shenstone's saying of Pope that he had the art of condensing sense more than anybody. Mr. Johnson said, "It is not true,

---

[1] Johnson gave various estimates of the number of lines of *The Traveller* which he had written. He told Reynolds that he had contributed not more than eighteen lines. In 1783 he marked as his own, at Boswell's request, only nine lines of which he said he could be sure. Hawkins remarks that he had been heard to say that he had written only three or four lines.

[2] Boswell quotes the lines in the published *Tour*. One couplet will suffice:

"Pride in their port, defiance in their eye,
I see the lords of human kind pass by."

sir. There is more sense in a line of Cowley, than in a page"
(or a sentence, or ten lines—I cannot be quite certain of the
very phrase) "of Pope." He maintained that Archibald, Duke
of Argyll, was a narrow man. I wondered at this; and observed
that his building so great a house at Inveraray was not like a
narrow man. "Sir," said he, "when a narrow man has resolved
to build a house, he builds it like another man. But Archibald,
Duke of Argyll, was narrow in his ordinary expenses, in his
quotidian expenses."

The distinction is very just. It is in the ordinary expenses of
life that a man's liberality or narrowness is to be discovered. I
never before had heard the word "quotidian" for "daily," and I
imagined it to be a word of Mr. Johnson's own fabrication. But
I have since found it in Dr. Young's *Night Thoughts*, Night Fifth:

Death's a destroyer of quotidian prey.

It rained very hard as we journeyed on after dinner.[3] I recollect the wind and rain and roar of brooks, which have since
been so nobly described in the *Journey to the Western Islands*.[4]

We got at night to Inveraray, to a most excellent inn. Even
here Mr. Johnson would not change his clothes. I put on a suit
of our landlord's.

The sight of good accommodation cheered us much. We
supped well; and after supper, Mr. Johnson, whom I had not
seen taste any fermented liquor during all our expedition, had
a gill of whisky brought to him. "Come," said he, "let me know
what it is that makes a Scotsman happy." He drank it all but
a drop, which I begged leave to pour into my glass, that I
might say we had drank whisky together.[5] I proposed Mrs.

---

[3] On October 28 Johnson wrote to Mrs. Thrale: "In all September we had, according
to Boswell's register, only one day and a half of fair weather; and October perhaps not
more."

[4] "The night came on while we had yet a great part of the way to go, though not so
dark but that we could discern the cataracts which poured down the hills on one side,
and fell into one general channel that ran with great violence on the other. The wind
was loud, the rain was heavy, and the whistling of the blast, the fall of the shower, the
rush of the cataracts, and the roar of the torrent, made a nobler chorus of the rough
music of nature than it had ever been my chance to hear before" (Johnson's *Journey*).

[5] "I never tasted whisky, except once for experiment at the inn in Inveraray, when I

Thrale should be our toast. He would not have *her* drank in whisky, but rather some insular lady; so we drank, I think, Miss Macpherson. He owned tonight that he got as good a room and bed as at an English inn.

I had here the comfort of a letter from my dear wife, of whom I had not heard for many weeks; and I had the regale of a letter from Mr. Garrick, in answer to mine to him from Inverness.[6] My feelings this night were as agreeable as can be imagined.

SUNDAY 24 OCTOBER. (Writing on 24 August 1782.) We passed the forenoon calmly and placidly. I prevailed on Mr. Johnson to read aloud Ogden's Sixth Sermon on Prayer, which he did with a distinct and agreeable solemnity. He praised my favourite preacher: his language, his acuteness, and said he fought infidels with their own weapons.

He wished to have more books; and upon inquiring if there were any in the house, he was told the waiter had some. They were brought to him. But I recollect none of them but Hervey's *Meditations*. Mr. Johnson thought slightingly of this admired book. He treated it with ridicule, and would not even allow the scene of the dying husband and father to be pathetic. I am not an impartial judge. For Hervey's *Meditations* were the delight of my dear, pious mother, and engaged my affections in my early years.[1] He read a passage concerning the moon ludicrously, and showed how easily he could, in the same style, make reflections on that planet, the very reverse of Hervey's, representing her as treacherous to mankind. He did this very well. But I have forgotten the particulars. He then played himself in making a Meditation on a Pudding, of which

---

thought it preferable to any English malt brandy" (Johnson's *Journey*). Boswell had forgotten that Johnson drank some brandy at Dunvegan (*ante*, p. 173).
[6] The two letters were printed at this point in the published *Tour*.
[1] James Hervey's *Meditations and Contemplations* composed one of the most popular religious books of the Eighteenth Century. Their character is indicated by some of the separate titles: "Meditations among the Tombs," "A Descant upon Creation," "Contemplations on the Starry Heavens." In the *Scots Magazine* for December 1758 appears "A Contemplative Walk at Moffat, on a Summer Night. A Sketch in Imitation of Hervey's Style," which appears to have been from Boswell's pen. He was then eighteen years old.

I, a little after he had ended, wrote down an imperfect note, the original of which I have preserved, and place as a loose leaf between this page and the opposite one.

A PUDDING

Flour that once waved in the golden grain and drank the dews of the morning. Milk pressed from the swelling udder by the gentle hand of the beauteous milkmaid, whose beauty and innocence might have recommended a worse draught; who, while she stroked the udder, indulged no ambitious thoughts of wandering in palaces, formed no plans for the destruction of her fellow-creatures. Let us consider: can there be more wanting to complete the Meditation on a Pudding? If more is wanting, more may be found. Salt which keeps the sea from putrefaction, that salt which is made the image of intellectual excellence, contributes to a pudding; and milk is drawn from the cow, that useful animal which eats the grass of the field, and supplies us with that which made the greatest part of the food of mankind in that age which the poets have agreed to call golden. It is made with an egg, that miracle of nature which the theoretical Burnet has compared to creation. An egg contains water within its beautiful smooth surface. An unformed mass, by the incubation of the parent, becomes a regular animal with bones and sinews and covered with feathers.

In a magazine, I think the Edinburgh weekly one, I found a saying of Mr. Johnson's, something to this purpose: that the happiest part of a man's life is what he passes lying in bed in the morning. I read it out to him. He said, "I may perhaps have said this, for nobody talks more laxly than I do." I think I ventured to suggest to him that this was dangerous from one of his authority.

I spoke of living in the country, and upon what footing one should be with neighbours. For my own part, I said I would not wish to be too easy, for then a man's time is never his own. He said it depended much on what kind of neighbours a country gentleman has, whether he should be on an easy footing or not; and to be sure it is plain there can be no general rule as to this. I told him a strange characteristic sally of Sir John Dalrymple upon this subject. He said to me, he never was happy in the country till he was not on speaking terms with any of his neighbours, which he contrived in different ways to bring about. "Lord Adam Gordon stuck long," said he. "At last the fellow poinded[2] my pigs, and then I got rid of him." "Nay, sir," said Mr. Johnson, "Lord Adam got rid of Sir John, and showed how little he valued him, by putting his pigs in the pound."

I told Mr. Johnson I was in some difficulty how to act at Inveraray. The Duchess of Argyll, I knew, hated me, on account of my zeal in the Douglas Cause.[3] But the Duke of Argyll had always been very civil to me, and had paid me a visit in London. They were now at the castle. Should I go and pay my respects there? Mr. Johnson was clear that I ought. But in his usual way, he was very shy of desiring to be there himself. His pride of character has ever made him keep aloof from any appearance of courting the great. Besides, he was impatient to get to Glasgow, where he expected letters. At the same time, he was secretly not unwilling to have attention paid him by so great a chieftain and so exalted a nobleman. He insisted I should not go to the castle this day before dinner, as it would look like asking an invitation. "But," said I, "if the Duke asks

---

[2] A Scots legal term; the published *Tour* has the English equivalent *pounded*.

[3] The complications of the Douglas Cause can hardly be unravelled in a footnote, but the text requires some elucidation. Lady Jane Douglas, sister of the Duke of Douglas, after remaining single until she was forty-eight, secretly married in 1746 Col. John Stewart, later baronet of Grandtully, but at that time a penniless Jacobite adventurer. It was maintained that on 10 July 1748, at Paris, Lady Jane had given birth to twin sons, Archibald and Sholto. Sholto died in his fifth year, but on the death of the Duke of Douglas, Archibald was declared heir to the estates and assumed the name of Douglas. An action was brought by the Duke of Hamilton, the heir-male, contending that Archibald Stewart Douglas was not the son of Lady Jane, but was a French child named Mignon, abducted by Col. Stewart from his parents in Paris. Both parties to the suit were minors, the true moving spirits being the dowager duchesses of Douglas and Hamilton. The Duchess of Douglas, Archibald Douglas's protector, was an old, shrewd, eccentric Scotswoman; the Duchess of Hamilton, a young and impulsive Irish girl, whose fabulous beauty, in the days when she was Elizabeth Gunning, had caused mobs to follow her in London. In July 1767 the Court of Session, by the casting vote of the Lord President, found Archibald Douglas to be *not* the child of Lady Jane Douglas. An appeal was made to the House of Lords, which on 27 February 1769 reversed the decision after strong speeches for Douglas by Lord Chancellor Camden and Lord Chief Justice Mansfield. Douglas was later raised to the peerage. Boswell, from the moment of his admission to the bar in 1766, had been a convinced and intemperate advocate of Douglas. He filled the newspapers with inflammatory paragraphs and published a short "novel," *Dorando*, a thinly veiled allegory of the Douglas Cause, in which uncomplimentary remarks were made concerning the Duchess of Hamilton. It remains only to add that the Duchess of Argyll of our text is the Duchess of Hamilton. Widowed in 1758, she had married in 1759 Col. John Campbell, who in 1770 succeeded to the Dukedom of Argyll.

us to dine with him tomorrow, shall we accept?" "Yes, sir,"
said he. I think he added, "to be sure." But he said, "He won't
ask us." I mentioned how disagreeable my company would be
to the Duchess. Mr. Johnson treated this objection with a
manly disdain. "That, sir," said he, "he must settle with his
wife." We dined well. I went to the castle just about the time
when I supposed the ladies would be gone from dinner. I sent
in my name, and was introduced. Found the amiable Duke
sitting at the head of his table, with Campbell of Airds and
several more gentlemen. I was very graciously received, drank
some claret, and gave some particulars of the curious journey
which I had been making with Dr. Johnson. When we rose
from table, the Duke came close to me, and said, "I hope you
and Dr. Johnson will dine with us tomorrow." I thanked his
grace, but told him Mr. Johnson was in a great hurry to get
back to London. The Duke, with an obliging complacency,
said, "He will stay one day; and I will take care he shall see
this place to advantage." I said I should be sure to let him
know his grace's invitation. This was as well as could be wished.
As I was going away, the Duke said, "Mr. Boswell, won't you
have some tea?" I thought it as well to put over the meeting
with the Duchess this night; so respectfully agreed. I was conducted to the drawing-room by the Duke, who announced my
name. But the Duchess took not the least notice of me. I did
not mind this, as the Duke was exceedingly civil. Lady Betty
Hamilton[4] made tea, and I had some. Miss Sempill, with whom
I was pretty well acquainted, hardly acknowledged me, I suppose for fear of offending the Duchess. Miss Campbell of Car-
rick talked a little with me.

I was accompanied to the inn by Mr. David Campbell,
Writer to the Signet, one of the clan, whom I found at his
chief's board. He sat a good while with Mr. Johnson and me,
and seemed to relish much Mr. Johnson's forcible conversa-

---

[4] The Duchess's only daughter by her first husband. She later made an unhappy marriage with the Earl of Derby.

tion. The Ayrshire election was mentioned. I told Mr. Johnson there were some gentlemen in the county who, from a notion of independency, resolved to oppose every candidate who was supported by the peers. "Foolish fellows," said he. "Don't they see that they are as much dependent upon the peers one way as t'other? The peers have only to *oppose* a candidate to get him success. It is said the only way to make a pig go forward is to pull him back by the tail. These people must be treated like pigs." He was much pleased with the Duke's invitation, and most readily accepted it.

MONDAY 25 OCTOBER. My acquaintance, the Rev. Mr. John Macaulay,[1] one of the ministers of Inveraray and brother to Mr. Kenneth at Cawdor, came to us this morning, and I think breakfasted with us. We then, accompanied by him, walked to the castle, where I presented Mr. Johnson to the Duke. We were shown through the house; and I never shall forget the enchanting impression made upon my fancy by some of the ladies' maids tripping about in neat morning dresses. After seeing nothing for a long time but rusticity, their elegance delighted me; and I could have been a knight-errant for them.[2] Such is my amorous constitution.

We then had a little low one-horse chair, in which I drove us about the place, Mr. Macaulay riding before us on a good large horse. Mr. Johnson was much pleased with the remarkable grandeur and improvements about Inveraray. He said, "What I admire here is the total defiance of expense." He thought the castle too low, and wished it had been a storey higher. I need not have said "he wished." It was only his opinion. We did not ascend Duniquoich.

When we came in before dinner, we found the Duke and some gentlemen in the hall. Mr. Johnson was much pleased with the large collection of arms, which are excellently dis-

---

[1] Lord Macaulay's grandfather.
[2] "On reflection, at the distance of several years, I wonder that my venerable fellow-traveller should have read this passage without censuring my levity."—BOSWELL.

posed there. I told what he had said to Sir Alexander Macdonald of his ancestors' not suffering their arms to rust. "Well,"
said the Doctor, "but let us be glad we live in times when arms
may rust. We can sit today at his grace's table without any risk
of being attacked, and perhaps sitting down again wounded."
(He expressed being wounded or maimed, by words which I
do not precisely remember.) The Duke placed him by himself
at table. I happened to sit in the middle, so that it was my duty
to give about the soup, which I did with all imaginable ease,
though conscious of the Duchess's peevish resentment. I was
in fine spirits, and offered her grace some. I was in the right
to be quite unconcerned, if I could. I was the Duke of Argyll's
guest, and he had nothing to do with the Duchess of Hamilton's foolish anger.

I knew it was not the rule here to drink to anybody. But
that I might have the satisfaction for once to look the Duchess
in the face, with a glass in my hand, I rose a little and with a
respectful air addressed her: "My lady Duchess, I have the
honour to drink your grace's good health." I think I repeated
all these words audibly and with a steady countenance. This
was rather too much. But she had set me at defiance.

She was very attentive to Mr. Johnson. I know not how a
middle state came to be mentioned. She asked Mr. Johnson
something about it. "Madam," said he, "your own relation Mr.
Archibald Campbell can tell you better about it. He was a
bishop of the Nonjurant Communion, and wrote a book upon
that subject." He engaged to get it for her grace. He gave a
full history of Mr. Archibald Campbell, which I am sorry I do
not recollect particularly.[3] He mentioned his saying of Lord
Townshend, "For though a Whig, he had humanity." He said
he had been bred a violent Whig, but afterwards kept better

---

[3] When Boswell was with Johnson at Oxford in the summer of 1784, Johnson wrote a
note on Campbell in a blank page of Boswell's Journal. This note, which Boswell dated
15 June 1784 (though under 9 June in *Life*, IV. 286), is preserved with the MS, page
667 verso. See the facsimile. There are no verbal differences between the MS and the
text as Boswell printed it, except that the nonsensical "He lived in 1743 or —44" of
the published text reads correctly in the MS, "died."

The Honourable Archibald Campbell, was
I believe the Nephew of the Marquis of Argyle.
He began life by engaging in Monmouth's rebellion,
and to escape the Law, lived sometime in Surinam.
When he returned, he became zealous for Episcopacy
and monarchy, and at the revolution adhered
not only to the Nonjurors, but to those who refused
to communicate with the Church of England
or to be present at any worship, where the [...]
for [...] mentioned as King. He was, I believe [...]
[...] once, apprehended in the reign of K. William, [...] once at the accession of George. He was
the familiar friend of Hickes and Nelson,
a man of letters, but injudicious, and very curious and inquisitive but credulous. He died
1743 at Æ. about 75 years old.

The above was supplied by
Dr Johnson at Oxford 15 June 178[...]
is not quite so full as the narrative [...]
[...]

NOTE ON THE HONOURABLE ARCHIBALD CAMPBELL,
WRITTEN AT OXFORD BY JOHNSON

367 in my hand, I rose ~~a little~~ and with a respectful air addressed her—My Lady Duchess, I have the honour to drink your Graces good health, ~~and~~ I repeated ~~all these~~ the words audibly & with a steady countenance. This was rather too much.

~~But she~~ let me ~~at~~ ~~silence~~ ~~Anyway~~ attentive to Dr Johnson. I know not now a Middle State came to be mentioned. ~~Her Grace~~ asked ~~Mr~~ him something about it. Madam (said he) your own relation Mr Archibald Campbell can tell you better about it. He was a bishop of the Nonjurant communion & wrote a book upon that subject & he engaged to get it for her Grace. ~~I have~~ a ~~first History~~ ~~bold Campbell~~ who company, and became a Tory. He said this with a fine smile, in pleasant allusion, as I thought, to the opposition between the political principles of the Duke's clan and his own.

Luxury was introduced. He defended it. "We have now," said he, "a splendid dinner before us" (or words to that effect). "Which of all these dishes is unwholesome?" The Duke asserted that he had observed the grandees of Spain diminished in their size by luxury. Mr. Johnson politely acquiesced in any observation which the Duke himself had made, but said that man must be very different from all other animals if he is diminished by good living, for the size of all other animals is increased by it. I said something of my belief in the second sight. The Duchess said, "I fancy (or "I suppose") you will be a Methodist." This was the only sentence she ever deigned to utter to me; and I take it for granted she thought it a good hit on my credulity in the Douglas Cause.

A Colonel Livingstone was there, the Member for the County of Argyll. He talked a bit vaguely; and the result was that Mr. Johnson afterwards remarked of him, "A mighty misty man, the Colonel."[4] I told Mr. Johnson a remark which I made. The Duke wanted to show a specimen of marble. He sent the Colonel for it, who brought a wrong piece; upon which he had to go back again to the other room, where it lay. He was conscious of an appearance of servility, but could not rebel. As he walked away, he whistled, to show his independency. Mr. Johnson thought this a nice trait of character.

He talked a great deal, and was so entertaining that Lady Betty Hamilton went and placed her chair next his, leaned upon it, and listened eagerly. It would have made a fine picture to have drawn the sage and her at this time in their several attitudes. He did not know all the while that it was a princess of the blood who thus listened to him. I told him afterwards. I never saw him so gentle and complaisant as this day.

---

[4] There is a large defect at the bottom of this page (669), involving this sentence and the preceding. There is no doubt as to Boswell's meaning or as to the identity of the person mentioned, but some of the words here printed may not be his own.

We went to tea. The Duke and I walked up and down the drawing-room, conversing. The Duchess persevered in her aversion to me, for which I really made allowance, considering how deeply she was interested for her son's cause, which I had opposed most heartily in every respect.

She made Mr. Johnson come and sit by her, while[5] she served him with tea. I heard her say something[6] of people being bad, and not what he thought them. He did not understand her, but I well knew it referred to me. I told him afterwards, and he thought it poor. She asked him why he made his journey so late in the year. "Why, madam," said he, "you know Mr. Boswell must attend the Court of Session, and it does not rise till the twelfth of August." She said, with spite, "I know *nothing* of Mr. Boswell." I heard this, and despised it. It was weak as well as impertinent. Poor Lady Lucy Douglas, to whom I mentioned it, observed, "She knew *too much* of Mr. Boswell."[7] I shall make no remark on her grace's speech. I indeed felt it as rather too severe; but when I recollected that my punishment was inflicted by so dignified a beauty, I had that kind of consolation which a man would feel who is strangled by a silken cord. Dr. Johnson was all attention to her grace. I never saw him so courtly. He had afterwards a droll expression upon her dignity of three titles: Hamilton, Brandon, Argyll. He called her a Duchess with three tails.[8]

He was well pleased with our visit to the Duke, who was exceedingly polite to him; and upon his complaining of the shelties, which he had hitherto rode, being too small for him, his grace told him he should have a good horse to carry him next day.

---

[5] The bottom of this page is missing, and cannot be supplied from the printed *Tour*. The words between "while" and "something" are an editorial guess.

[6] At the top of this page (672) appears a note indicating that Boswell was writing on 27 August 1782.

[7] MS defective. The next two sentences are supplied from the printed *Tour*; but the missing passage in the MS was probably only about half as long as this.

[8] The Duchess's first husband was Duke of Hamilton in the peerage of Scotland and Duke of Brandon in the peerage of Great Britain. Besides being a baroness in her own right, she was successively the wife of two dukes and the mother of four—probably a record.

Mr. John Macaulay passed the evening with us at our inn. . . . [9] at this, and challenged him hotly—"Mr. Macaulay, Mr. Macaulay! Don't you know it is very rude to cry eh!eh! when one is talking?" Poor Macaulay had nothing to say for himself. But the truth is, it was a sin of ignorance, or mere rusticity. Afterwards, when Mr. Johnson spoke of people whose principles were good but whose practice was faulty, Mr. Macaulay said he had no notion of people being in earnest in their good professions, whose practice was not suitable. The Doctor grew angry, and said, "Are you so ignorant of human nature, sir, as not to know that a man may[10] be very sincere in good principles, without having good practice?"

Dr. Johnson was unquestionably in the right; and whoever examines himself candidly will be satisfied of it, though the inconsistency between principles and practice is greater in some men than in others.

I recollect very little of this night's conversation. I am sorry that indolence came upon me towards the conclusion of our journey, so that I did not write down what passed with the same assiduity as during the greatest part of it.[11]

TUESDAY 26 OCTOBER. Mr. Macaulay breakfasted with us, nothing hurt or dismayed by his last night's correction. Being a man of good sense, he had a just admiration of Dr. Johnson.

Either yesterday morning or this, I communicated to Dr. Johnson, from Mr. Macaulay's information, the news that Dr. Beattie had got a pension of two hundred pounds a year. He sat up in his bed, clapped his hands, and cried, "O brave we!" —a peculiar exclamation of his when he rejoices.[1]

---

[9] Defect in the MS. "At our inn" is supplied from the printed text; but there are thirty or forty more words missing, to which there is nothing corresponding in the published *Tour*.

[10] Here the MS ends, and the remainder of the text is that of the third edition of the *Tour*.

[11] It should be noted that Boswell in the printed *Tour* makes no reference to the fact that he was writing this portion years after the events. Apparently he had kept some kind of memoranda, but his observation in the entry for 22 October (*ante*, p. 346) shows that they must have been very imperfect. He had, however, the benefit of Johnson's perusal through this portion.

[1] "Having mentioned, more than once, that my Journal was perused by Dr. Johnson,

As we sat over our tea, Mr. Home's tragedy of *Douglas* was mentioned. I put Dr. Johnson in mind that once, in a coffee-house at Oxford, he called to old Mr. Sheridan, "How came you, sir, to give Home a gold medal for writing that foolish play?" and defied Mr. Sheridan to show ten good lines in it. He did not insist they should be together, but that there were not ten good lines in the whole play. He now persisted in this. I endeavoured to defend that pathetic and beautiful tragedy, and repeated the following passage:

> ——————————————————Sincerity,
> Thou first of virtues! let no mortal leave
> Thy onward path, although the earth should gape,
> And from the gulf of hell destruction cry,
> To take dissimulation's winding way.

JOHNSON. "That will not do, sir. Nothing is good but what is consistent with truth or probability, which this is not. Juvenal, indeed, gives us a noble picture of inflexible virtue:

> Esto bonus miles, tutor bonus, arbiter idem
> Integer: ambiguae si quando citabere testis,
> Incertaeque rei, Phalaris licet imperet, ut sis
> Falsus, et admoto dictet perjuria tauro,
> Summum crede nefas animam praeferre pudori,
> Et propter vitam vivendi perdere causas."[2]

He repeated the lines with great force and dignity; then added, "And after this, comes Johnny Home with his *earth gaping*, and his *destruction crying*—pooh!"[3]

I think it proper to inform my readers that this is the last paragraph which he read."—BOSWELL. It is the editors' impression that the remainder of the Journal was not written out until the summer of 1785, when Boswell was revising his MS for the printer.

[2] "An honest guardian, arbitrator just,
Be thou; thy station deem a sacred trust.
With thy good sword maintain thy country's cause;
In every action venerate its laws:
The lie suborn'd if falsely urg'd to swear,
Though torture wait thee, torture firmly bear;
To forfeit honour, think the highest shame,
And life too dearly bought by loss of fame;
Nor, to preserve it, with thy virtue give
That for which only man should wish to live."
—BOSWELL. He attributes the translation to a "friend," i.e., Malone.

[3] "I am sorry that I was unlucky in my quotation. But notwithstanding the acuteness of Dr. Johnson's criticism, and the power of his ridicule, the tragedy of *Douglas* still continues to be generally and deservedly admired."—BOSWELL.

While we were lamenting the number of ruined religious buildings which we had lately seen, I spoke with peculiar feeling of the miserable neglect of the chapel belonging to the Palace of Holyrood House, in which are deposited the remains of many of the kings of Scotland, and of many of our nobility. I said it was a disgrace to the country that it was not repaired, and particularly complained that my friend Douglas, the representative of a great house and proprietor of a vast estate, should suffer the sacred spot where his mother lies interred to be unroofed, and exposed to all the inclemencies of the weather.[4] Dr. Johnson, who, I know not how, had formed an opinion on the Hamilton side in the Douglas Cause, slyly answered, "Sir, sir, don't be too severe upon the gentleman; don't accuse him of want of filial piety! Lady Jane Douglas was not *his* mother." He roused my zeal so much that I took the liberty to tell him he knew nothing of the cause, which I do most seriously believe was the case.

We were now "in a country of bridles and saddles," and set out fully equipped. The Duke of Argyll was obliging enough to mount Dr. Johnson on a stately steed from his grace's stable. My friend was highly pleased, and Joseph said, "He now looks like a bishop."

We dined at the inn at Tarbet, and at night came to Rossdhu, the beautiful seat of Sir James Colquhoun,[5] on the banks of Loch Lomond, where I, and any friends whom I have introduced, have ever been received with kind and elegant hospitality.

WEDNESDAY 27 OCTOBER. When I went into Dr. Johnson's room this morning, I observed to him how wonderfully courteous he had been at Inveraray, and said, "You were quite a fine gentleman, when with the Duchess." He answered,

[4] The earliest of Boswell's publications to be traced is a blank-verse poem, "An Evening Walk in the Abbey Church of Holyrood-house," which appeared in the *Scots Magazine* shortly before his eighteenth birthday. It expresses exactly the same sentiments as the present passage. Douglas resented the publication of these remarks in the *Tour*, and thereafter treated Boswell with great coldness.
[5] The father of Boswell's Kitty Colquhoun, to whom he had written verses and with whom he was at one time seriously in love.

in good humour, "Sir, I look upon myself as a very polite man"; and he was right, in a proper manly sense of the word. As an immediate proof of it, let me observe, that he would not send back the Duke of Argyll's horse without a letter of thanks, which I copied.

To his Grace the Duke of Argyll

Rossdhu, Oct. 27,[1] 1773.

MY LORD,—That kindness which disposed your grace to supply me with the horse, which I have now returned, will make you pleased to hear that he has carried me well.

By my diligence in the little commission with which I was honoured by the Duchess, I will endeavour to show how highly I value the favours which I have received, and how much I desire to be thought, my lord, your grace's most obedient, and most humble servant,

SAM. JOHNSON.

The Duke was so attentive to his respectable guest that on the same day he wrote him an answer, which was received at Auchinleck:

To Dr. Johnson, Auchinleck, Ayrshire

Inveraray, Oct. 27, 1773.

SIR,—I am glad to hear your journey from this place was not unpleasant, in regard to your horse. I wish I could have supplied you with good weather, which I am afraid you felt the want of.

The Duchess of Argyll desires her compliments to you, and is much obliged to you for remembering her commission. I am, sir, your most obedient humble servant,

ARGYLL.

I am happy to insert every memorial of the honour done to my great friend. Indeed, I was at all times desirous to preserve the letters which he received from eminent persons, of which, as of all other papers, he was very negligent; and I once proposed to him that they should be committed to my care, as his *custos rotulorum*. I wish he had complied with my request, as by that means many valuable writings might have been preserved that are now lost.[2]

---

[1] This letter and the next are erroneously dated "Oct. 29" in the text.
[2] "As a remarkable instance of his negligence, I remember some years ago to have found lying loose in his study, and without the cover, which contained the address, a letter to him from Lord Thurlow, to whom he had made an application as Chancellor, in be-

After breakfast, Dr. Johnson and I were furnished with a boat, and sailed about upon Loch Lomond and landed on some of the islands which are interspersed. He was much pleased with the scene, which is so well known by the accounts of various travellers that it is unnecessary for me to attempt any description of it.

I recollect none of his conversation, except that, when talking of dress, he said, "Sir, were I to have anything fine, it should be very fine. Were I to wear a ring, it should not be a bauble, but a stone of great value. Were I to wear a laced or embroidered waistcoat, it should be very rich. I had once a very rich laced waistcoat, which I wore the first night of my tragedy."

Lady Helen Colquhoun being a very pious woman, the conversation after dinner took a religious turn. Her ladyship defended the Presbyterian mode of public worship; upon which Dr. Johnson delivered those excellent arguments for a form of prayer which he has introduced into his *Journey*. I am myself fully convinced that a form of prayer for public worship is in general most decent and edifying. *Solemnia verba* have a kind of prescriptive sanctity, and make a deeper impression on the mind than extemporaneous effusions, in which, as we know not what they are to be, we cannot readily acquiesce. Yet I would allow also of a certain portion of extempore address, as occasion may require. This is the practice of the French Protestant churches. And although the office of forming supplications to the throne of heaven is, in my mind, too great a trust to be indiscriminately committed to the discretion of every minister, I do not mean to deny that sincere devotion may be experienced when joining in prayer with those who use no liturgy.

We were favoured with Sir James Colquhoun's coach to convey us in the evening to Cameron, the seat of Commissary

---

half of a poor literary friend [Alexander Macbean]. It was expressed in such terms of respect for Dr. Johnson that, in my zeal for his reputation, I remonstrated warmly with him on his strange inattention, and obtained his permission to take a copy of it; by which probably it has been preserved, as the original I have reason to suppose is lost."
—BOSWELL.

Smollett. Our satisfaction of finding ourselves again in a comfortable carriage was very great. We had a pleasing conviction of the commodiousness of civilization, and heartily laughed at the ravings of those absurd visionaries who have attempted to persuade us of the superior advantages of a *state of nature*.

Mr. Smollett was a man of considerable learning, with abundance of animal spirits; so that he was a very good companion for Dr. Johnson, who said to me, "We have had more solid talk here than at any place where we have been."

I remember Dr. Johnson gave us this evening an able and eloquent discourse on the origin of evil, and on the consistency of moral evil with the power and goodness of GOD. He showed us how it arose from our free agency, an extinction of which would be a still greater evil than any we experience. I know not that he said anything absolutely new, but he said a great deal wonderfully well; and perceiving us to be delighted and satisfied, he concluded his harangue with an air of benevolent triumph over an objection which has distressed many worthy minds: "This then is the answer to the question, πόθεν τὸ κακόν?"[3] Mrs. Smollett whispered me that it was the best sermon she had ever heard. Much do I upbraid myself for having neglected to preserve it.

THURSDAY 28 OCTOBER. Mr. Smollett pleased Dr. Johnson by producing a collection of newspapers in the time of the Usurpation, from which it appeared that all sorts of crimes were very frequent during that horrible anarchy. By the side of the high road to Glasgow, at some distance from his house, he had erected a pillar to the memory of his ingenious kinsman, Dr. Smollett; and he consulted Dr. Johnson as to an inscription for it. Lord Kames, who, though he had a great store of knowledge, with much ingenuity and uncommon activity of mind, was no profound scholar, had, it seems, recommended an English inscription. Dr. Johnson treated this with great contempt, saying, "An English inscription would be a

---

[3] "Whence is evil?"

disgrace to Dr. Smollett''; and in answer to what Lord Kames had urged as to the advantage of its being in English, because it would be generally understood, I observed that all to whom Dr. Smollett's merit could be an object of respect and imitation would understand it as well in Latin; and that surely it was not meant for the Highland drovers, or other such people who pass and repass that way.

We were then shown a Latin inscription proposed for this monument. Dr. Johnson sat down with an ardent and liberal earnestness to revise it, and greatly improved it by several additions and variations. I unfortunately did not take a copy of it as it originally stood, but I have happily preserved every fragment of what Dr. Johnson wrote.[1]

We had this morning a singular proof of Dr. Johnson's quick and retentive memory. Hay's translation of Martial was lying in a window. I said I thought it was pretty well done, and showed him a particular epigram, I think of ten, but am certain of eight, lines. He read it, and tossed away the book, saying, "No, it is *not* pretty well." As I persisted in my opinion, he said, "Why, sir, the original is thus" (and he repeated it); "and this man's translation is thus"; and then he repeated that also, exactly, though he had never seen it before, and read it over only once, and that too without any intention of getting it by heart.

Here a post-chaise, which I had ordered from Glasgow, came for us, and we drove on in high spirits. We stopped at Dumbarton, and though the approach to the castle there is very steep, Dr. Johnson ascended it with alacrity, and surveyed all that was to be seen. During the whole of our tour he showed uncommon spirit, could not bear to be treated like an old or infirm man, and was very unwilling to accept of any assistance; insomuch that, at our landing at Icolmkill, when Sir Allan Maclean and I submitted to be carried on men's shoulders from the boat to the shore, as it could not be brought quite

---

[1] Boswell proceeds to give the "fragments" by Johnson, and in a footnote prints the entire epitaph. Johnson's corrections were somewhat altered; as Boswell hints, for the worse.

close to land, he sprang into the sea and waded vigorously out.

On our arrival at the Saracen's Head Inn at Glasgow, I was made happy by good accounts from home; and Dr. Johnson, who had not received a single letter since we left Aberdeen, found here a great many, the perusal of which entertained him much. He enjoyed in imagination the comforts which we could now command, and seemed to be in high glee. I remember, he put a leg up on each side of the grate, and said, with a mock solemnity, by way of soliloquy but loud enough for me to hear it, "Here am I, an ENGLISH man, sitting by a *coal* fire."

FRIDAY 29 OCTOBER. The professors of the university being informed of our arrival, Dr. Stevenson, Dr. Reid, and Mr. Anderson breakfasted with us. Mr. Anderson accompanied us while Dr. Johnson viewed this beautiful city. He had told me that one day in London, when Dr. Adam Smith was boasting of it, he turned to him and said, "Pray, sir, have you ever seen Brentford?" This was surely a strong instance of his impatience and spirit of contradiction. I put him in mind of it today, while he expressed his admiration of the elegant buildings, and whispered him, "Don't you feel some remorse?"

We were received in the college by a number of the professors, who showed all due respect to Dr. Johnson; and then we paid a visit to the principal, Dr. Leechman, at his own house, where Dr. Johnson had the satisfaction of being told that his name had been gratefully celebrated in one of the parochial congregations in the Highlands, as the person to whose influence it was chiefly owing that the New Testament was allowed to be translated into the Erse language. It seems some political members of the Society in Scotland for Propagating Christian Knowledge, had opposed this pious undertaking, as tending to preserve the distinction between the Highlanders and Lowlanders. Dr. Johnson wrote a long letter upon the subject to a friend,[1] which being shown to them, made them ashamed, and

---

[1] William Drummond, bookseller in Edinburgh. Boswell printed the letter in the *Life* under its date, 13 August 1766.

afraid of being publicly exposed; so they were forced to a compliance. It is now in my possession, and is, perhaps, one of the best productions of his masterly pen.

Professors Reid and Anderson, and the two Messieurs Foulis, the Elzevirs of Glasgow, dined and drank tea with us at our inn, after which the professors went away; and I, having a letter to write, left my fellow-traveller with Messieurs Foulis. Though good and ingenious men, they had that unsettled speculative mode of conversation which is offensive to a man regularly taught at an English school and university. I found that, instead of listening to the dictates of the sage, they had teased him with questions and doubtful disputations. He came in a flutter to me and desired I might come back again, for he could not bear these men. "O ho! sir," said I, "you are flying to me for refuge!" He never, in any situation, was at a loss for a ready repartee. He answered, with quick vivacity, "It is of two evils choosing the least." I was delighted with this flash bursting from the cloud which hung upon his mind, closed my letter directly, and joined the company.

We supped at Professor Anderson's. The general impression upon my memory is that we had not much conversation at Glasgow, where the professors, like their brethren at Aberdeen, did not venture to expose themselves much to the battery of cannon which they knew might play upon them. Dr. Johnson, who was fully conscious of his own superior powers, afterwards praised Principal Robertson for his caution in this respect. He said to me, "Robertson, sir, was in the right. Robertson is a man of eminence, and the head of a college at Edinburgh. He had a character to maintain, and did well not to risk its being lessened."

SATURDAY 30 OCTOBER. We set out towards Ayrshire. I sent Joseph on to Loudoun, with a message that, if the Earl was at home, Dr. Johnson and I would have the honour to dine with him. Joseph met us on the road, and reported that the Earl "jumped for joy," and said," I shall be very happy to see them." We were received with a most pleasing courtesy by his lordship, and by the Countess his mother, who, in her ninety-fifth year, had all her faculties quite unimpaired. This was a very cheering sight to Dr. Johnson, who had an extraordinary desire for long life. Her ladyship was sensible and well-informed, and had seen a great deal of the world. Her lord had held several high offices, and she was sister to the great Earl of Stair.

I cannot here refrain from paying a just tribute to the character of John, Earl of Loudoun, who did more service to the county of Ayr in general, as well as to individuals in it, than any man we have ever had.[1] It is painful to think that he met with much ingratitude from persons both in high and low rank; but such was his temper, such his knowledge of "base mankind,"[2] that, as if he had expected no other return, his mind was never soured, and he retained his good humour and benevolence to the last. The tenderness of his heart was proved in 1745–6, when he had an important command in the Highlands, and behaved with a generous humanity to the unfortunate. I cannot figure a more honest politician; for, though his interest in our county was great, and generally successful, he not only did not deceive by fallacious promises, but was anxious that people should not deceive themselves by too sanguine expectations. His kind and dutiful attention to his mother was unremitted. At his house was true hospitality; a plain but a plentiful table; and every guest, being left at perfect freedom, felt himself quite easy and happy. While I live, I shall honour the memory of this amiable man.

At night, we advanced a few miles farther, to the house of Mr. Campbell of Treesbank, who was married to one of my wife's sisters, and were entertained very agreeably by a worthy couple.

SUNDAY 31 OCTOBER. We reposed here in tranquillity. Dr. Johnson was pleased to find a numerous and excellent col-

---

[1] He was Commander-in-Chief of the Forces in America, 1756–7.
[2] "'The unwilling gratitude of base mankind.'—POPE" (BOSWELL).

lection of books, which had mostly belonged to the Reverend Mr. John Campbell, brother of our host.[1] I was desirous to have procured for my fellow-traveller today the company of Sir John Cuninghame of Caprington, whose castle was but two miles from us. He was a very distinguished scholar, was long abroad, and during part of the time lived much with the learned Cunningham, the opponent of Bentley as a critic upon Horace. He wrote Latin with great elegance, and, what is very remarkable, read Homer and Ariosto through every year. I wrote to him to request he would come to us, but unfortunately he was prevented by indisposition.

MONDAY 1 NOVEMBER. Though Dr. Johnson was lazy and averse to move, I insisted that he should go with me and pay a visit to the Countess of Eglinton, mother of the late and present Earl. I assured him he would find himself amply recompensed for the trouble, and he yielded to my solicitations, though with some unwillingness. We were well mounted, and had not many miles to ride. He talked of the attention that is necessary in order to distribute our charity judiciously. "If thoughtlessly done, we may neglect the most deserving objects; and, as every man has but a certain proportion to give, if it is lavished upon those who first present themselves, there may be nothing left for such as have a better claim. A man should first relieve those who are nearly connected with him, by whatever tie; and then, if he has anything to spare, may extend his bounty to a wider circle."

As we passed very near the castle of Dundonald, which was one of the many residencies of the kings of Scotland, and in which Robert the Second lived and died, Dr. Johnson wished to survey it particularly. It stands on a beautiful rising ground, which is seen at a great distance on several quarters, and from whence there is an extensive prospect of the rich district of Cunninghame, the western sea, the Isle of Arran, and a part

---

[1] One of Boswell's early publications was an epitaph on the Rev. John Campbell. See *Scots Magazine*, April 1761 (xxiii.204).

of the northern coast of Ireland. It has long been unroofed; and, though of considerable size, we could not, by any power of imagination, figure it as having been a suitable habitation for majesty. Dr. Johnson, to irritate my old Scottish enthusiasm, was very jocular on the homely accommodation of "King Bob," and roared and laughed till the ruins echoed.

Lady Eglinton, though she was now in her eighty-fifth year, and had lived in the retirement of the country for almost half a century, was still a very agreeable woman. She was of the noble house of Kennedy, and had all the elevation which the consciousness of such birth inspires.[1] Her figure was majestic, her manners high-bred, her reading extensive, and her conversation elegant. She had been the admiration of the gay circles of life, and the patroness of poets.[2] Dr. Johnson was delighted with his reception here. Her principles in church and state were congenial with his. She knew all his merit, and had heard much of him from her son, Earl Alexander, who loved to cultivate the acquaintance of men of talents in every department.

All who knew his lordship will allow that his understanding and accomplishments were of no ordinary rate. From the gay habits which he had early acquired, he spent too much of his time with men, and in pursuits, far beneath such a mind as his. He afterwards became sensible of it, and turned his thoughts to objects of importance; but was cut off in the prime of his life.[3] I cannot speak but with emotions of the most affectionate regret, of one in whose company many of my early days were passed, and to whose kindness I was much indebted.

Often must I have occasion to upbraid myself that soon after our return to the mainland, I allowed indolence to prevail over

[1] Boswell here pays a compliment to his influential friend Lord Cassillis, who was a Kennedy, and a nephew of the Countess of Eglinton.

[2] Especially of Allan Ramsay, who presented her with an autograph MS of *The Gentle Shepherd*, which she gave to Boswell in 1777.

[3] Lord Eglinton was shot and killed by Mungo Campbell, a poacher on his estate, in 1769, at the age of forty-six. It was Eglinton who, in 1760, introduced Boswell "into the circles of the great, the gay, and the ingenious."

me so much as to shrink from the labour of continuing my Journal with the same minuteness as before;[4] sheltering myself in the thought that we had done with the Hebrides, and not considering that Dr. Johnson's memorabilia were likely to be more valuable when we were restored to a more polished society. Much has thus been irrecoverably lost.

In the course of our conversation this day, it came out that Lady Eglinton was married the year before Dr. Johnson was born; upon which she graciously said to him that she might have been his mother, and that she now adopted him; and when we were going away, she embraced him, saying, "My dear son, farewell!"[5] My friend was much pleased with this day's entertainment, and owned that I had done well to force him out.

TUESDAY 2 NOVEMBER. We were now in a country not only "of saddles and bridles," but of post-chaises; and having ordered one from Kilmarnock, we got to Auchinleck before dinner.

My father was not quite a year and a half older than Dr. Johnson, but his conscientious discharge of his laborious duty as a judge in Scotland (where the law proceedings are almost all in writing), a severe complaint which ended in his death, and the loss of my mother, a woman of almost unexampled piety and goodness, had before this time in some degree affected his spirits, and rendered him less disposed to exert his faculties; for he had originally a very strong mind and cheerful temper. He assured me he never had felt one moment of what is called low spirits, or uneasiness without a real cause. He had a great

---

[4] There is a lapse of memory here, for, as we have seen (p. 345, n. 1) it was at Lochbuie's in Mull that Boswell left off writing his Journal. This passage, one at the close of 25 October, and another after the entry for 11 November, show that he kept rough notes for at least a part of the remainder of the tour, and of Johnson's second visit to Edinburgh, through 11 November.

[5] Johnson preserves a bit which Boswell had forgotten: "She called Boswell the boy. 'Yes, Madam,' said I, 'we will send him to school.' 'He is already,' said she, 'in a good school'; and expressed her hope of his improvement" (Johnson to Mrs. Thrale, 3 Nov. 1773).

many good stories, which he told uncommonly well, and he was remarkable for "humour, *incolumi gravitate*," as Lord Monboddo used to characterize it. His age, his office, and his character had long given him an acknowledged claim to great attention, in whatever company he was; and he could ill brook any diminution of it. He was as sanguine a Whig and Presbyterian as Dr. Johnson was a Tory and Church of England man; and as he had not much leisure to be informed of Dr. Johnson's great merits by reading his works, he had a partial and unfavourable notion of him, founded on his supposed political tenets, which were so discordant to his own that, instead of speaking of him with that respect to which he was entitled, he used to call him "a Jacobite fellow." Knowing all this, I should not have ventured to bring them together, had not my father, out of kindness to me, desired me to invite Dr. Johnson to his house.

I was very anxious that all should be well; and begged of my friend to avoid three topics, as to which they differed very widely: Whiggism, Presbyterianism, and—Sir John Pringle.[1] He said courteously, "I shall certainly not talk on subjects which I am told are disagreeable to a gentleman under whose roof I am; especially, I shall not do so to *your father*."

Our first day went off very smoothly. It rained, and we could not get out; but my father showed Dr. Johnson his library, which, in curious editions of the Greek and Roman classics, is, I suppose, not excelled by any private collection in Great Britain. My father had studied at Leyden and been very intimate with the Gronovii and other learned men there. He was a sound scholar, and, in particular, had collated manuscripts and different editions of Anacreon, and others of the Greek lyric poets, with great care; so that my friend and he had much matter for conversation, without touching on the fatal topics of difference.

---

[1] Sir John Pringle's liberal religious views and his friendship with Benjamin Franklin were probably the reason for Johnson's prejudice against him. They never became acquainted.

Dr. Johnson found here Baxter's Anacreon, which he told me he had long inquired for in vain, and began to suspect there was no such book. Baxter was the keen antagonist of Barnes. His life is in the *Biographia Britannica*. My father has written many notes on this book, and Dr. Johnson and I talked of having it reprinted.

WEDNESDAY 3 NOVEMBER. It rained all day, and gave Dr. Johnson an impression of that incommodiousness of climate in the West, of which he has taken notice in his *Journey*; but, being well accommodated and furnished with variety of books, he was not dissatisfied.

Some gentlemen of the neighbourhood came to visit my father, but there was little conversation. One of them asked Dr. Johnson how he liked the Highlands. The question seemed to irritate him, for he answered, "How, sir, can you ask me what obliges me to speak unfavourably of a country where I have been hospitably entertained? Who *can* like the Highlands? I like the inhabitants very well." The gentleman asked no more questions.

Let me now make up for the present neglect by again gleaning from the past. At Lord Monboddo's, after the conversation upon the decrease of learning in England, his lordship mentioned *Hermes* by Mr. Harris of Salisbury, as the work of a living author for whom he had a great respect. Dr. Johnson said nothing at the time, but when we were in our post-chaise, told me he thought Harris "a coxcomb." This he said of him not as a man but as an author; and I give his opinions of men and books, faithfully, whether they agree with my own or not. I do admit, that there always appeared to me something of affectation in Mr. Harris's manner of writing; something of a habit of clothing plain thoughts in analytic and categorical formality. But all his writings are imbued with learning; and all breathe that philanthropy and amiable disposition, which distinguished him as a man.[1]

---

[1] "This gentleman, though devoted to the study of grammar and dialectics, was not so

At another time during our tour, he drew the character of a rapacious Highland chief with the strength of Theophrastus or La Bruyère; concluding with these words: "Sir, he has no more the soul of a chief than an attorney who has twenty houses in a street, and considers how much he can make by them."[2]

He this day, when we were by ourselves, observed, how common it was for people to talk from books; to retail the sentiments of others, and not their own; in short, to converse without any originality of thinking. He was pleased to say, "You and I do not talk from books."

THURSDAY 4 NOVEMBER. I was glad to have at length a very fine day, on which I could show Dr. Johnson the Place of my family, which he has honoured with so much attention in his *Journey*. He is, however, mistaken in thinking that the Celtic name, *Auchinleck*, has no relation to the natural appearance of it. I believe every Celtic name of a place will be found very descriptive. *Auchinleck* does not signify a *stony field*, as he has said, but a *field of flagstones*; and this place has a number of rocks which abound in strata of that kind. The "sullen dignity of the old castle," as he has forcibly expressed it, delighted him exceedingly. On one side of the rock on which its ruins stand runs the river Lugar, which is here of considerable breadth,

---

absorbed in it as to be without a sense of pleasantry, or to be offended at his favourite topics being treated lightly. I one day met him in the street, as I was hastening to the House of Lords, and told him I was sorry I could not stop, being rather too late to attend an appeal of the Duke of Hamilton against Douglas. 'I thought,' said he, 'their contest had been over long ago.' I answered, 'The contest concerning Douglas's filiation was over long ago; but the contest now is, who shall have the estate.' Then, assuming the air of 'an ancient sage philosopher,' I proceeded thus: 'Were I to *predicate* concerning him, I should say, the contest formerly was, What *is* he? The contest now is, What *has* he?'—'Right,' replied Mr. Harris, smiling; 'you have done with *quality*, and have got into *quantity*.'"—BOSWELL.

[2] The reader will recognize this paragraph and the preceding as repetitions. They were not, of course, repetitions in the published *Tour*, for Boswell deleted them (the first in the MS, the second after the text was set up) under the dates of their occurrence. (See *ante*, pp. 58 and 117.) Their inclusion here means (probably) that he had run back through the entire MS and reconsidered his deletions. The ultimate inclusion of the anecdote concerning Sir Alexander Macdonald is important, for it seems to have been to remove this very passage that Boswell cancelled leaf M4. He was therefore somewhat less than candid when he assured Macdonald that an offensive passage had been removed. Actually, he had merely transferred it to another place in the volume and pre-

and is bordered by other high rocks, shaded with wood. On the other side runs a brook, skirted in the same manner, but on a smaller scale. I cannot figure a more romantic scene.

I felt myself elated here, and expatiated to my illustrious mentor on the antiquity and honourable alliances of my family, and on the merits of its founder, Thomas Boswell, who was highly favoured by his sovereign, James IV of Scotland, and fell with him at the battle of Flodden Field; and in the glow of what, I am sensible, will, in a commercial age, be considered as genealogical enthusiasm, did not omit to mention what I was sure my friend would not think lightly of, my relation[1] to the Royal Personage, whose liberality, on his accession to the throne, had given him comfort and independence. I have, in a former page, acknowledged my pride of ancient blood, in which I was encouraged by Dr. Johnson; my readers therefore will not be surprised at my having indulged it on this occasion.

Not far from the old castle is a spot of consecrated earth, on which may be traced the foundations of an ancient chapel, dedicated to St. Vincent, and where in old times "was the place of graves" for the family. It grieves me to think that the remains of sanctity here, which were considerable, were dragged away and employed in building a part of the house of Auchinleck of the middle age, which was the family residence till my father erected that "elegant modern mansion," of which Dr. Johnson speaks so handsomely. Perhaps this chapel may one day be restored.

Dr. Johnson was pleased when I showed him some venerable old trees under the shade of which my ancestors had walked. He exhorted me to plant assiduously, as my father had done to a great extent.

As I wandered with my revered friend in the groves of

---

sented it without Macdonald's name. But no reader could ever have had any doubt as to the identity of the "rapacious Highland chief."

[1] Through his mother's family, the Erskines, Boswell was descended from John, 3rd Earl of Lennox, grandfather of Lord Darnley. Darnley's son, James I of England, was the common ancestor of George III and Prince Charles Edward. See n. 6, *ante*, p. 163.

Auchinleck, I told him that if I survived him, it was my intention to erect a monument to him here, among scenes which, in my mind, were all classical; for in my youth I had appropriated to them many of the descriptions of the Roman poets. He could not bear to have death presented to him in any shape, for his constitutional melancholy made the king of terrors more frightful. He turned off the subject, saying, "Sir, I hope to see your grandchildren!"

This forenoon he observed some cattle without horns, of which he has taken notice in his *Journey*, and seems undecided whether they be of a particular race. His doubts appear to have had no foundation, for my respectable neighbour, Mr. Fairlie, who, with all his attention to agriculture, finds time both for the classics and his friends, assures me they are a distinct species, and that, when any of their calves have horns, a mixture of breed can be traced. In confirmation of his opinion, he pointed out to me the following passage in Tacitus: "*Ne armentis quidem suus honor, aut gloria frontis*"[2] (*De Mor. Germ.* §5), which he wondered had escaped Dr. Johnson.

On the front of the house of Auchinleck is this inscription:

Quod petis, hic est;
Est Ulubris; animus si te non deficit aequus.[3]

It is characteristic of the founder; but the *animus aequus* is, alas! not inheritable, nor the subject of devise. He always talked to me as if it were in a man's own power to attain it; but Dr. Johnson told me that he owned to him, when they were alone, his persuasion that it was in a great measure constitutional, or the effect of causes which do not depend on ourselves, and that Horace boasts too much when he says, "*Æquum mi animum ipse parabo.*"[4]

FRIDAY 5 NOVEMBER. The Reverend Mr. Dun, our

---

[2] "Even the cattle have not their usual beauty or noble head."
[3] "What you seek is here, even in Ulubrae, if your mind is firm" (Horace, *Epistles*, I. xi.29–30). "Ulubrae, a town near the Pontine marshes of Latium, had been a byword among the Latin authors for its remoteness from Rome" (C. B. Tinker, *Young Boswell*, p. 9).
[4] Horace, *Epistles*, I.xviii.112.

parish minister, who had dined with us yesterday with some other company, insisted that Dr. Johnson and I should dine with him today. This gave me an opportunity to show my friend the road to the church, made by my father at a great expense for above three miles on his own estate, through a range of well-enclosed farms, with a row of trees on each side of it. He called it the *Via sacra*, and was very fond of it. Dr. Johnson, though he held notions far distant from those of the Presbyterian clergy, yet could associate on good terms with them. One of them[1] discovered a narrowness of information concerning the dignitaries of the Church of England, among whom may be found men of the greatest learning, virtue, and piety, and of a truly apostolic character. He talked before Dr. Johnson of fat bishops and drowsy deans; and, in short, seemed to believe the illiberal and profane scoffings of professed satirists or vulgar railers. Dr. Johnson was so highly offended that he said to him, "Sir, you know no more of our church than a Hottentot." I was sorry that he brought this upon himself.

SATURDAY 6 NOVEMBER. I cannot be certain whether it was on this day or a former that Dr. Johnson and my father came in collision. If I recollect right, the contest began while my father was showing him his collection of medals; and Oliver Cromwell's coin unfortunately introduced Charles the First, and Toryism. They became exceedingly warm and violent, and I was very much distressed by being present at such an altercation between two men, both of whom I reverenced; yet I durst not interfere. It would certainly be very unbecoming in me to exhibit my honoured father and my respected friend as intellectual gladiators, for the entertainment of the public; and therefore I suppress what would, I dare say, make an interesting scene in this dramatic sketch—this account of the transit of Johnson over the Caledonian Hemisphere.[2]

[1] The Rev. Mr. Dun himself, as the first edition shows. Boswell later suppressed the name out of consideration for the feelings of his old friend and tutor.

[2] Sir Walter Scott furnished Croker with a detailed and brilliant account of this conversation, but like all Scott's *Boswelliana*, it should be read as historical fiction, not as a

Yet I think I may, without impropriety, mention one circumstance, as an instance of my father's address. Dr. Johnson challenged him, as he did us all at Talisker, to point out any theological works of merit written by Presbyterian ministers in Scotland. My father, whose studies did not lie much in that way, owned to me afterwards that he was somewhat at a loss how to answer, but that luckily he recollected having read in catalogues the title of *Durham on the Galatians*; upon which he boldly said, "Pray, sir, have you read Mr. Durham's excellent commentary on the Galatians?" "No, sir," said Dr. Johnson. By this lucky thought my father kept him at bay, and for some time enjoyed his triumph; but his antagonist soon made a retort, which I forbear to mention.

In the course of their altercation, Whiggism and Presbyterianism, Toryism and Episcopacy, were terribly buffeted. My worthy hereditary friend, Sir John Pringle, never having been mentioned, happily escaped without a bruise.

My father's opinion of Dr. Johnson may be conjectured from the name he afterwards gave him, which was "Ursa Major." But it is not true, as has been reported, that it was in consequence of my saying that he was a *constellation* of genius and literature. It was a sly abrupt expression to one of his brethren on the bench of the Court of Session, in which Dr. Johnson was then standing, but it was not said in his hearing.

SUNDAY 7 NOVEMBER. My father and I went to public worship in our parish-church, in which I regretted that Dr. Johnson would not join us; for, though we have there no form of prayer nor magnificent solemnity, yet, as God is worshipped in spirit and in truth, and the same doctrines preached as in the Church of England, my friend would certainly have shown more liberality had he attended. I doubt not, however, but he employed his time in private to very good purpose. His uniform

---

record of fact. According to Scott, when Johnson challenged Lord Auchinleck to say what good Cromwell had ever done to his country, the old judge replied, "God, Doctor! he gart kings ken that they had a lith in their neck." (He taught kings that they had a joint in their necks.)

and fervent piety was manifested on many occasions during our tour which I have not mentioned. His reason for not joining in Presbyterian worship has been recorded in a former page.[1]

MONDAY 8 NOVEMBER. Notwithstanding the altercation that had passed, my father, who had the dignified courtesy of an old baron, was very civil to Dr. Johnson, and politely attended him to the post-chaise which was to convey us to Edinburgh.

Thus they parted.—They are now in another, and a higher, state of existence; and as they were both worthy Christian men, I trust they have met in happiness. But I must observe, in justice to my friend's political principles and my own, that they have met in a place where there is no room for Whiggism.

We came at night to a good inn at Hamilton. I recollect no more.

TUESDAY 9 NOVEMBER. I wished to have shown Dr. Johnson the Duke of Hamilton's house, commonly called the *Palace* of Hamilton, which is close by the town. It is an object which, having been pointed out to me as a splendid edifice from my earliest years, in travelling between Auchinleck and Edinburgh, has still great grandeur in my imagination. My friend consented to stop and view the outside of it, but could not be persuaded to go into it.

We arrived this night at Edinburgh, after an absence of eighty-three days. For five weeks together, of the tempestuous season, there had been no account received of us. I cannot express how happy I was on finding myself again at home.

WEDNESDAY 10 NOVEMBER. Old Mr. Drummond, the bookseller, came to breakfast. Dr. Johnson and he had not met for ten years. There was respect on his side, and kindness on Dr. Johnson's. Soon afterwards Lord Elibank came in, and

---

[1] The passage referred to is not in the original MS as we have it. When Johnson agreed to hear a Presbyterian prayer at Cawdor manse, Boswell writes in the published *Tour*: "This was a pleasing surprise to me; for he refused to go and hear Principal Robertson preach. 'I will hear him,' said he, 'if he will get up into a tree and preach; but I will not give a sanction, by my presence, to a Presbyterian assembly.'"

was much pleased at seeing Dr. Johnson in Scotland. His lordship said, hardly anything seemed to him more improbable. Dr. Johnson had a very high opinion of him. Speaking of him to me, he characterized him thus: "Lord Elibank has read a great deal. It is true, I can find in books all that he has read; but he has a great deal of what is in books, proved by the test of real life." Indeed, there have been few men whose conversation discovered more knowledge enlivened by fancy. He published several small pieces of distinguished merit, and has left some in manuscript, in particular an account of the expedition against Cartagena, in which he served as an officer in the Army. His writings deserve to be collected. He was the early patron of Dr. Robertson the historian, and Mr. Home the tragic poet; who, when they were ministers of country parishes, lived near his seat. He told me, "I saw these lads had talents, and they were much with me." I hope they will pay a grateful tribute to his memory.

The morning was chiefly taken up by Dr. Johnson's giving him an account of our tour. The subject of difference in political principles was introduced. JOHNSON. "It is much increased by opposition. There was a violent Whig, with whom I used to contend with great eagerness. After his death I felt my Toryism much abated." I suppose he meant Mr. Walmesley of Lichfield, whose character he has drawn so well in his Life of Edmund Smith.

Mr. Nairne came in, and he and I accompanied Dr. Johnson to Edinburgh Castle, which he owned was "a great place." But I must mention, as a striking instance of that spirit of contradiction to which he had a strong propensity, when Lord Elibank was some days after talking of it with the natural elation of a Scotchman, or of any man who is proud of a stately fortress in his own country, Dr. Johnson affected to despise it, observing that "it would make a good *prison* in ENGLAND."

Lest it should be supposed that I have suppressed one of his sallies against my country, it may not be improper here to correct a mistaken account that has been circulated as to his conversation this day. It has been said that, being desired to attend to the noble prospect from the Castle Hill, he replied, "Sir, the noblest prospect that a Scotchman ever sees is the high road that leads him to London." This lively sarcasm was thrown out at a tavern in London, in my presence, many years before.[1]

We had with us today at dinner at my house, the Lady Dowager Colville and Lady Anne Erskine, sisters of the Earl of Kellie; the Honourable Archibald Erskine, who has now succeeded to that title; Lord Elibank; the Reverend Dr. Blair; Mr. Tytler, the acute vindicator of Mary Queen of Scots, and some other friends.[2]

Fingal being talked of, Dr. Johnson, who used to boast that he had, from the first, resisted both Ossian and the Giants of Patagonia, averred his positive disbelief of its authenticity. Lord Elibank said, "I am sure it is not Macpherson's. Mr. Johnson, I keep company a great deal with you; it is known I do. I may borrow from you better things than I can say myself, and give them as my own; but if I should, everybody will know whose they are." The Doctor was not softened by this compliment. He denied merit to *Fingal*, supposing it to be the production of a man who has had the advantages that the present age affords, and said, "Nothing is more easy than to write enough in that style if once you begin."[3] One gentleman[4]

---

[1] At the Mitre, on 6 July 1763.

[2] The first edition reads, "and his son, the advocate."

[3] "I desire not to be understood as agreeing *entirely* with the opinions of Dr. Johnson, which I relate without any remark. The many imitations, however, of *Fingal*, that have been published, confirm this observation in a considerable degree."—BOSWELL.

[4] Alexander Fraser Tytler (later Lord Woodhouselee). The entire passage was softened after the first edition, which reads: "Young Mr. Tytler stepped briskly forward, and said, '*Fingal* is certainly genuine; for I have heard a great part of it repeated in the original.' Dr. Johnson indignantly asked him, 'Sir, do you understand the original?' TYTLER. 'No, sir.' JOHNSON. 'Why, then, we see to what this testimony comes. Thus it is.' He afterwards said to me, 'Did you observe the wonderful confidence with which young Tytler advanced, with his front ready *brazed*?'" Tytler resented this, and seems to have written Boswell an insulting letter. On 18 November 1785, Boswell consulted Malone and Courtenay, who told him that he must have an apology. He wrote, and on 30 November received a satisfactory reply. Meanwhile he had become involved in the much more serious controversy with Lord Macdonald.

in company expressing his opinion that *Fingal* was certainly genuine, for that he had heard a great part of it repeated in the original, Dr. Johnson indignantly asked him whether he understood the original; to which an answer being given in the negative, "Why then," said Dr. Johnson, "we see to what *this* testimony comes:—thus it is."

I mention this as a remarkable proof how liable the mind of man is to credulity, when not guarded by such strict examination as that which Dr. Johnson habitually practised. The talents and integrity of the gentleman who made the remark, are unquestionable; yet, had not Dr. Johnson made him advert to the consideration that he who does not understand a language cannot know that something which is recited to him is in that language, he might have believed, and reported to this hour, that he had "heard a great part of *Fingal* repeated in the original."

For the satisfaction of those on the north of the Tweed, who may think Dr. Johnson's account of Caledonian credulity and inaccuracy too strong, it is but fair to add that he admitted the same kind of ready belief might be found in his own country. He would undertake, he said, to write an epic poem on the story of Robin Hood, and half England, to whom the names and places he should mention in it are familiar, would believe and declare they had heard it from their earliest years.

One of his objections to the authenticity of *Fingal*, during the conversation at Ullinish, is omitted in my Journal, but I perfectly recollect it. "Why is not the original deposited in some public library, instead of exhibiting attestations of its existence? Suppose there were a question in a court of justice whether a man be dead or alive. You aver he is alive, and you bring fifty witnesses to swear it; I answer, 'Why do you not produce the man?'" This is an argument founded on one of the first principles of the law of evidence, which Gilbert would have held to be irrefragable.

I do not think it incumbent on me to give any precise decided opinion upon this question, as to which I believe more than some, and less than others. The subject appears to have now become very uninteresting to the public. That *Fingal* is not from beginning to end a translation from the Gaelic, but that *some* passages have been supplied by the editor to connect the whole, I have heard admitted by very warm advocates for its authenticity. If this be the case, why are not these distinctly ascertained? Antiquaries and admirers of the work may complain that they are in a situation similar to that of the unhappy gentleman whose wife informed him, on her death-bed, that one of their reputed children was not his; and, when he eagerly begged her to declare which of them it was, she answered, "*That* you shall never know," and expired, leaving him in irremediable doubt as to them all.

I beg leave now to say something upon second sight, of which I have related two instances, as they impressed my mind at the time. I own I returned from the Hebrides with a considerable degree of faith in the many stories of that kind which I heard with a too easy acquiescence, without any close examination of the evidence; but since that time my belief in those stories has been much weakened by reflecting on the careless inaccuracy of narrative in common matters, from which we may certainly conclude that there may be the same in what is more extraordinary. It is but just, however, to add that the belief in second sight is not peculiar to the Highlands and Isles.

Some years after our tour, a cause[5] was tried in the Court of Session, where the principal fact to be ascertained was whether a ship-master, who used to frequent the Western Highlands

---

[5] The cause of John Wilson, ironmonger in Glasgow, *versus* Archibald Maclean, merchant in Laggan, Mull, was tried in the Court of Session in July 1776. Wilson brought an action for payment of goods furnished by him to Maclean in 1771. Maclean produced a receipt signed by Captain John White, showing that the goods had been paid for. Wilson however alleged that the receipt was a forgery, Captain White having been drowned in 1770. Eighty witnesses gave evidence, supported by fifteen pieces of writing, that White was not drowned until October 1771; but a great many others swore that he had died twelve months earlier.

and Isles, was drowned in one particular year or in the year after. A great number of witnesses from those parts were examined on each side, and swore directly contrary to each other upon this simple question. One of them, a very respectable chieftain, who told me a story of second sight which I have not mentioned but which I too implicitly believed, had in this case, previous to this public examination, not only said, but attested under his hand, that he had seen the ship-master in the year subsequent to that in which the court was finally satisfied he was drowned. When interrogated with the strictness of judicial inquiry, and under the awe of an oath, he recollected himself better, and retracted what he had formerly asserted, apologizing for his inaccuracy by telling the judges, "A man will *say* what he will not *swear*." By many he was much censured, and it was maintained that every gentleman would be as attentive to truth without the sanction of an oath, as with it. Dr. Johnson, though he himself was distinguished at all times by a scrupulous adherence to truth, controverted this proposition; and, as a proof that this was not, though it ought to be, the case, urged the very different decisions of elections under Mr. Grenville's Act from those formerly made. "Gentlemen will not pronounce upon oath what they would have said, and voted in the House, without that sanction."

However difficult it may be for men who believe in preternatural communications, in modern times, to satisfy those who are of a different opinion, they may easily refute the doctrine of their opponents who impute a belief in second sight to superstition. To entertain a visionary notion that one sees a distant or future event, may be called superstition; but the correspondence of the fact or event with such an impression on the fancy, though certainly very wonderful, if proved, has no more connexion with superstition than magnetism or electricity.

After dinner various topics were discussed, but I recollect only one particular. Dr. Johnson compared the different talents of Garrick and Foote as companions, and gave Garrick greatly the preference for elegance, though he allowed Foote extraordinary powers of entertainment. He said, "Garrick is restrained by some principle, but Foote has the advantage of an unlimited range. Garrick has some delicacy of feeling; it is possible to put him out; you may get the better of him; but Foote is the most incompressible fellow that I ever knew: when you have driven him into a corner, and think you are sure of him, he runs through between your legs, or jumps over your head, and makes his escape."

Dr. Erskine and Mr. Robert Walker, two very respectable ministers of Edinburgh, supped with us, as did the Reverend Dr. Webster. The conversation turned on the Moravian missions, and on the Methodists. Dr. Johnson observed in general that missionaries were too sanguine in their accounts of their success among savages, and that much of what they tell is not to be believed. He owned that the Methodists had done good, had spread religious impressions among the vulgar part of mankind; but he said they had great bitterness against other Christians, and that he never could get a Methodist to explain in what he excelled others; that it always ended in the indispensable necessity of hearing one of their preachers.

THURSDAY 11 NOVEMBER. Principal Robertson came to us as we sat at breakfast; he advanced to Dr. Johnson, repeating a line of Virgil, which I forget. I suppose, either

> Post varios casus, per tot discrimina rerum,—

or

> —multum ille et terris jactatus, et alto.[1]

Everybody had accosted us with some studied compliment on our return. Dr. Johnson said, "I am really ashamed of the congratulations which we receive. We are addressed as if we had made a voyage to Nova Zembla, and suffered five persecutions in Japan." And he afterwards remarked that to see a man

---

[1] "Through various hazards and events we move."
"Long labours both by sea and land he bore."
—"DRYDEN" (BOSWELL).

come up with a formal air and a Latin line, when we had no fatigue and no danger, was provoking. I told him he was not sensible of the danger, having lain under cover in the boat during the storm; he was like the chicken that hides its head under its wing, and then thinks itself safe.

Lord Elibank came to us, as did Sir William Forbes. The rash attempt in 1745 being mentioned, I observed that it would make a fine piece of history. Dr. Johnson said it would. Lord Elibank doubted whether any man of this age could give it impartially. JOHNSON. "A man, by talking with those of different sides who were actors in it, and putting down all that he hears, may in time collect the materials of a good narrative. You are to consider, all history was at first oral. I suppose Voltaire was fifty years in collecting his *Louis XIV*, which he did in the way that I am proposing." ROBERTSON. "He did so. He lived much with all the great people who were concerned in that reign, and heard them talk of everything; and then either took Mr. Boswell's way, of writing down what he heard, or, which is as good, preserved it in his memory; for he has a wonderful memory." (With the leave, however, of this elegant historian, no man's memory can preserve facts or sayings with such fidelity as may be done by writing them down when they are recent.) Dr. Robertson said it was now full time to make such a collection as Dr. Johnson suggested; for many of the people who were then in arms were dropping off; and both Whigs and Jacobites were now come to talk with moderation. Lord Elibank said to him, "Mr. Robertson, the first thing that gave me a high opinion of you, was your saying in the Select Society,[2] while parties ran high, soon after the year 1745, that you did not think worse of a man's moral character for his having been in rebellion. This was venturing to utter a liberal sentiment while both sides had a detestation of each other."

---

[2] "A society for debate in Edinburgh, consisting of the most eminent men."—BOSWELL. Later in his memoirs (reprinted from the *European Magazine* for 1791 in F. A. Pottle's *Boswell's Literary Career*, 1929) he tells us that he was himself a member of this society.

Dr. Johnson observed that being in rebellion from a notion of another's right, was not connected with depravity; and that we had this proof of it, that all mankind applauded the pardoning of rebels, which they would not do in the case of robbers and murderers. He said, with a smile, that he wondered that the phrase of *unnatural* rebellion should be so much used, for that all rebellion was natural to man.

As I kept no journal of anything that passed after this morning,[1] I shall, from memory, group together this and the other days till that on which Dr. Johnson departed for London. They were in all nine days: on which he dined at Lady Colville's, Lord Hailes's, Sir Adolphus Oughton's, Sir Alexander Dick's, Principal Robertson's, Mr. Maclaurin's, and thrice at Lord Elibank's seat in the country, where we also passed two nights. He supped at the Honourable Alexander Gordon's, now one of our judges by the title of Lord Rockville; at Mr. Nairne's, now also one of our judges by the title of Lord Dunsinane; at Dr. Blair's, and Mr. Tytler's; and at my house thrice: one evening with a numerous company, chiefly gentlemen of the law; another with Mr. Menzies of Culdares, and Lord Monboddo, who disengaged himself on purpose to meet him; and the evening on which we returned from Lord Elibank's, he supped with my wife and me by ourselves.

He breakfasted at Dr. Webster's, at old Mr. Drummond's, and at Dr. Blacklock's; and spent one forenoon at my uncle Dr. Boswell's, who showed him his curious museum; and, as he was an elegant scholar, and a physician bred in the school of Boerhaave, Dr. Johnson was pleased with his company.

On the mornings when he breakfasted at my house, he had, from ten o'clock till one or two, a constant levee of various persons, of very different characters and descriptions. I could not attend him, being obliged to be in the Court of Session;

---

[1] He had a better reason than usual for the lapse in his record. The Winter Session of the Court began on 12 November, and he no doubt found that he had little time for writing after discharging his professional duties and entertaining Johnson.

but my wife was so good as to devote the greater part of the morning to the endless task of pouring out tea for my friend and his visitors.

Such was the disposition of his time at Edinburgh. He said one evening to me, in a fit of languor, "Sir, we have been harassed by invitations." I acquiesced. "Ay, sir," he replied; "but how much worse would it have been if we had been neglected?"

From what has been recorded in this Journal, it may well be supposed that a variety of admirable conversation has been lost, by my neglect to preserve it. I shall endeavour to recollect some of it, as well as I can.

At Lady Colville's, to whom I am proud to introduce any stranger of eminence, that he may see what dignity and grace is to be found in Scotland, an officer[2] observed, that he had heard Lord Mansfield was not a great English lawyer. JOHNSON. "Why, sir, supposing Lord Mansfield not to have the splendid talents which he possesses, he must be a great English lawyer from having been so long at the bar and having passed through so many of the great offices of the law. Sir, you may as well maintain that a carrier who has driven a pack-horse between Edinburgh and Berwick for thirty years does not know the road, as that Lord Mansfield does not know the law of England."

At Mr. Nairne's he drew the character of Richardson, the author of *Clarissa*, with a strong yet delicate pencil. I lament much that I have not preserved it: I only remember that he expressed a high opinion of his talents and virtues; but observed, that his perpetual study was to ward off petty inconveniencies and procure petty pleasures; that his love of continual superiority was such that he took care to be always surrounded by women, who listened to him implicitly and did not venture to controvert his opinions; and that his desire of

---

[2] Probably one of Lady Colville's brothers: either Captain Archibald Erskine, later 7th Earl of Kellie, or Lieutenant Andrew Erskine, Boswell's old companion and literary collaborator, who, however, had resigned his lieutenancy in 1769.

distinction was so great that he used to give large vails to the Speaker Onslow's servants that they might treat him with respect.

On the same evening, he would not allow that the private life of a judge in England was required to be so strictly decorous as I supposed. "Why then, sir," said I, "according to your account, an English judge may just live like a gentleman." JOHNSON. "Yes, sir—if he *can*."

At Mr. Tytler's, I happened to tell that one evening, a great many years ago, when Dr. Hugh Blair and I were sitting together in the pit of Drury Lane playhouse, in a wild freak of youthful extravagance I entertained the audience prodigiously by imitating the lowing of a cow. A little while after I had told this story, I differed from Dr. Johnson, I suppose too confidently, upon some point which I now forget. He did not spare me. "Nay, sir," said he, "if you cannot talk better as a man, I'd have you bellow like a cow."[3]

At Dr. Webster's he said that he believed hardly any man died without affectation. This remark appears to me to be well founded, and will account for many of the celebrated death-bed sayings which are recorded.

On one of the evenings at my house, when he told that Lord Lovat boasted to an English nobleman that though he had not his wealth, he had two thousand men whom he could at any time call into the field, the Honourable Alexander Gordon observed that those two thousand men brought him to the block. "True, sir," said Dr. Johnson, "but you may just as well argue, concerning a man who has fallen over a precipice to which he has walked too near, 'His two legs brought him to that.' Is he not the better for having two legs?"

---

[3] "As I have been scrupulously exact in relating anecdotes concerning other persons, I shall not withhold any part of this story, however ludicrous.—I was so successful in this boyish frolic, that the universal cry of the galleries was, '*Encore* the cow! *Encore* the cow!' In the pride of my heart, I attempted imitations of some other animals, but with very inferior effect. My reverend friend, anxious for my *fame*, with an air of the utmost gravity and earnestness, addressed me thus: 'My dear sir, I would *confine* myself to the *cow*!'"—BOSWELL.

At Dr. Blair's I left him in order to attend a consultation, during which he and his amiable host were by themselves. I returned to supper, at which were Principal Robertson, Mr. Nairne, and some other gentlemen. Dr. Robertson and Dr. Blair, I remember, talked well upon subordination and government; and, as my friend and I were walking home, he said to me, "Sir, these two doctors are good men, and wise men." I begged of Dr. Blair to recollect what he could of the long conversation that passed between Dr. Johnson and him alone this evening, and he obligingly wrote to me as follows:

March 3, 1785.

DEAR SIR,—As so many years have intervened since I chanced to have that conversation with Dr. Johnson in my house, to which you refer, I have forgotten most of what then passed, but remember that I was both instructed and entertained by it. Among other subjects, the discourse happening to turn on modern Latin poets, the Doctor expressed a very favourable opinion of Buchanan, and instantly repeated, from beginning to end, an ode of his entitled *Calendae Maiae* (the eleventh in his *Miscellaneorum Liber*), beginning with these words, "*Salvete sacris deliciis sacrae,*" with which I had formerly been unacquainted; but upon perusing it, the praise which he bestowed upon it as one of the happiest of Buchanan's poetical compositions, appeared to me very just. He also repeated to me a Latin ode he had composed in one of the Western Islands, from which he had lately returned. We had much discourse concerning his excursion to those islands, with which he expressed himself as having been highly pleased; talked in a favourable manner of the hospitality of the inhabitants, and particularly spoke much of his happiness in having you for his companion; and said that the longer he knew you, he loved and esteemed you the more. This conversation passed in the interval between tea and supper, when we were by ourselves. You, and the rest of the company who were with us at supper, have often taken notice that he was uncommonly bland and gay that evening, and gave much pleasure to all who were present. This is all that I can recollect distinctly of that long conversation. Yours sincerely,

HUGH BLAIR.

At Lord Hailes's, we spent a most agreeable day, but again I must lament that I was so indolent as to let almost all that passed evaporate into oblivion. Dr. Johnson observed there that it is wonderful how ignorant many officers of the army are, considering how much leisure they have for study and the acquisition of knowledge. I hope he was mistaken, for he maintained that many of them were ignorant of things belonging immediately to their own profession; "For instance, many cannot tell how far a musket will carry a bullet"; in proof of which, I suppose, he mentioned some particular person, for Lord Hailes, from whom I solicited what he could recollect of that day, writes to me as follows:

As to Dr. Johnson's observation about the ignorance of officers in the length that a musket will carry, my brother, Colonel Dalrymple, was present, and he thought that the Doctor was either mistaken, by putting the question wrong, or that he had conversed on the subject with some person out of service.

Was it upon that occasion that he expressed no curiosity to see the room at Dunfermline, where Charles I was born? "I know that he was born," said he; "no matter where." Did he envy us the birth-place of the king?

Near the end of his *Journey*, Dr. Johnson has given liberal praise to Mr. Braidwood's academy for the deaf and dumb. When he visited it, a circumstance occurred which was truly characteristical of our great Lexicographer. "Pray," said he, "can they pronounce any *long* words?" Mr. Braidwood informed him they could. Upon which Dr. Johnson wrote one of his *sesquipedalia verba*, which was pronounced by the scholars, and he was satisfied. My readers may perhaps wish to know what the word was, but I cannot gratify their curiosity. Mr. Braidwood told me it remained long in his school, but had been lost before I made my inquiry.[4]

Dr. Johnson one day visited the Court of Session. He thought the mode of pleading there too vehement, and too much addressed to the passions of the judges. "This," said he, "is not the Areopagus."

At old Mr. Drummond's, Sir John Dalrymple quaintly said

---

[4] "One of the best critics of our age 'does not wish to prevent the admirers of the incorrect and nerveless style which generally prevailed for a century before Dr. Johnson's energetic writings were known, from enjoying the laugh that this story may produce, in which he is very ready to join them.' He, however, requests me to observe, that 'my friend very properly chose a *long* word on this occasion, not, it is believed, from any predilection for polysyllables (though he certainly had a due respect for them), but in order to put Mr. Braidwood's skill to the strictest test, and to try the efficacy of his instruction by the most difficult exertion of the organs of his pupils.'"—BOSWELL. Probably Malone is the critic quoted.

the two noblest animals in the world were a Scotch Highlander and an English sailor. "Why, sir," said Dr. Johnson,
"I shall say nothing as to the Scotch Highlander, but as to
the English sailor, I cannot agree with you." Sir John said he
was generous in giving away his money. JOHNSON. "Sir, he
throws away his money, without thought and without merit.
I do not call a tree generous that sheds its fruit at every breeze."
Sir John having affected to complain of the attacks made upon
his *Memoirs*, Dr. Johnson said, "Nay, sir, do not complain. It
is advantageous to an author that his book should be attacked
as well as praised. Fame is a shuttlecock. If it be struck only
at one end of the room, it will soon fall to the ground. To keep
it up, it must be struck at both ends." Often have I reflected
on this since; and, instead of being angry at many of those who
have written against me, have smiled to think that they were
unintentionally subservient to my fame, by using a battledore
to make me *virum volitare per ora*.[5]

At Sir Alexander Dick's, from that absence of mind to which
every man is at times subject, I told, in a blundering manner,
Lady Eglinton's complimentary adoption of Dr. Johnson as
her son; for I unfortunately stated that her ladyship adopted
him as her son, in consequence of her having been married
the year *after* he was born. Dr. Johnson instantly corrected me.
"Sir, don't you perceive that you are defaming the Countess?
For, supposing me to be her son, and she was not married till
the year after my birth, I must have been her *natural* son."[6]
A young lady of quality,[7] who was present, very handsomely
said, "Might not the son have justified the fault?" My friend
was much flattered by this compliment, which he never forgot. When in more than ordinary spirits, and talking of his
journey in Scotland, he has called to me, "Boswell, what was

[5] "Fly to and fro on the lips of men."—Virgil, *Georgics*, III. 9.
[6] As a matter of fact, notwithstanding Lady Eglinton's assertion that she was married
"in the year eight," the *Scots Peerage* says that her marriage occurred in June 1709, only
three months before Johnson's birth.
[7] Lady Anne Lindsay, later Barnard, according to a note by Malone in his copy of the
Tour. She was the author of the well-known ballad, *Auld Robin Gray*.

it that the young lady of quality said of me at Sir Alexander Dick's?" Nobody will doubt that I was happy in repeating it.

My illustrious friend, being now desirous to be again in the great theatre of life and animated exertion, took a place in the coach which was to set out for London on Monday the 22d of November. Sir John Dalrymple pressed him to come on the Saturday before to his house at Cranston, which being twelve miles from Edinburgh, upon the middle road to Newcastle (Dr. Johnson had come to Edinburgh by Berwick, and along the naked coast), it would make his journey easier, as the coach would take him up at a more seasonable hour than that at which it sets out. Sir John, I perceived, was ambitious of having such a guest; but, as I was well assured that at this very time he had joined with some of his prejudiced countrymen in railing at Dr. Johnson, and had said he wondered how any gentleman of Scotland could keep company with him, I thought he did not deserve the honour; yet, as it might be a convenience to Dr. Johnson, I contrived that he should accept the invitation, and engaged to conduct him.[8] I resolved that, on our way to Sir John's, we should make a little circuit by Rosslyn Castle and Hawthornden, and wished to set out soon after breakfast; but young Mr. Tytler came to show Dr. Johnson some essays which he had written, and my great friend, who was exceedingly obliging when thus consulted, was detained so long that it was, I believe, one o'clock before we got into our post-chaise. I found that we should be too late for dinner at Sir John Dalrymple's, to which we were engaged; but I would by no means lose the pleasure of seeing my friend at Hawthornden—of seeing *Sam Johnson* at the very spot where *Ben Jonson* visited the learned and poetical Drummond.

---

[8] Boswell's original dislike for Sir John Dalrymple was increased by an incident which he records in his journal for 22 January 1782: "He published a scurrilous pamphlet against Lord Barrington and then refused a challenge from his lordship, which I think should exclude him from the company of every gentleman." (The pamphlet was *Three Letters to the Right Hon. Viscount Barrington*, 1778.) It was really not very daring of Boswell to attack Sir John in print so violently, since he knew there was no danger of a challenge from that quarter!

We surveyed Rosslyn Castle, the romantic scene around it, and the beautiful Gothic chapel, and dined and drank tea at the inn; after which we proceeded to Hawthornden and viewed the caves; and I all the while had *Rare Ben* in my mind, and was pleased to think that this place was now visited by another celebrated wit of England.

By this time "the waning night was growing old," and we were yet several miles from Sir John Dalrymple's. Dr. Johnson did not seem much troubled at our having treated the baronet with so little attention to politeness; but when I talked of the grievous disappointment it must have been to him that we did not come to the *feast* that he had prepared for us (for he told us he had killed a seven-year-old sheep on purpose), my friend got into a merry mood, and jocularly said, "I dare say, sir, he has been very sadly distressed. Nay, we do not know but the consequence may have been fatal. Let me try to describe his situation in his own historical style. I have as good a right to make *him* think and talk as he has to tell us how people thought and talked a hundred years ago, of which he has no evidence. All history, so far as it is not supported by contemporary evidence, is romance.—Stay now.—Let us consider!" He then (heartily laughing all the while) proceeded in his imitation, I am sure to the following effect, though now, at the distance of almost twelve years, I cannot pretend to recollect all the precise words:

Dinner being ready, he wondered that his guests were not yet come. His wonder was soon succeeded by impatience. He walked about the room in anxious agitation; sometimes he looked at his watch, sometimes he looked out at the window with an eager gaze of expectation, and revolved in his mind the various accidents of human life. His family beheld him with mute concern. "Surely," said he, with a sigh, "they will not fail me." The mind of man can bear a certain pressure; but there is a point when it can bear no more. A rope was in his view, and he died a Roman death.[9]

---

[9] "'Essex was at that time confined to the same chamber of the Tower from which his father Lord Capell had been led to death, and in which his wife's grandfather [actually great-grandfather] had inflicted a voluntary death upon himself. When he saw his friend carried to what he reckoned certain fate, their common enemies enjoying the spectacle, and reflected that it was he who had forced Lord Howard upon the con-

It was very late before we reached the seat of Sir John Dalrymple, who, certainly with some reason, was not in very good humour. Our conversation was not brilliant. We supped, and went to bed in ancient rooms which would have better suited the climate of Italy in summer than that of Scotland in the month of November.

I recollect no conversation of the next day worth preserving, except one saying of Dr. Johnson, which will be a valuable text for many decent old dowagers, and other good company in various circles to descant upon. He said, "I am sorry I have not learnt to play at cards. It is very useful in life; it generates kindness and consolidates society." He certainly could not mean deep play.

My friend and I thought we should be more comfortable at the inn at Blackshiels, two miles farther on. We therefore went thither in the evening, and he was very entertaining; but I have preserved nothing but the pleasing remembrance, and his verses on George the Second and Cibber,[10] and his epitaph on Parnell,[11] which he was then so good as to dictate to me. We breakfasted together next morning, and then the coach came and took him up. He had as one of his companions in it as far as Newcastle, the worthy and ingenious Dr. Hope, botanical professor at Edinburgh. Both Dr. Johnson and he used to speak of their good fortune in thus accidentally meeting; for they had much instructive conversation, which is always a most valuable enjoyment, and, when found where it is not expected, is peculiarly relished.

I have now completed my account of our tour to the Hebrides. I have brought Dr. Johnson down to Scotland, and seen

---

fidence of Russell, he retired, and by a *Roman death*, put an end to his misery.' Dalrymple's *Memoirs of Great Britain and Ireland*, Vol. I, p. 36."—BOSWELL.

[10] Printed in the *Life of Johnson* in the brief account of the year 1740:
> "Augustus still survives in Maro's strain,
> And Spenser's verse prolongs Eliza's reign;
> Great George's acts let tuneful Cibber sing;
> For Nature form'd the Poet for the King."

[11] Also printed in the *Life of Johnson*, in the discussion of the *Life of Parnell*, under the year 1781.

him into the coach which in a few hours carried him back into England. He said to me often that the time he spent in this tour was the pleasantest part of his life, and asked me if I would lose the recollection of it for five hundred pounds. I answered I would not; and he applauded my setting such a value on an accession of new images in my mind.

Had it not been for me, I am persuaded Dr. Johnson never would have undertaken such a journey; and I must be allowed to assume some merit from having been the cause that our language has been enriched with such a book as that which he published on his return; a book which I never read but with the utmost admiration, as I had such opportunities of knowing from what very meagre materials it was composed.

But my praise may be supposed partial; and therefore I shall insert two testimonies not liable to that objection, both written by gentlemen of Scotland, to whose opinions I am confident the highest respect will be paid: Lord Hailes and Mr. Dempster.

To James Boswell, Esq.

New Hailes, 6th Feb. 1775.

Sir,—I have received much pleasure and much instruction from perusing the *Journey* to the Hebrides.

I admire the elegance and variety of description, and the lively picture of men and manners. I always approve of the moral, often of the political, reflections. I love the benevolence of the author.

They who search for faults may possibly find them in this, as well as in every other work of literature.

For example, the friends of the old family say that the era of planting is placed too late, at the Union of the two kingdoms. I am known to be no friend of the old family, yet I would place the era of planting at the Restoration, after the murder of Charles I had been expiated in the anarchy which succeeded it.

Before the Restoration, few trees were planted, unless by the monastic drones; their successors (and worthy patriots they were), the barons, first cut down the trees, and then sold the estates. The gentleman at St. Andrews, who said that there were but two trees in Fife, ought to have added that the elms of Balmerino were sold within these twenty years to make pumps for the fire-engines.

In J. Major *De Gestis Scotorum*, L. i. C. 2., last edition, there is a singular passage:

"Davidi Cranstoneo conterraneo, dum de prima Theologiae licentia foret, duo ei consocii et familiares, et mei cum eo in artibus auditores, scilicet Jacobus Almain Senonensis, et Petrus Bruxcellensis, Praedicatorii Ordinis, in Sorbonae curia die Sorbonico coram commilitonibus suis publice objecerunt, quod pane avenaceo plebeii Scoti, sicut a quodam religioso intellexerant, vescebantur, ut virum, quem cholericum noverant, honestis salibus tentarent, qui hoc inficiari tanquam patriae dedecus nisus est."[12]

Pray introduce our countryman, Mr. Licentiate David Cranston, to the acquaintance of Mr. Johnson.

The syllogism seems to have been this:

They who feed on oatmeal are barbarians;

But the Scots feed on oatmeal:

Ergo ——

The licentiate denied the *minor*. I am, sir, your most obedient servant,

DAV. DALRYMPLE.

To James Boswell, Esq., Edinburgh

Dunnichen, 16th February, 1775.

MY DEAR BOSWELL,—I cannot omit a moment to return you my best thanks for the entertainment you have furnished me, my family, and guests, by the perusal of Dr. Johnson's *Journey to the Western Islands*; and now for my sentiments of it. I was well entertained. His descriptions are accurate and vivid. He carried me on the tour along with him. I am pleased with the justice he has done to your humour and vivacity. "The noise of the wind being all its own," is a *bon mot* that it would have been a pity to have omitted, and a robbery not to have ascribed to its author.[13]

There is nothing in the book, from beginning to end, that a Scotchman need to take amiss. What he says of the country is true, and his observations on the people are what must naturally occur to a sensible, observing, and reflecting inhabitant of a *convenient* metropolis, where a man on thirty pounds a year may be better accommodated with all the little wants of life than Coll or Sir Allan. He reasons candidly about the second sight, but I wish he had inquired more before he ventured to say he even doubted of

---

[12] "When my fellow-countryman, David Cranston, was taking his first course of theology, he had as fellow-students and bosom-friends James Almain of Sens and Peter of Brussels, a Dominican, who along with him attended the arts class under me. These men, in the course of a discussion on Founder's Day in the courtyard of the Sorbonne, taunted him publicly before his fellows by maintaining that the common people of Scotland (as they had been assured by a certain religious) ate oaten bread. This they did, knowing him to be quick-tempered and purposing to tease him with a fair joke; but he strove to repel the charge as if it had brought disgrace on his country." (Translation by Archibald Constable, revised, *Pub. Scottish Hist. Soc.*, x. 10. Two mistakes in the Latin have been silently corrected.)

[13] "The winter in Coll is never cold, but very tempestuous. I know not that I ever heard the wind so loud in any other place; and Mr. Boswell observed that its noise was all its own, for there were no trees to increase it"(Johnson's *Journey*).

the possibility of such an unusual and useless deviation from all the known laws of nature. The notion of the second sight I consider as a remnant of superstitious ignorance and credulity, which a philosopher will set down as such till the contrary is clearly proved, and then it will be classed among the other certain, though unaccountable, parts of our nature, like dreams, and —I do not know what.

In regard to the language, it has the merit of being all his own. Many words of foreign extraction are used, where, I believe, common ones would do as well, especially on familiar occasions. Yet I believe he could not express himself so forcibly in any other style. I am charmed with his researches concerning the Erse language and the antiquity of their manuscripts. I am quite convinced; and I shall rank Ossian and his Fingals and Oscars amongst the nursery tales, not the true history of our country, in all time to come.

Upon the whole, the book cannot displease, for it has no pretensions. The author neither says he is a geographer, nor an antiquarian, nor very learned in the history of Scotland, nor a naturalist, nor a fossilist. The manners of the people and the face of the country are all he attempts to describe or seems to have thought of. Much were it to be wished that they who have travelled into more remote, and of course more curious, regions, had all possessed his good sense. Of the state of learning, his observations on Glasgow University show he has formed a very sound judgment. He understands our climate too, and he has accurately observed the changes, however slow and imperceptible to us, which Scotland has undergone in consequence of the blessings of liberty and internal peace. I could have drawn my pen through the story of the old woman at St. Andrews, being the only silly thing in the book. He has taken the opportunity of ingrafting into the work several good observations, which I dare say he had made upon men and things before he set foot on Scotch ground, by which it is considerably enriched.[14] A long journey, like a tall May-pole, though not very beautiful itself, yet is pretty enough when ornamented with flowers and garlands; it furnishes a sort of cloak-pins for hanging the furniture of your mind upon; and whoever sets out upon a journey without furnishing his mind previously with much study and useful knowledge erects a May-pole in December, and puts up very useless cloak-pins.

I hope the book will induce many of his countrymen to make the same jaunt, and help to intermix the more liberal part of them still more with us, and perhaps abate somewhat of that virulent antipathy which many of them entertain against the Scotch; who certainly would never have formed those *combinations* which he takes notice of, more than their ancestors, had they not been necessary for their mutual safety (at least for their success) in

---

[14] "Mr. Orme, one of the ablest historians of this age, is of the same opinion. He said to me, 'There are in that book thoughts, which, by long revolution in the great mind of Johnson, have been formed and polished—like pebbles rolled in the ocean!' "— BOSWELL.

a country where they are treated as foreigners. They would find us not deficient, at least in point of hospitality, and they would be ashamed ever after to abuse us in the mass.

So much for the tour.—I have now, for the first time in my life, passed a winter in the country; and never did three months roll on with more swiftness and satisfaction. I used not only to wonder at, but pity, those whose lot condemned them to winter anywhere but in either of the capitals. But every place has its charms to a cheerful mind. I am busy planting and taking measures for opening the summer campaign in farming; and I find I have an excellent resource, when revolutions in politics perhaps, and revolutions of the sun for certain, will make it decent for me to retreat behind the ranks of the more forward in life.

I am glad to hear the last was a very busy week with you.[15] I see you as counsel in some causes which must have opened a charming field for your humorous vein. As it is more uncommon, so I verily believe it is more useful than the more serious exercise of reason; and, to a man who is to appear in public, more éclat is to be gained, sometimes more money too, by a *bon mot* than a learned speech. It is the fund of natural humour which Lord North possesses that makes him so much the favourite of the House, and so able, because so amiable, a leader of a party.

I have now finished *my* Tour of Seven Pages. In what remains, I beg leave to offer my compliments, and those of *ma très chère femme*,[16] to you and Mrs. Boswell. Pray unbend the busy brow and frolic a little in a letter to, my dear Boswell, your affectionate friend,

GEORGE DEMPSTER.[17]

I shall also present the public with a correspondence with the Laird of Raasay, concerning a passage in the *Journey to the Western Islands*, which shows Dr. Johnson in a very amiable light.

To James Boswell, Esq.

Raasay, April 10th, 1775.

DEAR SIR,—I take this occasion of returning you my most hearty thanks for the civilities shown to my daughter by you and Mrs. Boswell.[18] Yet, though she has informed me that I am under this obligation, I should very

---

[15] "This was a busy and a gainful week to me. I received twenty-seven guineas in fees, two more than I had ever received in one week before" (Boswell's Journal, 11 February 1775).

[16] Dempster had married Rose Heming in September 1774.

[17] "Every reader will, I am sure, join with me in warm admiration of the truly patriotic writer of this letter. I know not which most to applaud,—that good sense and liberality of mind, which could see and admit the defects of his native country, to which no man is a more zealous friend; or that candour, which induced him to give just praise to the minister whom he honestly and strenuously opposed."—BOSWELL.

[18] Flora MacLeod visited Edinburgh during the winter and spring of 1775, as we find in Boswell's Journal for that period.

probably have deferred troubling you with making my acknowledgments at present if I had not seen Dr. Johnson's *Journey to the Western Isles*, in which he has been pleased to make a very friendly mention of my family, for which I am surely obliged to him, as being more than an equivalent for the reception you and he met with. Yet there is one paragraph I should have been glad he had omitted, which I am sure was owing to misinformation; that is, that I had acknowledged MacLeod to be my chief, though my ancestors disputed the pre-eminence for a long tract of time.

I never had occasion to enter seriously on this argument with the present laird or his grandfather, nor could I have any temptation to such a renunciation from either of them. I acknowledge, the benefit of being chief of a clan is in our days of very little significance, and to trace out the progress of this honour to the founder of a family of any standing, would perhaps be a matter of some difficulty.

The true state of the present case is this: the MacLeod family consists of two different branches: the MacLeods of Lewis, of which I am descended, and the MacLeods of Harris. And though the former have lost a very extensive estate by forfeiture in King James the Sixth's time, there are still several respectable families of it existing, who would justly blame me for such an unmeaning cession, when they all acknowledge me head of that family; which though in fact it be but an ideal point of honour, is not hitherto so far disregarded in our country but it would determine some of my friends to look on me as a much smaller man than either they or myself judge me at present to be. I will, therefore, ask it as a favour of you to acquaint the Doctor with the difficulty he has brought me to. In travelling among rival clans, such a silly tale as this might easily be whispered into the ear of a passing stranger; but as it has no foundation in fact, I hope the Doctor will be so good as to take his own way in undeceiving the public—I principally mean my friends and connexions, who will be first angry at me, and next sorry to find such an instance of my littleness recorded in a book which has a very fair chance of being much read. I expect you will let me know what he will write you in return, and we here beg to make offer to you and Mrs. Boswell of our most respectful compliments. I am, dear sir, your most obedient humble servant,

JOHN MACLEOD.

To the Laird of Raasay

London, May 8, 1775.

DEAR SIR,—The day before yesterday I had the honour to receive your letter, and I immediately communicated it to Dr. Johnson. He said he loved your spirit, and was exceedingly sorry that he had been the cause of the smallest uneasiness to you. There is not a more candid man in the world than he is, when properly addressed, as you will see from his letter to you, which I now enclose. He has allowed me to take a copy of it, and he says you may read it to your clan, or publish it if you please. Be assured, sir, that I shall take care of what he has entrusted to me, which is to have an acknowledgment of his error inserted in the Edinburgh newspapers. You will, I dare say, be fully satisfied with Dr. Johnson's behaviour. He is desirous to know that you are; and therefore when you have read his acknowledgment in the papers, I beg you may write to me; and if you choose it, I am persuaded a letter from you to the Doctor also will be taken kind. I shall be at Edinburgh the week after next.

Any civilities which my wife and I had in our power to show to your daughter, Miss MacLeod, were due to her own merit, and were well repaid by her agreeable company. But I am sure I should be a very unworthy man if I did not wish to show a grateful sense of the hospitable and genteel manner in which you were pleased to treat me. Be assured, my dear sir, that I shall never forget your goodness, and the happy hours which I spent in Raasay.

You and Dr. MacLeod were both so obliging as to promise me an account in writing of all the particulars which each of you remember concerning the transactions of 1745–6.[19] Pray do not forget this, and be as minute and full as you can; put down everything; I have a great curiosity to know as much as I can, authentically.

I beg that you may present my best respects to Lady Raasay, my compliments to your young family, and to Dr. MacLeod, and my hearty good wishes to Malcolm, with whom I hope again to shake hands cordially. I have the honour to be, dear sir, your obliged and faithful humble servant,

JAMES BOSWELL.

ADVERTISEMENT, written by Dr. Johnson, and inserted by his desire in the Edinburgh newspapers:—referred to in the foregoing letter.[20]

The author of the *Journey to the Western Islands*, having related that the MacLeods of Raasay acknowledge the chieftainship or superiority of the MacLeods of Skye, finds that he has been misinformed or mistaken. He means in a future edition to correct his error, and wishes to be told of more, if more have been discovered.

Dr. Johnson's letter was as follows:

To the Laird of Raasay

DEAR SIR,—Mr. Boswell has this day shown me a letter in which you complain of a passage in the *Journey* to the Hebrides. My meaning is mistaken. I did not intend to say that you had personally made any cession of the rights of your house, or any acknowledgment of the superiority of Mac-

---

[19] See p. 150 n. 26.
[20] "The original MS is now in my possession."—BOSWELL. It is not among the Malahide papers.

Leod of Dunvegan. I only designed to express what I thought generally admitted: that the house of Raasay allowed the superiority of the house of Dunvegan. Even this I now find to be erroneous, and will therefore omit or retract it in the next edition.

Though what I had said had been true, if it had been disagreeable to you, I should have wished it unsaid, for it is not my business to adjust precedence. As it is mistaken, I find myself disposed to correct, both by my respect for you and my reverence for truth.

As I know not when the book will be reprinted, I have desired Mr. Boswell to anticipate the correction in the Edinburgh papers. This is all that can be done.

I hope I may now venture to desire that my compliments may be made, and my gratitude expressed, to Lady Raasay, Mr. Malcolm MacLeod, Mr. Donald Macqueen, and all the gentlemen and all the ladies whom I saw in the island of Raasay; a place which I remember with too much pleasure and too much kindness not to be sorry that my ignorance or hasty persuasion should, for a single moment, have violated its tranquillity.

I beg you all to forgive an undesigned and involuntary injury, and to consider me as, sir, your most obliged, and most humble servant,

London, May 6, 1775.   SAM. JOHNSON.[21]

It would be improper for me to boast of my own labours, but I cannot refrain from publishing such praise as I received from such a man as Sir William Forbes of Pitsligo, after the perusal of the original manuscript of my Journal.

To James Boswell, Esq.

Edinburgh, March 7, 1777.

MY DEAR SIR,—I ought to have thanked you sooner for your very obliging letter, and for the singular confidence you are pleased to place in me, when you trust me with such a curious and valuable deposit as the papers you have sent me.[22] Be assured I have a due sense of this favour, and shall faithfully and carefully return them to you. You may rely that I shall neither copy any part, nor permit the papers to be seen.

---

[21] "Raasay was highly gratified, and afterwards visited [in August 1782] and dined with Dr. Johnson, at his house in London."—BOSWELL.

[22] "In justice both to Sir William Forbes and myself, it is proper to mention that the papers which were submitted to his perusal contained only an account of our tour from the time that Dr. Johnson and I set out from Edinburgh (p. [32]), and consequently did not contain the elogium on Sir William Forbes (p. [13]), which he never saw till this book appeared in print; nor did he even know, when he wrote the above letter, that this Journal was to be published."—BOSWELL. This note was added in the second edition in consequence of a remark in Lord Macdonald's letter to Boswell of 26 November 1785: ". . . Having read a letter from a respectable person annexed to your publication who gives his sanction and approbation to the work in which he must have discovered his own just panegyric, I think it is time to justify myself. . . ."

They contain a curious picture of society, and form a journal on the most instructive plan that can possibly be thought of; for I am not sure that an ordinary observer would become so well acquainted either with Dr. Johnson, or with the manners of the Hebrides, by a personal intercourse, as by a perusal of your Journal.

I am very truly, dear sir, your most obedient and affectionate humble servant,

WILLIAM FORBES.

When I consider how many of the persons mentioned in this tour are now gone to "that undiscovered country, from whose bourne no traveller returns," I feel an impression at once awful and tender.—*Requiescant in pace!*

It may be objected by some persons, as it has been by one of my friends, that he who has the power of thus exhibiting an exact transcript of conversations is not a desirable member of society. I repeat the answer which I made to that friend: "Few, very few, need be afraid that their sayings will be recorded. Can it be imagined that I would take the trouble to gather what grows on every hedge, because I have collected such fruits as the *nonpareil* and the *bon chrétien?*"[23]

On the other hand, how useful is such a faculty if well exercised! To it we owe all those interesting apophthegms and memorabilia of the ancients, which Plutarch, Xenophon, and Valerius Maximus have transmitted to us. To it we owe all those instructive and entertaining collections which the French have made under the title of *Ana*, affixed to some celebrated name. To it we owe the *Table Talk* of Selden, the *Conversation* between Ben Jonson and Drummond of Hawthornden, Spence's *Anecdotes* of Pope, and other valuable remains in our own language. How delighted should we have been if thus introduced into the company of Shakespeare and of Dryden, of whom we know scarcely anything but their admirable writings! What pleasure would it have given us to have known their petty habits, their characteristic manners, their modes of composition, and their genuine opinion of preceding writ-

---

[23] Defined in Johnson's Dictionary as, respectively, a kind of apple and a kind of pear.

ers and of their contemporaries! All these are now irrecoverably lost. Considering how many of the strongest and most brilliant effusions of exalted intellect must have perished, how much is it to be regretted that all men of distinguished wisdom and wit have not been attended by friends, of taste enough to relish and abilities enough to register their conversation:

> Vixere fortes ante Agamemnona
> Multi, sed omnes illacrymabiles
> Urgentur, ignotique longa
> Nocte, carent quia vate sacro.[24]

They whose inferior exertions are recorded, as serving to explain or illustrate the sayings of such men, may be proud of being thus associated, and of their names being transmitted to posterity, by being appended to an illustrious character.

Before I conclude, I think it proper to say that I have suppressed[25] everything which I thought could *really* hurt any one now living. Vanity and self-conceit indeed may sometimes suffer. With respect to what *is* related, I considered it my duty to "extenuate nothing, nor set down aught in malice"; and

---

[24] "Great men lived, many of them, before Agamemnon; but unwept and unknown, they are all buried in eternal night, lacking their bard."—Horace, *Odes*, IV. ix. 25–8.

[25] "Having found on a revision of the first edition of this work that, notwithstanding my best care, a few observations had escaped me which arose from the instant impression, the publication of which might perhaps be considered as passing the bounds of a strict decorum, I immediately ordered that they should be omitted in the subsequent editions. I was pleased to find that they did not amount in the whole to a page. If any of the same kind are yet left, it is owing to inadvertence alone, no man being more unwilling to give pain to others than I am.

"A contemptible scribbler, of whom I have learned no more than that, after having disgraced and deserted the clerical character, he picks up in London a scanty livelihood by scurrilous lampoons under a feigned name, has impudently and falsely asserted that the passages omitted were *defamatory*, and that the omission was not voluntary but compulsory. The last insinuation I took the trouble publicly to disprove; yet, like one of Pope's dunces, he persevered in 'the lie o'erthrown.' As to the charge of defamation, there is an obvious and certain mode of refuting it. Any person who thinks it worth while to compare one edition with the other, will find that the passages omitted were not in the least degree of that nature, but exactly such as I have represented them in the former part of this note, the hasty effusion of momentary feelings which the delicacy of politeness should have suppressed."—BOSWELL. The "contemptible scribbler" was John Wolcot, who wrote under the pseudonym of Peter Pindar. Boswell's "public disproof" was a letter published in the *Gentleman's Magazine* for April, 1786, and earlier in the newspapers. Wolcot had made the charge in his *Poetical and Congratulatory Epistle to James Boswell*; he "persevered in the lie o'erthrown" in his *Bozzy and Piozzi*.

with those lighter strokes of Dr. Johnson's satire, proceeding from a warmth and quickness of imagination, not from any malevolence of heart, and which, on account of their excellence, could not be omitted, I trust that they who are the subject of them have good sense and good temper enough not to be displeased.

I have only to add that I shall ever reflect with great pleasure on a tour which has been the means of preserving so much of the enlightened and instructive conversation of one whose virtues will, I hope, ever be an object of imitation, and whose powers of mind were so extraordinary that ages may revolve before such a man shall again appear.

APPENDIX

APPENDIX

[See pp. 6 and 157.]

James Boswell to Lord Elibank

London, 22 April 1773.

MY DEAR LORD,—This letter is intended as a *happy prologue to a swelling act*. It is to announce to your lordship that I do now seriously believe that our illustrious friend Mr. Samuel Johnson will visit Scotland this year. I know your lordship's high respect for him, and your warm admiration of his wonderful genius; and therefore I need only hint to you that your throwing out to me a little of what you feel in abundance will, when read to him with my enthusiasm, fortify that resolution, which, I flatter myself, is already very strong. He talks of coming to Edinburgh about the beginning of August, that he may just see our courts of justice, and then he and I may set out directly on a tour through Scotland, particularly to see the Highlands and some of the Islands; after which we shall return to Edinburgh, where (and at your lordship's country seat) we must try to keep him as long as we can. I shall not be many more weeks in London at this time, so I beg that your lordship may send me an epistle full of insensible attraction for Mr. Johnson without delay. I have often told your lordship what influence you have with him; and my Johnsoniana contain compliments by him to your lordship more valuable than any titles which princes confer. I have the honour to be, my dear lord,

Your obliged humble servant.

Lord Elibank to James Boswell

August 21st, 1773.

DEAR BOSWELL,—I flew to Edinburgh the moment I heard of Mr. Johnson's arrival; but so defective was my intelligence that I came too late.

It is but justice to believe that I could never forgive myself, nor deserve to be forgiven by others, if I was to fail in any mark of respect to that very great genius.—I hold him in the highest veneration; for that very reason I was resolved to take no share in the merit, perhaps guilt, of enticing him to honour this country with a visit.—I could not persuade myself there was anything in Scotland worthy to have a summer of Samuel Johnson bestowed on it; but since he has done us that compliment, for heaven's sake inform me of your motions. I will attend them most religiously; and though I should regret to let Mr. Johnson go a mile out of his way on my account, old as I am, I shall be glad to go five hundred miles to enjoy a day of his company. Have the charity to send a council-post[1] with intelligence; the post does not suit us in the country. At any rate write to me. I will attend you in the North, when I shall know where to find you. I am, my dear Boswell, your sincerely obedient humble servant,

ELIBANK.

---

[1] "A term in Scotland for a special messenger, such as was formerly sent with dispatches by the lords of the council."—BOSWELL.

INDEX

INDEX

General subject headings are digested alphabetically and grouped in two articles: SCOTLAND AND THE SCOTCH and JOHNSON, SAMUEL, Part II (Sayings and Opinions). (In devising these subject headings we have received much assistance from Dr. R. W. Chapman's admirable index to the *Tour to the Hebrides.*) Observations on persons and places should be looked for under the proper names in question. Churches, inns, colleges, mountains, etc., are not grouped under larger territorial designations, but are given separate articles. Peers and peeresses, Lords of Session and their wives are indexed under titles, the titles chosen being usually those proper to 1785; but this rule has been broken when a person is better known by an earlier title or a family name (e.g., Lady Jane Douglas, Francis Bacon). The following abbreviations are employed: D. (Duke), E. (Earl), M. (Marquess), V. (Viscount), JB (James Boswell), SJ (Samuel Johnson).

Johnson, Esther (Swift's "Stella"), 206
Johnson, Michael, father of SJ, 3, 39, 174
JOHNSON, SAMUEL

[Part I, *Character*; Part II, *Sayings and Opinions*; Part III, *Writings*.]

I. *Character*. JB's character of, 6–10; appearance, 14 (not horrid), 81 (compared to elephant), 127 ("like a magnificent Triton"), 253 (on horseback), 284 ("eremitical"), 314 (in Highland dress), 359 (like a bishop); liking for post-chaises, 6; drinks no fermented liquor, 11, 43, 96, 173–4: *but see* 173 and 348–9; tea-drinking, 12; deafness, 15, 161, 256; reciter of scraps of verse, 26; writes poetry more easily than *Dictionary*, 29; reverence, 41, 143; composes rapidly, 45; inattention to established manners, 47; silent in company, 50; loudness of voice, 7–8, 53; politeness, 57, 359–60; strength and endurance, 58, 105, 217, 322, 363–4; bad humour, 68, 110, 112–13; respect for rank, 74, 355, 356; little taste for rural beauties, 81; talks "*ostentatiously*," 91; instructs himself in conversation, 96–7; imitates kangaroo, 98 n.6; eloquence, 102, 170; benevolence, 103, 394; feudal, 103, 109; mind not equipped to weigh minute particulars, 110; resolution and tranquillity, 118, 250–1, 347, 348; accuracy, 142; horror of bones, 143, 319; impatience, 158, 236; a "buck," 159, 161, 165, 226; a Tory, not a Jacobite, 162–3; weakness of sight, 165, 321; laziness, 169, 192, 367; wears no night-cap, 173, 233–4, 297; melancholy, 174; variety of knowledge, 174–5, 208; unwilling to have birthday mentioned, 183; contracts names of friends, 189, 297; laughter, 211–12, 368, 392; more spirit of adventure than JB, 227; "honest man," 230–1, 297, 299; "like a great mill," 231; fasted for two days, 252; impetuosity, 257; sceptical of round numbers, 267; minute observation, 293; no alertness, 294; talks to himself, 297–8; no ear for music, 305; incredulous, 325; "hogshead of sense," 342; "dungeon of wit," 345; talks laxly, 350; too proud to court the great, 351; gentle and complaisant, 355; negligent of his papers, 360; remarkable memory, 363; spirit of contradiction, 364, 378; readiness in repartee, 365; desire for long

life, 366; does not talk from books, 372; fear of death, 374; "Ursa Major," 376; refuses to attend Presbyterian worship, 376–7; habit of strict examination, 380; reverence for truth, 382, 400; love of long words, 389; candour, 398

II. *Sayings and Opinions*. Acting, 21–2, 28–9, 93–4; anecdotes, loves, 22; animal substances uncleanly, 176; Atlantic, crossed in open boat, 128; Atonement, The, 63–4; authors, benefited by attacks, 238–9, 390; —, competition good for, 50; biography, 55, 202, 204; "Borough-English," 311; butchery, 208–9; card-playing, 393; charity, 367; chieftainship, 117; churches and kirks, 24; civilized men, superiority of, 92–3; clergy, Scottish and English, 215–16, 245, 375; composition, 23, 44–5; country gentlemen, 78; "country of saddles and bridles," 309; creeds and confessions, 87; cucumbers, 259; cunning, 177–8; death, 155, 245, 307; death-bed behaviour, 203–4, 387; dedications, 253–4; "depeditation," 97; "doggedly," 23; dress, 361; dressing, 45; drinking, 39–40, 119, 314; duel, trial by, 12–13; duelling, 190–1; education, 60, 71, 174, 241; emigration, 15, 54; endings of letters, 203; "*English* man by a *coal* fire," 364; entails, 73; Erse poetry, 204–5; "*Et hoc secundum sententiam philosophorum est esse beatus*," 268; evil, origin of, 85, 362; fencing, 44; fools, spaniel and mule, 187–8; fornication, 167–8; fraud, difficulty of proving, 311–12; French credulity, 323; — literature, 299–300; general terms, 76; good breeding, 57; grace before breakfast, 90; gratitude, 193; gunpowder, 91; Hanover, house of, 236; happiness, 155, 268; hereditary offices, 87; history of the '45, 384; "Inch Boswell," 322; inscriptions, English and Latin, 118, 363; intelligence of Highlanders, 113; judges, private life of, 387; judicial oaths, 382; language, 186; Latin, study of, 103; law and tragic poetry, man could apply mind equally to, 19–20; laziness, 192; learning, decrease of, 55–6; — in Scotland, 37–8; legal ethics, 14–15; lepers, 36 n.6; literary property, 32, 49; literature and criticism, 189, 299–300; "little-houses," 291–2: *see also* "little-houses" *s.v.* SCOTLAND AND THE SCOTCH; luxury, 355;